38011   55   195559   7

THE HIG   KT-382-337

BLOOMSBURY
GOOD READING GUIDE

DORNOCH ACADEMY
LIBRARY

REF

820.3

BLOOMSBURY
GOOD READING GUIDE

This edition edited by
Nick Rennison

Original Author
Kenneth McLeish

[DORNOCH ACADEMY]

BLOOMSBURY

To my parents,
who introduced me to the
pleasure of reading

This fifth edition of the
Good Reading Guide
is edited by
Nick Rennison.

The *Good Reading Guide* was
conceived and written by the late
Kenneth McLeish
and published in four editions.

All rights reserved; no part of this publication may be reproduced, stored in a retrieval system, or transmitted in any form or by any means, electronic, mechanical, photocopying or otherwise, without the prior written permission of the Publishers.

Bloomsbury Publishing Plc,
38 Soho Square, London, W1D 3HB

www.bloomsburymagazine.com
Bloomsbury's website offers booklovers the chance to participate in the literary life online. Its features include a monthly magazine, advice for reading groups, a research centre and a writers' almanac. Most books mentioned in the *Good Reading Guide*, where still in print, can be purchased through the online bookshop.

The moral right of the author has been asserted.

Copyright © 1988, 1990, 1994, 1996, 2001 the estate of Kenneth McLeish

Additional text for this edition copyright © 2001 Bloomsbury Publishing Plc

A CIP entry for this book is available from the British Library.

ISBN 0 7475 5933 3

10 9 8 7 6 5 4 3

Index by Hilary Bird
Typeset by Hewer Text Ltd, Edinburgh
Printed and bound in Great Britain by Clays Ltd, St Ives plc

CONTENTS

How to Use this Book

The *Bloomsbury Good Reading Guide* seeks to answer two main questions: 'Which book should I read?' and 'Which book should I read next?' The bulk of the text consists of articles on some 375 authors, describing the kind of books they wrote, listing titles and suggesting books (by the same authors and by others) which might make interesting follow-ups. Scattered through this guide are some 90 **Read on a Theme** menus of suggested reading. They are straightforward lists of about seven or eight books of a similar kind, ranging from *Action Thrillers* (p 2) to *Weepies* (p 293). There are also nine double-page features, **Startpoints**, each of which covers a particular category of reading, with a large number of suggestions and follow-ups. In alphabetical sequence, they are: **Autobiography**, **Biography**, **Crime**, **Historical Novels**, **Letters and Diaries**, **Poetry**, **Science Fiction and Fantasy**, **Thrillers** and **Travel**. There are also twelve **Pathways,** which take a very well-known novel and set off in different directions from this same starting point. Anyone who follows the suggestions in a Pathway, and the 'Read Ons' from *those* suggestions, will end up reading dozens of books, both obvious follow-ups and unexpected ones, but all related in some way to the original selection.

The text contains no literary criticism. I wanted to describe books, not to be clever at their expense. In particular, I tried to avoid ranking authors by 'literary merit', on assessments of whether their work is 'great' or 'light'. The length of each entry depends solely on how much needed to be said. If this had been a travel guide, New York might well have enjoyed more space than the commuter village up the line – but that would have had no bearing on where one might choose to live.

None the less, this fifth edition does include an embryonic rating system. Rather than emulate hotel guides and load the book with symbols, I've limited myself to two only, and awarded them sparingly. The symbol ☆ means that the book in question is highly recommended, while ★ means that, in my opinion, it is a masterpiece.

Throughout the text, ▷ before someone's name means that that person has a main entry of his or her own. All books mentioned in the *Good Reading Guide* were written in English or are widely available in translation. We have tried to cover as wide a range of writers of English as possible, and have included authors from Australia, Canada, New Zealand, the Republic of Ireland, South Africa and the US, as well as the UK. Some books are published under different titles in the US. If this is the case, the UK title is given first, followed by the US title: Daphne Du Maurier, *The Apple Tree/Kiss Me Again, Stranger*. Books originally written in a foreign language are listed by their English titles. Original titles follow in brackets where they may be familiar to readers or where they may be used for some English editions. Examples are Émile Zola, *The Boozer* (*L'assommoir*) or André Gide, *The Pastoral Symphony* (*La symphonie pastorale*).

Main author articles are listed alphabetically by surname. Each contains some or all of four different strands of information:

1 a paragraph about the author's work and style in general
2 a detailed description of a particular book which is a good example of the author's work
3 a list of main books by the same author
4 suggestions for follow-up reading:
   ● by the same author
   ▶ by others

In this fifth edition of the *Good Reading Guide* we have updated entries to include books (and alas, deaths) occurring since the last edition, and we have revised entries (some substantially), added new titles and menus and added nearly fifty authors new to the guide. To accommodate these changes we have, regretfully, excluded a small number of writers who appeared in earlier editions but whose popularity has waned significantly. We welcome ideas, comments and suggestions for any future editions. Please write to me, care of the publishers.

The cut-off date for inclusion in this fifth edition of the *Good Reading Guide* was June 2001. The final choice of books and authors, the comments and the text have been my responsibility. I take the blame. But many people have helped. This is the first edition of the *Good Reading Guide* in which the revisions and changes have not been made by the original author, the late Kenneth McLeish. However, much of the book remains, in essence, his work. Many of the entries he wrote for earlier editions were so concise, witty, informative and insightful that it seemed both presumptuous and unnecessary to change them. Susan Osborne has a knowledge of contemporary fiction second to none and the Read on a Theme menus have benefited enormously from her many suggestions. Steve Andrews is a walking encyclopedia of information and opinion about science fiction, and I am grateful for his advice and suggestions in a genre where I make no claims to expertise. Richard Shephard contributed many suggestions for Read Ons in American fiction and outlined the entries on half a dozen contemporary US novelists for me. Niamh Marnham proved inventive and imaginative in suggesting both new Read on a Theme menus and ways of improving existing ones. I am very grateful to all four of them and to the many other people who have, over the years, suggested new authors and books to me. To name Noel Murphy, Hugh Pemberton, Gordon Kerr, Travis Elborough, John Magrath, Kevin Chappell, Linda Pattenden, Peter French, Brian Grist, Lucinda Rennison and Paul Skinner is to name only a few. To name more would be to run the risk of sounding like an Oscar-winning actor thanking his entire acquaintance for contributions to his career. But many others have done for me what this *Good Reading Guide* hopes to do for anybody who uses it – pointed me in the direction of rewarding and enjoyable novels which I would not otherwise have had the good fortune to read.

Nick Rennison
July 2001

KEY TO THE SYMBOLS

☆ Highly recommended
★ Masterpiece

Read On symbols:
● Other books by the same author
▶ Similar books by other authors
▷ A book by an author who features in the *Good Reading Guide*

INTRODUCTION

Reading is one of the most satisfying of all human skills. We can survive – people *do* survive – perfectly well without it, and yet many would list it high among the things which make life worth living. Even such eager readers, however, can be daunted by the sheer number of books on offer. Libraries and bookshelves are stuffed with treasures; like explorers in some vast, landmarkless new continent, we hardly know where to turn. Hence this book: a guide not to countries, but to books.

Yet, as the 21st century dawns, books (it is claimed) are under threat again. It is not the kind of threat that they have faced before. Books have regularly faced the wrath of cultural dictators in past centuries. The Nazis have been by no means the only burners of books. Ideologues of all kinds have seen books as potentially subversive and attempted to curb their influence. Yet books and literature have survived their attentions

Today books may be in danger of a quite different and even more serious kind. They may be threatened by a combination of indifference and technology. No more than a century after the arrival of universal education in the Western world, and a mere sixty years since the invention of the cheap paperback, fewer books are being read than ever before. The majority of literate adults hardly open a book from the end of their schooldays till the day they die. We begrudge spending on a book the same sort of money we pay for a video, cassette or CD. We spend four or five times that amount on computer games. If we want to 'read', we buy newspapers or magazines, where the contents are sliced up into self-contained, pre-digested gobbets to suit our short concentration spans. All over the literate world, libraries are losing funding, cutting back their collections, closing down.

The interactive CDs of the early 1990s were only the first harbingers of momentous changes in the ways in which words and information can be accessed. The extraordinary growth of the Internet in the last five years has seen more and more texts available through one's PC. It is no longer necessary to go to a bookshop or a library to track down literature as different as a Shakespeare play and a novel by Edgar Rice Burroughs, a poem by Tennyson and a Sherlock Holmes short story. You can locate, if you wish, the work of the Church Fathers or Jane Austen's *Pride and Prejudice*, the *Book of Mormon* or Cervantes in Spanish in a matter of moments. They are all out there in the rapidly expanding realm of cyberspace.

The way in which we read may well be changing. The latest generation of small book-sized computers enable you to read in an armchair, or sitting in bed, instead of bolt upright at a table. Today's children, brought up from infancy to use computers as tools for both learning and entertainment, may well find scrolling a handier way to move through a text than turning pages.

Books themselves, as physical objects, may well be about to change. This is not a cause for overmuch alarmist hand-wringing by old fogeys. They have changed before – from scrolls to piles of pages, for example. Things only become sinister when we squeeze out of our lives not books themselves, but their contents. The ancient world used to regard books as the memory of the whole human race. In Roman times, the library at Alexandria was thought to contain every piece of knowledge our species had amassed till then. A thousand years later, the university library at Isfahan had the same status in the Islamic world. Even the smallest library today contains far more knowledge than any one person could ever remember. Non-fiction books extend our knowledge and our memory. If they disappeared overnight, if we had to take our knowledge solely from such sources as the media, we would soon become different people.

This is just as true of fiction. We live in an age where 'fiction' means, mainly, films, TV soaps, drama series and sitcoms. Literary fiction is a minority pleasure. And there are those who would deny it any place at all in our scientific, rational, materialistic society. When Ruth Lawrence, a mathematical prodigy of some 15 years ago, went to Oxford at the age of 12, her father announced to the press that he and his wife had 'educated' her without any reference to 'literature' whatever. 'Not only does literature not help you to improve your life,' he said, 'it positively impedes you. I feel there's a kind of obscenity in the way most literature attempts to lead people's lives vicariously and purports to show their innermost feelings. We should live our lives for ourselves.'

Feelings – those are the key to it. The implication seems to be that any part of us which is intellectual can be stimulated, nourished and guided, but that every non-cerebral impulse should be left to blossom, or wither, for itself. The notion is nonsense. The usual way to 'live' our emotions, to release their potential, is by sharing them, by communication with other people. Each individual's emotional makeup is as unique – as personal – as a gene pattern, but we spend our whole lives trying to match them with others, and we draw strength and comfort both from the similarities we find and from the differences. Two of the most exciting activities of human life are finding occasions for such emotional dialogue, and pondering the results. We talk to parents, lovers, children, friends, strangers, in a constant attempt to find out their feelings, to measure our response to life against theirs. It is a form of growth, of education. The more we find in common with others, the more we learn about ourselves. This is living our emotions not 'vicariously', but for ourselves, in company.

No other human being should be excluded from our emotional company. And literature is the ideal way to enter the emotional experience of a vast range of people, from all countries, all periods, all kinds of society. I know Dickens's London, P.G. Wodehouse's Blandings Castle and the 'mean streets' walked by US private eyes as well as my own back garden – not because I've been there but because I recognize the way people feel in them and the way the authors distil those feelings into words.

This is neither as cosy as it sounds, nor living one's life 'vicariously'. If we tried to remake ourselves in the image of Bertie Wooster, David Copperfield or Philip Marlowe, it would certainly be dangerous, because we would be surrendering our emotional identity to become what we read. If there were any risk of this, it would be wise for us to leave fiction alone. But to abandon books because we think that Shakespeare, Tolstoy, Dickens, Austen, the Brontë sisters – not to mention the vast range of contemporary novelists – have nothing useful to tell us is to impoverish ourselves.

I began by comparing the *Bloomsbury Good Reading Guide* to the kind of guidebooks we buy to countries of the world. The world of books is boundless, and is crammed with human beings of every profession, viewpoint, character, moral and ethical persuasion. It covers not only everything that has happened in 'real' human existence, but the infinite possibilities of the imagination. To anyone standing outside, this can seem daunting. But, as any reader knows, once you start exploring, the experience becomes ever more addictive and enriching. To refuse to enter the country at all, or to walk through it without glancing to right or left, is to deny oneself not just pleasure, but enormous self-enhancement.

A

ACHEBE, Chinua (born 1930)
Nigerian novelist

☆ *Things Fall Apart* (1958), Achebe's best-known novel, is a story of the people of Umuofia on the River Niger, and especially of Okonkwo, a rich and headstrong elder. Okonkwo wins respect among his people by a magnificent wrestling-throw when he is 18, and keeps it by his hard work as a farmer, his love for the land. Then, by accident, he kills a relative, and is forced by custom to live out of the village for seven years. While he is away Christian missionaries come. They speak through interpreters, understand nothing of the people's beliefs and are followed by white commissioners whose laws destroy the society they were devised to 'civilize'. Achebe's points are blunt, and (for ex-colonialists) shamingly unanswerable. But his novel's main fascination is not political but social. Through his direct, uncomplicated scenes, reverberant as poetry, Achebe reveals his people's inner lives.

Achebe's other novels include No Longer at Ease, Arrow of God *and* Anthills of the Savannah.

> **READ ON**

- ● *A Man of the People* (a satirical, bitter farce about what happens when white imperialists leave and black politicians set up a state on 'Western' lines).
- ▶ to *Things Fall Apart*: Amos Tutuola, *My Life in the Bush of Ghosts* (making a denser, more Homeric use of Nigerian folk styles); ▷ Ben Okri, *The Famished Road*; ▷ I.B. Singer, *Satan in Goray*,
- ▶ to Achebe's later, and politically much more savage work: ▷ V.S. Naipaul, *A Bend in the River*; Wole Soyinka, *The Interpreters*.

ACKROYD, Peter (born 1949)
British writer

Ackroyd is a biographer as well as a novelist – his *Dickens* is 1200 pages long, sumptuously detailed, and acclaimed – and his fiction benefits from a researcher's eye for extraordinary and revealing detail about the past. Often, he blends a modern story with a historical one, and characters from the past move in and out of the contemporary narrative like ghosts. He sets many stories in London (he is the author of a recent 'biography' of the city), and superbly evokes its people and atmosphere, both today and in different periods of the past.

HAWKSMOOR (1985)

This remains the most exhilarating and adventurous of Ackroyd's explorations of a London in which past and present endlessly intertwine. A contemporary detective (the namesake of the 17th-century architect) is driven towards a mystical encounter with forces from the past through his investigations of a series of murders in London churches. Part of the narrative is written in a prose which demonstrates Ackroyd's chameleon-like ability to mimic the English of past centuries and its rhythms.

Ackroyd's other novels include Chatterton *(about the 18th-century literary forger who committed suicide at the age of 18),* The House of Doctor Dee *(in which the central character inherits a Clerkenwell house once owned by the Elizabethan magus John Dee),* The Last Testament of Oscar Wilde *and* English Music. *He has also written poetry, and prize-winning biographies of T.S. Eliot and William Blake.* Dan Leno and the Limehouse Golem *(blending the stories of the real Dan Leno, 'the funniest man in England' in 19th-century music-hall, such literary figures as George Gissing and Karl Marx, and the mysterious serial killer of the 1890s nicknamed the 'Limehouse Golem') and* Milton in America *are more recent novels.*

> READ ON

▶ to *Hawksmoor*: David Liss, *A Conspiracy of Paper*; Iain Pears, *An Instance of the Fingerpost*; ▷ Iain Sinclair, *White Chappell, Scarlet Tracings*.
▶ to Ackroyd's work in general: ▷ Michael Moorcock, *Mother London*; ▷ Iain Sinclair, *Downriver*; ▷ Rose Tremain, *Restoration*; ▷ Jeanette Winterson, *Sexing the Cherry*.

READ ON A THEME: ACTION THRILLERS

▷ Tom Clancy, *The Hunt for Red October*
  Clive Cussler, *Flood Tide*
  Daniel Easterman, *The Jaguar Mask*
▷ Ken Follett, *Code to Zero*
▷ Frederick Forsyth, *The Day of the Jackal*
  Jean-Christophe Grangé, *Blood Red Rivers*
  Martin Cruz Smith, *Havana Bay*

See also: High Adventure; Historical Adventure; Spies and Double Agents; Terrorists/ Freedom Fighters

---

ADAMS, Douglas (1952–2001)
British novelist

Adams began his career as a radio joke-writer, and also worked for the TV science fiction series *Doctor Who*. He made his name with a series of genial science fiction spoofs, beginning with *The Hitchhiker's Guide to the Galaxy* (1979). In this, Earthman Arthur Dent, informed that his planet is about to be vapourized to make room for a hyperspace bypass, escapes by stowing away on an alien spacecraft. This is the beginning of a wild journey through time and space, in the course of which he meets the super-cool President of the Galaxy, Zaphod Beeblebrox, discusses the coastline of Norway with Slartibartfast (who won prizes for designing it), watches the apocalyptic floor-show in the Restaurant at the End of the Universe, and discovers the answer to the 'ultimate question about life, the universe and everything'. The other *Hitchhiker* books (self-contained sequels) are *The Restaurant at the End of the Universe*; *Life, the Universe and Everything*; *So Long, and Thanks for All the Fish*; and *Mostly Harmless*. In 1987 Adams began a second series, this time starring Dirk Gently, an intergalactic private eye who has to cope not only with the usual quota of blondes and hoodlums, but with electronic monks, thinking horses, the space-time continuum and an uneasy feeling that he is no more than a bystander in his own bad dreams. The Gently books are *Dirk Gently's Holistic Detective Agency* and *The Long Dark Teatime of the Soul*. In his later years Adams largely turned away from the printed page to concentrate on projects in other media but the *Hitchhiker* books remain as the most inspired of all science fiction spoofs.

> READ ON

▶ Science fiction spoofs in similarly lunatic vein: ▷ Harry Harrison, *The Stainless Steel Rat*; Robert Asprin, *Phules Company*.
▶ Fantasy spoofs: ▷ Terry Pratchett, *The Colour of Magic*; Robert Asprin, *Another Fine Myth*; Robert Rankin, *The Anti-Pope* (and others in the Brentford series).

READ ON A THEME: ADOLESCENCE

　Alain-Fournier, *Le Grand Meaulnes*
▷ Beryl Bainbridge, *A Quiet Life*
▷ Colette, *The Ripening Seed*
▷ Miles Franklin, *My Brilliant Career*
　Jane Gardam, *Bilgewater*
　Lesley Glaister, *Digging to Australia*
　S.E. Hinton, *That Was Then, This Is Now*
　Hanif Kureishi, *The Buddha of Suburbia*
　Harper Lee, *To Kill a Mockingbird*
▷ J.D. Salinger, *The Catcher in the Rye*
　Sue Townsend, *The Secret Diary of Adrian Mole, aged 13 ¾*
▷ Rose Tremain, *The Way I Found Her*
▷ Antonia White, *Frost in May*
　Edmund White, *A Boy's Own Story*.

See also: Children; Eccentric Families; Parents and Children; Schools; Teenagers

READ ON A THEME: AFRICA

▷ Chinua Achebe, *Things Fall Apart*
　Ronan Bennett, *The Catastrophist*
　Paul Bowles, *The Sheltering Sky*
▷ William Boyd, *A Good Man in Africa*

Justin Cartwright, *Masai Dreaming*
Giles Foden, *The Last King of Scotland*
▷ Nadine Gordimer, *None To Accompany Me*
▷ Barbara Kingsolver, *The Poisonwood Bible*
▷ Ben Okri, *The Famished Road*
　Wole Soyinka, *The Season of Anomie*
▷ Evelyn Waugh, *Scoop*

ALLENDE, Isabel (born 1942)
Peruvian-born Chilean novelist

Allende's first novel, ☆ *House of the Spirits* (1985), was a glowing family tapestry in the magic-realist manner of ▷ Márquez's *One Hundred Years of Solitude*, spanning five generations and thronged with larger-than-life characters and supernatural events. She followed this vein in *Eva Luna* (1989), which is particularly evocative of life on a decaying hacienda deep in the tropical bush. Her finest book, *Of Love and Shadows* (see below) adds politics to the magic-realist mixture, to devastating effect. *Paula* (1995) is a moving account of the death of Allende's daughter which opens out into the story of her own life and the political tragedies of Chile. *Aphrodite* (1998) is an unclassifiable celebration of food, sex and sensuality which reflects the same delight in the physical world that runs through all her fiction.

OF LOVE AND SHADOWS (1987)
Irene Beltran, a journalist, and her photographer-lover Francisco Leal are investigating the disappearance of a disturbed, possibly saintly adolescent. In the jackbooted dictatorship in which they live, however, the child is not simply missing but 'disappeared', one of thousands snatched by the authorities who will never be seen again. Allende surrounds her main characters with a web of fantastic personal history in true magic-realist style. But the further the investigators thread their way through the sadism and ruthlessness of the labyrinthine fascist state, the more fact begins to swallow fairy tale. The investigators themselves begin to lose reality – their love-affair becomes a swooning parody of romantic fiction – but what they discover grows more and more uncomfortably like real South American life, like nightmare fleshed.

Allende has also published The Stories of Eva Luna, *a set of long short stories which forms a pendant to* Eva Luna.

⎡ READ ON ⟩

● *Eva Luna.*
▶ Alejo Carpentier, *The Chase.* ▷ Stephen Dobyns, *The Two Deaths of Señora Puccini*; Oscar Hijuelos, *The Fourteen Sister of Emilio Montez O'Brien.* ▷ Mario Vargas Llosa, *Captain Pantoja and the Special Service* gives a more farcical view of Allende's terrifying, haunted world.

READ ON A THEME: **ALL-ENGULFING FAMILIES**

▷ **Anita Brookner**, *Family and Friends*
▷ **Angela Carter**, *The Magic Toyshop*
▷ **William Faulkner**, *The Sound and the Fury*
  Anne Fine, *Telling Liddy*
▷ **Margaret Forster**, *The Battle for Christabel*
▷ **John Galsworthy**, *The Forsyte Saga*
  Lesley Glaister, *Digging to Australia*
▷ **François Mauriac**, *The Nest of Vipers*
▷ **Christina Stead**, *The Man Who Loved Children*

See also: Eccentric Families; Many Generations

ALLINGHAM, Margery (1905–66)
British novelist

Allingham wrote 'crime fiction' only in the sense that each of her books contains the step-by-step solution of a crime, and that their hero, Albert Campion, is an amateur detective whose amiable manner conceals laser intelligence and ironclad moral integrity. But instead of confining Campion by the boundaries of the detective-story genre, Allingham put him in whatever kind of novel she felt like writing. Some of her books (*More Work for the Undertaker*; *The Beckoning Lady*) are wild, ▷ Wodehousian farce, others (*Sweet Danger*; *Traitor's Purse*) are ▷ Buchanish, ▷ Amblerish thrillers. Her best books are those of the 1940s and 1950s, and especially two set in an atmospheric, cobble-stones-and-alleyways London filled with low-life characters as vivid as any in ▷ Dickens, *The Tiger in the Smoke* (see below) and *Hide My Eyes*.

THE TIGER IN THE SMOKE (1952)
Like all of Allingham's novels, this is not a conventional whodunnit, although it contains plenty of mysteries that demand solutions. Jack Havoc, the 'tiger' of the title, escapes from jail and the hunt for this violent convict takes place in an eerie and fog-enshrouded London which Allingham brilliantly evokes. Campion and other characters familiar from Allingham's work loom in and out of the fog as the action moves inexorably towards a violent conclusion.

Allingham's other Campion books include Coroner's Pidgin, Police at the Funeral, Look to the Lady *and the short-story collections* Mr Campion and Others *and* Take Two at Bedtime. *After Allingham's death, her husband P. Youngman Carter wrote two further Campion novels, one of which,* Mr Campion's Farthing, *is up to his wife's most sparkling standard.*

READ ON ▷

● *Death of a Ghost* (set in London's eccentric art-community and involving – what else? – forged paintings); *Hide My Eyes*.
▷ **Michael Innes**, *The Daffodil Affair*, ▷ **Edmund Crispin**, *The Case of the Gilded Fly*, **H.R.F. Keating**, *A Rush on the Ultimate*.

READ ON A THEME: **ALL THE WORLD'S A STAGE**
(books about theatre)

▷ Beryl Bainbridge, *An Awfully Big Adventure*
  Caryl Brahms and S.J. Simon, *A Bullet in the Ballet*
▷ Angela Carter, *Wise Children*
▷ Robertson Davies, *Tempest-Tost*
▷ Charles Dickens, *Nicholas Nickleby* (Nicholas's adventures with the Crummles)
▷ Thomas Keneally, *The Playmaker*
▷ J.B. Priestley, *The Good Companions*
▷ Mary Renault, *The Mask of Apollo*
▷ Barry Unsworth, *Morality Play*

READ ON A THEME: **ALTERED STATES (CHEMICAL FICTION)**

▷ J.G. Ballard, *Cocaine Nights*
  William Burroughs, *Junky*
▷ Bret Easton Ellis, *Glamorama*
▷ Jay McInerney, *The Story of My Life*
  Kevin Sampson, *Powder*
  Alexander Trocchi, *Cain's Book*
▷ Irvine Welsh, *Trainspotting*

AMBLER, Eric (1909–98)
British novelist and screenwriter

Ambler worked in advertising, the film industry and the secret service before becoming a full-time novelist. The deadpan style of his thrillers lets him move easily from violence to farce, and he either sets his books in exotic places (the Levant, the Far East, tropical Africa), or else makes familiar European locations seem exotic as the scene of sinister and unlikely goings-on. His central characters are minor crooks, conmen, or innocent bystanders trapped by circumstances or curiosity into a chain of bizarre and dangerous events. His supporting casts are crammed with improbable, unsavoury specimens, very few of whom are quite what they seem to be. Films and TV series have made this kind of thriller endlessly familiar. But Ambler was one of the first to write it, and he is still among the best. As John le Carré once said, he is 'the source on which we all draw'.

THE MASK OF DIMITRIOS (1939)
Although later thrillers continued to be successful (*The Light of Day*, for instance, published in 1962 was made into the movie *Topkapi*), Ambler's best and most characteristic thrillers belong to the low, dishonest decade of the 1930s. In *The Mask of Dimitrios* Charles Latimer, a bored writer, sets out to track down an elusive Levantine criminal and finds that his search for the truth about Dimitrios Makropolous leads him into dangerous territory. Propelled by chance and curiosity from his own comfortable world, Latimer is suddenly surrounded by endless deceits and random violence.

Ambler's other thrillers include Cause for Alarm, Epitaph for a Spy, Journey into Fear, Passage of Arms, The Schirmer Inheritance *and* To Catch a Spy. *He also wrote thrillers (eg* The Maras Affair*;* Charter to Danger*) in collaboration with* Charles Rodda, *published under the name Eliot Reed. They are more straightforward, but no less gripping, than his solo books.*

READ ON

- **to *The Mask of Dimitrios*: ▷ Graham Greene, *Stamboul Train*, ▷ John le Carré, *Single and Single*.**
- **to Ambler's work in general: ▷ Len Deighton, *Horse Under Water*; Lionel Davidson, *The Night of Wenceslas*; Richard Condon, *The Manchurian Candidate*.**

AMIS, Kingsley (1922–95)

British writer of novels, poems and non-fiction

In the 1950s, when Amis's writing career began, British writers of all kinds – the 'angry young men' – had begun to rant in plays, films and novels about the unfairness, snobbishness and priggishness of life. Whingeing became an artistic form – and Amis' novels showed its funny side. The working-class hero of *Lucky Jim* (1954) tries to conform with his madrigal-singing, right-newspaper-reading, wine-savouring university colleagues, and in the process shows them up for the pretentious fools they are. The central character of *That Uncertain Feeling*, a small-town librarian, thinks that devastating sexual charm will carry him to the pinnacle of local society; the results are farcical. The hero of *Take a Girl Like You* (1960) finds it hard to persuade anyone else in his circle that 'free love' and 'the swinging sixties' are the good things glossy magazines crack them up to be. In the 1960s and 1970s Amis' farcical fires burned low. He began to affect a ponderous, self-consciously right-wing fuddy-duddiness, and abandoned satire for books of other kinds (a ghost story, a James Bond spy story and several science fiction books). In the 1980s, however, he returned to the satirical muttering which he always did better than any of his imitators – and his more recent books (beginning with *The Old Devils*: see below) are among his funniest.

THE OLD DEVILS (1986)

A group of old men, acquaintances for over 40 years, meet daily in a Welsh bar to grumble. They are obsessed by failure, their own and the world's. They are especially vitriolic about other people's success – and their discomfort with the world is brought to a peak when one of their 'friends', a famous TV Welshman and an expert on a Dylan-Thomasish poet, comes to settle in the town.

The best of Amis's comic novels not mentioned above are One Fat Englishman, Ending Up, The Folks Who Live on the Hill *and* Difficulties With Girls *(a 1988 sequel to* Take a Girl Like You*). The best of his serious novels are* The Anti-Death League, *about a top-secret army unit whose aim is to abolish death, and* The Alteration, *set in a fantasy contemporary Britain in which modern science and modern religion have never happened, so that we are still organizing our lives in medieval ways. His* Memoirs *are gleefully malicious pen-portraits of two dozen former friends, devastatingly satirical or distasteful according to your mood.*

READ ON ▷

● *Jake's Thing*; *Stanley and the Women*; *The Russian Girl*.
▶ ▷ Malcolm Bradbury, *Eating People is Wrong*. ▷ A.N. Wilson, *Love Unknown*.
Christopher Hope, *Serenity House*. ▷ Tom Sharpe, *Porterhouse Blue*. ▷ William
Boyd, *A Good Man in Africa*. Howard Jacobson, *Peeping Tom*. William Cooper,
Scenes from Provincial Life.

AMIS, Martin (born 1949)
British novelist

Amis's books are icily satirical, cold with rage at the physical and moral sleaziness
of the human race. His characters' preoccupations are sex, food, money and
success, and they are tormented by failure to win, or keep, all four. Ronald
Firbank and ▷ F. Scott Fitzgerald found similar prancing emptiness in the 'gay
young things' of the 1920s. Amis matches those writers' bilious wit and parades
his dazzlingly inventive prose style in his pages but adds a pungent view of his
own: that the entire generation born after the creation of nuclear weapons is
maimed beyond cure, a race of psychotic moral mutants. Few contemporary
writers treat such repulsive subject matter so dazzlingly. Amis's novels are
compulsively nasty, superbly hard to like.

MONEY (1984)
This is the 'suicide note' of an obese, deranged and despairing film
director, stumbling through a New York inferno of fast food, pornography,
violence and moronic greed. He is a lunatic in a world that has gone mad;
when he opens his mouth to scream, his voice is drowned in the
megametropolitan carnival, the dance of death that is (for Amis, at least)
contemporary America.

Amis's other novels are The Rachel Papers, Dead Babies, Other People,
Success, Time's Arrow, The Information *and* Night Train. The Moronic Inferno
*is a bilious travelogue about the US, a marvellously raw, non-fiction counterpart
to* Money. Einstein's Monsters *and* Heavy Water *contain short stories.* Experience *is a remarkable memoir, particularly affecting and moving (not words
usually applied to Amis's work) in its portrait of his relationship with his father,
Kingsley Amis.* War Against Cliché *is a collection from thirty years of literary
journalism.*

READ ON ▷

● *London Fields* (about a man in apocalypse-hurtling 1999 London trying to write a
novel about a woman trying to arrange her murder by a slob of a man fantasizing
about winning the world darts championship).
▶ Terence Blacker, *Fixx*, ▷ Iain Banks, *The Wasp Factory*, Madison Smartt Bell, *The
Year of Silence*. ▷ Saul Bellow, *Mr Sammler's Planet*. ▷ Jay McInerney, *Model
Behaviour* ▷ Will Self, *My Idea of Fun*; ▷ Vladimir Nabokov, *Despair*.

READ ON A THEME: ANCIENT GREECE AND ROME

Greece:
    Hilary Bailey, *Cassandra, Princess of Troy*
▷ William Golding, *The Double Tongue*
    Tom Holt, *Olympiad*
▷ Homer, *Odyssey*
    Naomi Mitchison, *The Corn King and the Spring Queen*
▷ Mary Renault, *The King Must Die*
▷ Gore Vidal, *Creation*

Rome:
    Lindsey Davies, *The Iron Hand of Mars*
▷ Robert Graves, *I, Claudius*
    Allan Massie, *Tiberius*
    Steven Saylor, *Roman Blood*
▷ Thornton Wilder, *The Ides of March*
▷ Marguerite Yourcenar, *Memoirs of Hadrian*

See also: The Bible; The Middle Ages; Other Peoples, Other Times; Renaissance Europe.

READ ON A THEME: THE ANIMAL KINGDOM

    Richard Adams, *Watership Down*
    Aeron Clement, *The Cold Moons*
    Paul Gallico, *The Snow Goose*
▷ Ernest Hemingway, *Fiesta/The Sun Also Rises*
    William Horwood, *Duncton Wood*
▷ Jack London, *White Fang*
    Henry Williamson, *Tarka the Otter*

READ ON A THEME: ART FOR WHOSE SAKE?

(painters; fakers; patrons; art enthusiasts)
▷ Margery Allingham, *Death of a Ghost*
    Joyce Cary, *The Horse's Mouth*
    Tracy Chevalier, *Girl with a Pearl Earring*
    Michael Frayn, *Headlong*
    Lesley Glaister, *Sheer Blue Bliss*
▷ Alan Hollinghurst, *The Folding Star*
▷ Wyndham Lewis, *Tarr*
    Shena Mackay, *The Artist's Widow*
▷ W. Somerset Maugham, *The Moon and Sixpence*
    Arturo Perez-Reverte, *The Flanders Panel*
    Irving Stone, *The Agony and the Ecstasy*

ASIMOV, Isaac (1920–92)
US writer of novels, short stories and non-fiction

Asimov published his first story at 19, and went on to write over 300 books, ranging from Bible guides and history text books to the science fiction novels and stories for which he is best known. Much of his most seminal science fiction work was written in the 1940s when he (and others) came under the editorial wing of John W. Campbell, the pulp magazine man who virtually defined science fiction as Hollywood now depicts it. Strongly plotted and concentrating on ideas more than style, Asimov's novels and stories invite the reader to collaborate in the unfolding of concepts like the famous 'Three Laws of Robotics.' Asimov's down-to-earth, logical thinking means that his works are often the stuff of real science – the 'three laws', for example, have been used as the basis of real-life robot programming.

THE FOUNDATION SAGA (1951–93)
The first three books, a self-contained trilogy, appeared in the 1950s; Asimov added the remaining volumes 30 years later. The Saga is 'space opera' (science fiction soap opera) on a huge scale, an account of political manoeuvrings among nations and civilizations of the far future. Hari Seldon, a professor of psycho-history (statistical and psychological prediction of the future) foresees a disastrous era of war in the galactic empire, and establishes two Foundations on the galaxy's edge, dedicated to safeguarding civilized knowledge until it is again required. The Saga describes the nature and work of each Foundation, their uniting to defeat external threat (from an alien intelligence, 'the Mule') and their subsequent internecine struggles. For, like all human constructs, they are themselves prey to emotion and irrationality, to a bias which can lead towards dark as well as light.

The Foundation novels are Foundation, Foundation and Empire *and* Second Foundation. *Books in the continuation series are* Prelude to Foundation, Foundation's Edge, Foundation and Earth *and the posthumous* Forward the Foundation. *Asimov's other science fiction novels include* Pebble in the Sky, The Stars Like Dust *and* The Currents of Space *(all on themes related to the Foundation Saga).*

> **READ ON**

- Asimov's other major achievement is the robot sequence of books *I, Robot, The Rest of the Robots, The Caves of Steel, The Naked Sun* and *The Robots of Dawn*. His story 'Nightfall' (from a collection of that title) has several times been voted the best science fiction short story ever written.
- ▶ to the Foundation Saga: ▷ Iain M. Banks, *Consider Phlebas* (and the other Culture novels); Gordon R. Dickson, *Tactics of Mistake* (and others in the Dorsai sequence); ▷ Robert A. Heinlein, *The Man Who Sold the Moon*; Peter F. Hamilton, *The Reality Dysfunction*.
- ▶ to *The Caves of Steel/The Naked Sun*: Alfred Bester, *The Demolished Man*; Larry Niven, *The Long Arm of Gil Hamilton*.
- ▶ Other examples of Golden Age, John W. Campbell-inspired science fiction: Robert Heinlein, *Methuselah's Children*; A.E. Van Vogt, *The Voyage of the Space Beagle*.

ATKINSON, Kate (born 1951)
British novelist

Kate Atkinson writes family sagas but they are family sagas unlike any others to be found on the shelves of a library or bookshop. The narrative bounces back and forth between decades, the language and imagery are often poetical and allusive, boundaries between what is 'real' and what is 'unreal' in the stories blur. Eccentricity and quirkiness intrude on ordinary lower-middle-class domesticity and the books are often very funny. Her first novel *Behind the Scenes at the Museum* (1994) is the story of Ruby Lennox, growing up in the family home above a pet shop in York in the 1950s and 1960s. Her womanizing father and her disgruntled mother, dreaming of a Hollywood glamour that would have been preferable to Yorkshire home life, are strongly created characters, as are the other members of the family. Ruby reaches back into the past in search of explanations for family flaws and frailties and the narrative zigzags between the generations, from her great-grandmother's affair with a French photographer to the unruly circumstances of her own life. The book was a great commercial and critical success, becoming both a bestseller and Whitbread Book of the Year. Kate Atkinson has since written two further novels, *Human Croquet* (1997), the extravagantly told story of a family whose glory days are in the past, and *Emotionally Weird* (2000), about a mother and daughter holed up in a decaying family home and telling one another stories of their own and others' lives.

> READ ON

● *Human Croquet.*
▶ ▷ Angela Carter, *Wise Children*; ▷ Margaret Atwood, *The Blind Assassin*; ▷ Esther Freud, *Gaglow*; Zadie Smith, *White Teeth.*

ATWOOD, Margaret (born 1939)
Canadian writer of novels, short stories and poems

Atwood is a poet as well as a novelist, and her gifts of precise observation and exact description illuminate all her work. She is fascinated by the balance of power between person and person, and by the way our apparently coherent actions and sayings actually float on a sea of turbulent unseen emotion. Her books often follow the progress of relationships, or of one person's self-discovery. The heroine of *Life Before Man*, for example, is caught up in a sexual quadrilateral (one of whose members, her lover, has just committed suicide), and our interest is as much in seeing how she copes with her own chaotic feelings as in the progress of the affair itself. In *Cat's Eye* (1989), a middle-aged painter returns to Toronto, remembers her dismal childhood and adolescence there, and finally comes to terms with the bully who made her life miserable as a schoolchild and with that bully's appalling, manipulative mother. Many writers have tackled similar themes, but Atwood's books give a unique impression that each moment, each feeling, is being looked at through a microscope, as if the swirling, nagging 'real' world has been momentarily put aside for something more urgent which may just – her characters consistently put hope above experience – make sense of it.

☆ THE HANDMAID'S TALE (1985)

This dazzling dystopian novel, at once Atwood's most savage book and a departure from her usual Canadian stamping grounds, is set in the 21st-century Republic of Gilead. In this benighted state, fundamentalist Christianity rules and the laws are those of Genesis. Women are chattels: they have no identity, no privacy and no happiness except what men permit them. Offred, for example, is a Handmaid, and her life is devoted to one duty only: breeding. In Gilead public prayers and hangings are the norm; individuality – even looking openly into a man's face or reading a woman's magazine – is punished by mutilation, banishment or death. The book shows Offred's struggle to keep her sanity and her identity in such a situation, and her equivocal relationship with the feminist Underground which may be Gilead's only hope.

Atwood's other novels include Surfacing, The Edible Woman, Bodily Harm *and* The Robber Bride. Dancing Girls, Wilderness Tips *and* Bluebeard's Egg *contain short stories.* The Journals of Susannah Moodie *and* True Stories *are poetry collections, and her* Selected Poems *are also available.* Good Bones *is a collection of funny, feminist retellings of such fables as* The Little Red Hen, Cinderella *and* Hamlet.

READ ON ▷

- *Alias Grace* (an exploration of women's sexuality and social roles wrapped up in a gripping story of a 19th-century housemaid who may or may not have been a murderess); *The Blind Assassin* (an old woman recalls her life, lived in the shadow of her flamboyant, doomed sister and the sensational novel the sister wrote).
- ▶ to *The Handmaid's Tale*: ▷ George Orwell, *1984.*
- ▶ to *Surfacing*: ▷ Angela Carter, *Heroes and Villains*; ▷ Carol Shields, *The Stone Diaries.*
- ▶ to *Cat's Eye*: ▷ Bernice Rubens, *Our Father*; Lynne Reid Banks, *Children at the Gate*; ▷ Alison Lurie, *Imaginary Friends.*
- ▶ to Atwood's work in general: ▷ Doris Lessing, *Martha Quest*; ▷ Nadine Gordimer, *A Sport of Nature*; ▷ Saul Bellow, *Herzog.*

AUSTEN, Jane (1775–1817)
British novelist

Austen loved the theatre, and the nearest equivalents to her novels, for pace and verve, are the social comedies of such writers as Sheridan or Goldsmith. The kind of novels popular at the time were epic panoramas (like those of ▷Sir Walter Scott), showing the human race strutting and swaggering amid stormy weather in vast, romantic landscapes. Austen preferred a narrower focus, concentrating on a handful of people busy about their own domestic concerns. Her books are about the bonds which draw families together and the ambitions and feelings (usually caused by grown-up children seeking marriage partners) which divide them. Her plots fall into 'acts', like plays, and her dialogue is as precise and witty as in any comedy of the time. But she offers a delight available to no playwright: that of the author's own voice, setting the scene, commenting on and shaping events. She is like a bright-eyed, sharp-tongued relative sitting in a corner of the room watching the rest of the family bustle.

★☆ PRIDE AND PREJUDICE (1813)

Genteel Mr and Mrs Bennet and their five grown-up daughters are thrown into confusion when two rich, marriageable young men come to live in the neigh-bourhood. The comedy of the story comes from Mrs Bennet's mother-hen-like attempts at matchmaking, and the way fate and the young people's own inclinations make things turn out entirely differently from her plans. The more serious sections of the novel show the developing relationship between Elizabeth Bennet, the second daughter, and cold, proud Mr Darcy. Although secondary characters (henpecked Mr Bennet, snobbish Lady Catherine de Bourgh, Eliza-beth's romantic younger sister Lydia, the dashing army officer Wickham and the toady Mr Collins) steal the limelight whenever they appear, the book hinges on half a dozen magnificent set-piece scenes between Elizabeth and Darcy, the two headstrong young people the reader longs to see realizing their love for one another and falling into one another's arms.

Apart from a number of unfinished works (eg The Watsons; Sanditon), *Austen's output consists of six novels:* Northanger Abbey *(a spoof of romantic melodrama, unlike any of her other books),* Sense and Sensibility, Pride and Prejudice, Mansfield Park, Emma *and* Persuasion.

READ ON >

- *Emma* (about a young woman so eager to manage other people's lives that she fails, for a long time, to realize where her own true happiness lies); *Mansfield Park* (a darker comedy about a girl brought up by a rich, charming family who is at first dazzled by their easy brilliance, then comes to see that they are selfish and foolish, and finally, by unassuming persistence, wins through to the happiness we have hoped for her).
- ▶ to *Pride and Prejudice*: Emma Tennant, *Pemberley* (ripely romantic sequel, not terribly Austenish but fun for Elizabeth/Darcy lovers); ▷ Mrs Gaskell, *Wives and Daughters*.
- ▶ to *Mansfield Park*: Joan Aiken, *Mansfield Revisited* – the best of many attempts to use Austen's characters and equal Austen's style.
- ▶ to Austen's work in general: ▷ William Thackeray, *Vanity Fair*; ▷ E.M. Forster, *A Room With a View*; ▷ Alison Lurie, *Only Children*; ▷ Barbara Pym, *Excellent Women*; the short stories of ▷ Anton Chekhov and ▷ Katherine Mansfield.

AUSTER, Paul (born 1947)
US writer

Born in Newark, New Jersey, Auster travelled in Europe before enrolling at Columbia University. Following an exchange year spent in Paris, he returned to Columbia in 1968, writing journalism while student riots, anti-war demonstrations and the summer of love hangover raged around him. His first book, *Squeeze Play* (1982), was a pastiche of a crime novel. Curiously, the author's name was listed as Paul Benjamin, a name given to a character in the 1995 film 'Smoke', scripted by Auster. Auster's key work is *The New York Trilogy* (1987, although the individual books appeared separately in 1985 and 1986 as *City of Glass*, *Ghosts* and *The Locked Room*) and this was once again a sly deconstruction job on the detective novel. The *Trilogy* is a more complex narrative than *Squeeze Play*, one in which reader, author and sleuth seem to exchange roles in a strange kind of

AUTOBIOGRAPHY

Writing an autobiography gives you the chance to relive your own life – and to edit it to suit yourself. Although we readers may think that an autobiography allows us inside the writer's head, this is an illusion. We see only what we are allowed to see, and who is to tell how much is fiction, how much is fact? Often (though there are exceptions, for example Charles Chaplin's *My Autobiography*, 1964), the better-known the person, the less interesting the book. Generals' and politicians' memories tend to rehash old battles; showbiz autobiographies tend to revive old triumphs and pay off old scores. Some writers have made a speciality out of autobiography (see for example Blishen below) and because their books concentrate on place and other people's characters as much as their own, they are often the most enjoyable of all.

Amis, Martin, (born 1949) *Experience* (2000). ▷ *Enfant terrible* of English fiction has now reached middle age, and this reflective book, moving in its meditations on time and loss, is one of the results. Very candid, funny and revealing.

Angelou, Maya (born 1928), *I Know Why the Caged Bird sings* (1969). Singer, dancer and black rights activist tells scathing story of growing up in racist Southern US. Also: *Gather Together in My Name*; *Singin' and Swingin' and Gettin' Merry Like Christmas*; *The Heart of a Woman*; *All God's Children Need Travelling Shoes*.

Blishen, Edward (born 1920), *Roaring Boys* (1955). First of Blishen's self-contained books of autobiography, each taking one aspect of his life. This one is about teaching in a tough slum school in the years after World War II. Also: *A Cack-Handed War*; *Sorry, Dad*; *Shaky Relations*; *Donkey Work*.

Brittain, Vera (1893–1970), *Testament of Youth* (1933). Upper-middle-class young woman becomes battlefield nurse in World War I and finds her attitudes to herself and her society completely changed. A classic. Also: *Testament of Friendship*; *Testament of Experience*.

Chang, Jung, *Wild Swans* (1991). The author grew up in Mao's China, only escaping to study abroad after cultural Revolution. Through her own story and those of her mother and grandmother, she tells the unhappy story of China in the 20th century.

Douglass, Frederick, *Narrative of the Life of an American Slave* (1845). Moving recollections of life as a slave in the pre-Civil War South by man who went on to become the first great African–American orator and leader.

Durrell, Gerald (1925–95), *My Family and Other Animals* **(1956)**. Idyllic childhood of young naturalist in 1930s Corfu. The animals are described with zestful seriousness; the humans are like the cast of some eccentric farce. A classic. Also: *Birds, Beasts and Relatives*; *Fillets of Place*.

Feynman, Richard, *Surely You're Joking, Mr. Feynman* **(1985)**. Endearing, entertaining and intellectually stretching memoir by Nobel Prize-winning physicist who added new realms of meaning to the word 'eccentric'.

Frame, Janet (born 1924), *An Autobiography* **(1990)**. Compendium of three books: *To the Island*, about growing up in rural New Zealand, *An Angel at my Table*, a scarring account of eight years in a mental hospital, and *The Envoy from Mirror City*, about trying to make a career as a writer, falling in love and finding happiness at last.

Gosse, Edmund, *Father and Son* **(1907).** Classic account of two generations clashing in the story of Gosse's relationship with his God-fearing, terrifying father and his attempts to fashion his own character.

Holroyd, Michael, *Basil Street Blues* **(1999)**. Acclaimed biographer of Strachey and Shaw turns the spotlight on his own eccentric family in a richly enjoyable, very funny book.

Keenan, Bryan, *An Evil Cradling* **(1992)**. Keenan turns his terrible experiences as a hostage in Beirut into a luminous, beautifully written account of suffering, friendship and forgiveness.

Levi, Primo, *If This Is a Man* **(1987**). Levi's unsparing memoir of life in Auschwitz forces us to contemplate both the depths and the heights of the human spirit.

McCourt, Frank (born 1930) *Angela's Ashes* **(1996)**. Compelling story of surviving, with humour and humanity intact, a childhood spent in poverty and deprivation in 1930s and 1940s Limerick. Sometimes harrowing, often very funny. *'Tis* is a sequel continuing McCourt's story after he emigrated to New York as a young man.

Wolff, Tobias, *This Boy's Life* **(1999)**. How to survive the perils and pleasures of a typical American adolescence when you're living in a very untypical (for the 1950s) family.

Also recommended: Andrea Ashworth, *Once in a House on Fire*; Diana Athill, *Stet*; Brendan Behan, *Borstal Boy*; Bruce Chatwin, *What Am I Doing Here?*; Robert Graves, *Goodbye to All That*; Ben Hamper, *Rivethead*; Laurie Lee, *As I Walked Out One Midsummer Morning*; Vladimir Nabokov, *Speak, Memory*; Lorna Sage, *Bad Blood*; Wole Soyinka, *Ake*; Peter Ustinov, *Dear Me*; Joan Wyndham, *Love Lessons*.

free-for-all. In the first segment, Quinn, a writer of detective stories, is summoned by someone who wants to get hold of a character called Paul Auster. *Ghosts* sees a detective named Blue hired by White to tail Black and, again, identities seem elastic and fluid. The third volume has the narrator following a friend, the writer Fanshawe who has vanished, leaving behind not only his writing but also his wife and child. Before long, the mysterious Fanshawe is the one doing the following and the narrator the one being pursued.

Auster's other novels include In the Country of Last Things *(in which a woman searches for her brother in a crumbling, post-apocalyptic city),* The Music of Chance *(in which a professional gambler drifts across America winning and losing at cards)* Mr. Vertigo, Moon Palace, Leviathan, The Invention of Solitude *and* Timbuktu. The Art of Hunger *consists of essays, largely on literary subjects.*

> READ ON >

● *The Invention of Solitude.*
▶ Robert Coover, *Ghost Town* (undermines the Western genre just as Auster undermines the detective story); ▷ Don DeLillo, *Running Dog*; ▷ Thomas Pynchon, *The Crying of Lot 49*; Cameron McCabe, *The Face on the Cutting Room Floor* (very different in style and setting but also takes apart the conventions of the detective story to great effect).

READ ON A THEME: AUSTRALIA

▷ Murray Bail, *Eucalyptus*
▷ Peter Carey, *Oscar and Lucinda*
▷ Bruce Chatwin, *The Songlines*
   David Foster, *The Glade Within the Grove*
▷ Miles Franklin, *My Brilliant Career*
   Howard Jacobson, *Redback*
▷ Thomas Keneally, *Woman of the Inner Sea*
▷ David Malouf, *Remembering Babylon*
▷ H.H. Richardson, *The Getting of Wisdom*
▷ Jane Rogers, *Promised Lands*
▷ Patrick White, *A Fringe of Leaves*
   Tim Winton, *Cloudstreet*

READ ON A THEME: AUTOBIOGRAPHIES AND MEMOIRS (GHOSTED!)

   Margaret George, *The Memoirs of Cleopatra*
▷ Robert Graves, *I, Claudius*
▷ Joseph Heller, *God Knows* (King David of Israel)
   Stephen Marlowe, *The Memoirs of Christopher Columbus*
   Rosalind Miles, *I, Elizabeth*
   Robert Nye, *The Voyage of the Destiny* (Sir Walter Raleigh)
   Augusto Roa Bastos, *I, The Supreme* (Francia, dictator of Paraguay)

B

BAIL, Murray (born 1941)
Australian writer

In two books, Murray Bail proved himself to be a comic novelist of invention and originality, employing farce and absurdity as pinpricks to deflate the pretensions of his characters. *Homesickness* (1980) shows a group of unlikeable tourists and their pilgrimage around the world in search of, one assumes, the mind-broadening effects that travel supposedly brings. Instead what they get is an endless succession of featureless airports and soulless hotels. And visits to a sequence of bizarre museums – a Corrugated Iron museum, an Institute of Marriage where a slice of Queen Victoria's wedding cake is on display, a Museum of Legs. Bail's deadpan recounting of their travels adds to the sense of the tourists' alienation from any real experience of the places they visit. *Holden's Performance* (1987) is the story of an innocent abroad in Australia, an Antipodean Candide who bulldozes his way through life, matter-of-factly observing the antics of the cast of rogues, eccentrics and weirdos that Bail assembles around him. In 1998, after a long silence, Bail published a third novel, *Eucalyptus*, which has none of the comic absurdity of the first two. Instead the book is an unusual love story and a fable about the power of storytelling in which a farmer promises his daughter to anyone who can name all the species of eucalyptus tree on his land. Suitors come and go but the daughter is attracted only by a young man whom she encounters amidst the trees and who tells her a succession of stories about distant lands and cities. A contemporary variant on a classic fairy tale theme, *Eucalyptus* is told in a sensuous, detailed prose that gives substance to a novel that might otherwise have risked affectation and pretentiousness.

> **READ ON**

▷ **Peter Carey, *Oscar and Lucinda*;** ▷ **David Malouf, *The Conversations at Curlow Creek*;** ▷ **Italo Calvino, *Invisible Cities*.**

BAILEY, Paul (born 1937)
British novelist

Bailey's novels explore despair, paranoia and the redemptive promise of love in spare, bleak prose. *At the Jerusalem* (1967) is set in an old people's home; in *A Distant Likeness* (1973) obsession with the crime he is investigating triggers a policeman's delusion and madness. The hero of *Gabriel's Lament* (1986) is a middle-aged man, entirely dominated by his widower father, who finds release only after the old man dies. *Sugar Cane* (1993) examines two lives: those of the venereologist Esther Potocki and the male prostitute 'Stephen'. *Kitty and Virgil*

(1998) is a poignant, cleverly constructed and unusual love story which slowly unveils the relationship between Kitty Crozier, who works for a London publisher, and Virgil Florescu, a poet escaped from the Ceausecus' Romania.

READ ON >

- *Old Soldiers*, *Peter Smart's Confessions* (an actor teeters on the edge of insanity).
- ▶ David Cook, *Happy Endings*; ▷ John Updike, *The Poorhouse Fair*; ▷ Susan Hill, *The Bird of Night*.

BAINBRIDGE, Beryl (born 1934)
British novelist

In British music-hall and stand-up comedy, there is a tradition of using flat, unemotional words to recount the disasters that happen to perfectly ordinary people, whose boring lives conceal passions and aspirations the speaker can only hint at. Bainbridge's short, dialogue-filled novels do the same thing in print. They are horror stories told like everyday gossip, and their downbeat wit and plain style are essential to the effect. *The Bottle-factory Outing* (1974) is about two women, pathologically jealous of one another, who share a flat and make plans for the seductions and other delights of a works outing – which turns out darkly different from anything either suspected. *Another Part of the Wood* (1992) is about a group of friends bickering on a doomed joint holiday in a Welsh forest cottage. In several books, Bainbridge uses real historical characters, imagining for them the same kind of chance-ridden, often desperate lives as those of her invented people. *Young Adolf* (1978) sends Hitler to a tatty 1919 Liverpool boarding house filled with Bainbridge eccentrics. *The Birthday Boys* (1991) is a retelling, a chapter by each of the men involved, of Scott's disastrous 1910–12 Antarctic expedition.

MASTER GEORGIE (1998)
The best and bleakest of Bainbridge's historical fictions, this is the story of Liverpudlian surgeon and photographer George Hardy, who volunteers to take his medical skills to the war in the Crimea. Accompanied by an eccentric entourage of family and friends, including Myrtle, his adoring adoptive sister and Dr. Potter, his increasingly troubled brother-in-law, George flounders through the death and disease of the war in search of meanings that aren't there. Told in a series of narrative voices – including those of Myrtle and Dr. Potter – this is a dark, laconic and moving story that long remains in the mind.

Bainbridge's other novels include A Quiet Life, Harriet Said, The Dressmaker, Sweet William, Injury Time *and* Watson's Apology.

READ ON >

- *An Awfully Big Adventure* (set in shabby provincial theatre in the bleak 1950s). *Every Man for Himself* (Bainbridge's typically idiosyncratic take on the Titanic disaster).
- ▶ ▷ Paul Bailey, *Sugar Cane* ▷ Ian McEwan, *The Cement Garden*; Alice Thomas Ellis, *The Inn at the Edge of the World* ▷ Hilary Mantel, *Fludd*.

BAKER, Nicholson (born 1957)
US writer

The minutiae of life, the tiny details that form the background to most fiction, are brought into the foreground in the early novels of Nicholson Baker. Little happens in a conventional narrative sense but the reader's interest is held by Baker's playfulness with language, his odd, oblique observations and his digressions. In *Room Temperature* (1990) the novel's only action (if that is the right word) is the feeding of a baby. *The Mezzanine* (1988) centres on the short escalator journey of an office worker to the floor on which he works. This makes the books sound dull and they are anything but. They are short books and Baker crams them with the most extraordinary, offbeat information and speculation, often contained in elaborate footnotes in which the word count substantially outmatches that in the main text. What is the physics behind the breaking of shoelaces and why does one break and not the other? Are the hot-air blowers in public toilets really more sanitary than towels? Why and how do straws float in milk? These are the kinds of questions that exercise Baker's protagonists. They also lavish their verbal ingenuity on the praise of perforations and the design of Jiffy-Pop cartons. Some readers will find Baker's knowing ironies and reflections, his stream of consciousness for the designer-label generation deeply irritating. Others will be beguiled by his wit, the attention he gives to the everyday and the way books like *The Mezzanine* and *Room Temperature* reveal the idle, insignificant internal monologues and debates we all conduct as we go about our lives.

THE FERMATA (1994)
After his early novels, Baker gained a certain notoriety by turning his obsessive attention to sex. *Vox* (1992), explicitly detailed about the delights of telephone sex, was followed by *The Fermata*. This is the story of an office temp, Arno Strine, who has the ability to freeze time at the snap of his fingers. He uses this ability to explore erotic possibilities not otherwise available to him, undressing women at will, playing sexual practical jokes on those frozen. Attacked for misogyny by critics who seemed to mistake Baker's views for those of his fictional character, *The Fermata* is actually a witty and clever analysis of the whole idea of pornography and the pornographic gaze, showing a subtle awareness of the issues involved which escaped most of his critics.

Baker's other books (fiction and non-fiction) include *U and I, The Size of Thoughts, The Everlasting Story of Nory* and *Double Fold*.

> **READ ON**

▶ to *The Fermata*: ▷ Will Self, *Cock and Bull*.
▶ to Baker's other fiction: ▷ John Updike, *Couples*; Gilbert Sorrentino, *Imaginative Qualities of Actual Things*.

BALDWIN, James (1924–87)
US writer of novels, plays and non-fiction

In a series of non-fiction books (*Notes of a Native Son*; *The Fire Next Time*; *No Name in the Street*), Baldwin described the fury and despair of alienated US blacks, urging revolution as the only way to maintain racial identity in a hostile environment. His plays and novels tackle the same theme, but add two more, equally passionate: the way fundamentalist Christianity is a destructive force, and the quest for sexual identity in an amoral world. *Go Tell it on the Mountain* (1953) is a novel about a poor Harlem family torn apart by the pressures of born-again Christianity. *Another Country* (1962) shows people living lives of increasing desperation in a corrupt, all-engulfing and terrifying New York. *Giovanni's Room* (1956) is about an American in Paris, having to choose between his mistress and his (male) lover.

Baldwin's other novels are Tell Me How Long the Train's Been Gone, If Beale Street Could Talk *and* Evidence of Things Not Seen*; his short stories are in* Going to Meet the Man. *His plays include* The Amen Corner *and* Blues for Mr Charlie, *and his other non-fiction books are* Nobody Knows My Name, Nothing Personal *(with photos by Richard Avedon) and* A Rap on Race *(with Margaret Mead).*

> READ ON

▶ In Ralph Ellison's *Invisible Man* a rootless black American travels the US in search of identity, and finally – as the book becomes increasingly surreal – continues his quest in hell.

▶ Richard Wright's *Native Son*, first published in 1940, is the story of a young black man driven to crime and murder by racism and deprivation.

▶ Chester Himes's detective novels (e.g. *Cotton Comes to Harlem*) are set in a wildly vibrant and violent Harlem and, crime plots apart, are as unsparing as any of Baldwin's books.

▶ Maya Angelou's autobiographical sequence, beginning with *I Know Why the Caged Bird Sings*, gives sunnier reactions to equally abrasive Southern US black experience.

▶ Books as bleak as Baldwin's about the conjunction of sex, violence and despair: Jean Genet, *Querelle of Brest*; John Rechy, *The City of Night*; John Edgar Wideman, *A Glance Away*.

BALLARD, J.G. (James Graham) (born 1930)
British novelist

Ballard's pessimism about the human race and our capacity for violence and destruction reveals itself in novels which are usually designated science fiction but which stretch the limits of the genre almost to breaking point. Each of these novels takes an aspect of the way we treat the planet, and each other, and extends it towards catastrophe. In some books (e.g. *The Drowned World*, about the melting of the polar ice-caps,) human actions trigger natural disaster. In others (e.g. *Concrete Island*, about a man trapped on a motorway island, and *High Rise*, about the effects on human nature of living in ever-higher tower-blocks) we laboriously reconstruct the world as a single, megalopolitan prison-cell. *Crash*, which gained a new notoriety as a consequence of David Cronenberg's 1996 film version, delves into dark realms of the psyche in its examination of the sexual allure of car crashes and adds new realms of meaning to the word 'auto-eroticism.' Apart from science fiction, Ballard is best known for *Empire of the Sun* (1984), a powerful autobiographical novel about a young teenager in a World War II Japanese internment camp, and its sequel *The Kindness of Women* (1991), about the same boy as a young adult looking for love in post-World War II

England. More recent novels, like *Cocaine Nights* (1996) and *Super-Cannes* (2000), straddle the gap between social analysis and social prediction in their depictions of sex and drugs-fuelled decadence. In *Cocaine Nights* the investigation of a fatal fire in an upmarket Spanish resort reveals violence and anarchy lurking beneath a civilized veneer. In *Super-Cannes* an apparently utopian business community in the south of France, 'an ideas laboratory for the new millennium', is the setting for unsettling mind-games and eventual violence.

Ballard's other books include The Four-Dimensional Nightmare, Hello America *(about European explorers of the future rediscovering a long abandoned US) and* The Atrocity Exhibition/Love and Napalm: Export USA, *a tortured, surrealist meditation on politics, sex and automobile disasters.* The Voices of Time, Myths of the Near Future, Low-flying Aircraft *and the linked volume* The Vermilion Sands *are collections of short stories.*

READ ON >

● *The Day of Creation* (about a scientist trying to find water in drought-stricken Africa, who sees a new river appear miraculously, becomes obsessed with it, and travels up it to find its source and hopefully understand himself). *Rushing to Paradise* (about a post-apocalypse utopia run by a mad, fundamentalist feminist).
▶ William Burroughs, *The Soft Machine*; ▷ Will Self, *My Idea of Fun*; ▷ Philip K. Dick, *Valis*.

BALZAC, Honoré de (1799–1850)
French novelist

Photography was invented during Balzac's lifetime, and there was talk of using it to produce an encyclopedia of human types, catching each trade, profession and character in a suitable setting and at a particularly revealing moment. Balzac determined to do much the same thing in prose: to write a set of novels which would include people of every possible kind, described so minutely that the reader could envisage them as clearly as if they had been photographed. He called the project *The Human Comedy*, and although he died before completing it, it still runs to some 90 pieces of fiction – which can be read separately – and includes over 2000 different characters.

★ OLD GORIOT (LE PÈRE GORIOT) (1834)
Goriot is a lonely old man obsessed by love for his two married daughters. He lives in a seedy Parisian boarding-house (whose contents and inhabitants Balzac meticulously describes), and gradually sells all his possessions, and even cuts down on food, to try to buy his daughters' love with presents. They treat him with a contempt he never notices – in fact everyone despises him except Rastignac, a student living in the same house. Goriot's death-bed scene, where he clutches Rastignac's hand thinking that his daughters have come to visit him at last, is one of Balzac's most moving passages, a deliberate evocation of King Lear's death in Shakespeare's play.

The best-known novels from The Human Comedy *are* César Birotteau *(about a shopkeeper destroyed by ambition),* Eugénie Grandet *(a love story, one of Balzac's few books with a happy ending), and* Cousin Bette *(about a man whose obsessive philandering tears his family apart).* Droll Tales *is a set of farcical short stories, similar to those in Giovanni Boccaccio's* Decameron *or* The Arabian Nights.

READ ON ▷

- *The Curé of Tours* (a similarly detailed, and almost equally moving, study of desolate old age).
- ▶ to Balzac's power and emotional bleakness: ▷ Émile Zola, *Nana*; ▷ François Mauriac, *The Woman of the Pharisees*; Theodore Dreiser, *An American Tragedy*; ▷ Carson McCullers, *The Ballad of the Sad Café*; Hugh Walpole, *The Old Ladies*.
- ▶ to his vision of the 'ant-hill of human aspiration', the senseless, self-destructive bustle of affairs: ▷ Charles Dickens, *Dombey and Son*; George Gissing, *New Grub Street*.

BANKS, Iain (born 1954)
British novelist

As 'Iain Banks', Banks writes literary novels, each of them fuelled with dark, obsessive imaginings. His first novel *The Wasp Factory* (1984) was a disturbing but compelling announcement of his themes. It is the story, in his own words, of Frank Cauldhame, a teenage killer, living with his father on a remote Scottish island where he practises bizarre sacrificial rituals to protect himself against perceived threats. Extremely graphic in its description of blood, death and violence, it is not a book for the easily queasy but creates its own imagined world with great power. *The Bridge* (1986) explores the fantasies of a man about to die after a car-crash – and is set partly on a nightmarish Forth Bridge, partly in the hero's memories of his Scottish childhood, and partly in a mad sword-and-sorcery fantasy adventure into which his fevered imagination projects him. *Complicity* (1993) is about the dilemma of a journalist accused of being a serial killer: will he take the blame, or defend himself by revealing the truth which is at present known to only two people, himself and his best friend, the real killer? *The Business* (1999) is a tale of corruption and conspiracy in a shadowy, centuries-old organization devoted to the making of money. As 'Iain M. Banks', Banks writes science fiction, filled with the same wild humour and bizarre imagination. The 'Culture' novels tell of a future society in which technological advance has created super-beings of great longevity and almost limitless capacities. The advanced inhabitants of the Culture come into contact and often conflict with other less-developed societies throughout the galaxies. Banks's science fiction is basically space opera but space opera with an intelligence and sophistication it doesn't usually possess.

READ ON ▷

- novels: *Canal Dreams, Espedair Street, The Crow Road, Whit*; science fiction: *Use of Weapons, Consider Phlebas, The Player of Games, Excession, Inversions, Look to Windward*.
- ▶ to Banks's literary novels: ▷ Ian McEwan, *The Comfort of Strangers* ▷ Martin Amis, *The Information;* Clive Barker, *The Damnation Game;* ▷ Alasdair Gray, *Lanark*. To his science fiction: Peter F. Hamilton, *The Reality Dysfunction;* Ken McLeod, *The Star Fraction*; Robert Sheckley, *The Alchemical Marriage of Alistair Crompton*.

BARKER, PAT (born 1943)
British novelist

Barker's early novels told, in a no-nonsense, brisk way, about the lives of ordinary people, usually women, poor and in the North of England. In the 1990s she used the same blunt precision on a completely different subject, the experience of fighting men in the First World War, and produced the award-winning trilogy *Regeneration* (1991), *The Eye in the Door* (1993) and *The Ghost Road* (1995). Mixing wholly fictional characters like the anti-heroic Billy Prior with real characters such as the poets Siegfried Sassoon and Wilfred Owen and the psychiatrist William Rivers, Barker succeeded in re-imagining the First World War for a new generation of readers. These novels enter into the heads of young men forced to cause, endure and deal with horrors beyond imagining: in short, not the bravado but the waste of war. Our great-grandparents brought back tales like these, and Owen turned them into lacerating poems; Barker's books strip away time and distance, giving voices to shadows and the inarticulate, so that you feel that this is exactly what it must have been like to live these nightmares. Since completing her First World War trilogy Pat Barker has returned to something like the territory of her earlier fiction with *Another World* (1998) and *Border Crossing* (2001) in which a child psychiatrist working in the north of England is drawn back into a terrible crime in the past.

> **READ ON**

- ● Barker's earlier novels include **Union Street** (filmed as **Stanley and Iris,** with Robert de Niro and Jane Fonda) and the particularly fine **Blow Your House Down.**
- ▶ to the trilogy: Erich Maria Remarque, **All Quiet on the Western Front** (renowned 1930s novel about German squaddies in the First World War); ▷ Sebastian Faulks, **Birdsong**; ▷ Norman Mailer, **The Naked and the Dead** (about bewildered young airmen in the Second World War).
- ▶ to Barker's work in general: ▷ Helen Dunmore, **With Your Crooked Heart** ▷ Margaret Forster, **Mother Can You Hear Me?**; Jane Gardam, **Bilgewater**; Anne Fine, **Telling Liddy.**

BARNES, Julian (born 1946)
British novelist

Barnes worked as editorial assistant on the Oxford English Dictionary, and as a drams critic, before becoming a full-time writer in his early 30s. After two enjoyable but ordinary novels, *Metroland* and *Before She Met Me*, he hit form in 1984 with ☆ *Flaubert's Parrot*. This is a dazzlingly ironical book about a biographer of ▷ Flaubert so obsessed with his subject, so eager to investigate every piece of fluff on Flaubert's carpet or tea-stain on his crockery, that the quest utterly and ludicrously swallows his own identity. In 1986 Barnes followed this with a tour de force of an entirely different kind, *Staring at the Sun*. The heroine (who lives from the 1930s to the 2020s) is offered three main choices in her life, and after twice making the wrong decision (settling for the conventional) she uproots herself in old age, learns to fly and sets off to visit the Seven Wonders of the modern world. In *A History of the World in 10½ Chapters* (1989), Barnes describes a number of skin-of-the-teeth escapes for the human race, epic voyages from life-threatening reality to one mirage of the radiant future after another: Noah's Ark, the raft of the Medusa, a boatful of Jewish refugees, a film crew in the Amazon rain forest. The book also meditates on love – which, in Barnes's most ironical shift of all, may be the solution to the human dilemma, a solution all his characters are too self-obsessed to see. *Talking It Over* (1991) explores an adulterous affair from the point of view of each of the people involved. *Love, Etc* (2000) returns to the same three characters ten years after the events described in *Talking It Over*. *England, England* (1998) is a knowing, sophisticated and often very funny satire on ideas of Englishness. A megalomaniac tycoon creates a theme-park England on the Isle of Wight, filled with all those things deemed quintessentially English, and the fantasy land gradually supersedes the real England.

As well as novels under his own name, Barnes also writes private-eye thrillers as 'Dan Kavanagh'. They include Duffy, Going to the Dogs *and* Putting the Boot In. Letters from London, 1990–95 *is a collection of ruminant, witty journalism about post-Thatcher London and the chattering classes.* Cross Channel *is a collection of meaty short stories.*

> **READ ON**

▶ to *Flaubert's Parrot*: ▷ Vladimir Nabokov, *Pale Fire*.
▶ to *Staring at the Sun*: ▷ Gabriel García Márquez, *Love in the Time of Cholera*.
▶ to *A History of the World in 10½ Chapters*: ▷ Michèle Roberts, *The Book of Mrs Noah*.
▶ to Barnes's other works: Jonathan Coe, *What a Carve Up!*; ▷ Ian McEwan, *Enduring Love*.

BARTH, John (born 1930)
US novelist

Barth is a professor of English, and his novels are academic delights: intellectual bran-tubs crammed with allusions, jokes, puns, throwaway theories, parodies, bizarre historical research and fantasy. *The Sot-Weed Factor* (1960) is a sprawling picaresque fiction set in early 18th-century England and colonial Maryland. In *Giles Goat-boy* (1967), a Messiah-figure and a devil-figure battle it out for the hearts and minds of people in a US university which is also the universe, and in the process we are shown every kind of metaphysical, dogmatic and alchemical hocus-pocus that has ever haunted the human mind. Many would see Barth as an archetypally 60s writer and it was that decade that brought him his greatest popular success but he has continued to produce multi-layered, ambitious and enjoyable novels. *Letters* (1979) is, according to its author, 'an old-time epistolary novel by seven fictitious drolls and dreamers, each of which imagines himself factual.' In *The Last Voyage of Somebody the Sailor* (1991), a 20th-century author who is also a sailor slips through a time-loop from modern Maryland to the fantastical Baghdad of Sinbad the Sailor – and for nearly 600 pages the two environments are deliriously rammed together as if they had been thrown into some kind of literary blender.

Barth's other books include The Floating Opera, The End of the Road, Chimera, *and two concerned specifically with sailing,* Sabbatical *(in which a couple sailing round Chesapeake Bay become identified with every mythical sailor ever heard of) and* The Tidewater Tales *(whose heroes, a writer and a tale-collector, set sail in a boat called Story).* Lost in the Funhouse *contains short stories;* The Friday Book *collects essays and reviews.*

READ ON ▷

▶ to *Giles Goat-boy*: ▷ Robert A. Heinlein, *Stranger in a Strange Land* (for the Messianic theme); ▷ Robertson Davies, *The Rebel Angels* (first book of the Cornish Trilogy, for the theme of the crazed university).

▶ to Barth's work in general: ▷ Thomas Pynchon, *Mason & Dixon*; T.Coraghessan Boyle, *Water Music*; David Foster Wallace, *Infinite Jest*; Donald Barthelme, *Snow White*.

READ ON A THEME: **BATTLING WITH LIFE**

(people at odds with the society around them)
▷ James Baldwin, *Go Tell it on the Mountain*
  T. Coraghessan Boyle, *The Tortilla Curtain*
▷ Peter Carey, *Oscar and Lucinda*
▷ Charles Dickens, *Oliver Twist*
▷ Thomas Hardy, *Jude the Obscure*
▷ Nathaniel Hawthorne, *The Scarlet Letter*
▷ W. Somerset Maugham, *Of Human Bondage*
▷ John Steinbeck, *The Grapes of Wrath*
▷ Émile Zola, *Nana*

See also: Emotionally Ill-at-Ease; Perplexed by Life; Revisiting One's Past

---

BECKETT, Samuel (1906–89)
Irish writer

Novelist, poet and playwright, Beckett produced work both in French and English, issuing translations as he went along. Most of his novels, and his best-known play *Waiting for Godot*, first appeared in French. As a young man he was ▷ Joyce's secretary, and his work owes debts to the monologue which ends *Ulysses* and to the dream-narratives of *Finnegans Wake*. His subject is the futility of human existence, and his characters (the narrators of his books) are tramps, cripples and the insane. His works would be unendurably bleak – many readers find them so – if they were not lit with a fantastical, death-defying black humour and marked by an almost obsessive interest in the potential and limits of language.

Beckett's main novels are Murphy, Watt *and the trilogy* Molloy, Malone Dies *and* The Unnameable. *His plays include* Waiting for Godot, Endgame, Krapp's Last Tape *and* Happy Days. *His poems are in* Collected Poems in English and French. More Pricks than Kicks *is a collection of early, Joycean short stories.*

READ ON ▷

▶ James Joyce, *Ulysses;* Julio Cortazar, *Hopscotch*; Georges Perec, *A Void*; B.S. Johnson, *House Mother Normal*.

BEERBOHM, Max (1876–1956)
British artist and writer

A caricaturist and satirist, Beerbohm published cartoons, parodies, essays and articles ridiculing literary and social figures of the day. His only novel, ☆*Zuleika Dobson* (1911) is a send-up of the university-set romantic novels of the day. Beerbohm turns the genre's conventions on their heads. His Oxford under-graduates, whether gentlemen (world-weary and overbred) or scholars (weedy and obsessive), think of nothing but themselves, until Zuleika, the beautiful grand-daughter of the Warden of Judas College, sweeps into the university and every male in the place (even the statues on their pedestals) starts swooning for love of her.

> READ ON ⟩

● *Seven Men* (short stories).
▶ Nancy Mitford, *Don't Tell Alfred*; ▷ Evelyn Waugh, *Decline and Fall*; Oscar Wilde, *The Picture of Dorian Gray* takes a darker view of similarly self-obsessed characters.

READ ON A THEME: BEFORE THE NOVEL

The novel as we know it was perfected in the 18th century. These books preceded it – but are novels in all but name.
  Apuleius (2nd century), *The Golden Ass*
  John Bunyan (17th century), *Pilgrim's Progress*
  Cervantes (16th century), *Don Quixote*
▷ Homer (c9th century BCE), *The Odyssey*
  Thomas Malory (15th century), *Morte d'Arthur*
  Petronius (1st century), *Satyricon*
▷ François Rabelais (16th century), *Gargantua* and *Pantagruel*

READ ON A THEME: BEFORE THE WEDDING

  John Berger, *To the Wedding*
  Isabel Colegate, *Statues in a Garden*
▷ Roddy Doyle, *The Snapper*
▷ Carson McCullers, *The Member of the Wedding*
  David Nobbs, *A Bit of a Do*
▷ Carol Shields, *The Republic of Love*
▷ Eudora Welty, *Delta Wedding*

BELLOW, Saul (born 1915)
US novelist and playwright

In Bellow's view, one of the most unexpected aspects of life in the modern world, and particularly in the post-Christian West, is that many people have lost all sense of psychological and philosophical identity. All Bellow's leading characters feel alienated from society. Some are content to suffer; others try to assert themselves, to invent an identity and live up to it – an attempt which is usually both bizarre and doomed. The hero of *The Adventures of Augie March* (1953), trying to model himself on one of ▷Hemingway's men of action, takes his girl-friend lizard-hunting in Mexico with a tame eagle, and is amazed when she leaves him. The hero of *Henderson the Rain King* (1959) goes on safari to darkest Africa, only to be taken prisoner by a remote people who think him a god-king and mark him for sacrifice. All of Bellow's fiction is written in a rich and expansive prose and the exuberance of his imagination, clear both in description and in the creation of character, adds life and energy to what is already philosophically intriguing.

★ HUMBOLDT'S GIFT (1975)

The book's hero, Charlie Citrine, is a wise-cracking, street-wise failure. He is a writer whose inspiration has run out, a husband whose wife is divorcing him and whose mistress despises him, an educated man terrified of brainwork. Unexpectedly, a legacy from a dead friend, a drunken, bawdy poet, turns out not to be the worthless pile of paper everyone imagines but a scenario which forms the basis for a hugely successful film. Wealth is now added to Citrine's problems, and he is battened on by tax officials, accountants, salesmen and an unsuccessful crook who tries to extort from him first money and then friendship. As the novel proceeds, Citrine keeps nerving himself to make the decision – any decision – that will focus his life, and is hampered each time by ludicrous circumstances and by the contrast between his own inadequacy and the memory of his larger-than-life, dead friend.

Bellow's other full-length novels are Mr Sammler's Planet, Herzog, The Dean's December *and* More Die of Heartbreak. *Publication of* Ravelstein, *a novel of mortality and friendship, in 2000 showed that old age had brought little diminution of Bellow's creative zest and imagination.* Dangling Man, The Victim, Seize the Day, A Theft, The Bellarosa Connection *and* The Actual *are mid-length novellas, and his short stories are collected in* Mosby's Memoirs, Something to Remember Me By *and* Him With the Foot in His Mouth. It All Adds Up *is a fat, juicy collection of non-fiction. He has also written plays and a fascinating political memoir about a visit to Israel,* To Jerusalem and Back.

> READ ON ▷

- *Herzog* **(about a panic-stricken intellectual who revisits the scenes of his past life trying to find clues to his psychological identity: cue for a magnificent travelogue through the city of Chicago, Bellow's consistent inspiration and this book's other central 'character').**
- ▶ **to Bellow's theme of people searching for identity:** ▷ **Albert Camus,** *The Fall*; ▷ **William Golding,** *The Paper Men*; **Bernard Malamud,** *A New Life*; ▷ **Margaret Atwood,** *Surfacing*.
- ▶ **to Bellow's work in general:** ▷ **Philip Roth,** *American Pastoral*; **Henry Roth,** *Call It Sleep*; ▷ **Mordecai Richler,** *Barney's Version*.

BENNETT, Arnold (1867–1931)
British novelist and non-fiction writer

Bennett worked as a journalist (he once edited *Woman's Own*), and then spent eight years in Paris, setting himself up as playwright, novelist and essayist. He was a workaholic, writing hundreds of thousands of words each year, and much of his output was pot-boiling. But his best novels and stories, set in the area he called 'the Five Towns' (Stoke-on-Trent and its surrounding conurbations), are masterpieces. They deal in a realistic way with the lives and aspirations of ordinary people (factory hands, shop assistants, housewives), but are full of disarming optimism and fantasy. Bennett's characters have ambitions; they travel, they read, they dream. Apart from the Five Towns novels his best-known works are two books originally written as magazine-serials: *The Card* (about a bouncy young man whose japes outrage provincial society but who ends up as mayor) and *The Grand Babylon Hotel*, a set of linked stories about the guests and staff in a luxury hotel.

THE OLD WIVES' TALE (1908)
The lives of two sisters are contrasted: vivacious Sophia and steady Constance. Sophia feels constricted by life in the Five Towns, falls for a handsome wastrel and elopes with him to Paris, where he deserts her. Constance meanwhile marries a clerk in her father's shop, and settles to a life of bored domesticity. The novel charts the sisters' lives, and includes memorable scenes of the 1870 siege of Paris in the Franco-Prussian War. Its concluding section unites the sisters, now elderly, and shows, as their lives draw to a close, that those lives were all they had, that neither achieved anything or made any impact on the world.

The Five Towns novels are Anna of the Five Towns, The Old Wives' Tale, Clayhanger, Hilda Lessways, These Twain *and* The Roll Call. Riceyman Steps, *which tells the tragedy of a miserly second-hand bookseller in London's Clerkenwell, is grimmer and more* ▷ *Zolaesque.*

READ ON ▷

● *Clayhanger; Riceyman Steps.*
▶ ▷ **D.H. Lawrence,** *The Rainbow;* ▷ **H.G. Wells,** *Ann Veronica;* **Theodore Dreiser,** *Sister Carrie;* ▷ **W. Somerset Maugham,** *Of Human Bondage.* ▷ **J.B. Priestley,** *Angel Pavement;* **Sherwood Anderson,** *Winesburg, Ohio* **(a set of stories about a US small town whose people's feelings and lives echo those of Bennett's characters).**

BENSON, E.F. (Edward Frederic) (1867–1940)
British novelist and non-fiction writer

Benson came from one of the most illustrious of all Victorian families. His father was an Archbishop of Canterbury; one of his brothers was a high-ranking Cambridge don; another was a Roman Catholic monsignor; his sister was one of the first women to take a first at Oxford. As a young man, Benson was a dandy, a friend of Oscar Wilde – and published a scandalously homoerotic novel about public-school life. He wrote over 120 books altogether, and is best remembered today for acid social comedies, and particularly for the 'Mapp and Lucia' series, televized with enormous success in the mid-1980s. Their characters are well-to-do, middle-class Edwardians, whose chief interest in life is social one-upmanship. One's bridge party, one's garden, one's paintings or one's recipes must simply outclass everyone else's, and if there is the slightest risk of failure, devious means must be employed.

☆ MAPP AND LUCIA (1935)

In previous books in the series we met Lucia, social queen of the little town of Riseholme, and Miss Mapp, who holds the same position in Tilling. Now Lucia moves to Tilling for the summer with her friend Georgie Pillson, rents Mapp's beloved house Mallards, and proceeds to upstage Mapp socially at every moment and in every way. The war between the ladies is fought at garden parties, poetry evenings and dinner-parties, and finally reaches its climax – one of Benson's most preposterous inventions – on an upturned table in the English Channel.

Benson's other comic novels, similar in themes and wit to the 'Lucia' books, include the 'Dodo' series and the (slightly) more serious Mrs Ames *and* Secret Lives.

> READ ON

- ● *Queen Lucia*; *Paying Guests*.
- ▶ Tom Holt, *Lucia in Wartime* and *Lucia Triumphant* (sequels, as good as Benson at his best).
- ▶ Comparable books of high social comedy, 1930s–1950s set: ▷ P.G. Wodehouse, *Life at Blandings*; ▷ Evelyn Waugh, *Vile Bodies*; Nancy Mitford, *Love in a Cold Climate*.

READ ON A THEME: THE BIBLE

Old Testament
  Jenny Diski, *Only Human*
▷ Robert Heinlein, *Job*
▷ Joseph Heller, *God Knows*
▷ Thomas Mann, *Joseph and His Brothers*
▷ Jeanette Winterson, *Boating for Beginners*

New Testament
▷ Anthony Burgess, *The Kingdom of the Wicked*
▷ Jim Crace, *Quarantine*
▷ Norman Mailer, *The Gospel According to the Son*
  George Moore, *The Brook Kerith*
▷ Michèle Roberts, *The Wild Girl*
  Jose Saramago, *The Gospel According to Jesus Christ*
  Henryk Sienkiewycz, *Quo Vadis?*

See also: Ancient Greece and Rome; Other Peoples, Other Times

---

BINCHY, MAEVE (born 1940)
Irish novelist

Maeve Binchy is usually classified as a 'romance' writer but this classification can obscure her skill and versatility. Many romance writers appear to write the same novel over and over again. Every Maeve Binchy novel is different, although all demonstrate her humour and humanity. Whether writing about a family in a small Irish village (*The Glass Lake*), a Dublin woman who only becomes her true self

BIOGRAPHY

Next to fiction, biography is the most popular of all forms of literature. More 'Lives' are written, bought and borrowed from libraries than at any other time in history; some people read nothing else. Some biographies (for example, Martin Gilbert's multi-volume *Churchill*) are works of documentary history, with every phrase checked and verified from first-hand accounts. Others set out to explain their subject, to puzzle out his or her psychological identity as well as narrating the life. Others again (the celeb biographies which enjoy their brief shelf-life) are chiefly for fans: memoirs or snapshots whose main purpose is to remind, not tell. The best biographies, perhaps, do all these jobs at once, so that you end up entertained as well as informed, enriched by what you read.

Ackroyd, Peter, *The Life of Thomas More* (1998). Novelist and biographer of several great Londoners (Dickens, Blake) turns his attention to the man for all seasons and comes up with a novel but convincing portrait.

Boswell, James, ★☆ *The Life of Samuel Johnson, Ll.D.* (1791). Classic known by all but read by few. Wonderful, word-by-word accounts of Johnson's table talk, evocative scene-setting, full of personal affection for its subject. Like a window thrown open on 18th-century London.

Ellmann, Richard, *James Joyce* (1968). Magisterial interpretation of the life and work of Ireland's greatest novelist and exile.

Garrow, David J., *Bearing the Cross* (1987). Biography of Martin Luther King, Jr, good on the man, outstanding on the political and social background; and blunt about the legend.

Hamilton, Nigel, *Monty* (1981–6). Three-volume account of the dazzling Second World War general who succumbed to megalomania and melancholy in later life, when peace left him with no role to play.

Holmes, Richard, *Coleridge: Early Visions* (1989) and *Coleridge: Darker Reflections* (1998). Two vividly readable volumes which bring to life the pathos and achievement of Coleridge's struggle to subdue his addiction and fulfil the extraordinary promise of his youth.

Holroyd, Michael, *Lytton Strachey* (1968). Strachey was himself an innovative biographer (see *Eminent Victorians*, 1918), but is also interesting as a member of the Bloomsbury Group, an extraordinarily self-obsessed collection of early 20th-century British writers, artists, critics, autobiographers, biographers and diarists. Holroyd brilliantly untangles their relationships, while still managing to focus on Strachey.

Kershaw, Ian, *Hitler: Hubris 1889–1936* (1998) and *Hitler: Nemesis 1936–1945* (2000). After nearly fifty years Alan Bullock's biography of Hitler has finally been supplanted as the standard work by Kershaw's chilling, two-volume examination of the creation and career of a tyrant.

Lahr, John, *Prick Up Your Ears* (1978). The short life and violent death of legendary playwright Joe Orton evoked, together with his claustrophobic and eventually fatal relationship with Kenneth Halliwell.

Motion, Andrew, *Philip Larkin* (1993). Motion, himself a poet and a friend and colleague of Larkin, undertook the difficult task of a biography of an intensely private man and produced one of the best lives of a poet in years.

Pimlott, Ben, *The Queen* (1996). Most recent royal biographies have been exercises in prurience, banality or both – here's one of the few written with genuine intelligence and insight.

Tillyard, Stella, *Aristocrats* (1994). Entertaining and successful multi-biography in which Tillyard recreates the upper-class 18th-century world of the four Lennox sisters.

Also recommended: Claire Tomalin, *Mrs Jordan's Profession*; Antonia Fraser, *Cromwell: Our Chief of Men*; Vincent Cronin, *Napoleon*; Amanda Foreman, *Georgiana, Duchess of Devonshire*; Robert Blake, *Disraeli*; Patrick French, *Younghusband*; Gitta Sereny, *Albert Speer*; Dava Sobel, *Longitude*; Victoria Glendinning, *Jonathan Swift*; Denis Mack Smith, *Mussolini*; Bernard Crick, *George Orwell: A Life*.

when she spends time away from Dublin and her home (*Tara Road*) or two old friends whose friendship becomes something more as they struggle to achieve their ambition of running the best catering company in Dublin (*Scarlet Feather*), Binchy provides affectionate and compelling tapestries of ordinary people's lives and loves.

Maeve Binchy's other novels include Circle of Friends, Echoes, Evening Class, The Firefly Summer, Light a Penny Candle *and* Silver Wedding. The Lilac Bus *is a set of linked short stories about the passengers who travel regularly on a small country bus*. Victoria Line, Central Line *is a collection of short stories about passengers on the Tube*.

READ ON $\triangleright$

● *Echoes.*
▶ Rosamunde Pilcher, *The Shell Seekers*; $\triangleright$ Edna O'Brien, *The Country Girls*; Patricia Scanlan, *Promises, Promises*; Clare Boylan, *Holy Pictures*; Cathy Kelly, *She's The One.*

READ ON A THEME: BLACK BRITONS

Diran Adebayo, *Some Kind of Black*
David Dabydeen, *The Intended*
Bernardine Evaristo, *The Emperor's Babe*
Hanif Kureishi, *The Buddha of Suburbia*
Andrea Levy, *Never Far From Nowhere*
Meera Syal, *Anita & Me*
Zadie Smith, *White Teeth*
Stephen Thompson, *Toy Soldiers*

BLINCOE, Nicholas (born 1966)
British novelist

Writing novels that veer wildly and entertainingly from black comedy to graphically described violence and action, Nicholas Blincoe has been one of the stars of a new wave of British crime fiction in the last ten years. Drawing on the traditions of American pulp and noir fiction rather than the (mostly) cosier conventions of the average British crime novel, he has written several books that bristle with sharp prose and snappy, streetwise dialogue. His first book, *Acid Casuals* (1997), the story of a transsexual's bloody return to her native Manchester and the drugs scene there, was followed by *Jello Salad* (1997), set in a Soho peopled almost exclusively by drug-fried addicts and homicidal maniacs. Fast-paced and imaginative, they treated even the most gruesome violence with black comic detachment. *The Dope Priest* (1999) saw Blincoe move his setting from Britain to the Middle East but continue to provide a cocktail of thrills, farce and drug-fuelled mayhem. In 2000 Blincoe was one of the editors of the anthology of young British writers *All Hail the New Puritans* which began with a manifesto stating (among other things) that, 'As faithful representations of the present, our texts will avoid all improbable or unknowable speculations on the past or the future.' His own novels have, arguably, not been especially 'faithful representations of the present' but they have been no less enjoyable for that.

READ ON >

▶ James Hawes, *White Merc with Fins*; Jeremy Cameron, *Vinnie Got Blown Away*; Colin Bateman, *Cycle of Violence*; Charles Higson, *King of the Ants*.

BLISH, James (1921–75)
US novelist

Blish's many science fiction books for children include a dozen novels based on the TV series *Star Trek*. His adult books range from space opera – for example the 'Cities in Flight' novels, in which a mechanism is devised to spin whole sections of the Earth's surface into space, where their inhabitants eagerly or apprehensively set about reinventing their own lives – to more serious works such as the 'After Such Knowledge' tetralogy, using the forms and styles of science fiction to discuss complex philosophical and religious ideas.

A CASE OF CONSCIENCE (1959)
This book, one of the 'After Such Knowledge' novels, is claimed by some readers to be not only Blish's masterpiece, but one of the finest books in the science fiction genre. A Jesuit Earth-scientist on an unexplored, paradisal planet wonders whether the fact that he is a human being, one of God's supreme creations, gives him superiority over the alien inhabitants, who are an ethical but godless race of intelligent lizards. He decides that the planet is a creation of the Devil – and then has to face the idea that this is heresy, since only God is able to create.

The other books in the 'After Such Knowledge' series (all self-contained) are Black Easter, Doctor Mirabilis *and* The Day After Judgement. *The 'Cities in Flight' novels are* They Shall Have Stars, A Life for the Stars, Earthman Come Home *and* A Clash of Cymbals.

READ ON >

▶ to *A Case of Conscience*: ▷ Philip K. Dick, *The Divine Invasion*; ▷ Michael Moorcock, *Behold the Man*; Keith Roberts, *Kiteworld*; Mary Doria Russell, *The Sparrow*.
▶ to Cities in Flight series: Brian Aldiss, *Non-Stop*; Michael Coney, *The Ultimate Jungle*; Garry Kilworth, *The Night of Kadar*.

BÖLL, Heinrich (1917–85)
German novelist and non-fiction writer

For decades after the Second World War and the 'economic miracle' which followed it, German novelists hovered over their country like doctors examining a particularly interesting patient. How could any nation be so outwardly flourishing and seem so dead inside? Böll, a Roman Catholic, linked the malaise of society with another kind of moral disintegration, the collapse of faith – but instead of preaching or hectoring he tried to alert his readers with bitter, savage satire. *The Safety Net*, for example, is about terrorism. *The Lost Honour of Katharina Blum* satirizes tabloid journalism and our obsession with 'news' in the story of a woman destroyed and driven to violence by the intrusions of the press. In *Group Portrait with Lady* (1971) Böll uses a 'documentary' method to assemble a picture of both an ordinary individual and the teeming German society of which she is part. The book's style is brisk, witty and apparently uncontroversial, so that it is not until the end that we realize just what Böll is saying about Germany's moral plight.

Böll's other novels include And Where Were You, Adam?, Billiards at Half Past Nine *and* Women in a River Landscape. *His short stories are in* Absent Without Leave, Traveller, if you Come to Spa, Children are Civilians Too *and* The Casualty. What's To Become of the Boy? *is a savage memoir of adolescence under the Nazis;* Irish Journal *describes his stay in Ireland in the 1960s, and his affection for the Celtic, Catholic culture he found there.*

READ ON ▷

- *Billiards at Half-past Nine* (a panoramic view of German society in the 50 years during and after World War II, focused on a single family); *The Clown* (a bleak study of one person's attempt to retain dignity, moral integrity and religious faith in a society where such qualities are no longer valued).
- ▶ Robert Musil, *Young Törless.* Nathalie Sarraute, *Portrait of an Unknown Man.*
- ▶ to Böll's work in general: ▷ Saul Bellow, *Mr. Sammler's Planet*; ▷ Günter Grass, *The Call of the Toad.*

READ ON A THEME: BOOZE AND BOOZERS

Charles Bukowski, *Tales of Ordinary Madness*
Joyce Cary, *The Horse's Mouth*
▷ Graham Greene, *The Power and the Glory*
Patrick Hamilton, *Hangover Square*
Charles Jackson, *The Lost Weekend*
▷ Malcolm Lowry, *Under The Volcano*
▷ Flann O'Brien, *The Poor Mouth*
George Pelecanos, *Down by the River Where the Dead Men Go*
Budd Schulberg, *The Disenchanted*

BORGES, Jorge Luis (1899–1987)
Argentinian short story writer and poet

Until the 1950s Borges worked as a librarian and was an admired poet. He had to give up librarianship when he went blind, but he always claimed that the 'darkness of his eyes' enabled him to see better in his writings. In the 1950s his 'fictions' began to appear in English, and his reputation spread world-wide. A 'fiction' is a short prose piece, ranging in length from a paragraph to a half-dozen pages. Some are short stories, in the manner of ▷ Kipling, Chesterton or ▷ Kafka (whom Borges translated into Spanish). Others are tiny surrealist meditations, zen-like philosophical riddles or prose-poetry. A 20th-century writer produces a version of *Don Quixote* for modern times – and it is identical, word for word, to the original. A man meets a mysterious stranger by a riverside, and finds that the stranger is himself. The library of the Tower of Babel is meticulously described. A man writes about the terrifying prison which traps him – and only at the end reveals its name: the world.

LABYRINTHS (ENGLISH EDITION 1962)
This is a generous anthology of Borges's work, and gives the flavour particularly of the 'fictions'.

Borges's stories and fictions are in A Universal History of Infamy, Fictions, The Aleph, Dreamings, The Book of Sand *and* Doctor Brodie's Report. *His* Selected Poems *were published in English translation in 1972.*

> READ ON

- ● *The Book of Imaginary Beings* **(descriptions of 120 fanciful creatures from the weirder recesses of the world's imagination: the chimera, the Cheshire cat, the chonchon, the lunar hare, the elephant that foretold Buddha's birth, the 36 lamed wufniks, Haokah the thunder-god, Youwakee the flying girl, and so on).**
- ▶ ▷ **Gabriel García Márquez,** *Innocent Erendira*; **G.K. Chesterton,** *The Man Who Was Thursday*; **Robert Coover,** *Pricksongs and Descants*; ▷ **Italo Calvino,** *Invisible Cities.*

BOWEN, Elizabeth (1899–1973)
Irish novelist and short story writer

Although Bowen's themes were emotional – loneliness; longing for love; lack of communication – she wrote in a brisk and faintly eccentric style (italicizing the most unlikely words, *for* example) which gives her stories an exhilarating feeling of detachment from the events and reactions they describe. She was especially skilful at evoking atmosphere in houses or locales – London streets and tube-stations during the 1940s Blitz, for example (the setting of 'Mysterious Kor', possibly her finest short story), become places of eerie fantasy rather than reality. Her concern, despite her characters' craving to preserve the social niceties, was to show 'life with the lid off' – and this, coupled with the unpredictability of her writing style, constantly edges her plots from realism through dream to nightmare.

☆ THE DEATH OF THE HEART (1938)
Portia, a naive 16–year-old orphan (in a more modern book she might be 12 or 13) goes to live with her stuffy half-brother and his brittle, insecure wife in fashionable 1930s London. Her innocence is in marked contrast to their world-weary sophistication, and they are as exasperated with her as she is with them. Then she falls in what she imagines to be love, and all parties are launched on an ever-bumpier emotional ride.

Bowen's other novels include The House in Paris, A World of Love *and* Eva Trout. *Her short stories are published in* Encounters, Ann Lee's, Joining Charles, The Cat Jumps *and the World War II collections* Look at All Those Roses *and* The Demon Lover. Bowen's Court *is an idiosyncratic but compelling account of her Anglo-Irish family's history.*

READ ON ▷

- *The Heat of the Day* (in which a doomed love affair is conducted against the backdrop of Second World War London); *Eva Trout*.
- ▶ to Bowen's novels: ▷ Henry James, *The Wings of the Dove*; ▷Angus Wilson, *The Middle Age of Mrs. Eliot*; ▷ Iris Murdoch, *The Sandcastle*.
- ▶ to Bowen's short stories: ▷ Elizabeth Taylor, *A Dedicated Man*; ▷John Fowles, *The Ebony Tower*; ▷ William Trevor, *The Collected Stories*.

BOYD, William (born 1952)
British novelist and screenwriter

Boyd began his career as an Oxford don and a film critic. His early books were serious farces, in the manner of ▷ Waugh's *A Handful of Dust* or *Sword of Honour*. He is particularly biting about ruling-class English idiocy, and the grotesquely inappropriate settings in which it flourishes. *A Good Man in Africa* (1981) detailed the last limp flourishes of colonialism through its portrait of Morgan Leafy, drunken and corrupt representative of Her Majesty's government in the imaginary African state of Kinjanja; *An Ice Cream War* (1982) was set in the forgotten African campaigns of the First World War; *Stars and Bars* (1984, later filmed with Daniel Day-Lewis), the most farcical of all, is about an English innocent seriously at a loss in the lunatic world of the arts in the US. In more recent novels Boyd has turned his attention to contemporary London. *Armadillo* (1998), half noirish thriller, half social satire, follows the story of an upwardly mobile insurance clams adjuster whose life rapidly becomes downwardly mobile when an apparently routine business appointment entangles him in deception and conspiracy.

THE NEW CONFESSIONS (1987)
The 'autobiography' of John James Todd, from inept adolescence at a hearty Scottish school, through ludicrous and ghastly First World War experiences, to a roller coaster career as one of the founding geniuses of German silent cinema. Throughout his life, Todd is obsessed by making a nine–hour epic based on Rousseau's *Confessions*, and is frustrated at every turn: by the coming of sound, the rise of Hitler, the Second World War and McCarthyism. Farcical incidents, but nonetheless a substantial, sombre study of a man in thrall to his own glittering opinion of his past.

Boyd's other books include Brazzaville Beach, The Blue Afternoon, On the Yankee Station *and* The Destiny of Natalie 'X' and Other Stories *(short stories) and* Nat Tate: An American Artist, *a short, spoof biography which gleefully highlights the idiocies and pretensions of the art world*

READ ON ▷

- *Brazzaville Beach*.
- ▶ to the early books: ▷ Anthony Powell, *What's Become of Waring?*; ▷ Malcolm Bradbury, *Stepping Westward*.
- ▶ to *The New Confessions*: Adam Thorpe, *Still*; ▷ Robertson Davies, *What's Bred in the Bone*; ▷ Len Deighton, *Close-up*.
- ▶ to *Armadillo*: ▷ Martin Amis, *The Information*.

BRADBURY, Malcolm (1932–2000)
British novelist and screenwriter

A university professor, Bradbury wrote sharp satires on academic life. The form and style of his first two novels were straightforward, but from *The History Man* onwards he began using experimental methods: fragmenting the plots into short scenes like those of TV plays, writing in the present tense, incorporating footnotes, commentaries and asides. The feeling is that each book is a game, meant to amuse the author as well as the reader – a feature which sets Bradbury apart from all other 'campus' novelists.

THE HISTORY MAN (1975)
The book – far funnier than the TV series it inspired – is set in a brutalist British 'new' university, all bare concrete and graffiti. Its hero is an equally abrasive 'new' academic, the sociologist Howard Kirk. Kirk thinks that sociology is the only study relevant to the modern world, and that it should be a vehicle for radical change. He also believes in sleeping with as many female staff and students as he can entice to bed. He preaches left-wing politics in his seminars, humiliates anyone he suspects of right-wing opinions (for example students who wear ties and call him 'Sir'), organizes sit-ins and strikes, and strides happily through the desta-bilized, quivering society he creates all round him.

Bradbury's other novels are Eating People is Wrong, Stepping Westward, All Dressed Up and Nowhere to Go, Why Come to Slaka, Rates of Exchange, Doctor Criminale *(journalist pursues mysterious philosopher through Europe) and* To the Hermitage, *in which a contemporary story of high-flying academics is intercut with a recreation of Enlightenment thinker Diderot's journey to the court of Catherine the Great*. Cuts *is a long short story,* Mensonge *a send-up of French lit-crit pretentiousness and* No, Not Bloomsbury *a collection of essays, articles and reviews.* Who Do You Think You Are? *collects short stories. He also wrote volumes of literary criticism and TV plays and adaptations of his own and other people's books, including novels by* ▷Evelyn Waugh *and* ▷Tom Sharpe.

> READ ON ▷

- *Stepping Westward* **(about a naive English lecturer on an exchange visit to a liberal western US campus).**
- ▶ **to** *The History Man***: Mary McCarthy,** *The Groves of Academe***; ▷ Vladimir Nabokov,** *Pnin***; Randall Jarrell,** *Pictures from an Institution***; ▷ John Barth,** *The End of the Road***.**
- ▶ **to** *Stepping Westward***: ▷ David Lodge,** *Changing Places* **▷ Tom Sharpe,** *Wilt* **and its glorious, tasteless sequels are campus farce rather than comedy: entertainment for its own gross sake without a whiff of satire.**

BRAGG, Melvyn (born 1939)
British writer

One of the best-known faces on arts TV for 30 years, Bragg has written some 20 novels, all meatily readable and all dealing with aspects of Englishness. Many are set in the Lake District, and explore themes of country life and the coming of industrialization in ways reminiscent of ▷Thomas Hardy or ▷D.H. Lawrence, recast in a more contemporary prose-style. Typical titles are *The Hired Man* (1969), *Josh Lawton* (1972), *Kingdom Come* (1980) and *The Maid of Buttermere* (1987). *A Time to Dance* (1990), about a man's obsessive passion for a younger woman, became a scandalous success as a TV series in 1992, principally because of what one critic called the 'bare-bottom count'. *Crystal Rooms* (1992) is a scathing portrait of the Thatcher London of the 1980s, complete with fatcat politicians, Garrick Club mediafolk, orphans begging in the streets, cynical stockbrokers and corrupt police. *Credo* (1996) was a very different novel to any Bragg had previously written but was the result of a long-cherished ambition to tell the story of the Christianization of the North of England in the 7th century. The result is one of the most satisfying historical novels of the last decade, rich in detail, character and conviction. In his last two novels, *The Soldier's Return* (1999) and *A Son of War* (2001) Bragg records the difficulties Sam Richardson has in adjusting to peacetime after service in the Second World War and his relationship with his growing son.

Bragg's other novels include Autumn Manoeuvres, The Silken Net, For Want of a Nail *and* Love and Glory. *He has also written biographies of Richard Burton* (Rich) *and Laurence Olivier.*

> **READ ON**

- ● *A Place in England.*
- ▶ to *Crystal Rooms:* ▷ Martin Amis, *London Fields*; Jonathan Coe, *What a Carve Up!*
- ▶ to Bragg's Cumbria-set books: Stanley Middleton, *The Daysman*; David Storey, *Saville*; ▷ D. H. Lawrence, *Sons and Lovers*.

BRINK, André (born 1935)
South African novelist

In the South Africa of the apartheid era it was impossible for an honest novelist to ignore the central tenet of crude racial injustice on which society was founded. All the country's finest novelists, from ▷ Nadine Gordimer to ▷ J.M. Coetzee, had to find their own fictional means to confront it. André Brink's novels have told very different stories in very different forms and voices. An historical novel of great poignancy, set in the 18th century, in which a white woman, wife of an explorer, and a black runaway slave are stranded in the South African wilderness and embark on a doomed love affair as they trek painfully back towards the Cape (*An Instant in the Wind*). A huge, intricately plotted story that borrows significantly from the thriller genre in its description of people caught up in a plot to assassinate the State President outside the gates of Cape Town Castle (*An Act of Terror*). The story of an ordinary, decent man drawn ever further into a quagmire of state corruption when he persists in the investigation of the death of a man he knew in police custody (*A Dry White Season*). All represent, in some ways, Brink's responses to the iniquities of apartheid. In the new South Africa Brink has continued to find interesting ways of exploring his country's past and present. In *Imaginings of Sand* South Africa is on the verge of its first democratic elections and an exile returns to the deathbed of her 103–year old grandmother. Through her grandmother and the stories, both personal and national, she tells, the returned exile learns new truths about the oppressions and deceits of history.

Stories and myths are at the heart of *Devil's Valley* (1998), an inspired mix of fantasy and realism in which Flip Lochner, a hard-drinking newspaperman, stumbles across a bizarre Boer community which has spent 150 years in isolation from the outside world. In this, as in all his pre- and post-apartheid fiction, Brink shows an acute political intelligence allied to the imagination of a fine storyteller.

READ ON >

- *Looking on Darkness (a black actor faces execution for the murder of his white lover).*
- ▶ J.M. Coetzee, *In the Heart of the Country*; ▷ Nadine Gordimer, *The Late Bourgeois World*; Breyten Breytenbach, *A Season in Paradise*; Alan Paton, *Cry, the Beloved Country.*

BRODKEY, Harold (1930–96)
US writer

One of the great vanishing acts in American letters, Brodkey, whose real name was Harold Weintraub, had his first collection of short fiction *First Love and Other Sorrows* published in 1957, to great acclaim. Brodkey announced that his next book would be a novel entitled *A Party for Animals*. Despite persistent rumours that this long-gestating work was on its way, it didn't actually arrive and the silence was broken only occasionally by the appearance of another story (often in *The New Yorker*) and, inevitably, more rumours. For years, tales about Brodkey circulated more frequently than tales by him. In 1985, when all but his most ardent fans had abandoned hopes of seeing a new Brodkey book, one actually appeared, a volume of stories entitled *Women and Angels* (1985). This was followed, in a rare burst of activity, by yet another collection, *Stories in an Almost Classical Mode* (1988). Brodkey's novel finally showed up in 1991, an auto-biographical work called *The Runaway Soul*. Accorded respectful, if often bemused, reviews, the book could not help but disappoint a public who by now felt that Brodkey's talent lay not so much in writing a novel as in not writing one. After two further works, *Profane Friendship*, a tale of sexual obsession, and the harrowing and self-explanatory *My Life, My Wife and AIDS* (1994), Brodkey died of an AIDS-related illness. Probably his finest book is the *Stories in an Almost Classical Mode*, a collection of finely honed masterpieces. Curiously, given his inability, or perhaps reluctance, to complete his novel, several of the stories are quite long ('Largely an Oral History of My Mother', at over 80 pages, is a novella, while 'The Abundant Dreamer', 'Angel', 'The Shooting Range', 'S.L.' and the title story are all between 40–50 pages), but each one is of a quality rarely found in modern fiction.

READ ON >

- to the short stories – ▶ Andre Dubus, *Selected Stories*; John Cheever, *The Collected Stories.*
- read on to *The Runaway Soul* – (different settings and different styles but similar theme of brilliant man's emergence from a troubled family into a threatening world) ▷ Saul Bellow, *The Adventures of Augie March*; Henry Roth, *Call It Sleep* (Roth is also the only US writer to suffer a longer case of writer's block than Brodkey – he published nothing for nearly 60 years).

BRONTË, Charlotte (1816–55)

BRONTË, Emily (1818–48)
British novelists

Much has been made of the Brontës' claustrophobic life in the parsonage at Haworth in Yorkshire, and of the way they compensated for a restricted and stuffy daily routine by inventing wildly romantic stories. Their Haworth life was first described by a novelist (▷ Mrs. Gaskell), and is as evocative as any fiction of the time. In some ways it colours our opinion of their work: for example, if the third sister, Anne, had not been a Brontë, few people would nowadays remember her novels, which are pale shadows of her sisters' books. But Charlotte and Emily need no biographical boosting. They were geniuses, with a (remarkably similar) fantastical imagination, a robust, melodramatic view of what a 'good story' ought to be, and a pre-Freudian understanding of the dark places of the soul. Their brooding landscapes and old, dark houses may have been drawn from life, but what they made of them was an original, elaborate and self-consistent world, as turbulent as dreams.

JANE EYRE (BY CHARLOTTE BRONTË, 1847)
The plot is a romantic extravaganza about a poor governess who falls in love with her employer Mr Rochester, is prevented from marrying him by the dark secret which shadows him, and only finds happiness on the last page, after a sequence of melodramatic and unlikely coincidences. The book's power is in its counterpointing of real and psychological events. We read about storms, fires, wild-eyed creatures gibbering in attics and branches tapping at the windows – but what we are really being shown is the turmoil in Jane's own soul, the maturing of a personality. This emotional progress, magnificently described, unifies the book and transmutes even its silliest events to gold.

★☆ WUTHERING HEIGHTS (BY EMILY BRONTË, 1847)
The story begins in the 1770s, when a rich Yorkshire landowner, Earnshaw, brings home a half-wild, sullen foundling he names Heathcliff. Heathcliff grows up alongside Earnshaw's own children, and falls in love with Cathy, the daughter. But he overhears her saying that she will never marry him because she is socially above him – and the rest of the novel deals with his elaborate revenge on her whole family and the way the emotional poison is eventually neutralized. As in *Jane Eyre*, desolate moorland and lonely, rain-lashed houses are used as symbols of the passions in the characters' hearts. Heathcliff, in particular, is depicted as if he were a genuine 'child of nature', the offspring not of human beings but of the monstrous mating of darkness, stone and storm.

All three sisters wrote Wordsworthy, nature-haunted poetry. Emily's only completed novel was Wuthering Heights; *Charlotte's were* Jane Eyre, The Professor *and* Villette; *Anne's were* Agnes Grey *and* The Tenant of Wildfell Hall.

READ ON ▷

● to *Jane Eyre*: *Wuthering Heights*.
● to *Wuthering Heights*: *Jane Eyre*.

▶ to *Jane Eyre*: ▷ Daphne Du Maurier, *Rebecca*; ▷ Jean Rhys, *Wide Sargasso Sea*; ▷ Margaret Mitchell, *Gone With the Wind*; George Douglas Brown, *The House With the Green Shutters*.

▶ to *Wuthering Heights*: Lin Haire-Sargeant, *Heathcliffe* (romance sequel); R.D. Blackmore, *Lorna Doone*; ▷ Thomas Hardy, *Tess of the d'Urbervilles*; ▷ Iris Murdoch, *The Unicorn* (about the turbulent passions of a more modern heroine).

BROOKNER, Anita (born 1928)
British novelist

As well as writing fiction, Brookner has worked as a lecturer and expert on fine art. Her novels are written in a stylish, witty, undemonstrative prose – one exactly suiting the characters of her people. They are middle-aged, upper-middle-class women (professors, librarians, novelists): well-off, well-tailored, well-organized and desperately lonely. Something has blighted their emotional lives, leaving them to order their comfortable, bleak existences as best they can, to fill their days. The books show us what brought them to their condition – usually the actions of others: husbands, parents or friends – and sometimes tell us how the problem is resolved. In 'well-made' stage and film dramas of the 1930s, women were always blinking back tears and bravely facing the future. Brookner's heroines, except that they have lost even the power to cry, try to do the same.

LOOK AT ME (1983)
Frances Hinton, librarian at a medical research institute, lives a disciplined, unvarying existence which she compares wistfully with what she imagines to be the exuberant, exciting lives of the research workers and others who use the books. She is 'taken up' by one of the most brilliant men, dazzling as a comet, and by his emotionally extrovert wife. She falls in love and imagines that she is loved in return. But what looks like being a sentimental education in fact teaches her only that all human beings are islands, and that unless we hoard our inner lives and treasure our privacy, we will lose even what peace of mind we have.

Brookner's other novels include A Start in Life, Providence, A Friend from England, Latecomers, Brief Lives, A Closed Eye, Incidents in the Rue Laugier, Falling Slowly and Undue Influence. *Her most recent novel* The Bay of Angels (2001) *reveals once again her unrivalled capacity to draw us into lives that are often pinched and circumscribed but that have their own small dramas and epiphanies. Anita Brookner is an expert on 18th- and 19th-century French art, and has published books about the painters Watteau, Greuze and David and* Soundings, *a collection of art history essays.*

> READ ON ▷

● *Hotel du Lac; A Family Romance.*
▶ Elizabeth Jane Howard, *Something in Disguise*; Edward Candy, *Scene Changing*; ▷ A.S. Byatt, *The Virgin in the Garden*; Jenny Diski, *Rainforest*; Susan Fromberg Shaeffer, *The Injured Party*.

BUCHAN, John (1875–1940)
British novelist

John Buchan combined a literary career with a life in public service, culminating in a five-year period as governor-general of Canada. As befits the works of an imperial administrator, his many novels celebrate British pluck and derring-do. His thrillers play virtuoso variations on the same basic plot. A stiff-upper-lipped hero (often Richard Hannay) discovers a conspiracy to End Civilization as We Know It, and sets out single-handed, or with the help of a few trusted friends, to frustrate it. He is chased (often by the police as well as by the criminals), and wins through only by a combination of physical courage and absolute moral certainty. The pleasure of Buchan's novels is enhanced by the magnificently described wild countryside he sets them in (usually the Scottish highlands or the plains of southern Africa), and by their splendid gallery of minor characters, the shop-keepers, tramps, local bobbies and landladies who help his heroes, often at enormous (if shrugged-off) personal risk.

★ THE THIRTY-NINE STEPS (1915)
Richard Hannay, returning from South Africa, is told by a chance American acquaintance of a plot to invade England. Soon afterwards the American is killed and Hannay is framed for his murder. To escape two manhunts, one by the conspirators and the other by the police, he takes to the hills, and only after 300 pages of breathtaking peril and hair's-breadth escapes does he succeed in saving his country and clearing his name.

Buchan's other thrillers include Huntingtower, John McNab *and* Witchwood *(all set in Scotland), and the Hannay books* Greenmantle, Mr Standfast, The Three Hostages *and* The Island of Sheep. *He also wrote a number of lively historical novels including* The Free Fishers, *set at the time of the Napoleonic Wars, and* The Blanket of the Dark, *an ingenious narrative built round a rightful heir to the Tudor throne and a plot to assassinate Henry VIII.*

> READ ON

- ● *Greenmantle*; *Mr Standfast*; *Prester John* **(an African adventure as exciting and bizarre as anything by ▷ H. Rider Haggard, whose *She* makes an excellent follow-up).**
- ▶ **Erskine Childers, *The Riddle of the Sands*; Geoffrey Household, *Rogue Male*.**

BURGESS, Anthony (1917–93)
British novelist and non-fiction writer

Originally a composer, Burgess began writing books in his mid-30s, and poured out literary works of every kind, from introductions to ▷Joyce (*Here Comes Everybody/Re Joyce*) to filmscripts, from opera libretti to book reviews. Above all he wrote several dozen novels, of a diversity few other 20th-century writers have ever equalled. They range from fictionalized biographies of Shakespeare (*Nothing Like the Sun*) and the early Christian missionaries (*The Kingdom of the Wicked*) to farce (the four Enderby stories, of which *Inside Mr Enderby* is the first and *Enderby's Dark Lady* is the funniest), from experimental novels (*The Napoleon Symphony*, about Napoleon, borrows its form from Beethoven's Eroica

Symphony) to semi-autobiographical stories about expatriate Britons in the Far East (*The Malaysian Trilogy*). The literary demands of Burgess's books vary as widely as their contents: the way he finds a form and style to suit each new inspiration is one of the most brilliant features of his work.

☆ A CLOCKWORK ORANGE (1972)

In a grim future Britain, society is divided into the haves, who live in security-screened mansions in leafy countryside, and the have-nots, who swagger in gangs through the decaying cities, gorging themselves on violence. The book is narrated by the leader of one such gang, and is written in a private language, a mixture of standard English, cockney slang and Russian. (Burgess provides a glossary, but after a few pages the language is easy enough to follow, and its strangeness adds to the feeling of alienation which pervades the book.) The young man has committed a horrific crime, breaking into a house, beating up its owner and raping his wife, and the police are 'rehabilitating' him. His true 'crime', however, was not action but thought – he aspired to a way of life, of culture, from which his class and lack of money should have barred him – and Burgess leaves us wondering whether his 'cure' will work, since he is not a brute beast (as the authorities claim) but rather the individuality in human beings which society has chosen to repress.

Burgess' other novels include a reflection on what he sees as the death throes of modern Western civilization, 1985, *a gentler,* ▷ *Priestleyish book about provincial English life earlier this century,* The Piano Players, *and* A Dead Man in Deptford (*an atmospheric novel about Christopher Marlowe – and Elizabethan theatre and espionage).* Little Wilson and Big God *and* You've Had Your Time *are autobiography,* Mozart and the Wolf Gang *is a 'celebration' for Mozart's bicentenary year,* Urgent Copy *and* Homage to Qwert Yuiop *are collections of reviews and literary articles and* The Devil's Mode *is a collection of short stories.*

| READ ON ▷ |

● *Earthly Powers* (a blockbuster embracing every kind of 20th-century 'evil', from homosexual betrayal to genocide, and the Church's reluctance or inability to stand aside from it).

▶ to *A Clockwork Orange*: ▷ Aldous Huxley, *Brave New World*; ▷ Margaret Atwood, *The Handmaid's Tale*; ▷ Russell Hoban, *Riddley Walker*.

▶ to Burgess's historical novels: ▷ Michèle Roberts, *The Wild Girl*; Patricia Finney, *Firedrake's Eye*.

▶ to *The Malaysian Trilogy*: ▷ Paul Theroux, *Jungle Lovers*.

▶ to the Enderby comedies: ▷ David Lodge, *Small World*; Peter De Vries, *Reuben, Reuben*.

BYATT, A. (Antonia) S. (Susan) *(born 1936)*
British novelist

Byatt was a university teacher for 20 years. Her work has many particularly 'academic' qualities: it is erudite, thoroughly researched and coolly authoritative. But it also springs surprises: she deals with intellectuals from the professional and upper middle classes, and shows how their conceits and self-control are undermined by passions and enthusiasms as hard to discipline as they are unexpected. *Shadow of a Sun* (1964) and *The Game* (1967) are each about women who feel eclipsed by more successful relatives: a novelist father in the first book, a sister in the second. (Margaret Drabble is Byatt's sister.) *The Virgin in the Garden* (1978) and its sequel *Still Life* (1985) are about two sisters balancing their passion for English literature and their belief that the truth about emotions and ideas is to be found in books with their discovery that real life, real experience, has many surprises and even more to offer them. *Babel Tower* (1996) follows some of the characters from these two novels into the turbulent personal and political world of the early 1960s. *The Biographer's Tale* (2000) revisits the relationship between literary scholars and the writers they study that was one of the subjects of *Possession* (see below). Phineas Nanson leaves the world of literary theory in pursuit of the facts about Scholes Destry Scholes who was himself the biographer of an eminent Victorian, Sir Elmer Boles. On his journey Phineas discovers not only that facts and fictions about a life can be difficult to entangle but that his own sense of himself is subject to endless change and revision.

POSSESSION (1990)
In this Booker Prize-winning novel Byatt unravels the interlocking lives of two present-day literary researchers who are themselves tracking the lives of two interlocking Victorian poets. As the two academics discover that the 19th century writers Randolph Ash and Charlotte LaMotte shared an illicit but all-consuming passion, they themselves stretch the emotional bonds they have placed upon their lives. This imaginative and engaging mixture of literary pastiche, detective story, romance and fairy tale remains Byatt's most substantial, most rewarding book.

> READ ON >

- *Angels and Insects* (two linked short novels, set in Victorian England and splendid on the clash between claustrophobic etiquette and the thrusting intellectual excitement of the time). *The Djinn in the Nightingale's Eye* (retellings of five fairy-tales), *The Matisse Stories*, *Elementals* (short stories).
- ▶ ▷ Angus Wilson, *Anglo-Saxon Attitudes*; ▷ Iris Murdoch, *The Sea, The Sea*; Elizabeth Jane Howard, *Falling*; ▷ Carol Shields, *Mary Swann*.

C

CALVINO, Italo (1923–85)
Italian novelist and short story writer

Calvino's first works followed the grim neo-realist tradition of the late 1940s, treating contemporary subjects in an unsparing, documentary way. But in the 1950s he decided to change his style, to write (as he put it) the kind of stories he himself might want to read. These were fantastic, surrealist tales, drawing on medieval legend, fairy stories, science fiction and the work of such 20th-century experimental writers as ▷Kafka and ▷Borges. The style is lucid and poetic; the events, however bizarre their starting-point, follow each other logically and persuasively; the overall effect is magical. In *Cosmicomics* huge space-beings play marbles with sub-atomic particles and take tea with one another as decorously as any Italian bourgeois family. The people in *The Castle of Crossed Destinies* are struck magically dumb and have to tell each other stories using nothing but tarot cards. *If on a Winter's Night a Traveller*, a sequence of interacting chapters from novels that never quite transform themselves into conventional narratives, is a playful examination (half post-modernist meta-fiction, half old-fashioned shaggy dog story) of the pleasures of books and reading. In *Invisible Cities* Marco Polo invents fantasy cities to tickle the imagination of Kubla Khan. Calvino's wide-eyed, bizarre fantasy has been imitated but never surpassed; he is one of the most entrancing writers of the century.

☆ OUR ANCESTORS (1951–9)

This book contains a full-length novel (*The Baron in the Trees*) and two long stories. In *The Baron in the Trees* a boy abandons the ground for the treetops and – in one of Calvino's most sustained and lyrical *tours de force* – lives an entire, fulfilled life without ever coming down to earth. In *The Cloven Viscount* a medieval knight is split in two on the battlefield – and each half goes on living independently, one good, one bad, deprived of the link which made them a whole human being and gave them moral identity. In *The Non-Existent Knight* an empty suit of armour takes on its own identity, fighting, discussing tactics, brawling – and forever yearning after the reality of life, the psychological and emotional fullness which it/he can never know.

Calvino's neo-realist books are The Path to the Nest of Spiders *(a novel) and* Adam, One Afternoon *(short stories). His fantasies are collected in* T Zero, Cosmicomics, Invisible Cities, Our Ancestors, The Castle of Crossed Destinies, Mr Palomar *and* The Watcher and Other Stories. Under the Jaguar Sun *(unfinished at his death) contains three stories on taste, hearing and smell, part of a projected set on the five senses.* Numbers in the Dark *is a posthumous collection of short 'fables', dialogues, essays and other gleanings from newspapers and magazines – an addict's treasure-hoard.* Italian Folktales *reworks traditional material in a similar, uniquely personal way.*

> READ ON

- *Invisible Cities*; *Cosmicomics.*
- ▶ ▷ Thomas Mann, *The Holy Sinner.* ▷ Jim Crace, *Continent.*
- ▶ Good short-story follow-ups: ▷ Jorge Luis Borges, *Fictions*; ▷ Angela Carter, *The Bloody Chamber.*

CAMUS, Albert (1913–60)
French novelist and non-fiction writer

Throughout his life, in newspaper articles, plays, essays and novels, Camus explored the position of what he called *l'homme révolté*, the rebel or misfit who feels out of tune with the spirit of the times. His characters recoil from the values of society. They believe that our innermost being is compromised by conformity, and that we can only liberate our true selves if we choose our own attitude to life, our day-to-day philosophy. Camus compared the human condition to that of Sisyphus in Greek myth, forever rolling a stone up a hill only to have it crash back down every time it reached the top – and said that the way to cope with this situation was to abandon ambition and concentrate on the here and now. But despite his uncompromising philosophy, his books are anything but difficult. His descriptions of sun-saturated Algeria (in *The Outsider*), rainy Amsterdam (in *The Fall*) or disease-ridden, rotting Oran (in *The Plague*) are fast-moving and evocative and he shows the way inner desolation racks his heroes with such intensity that we sympathize with every instant of their predicament and long, like them, for them to break through into acceptance, into happiness.

THE PLAGUE (1947)
Plague ravages the Algerian town of Oran. Quarantined from the outside world, the citizens cope with their tragedy as best they can, either clinging to the outward forms of social life (petty city ordinances; the formalities of religion) or pathetically, helplessly suffering. (For Camus's original readers, the novel was an allegory of France under wartime Nazi occupation). At the heart of the story are Dr Rieux (the story-teller) and a group of other intellectuals. Each has different feelings about death, and for each of them the plague is not only a daily reality, an external event which has to be endured, but a philosophical catalyst, forcing them to decide what they think about the world and their place in it.

As well as in novels, Camus set out his philosophy in two substantial essays, The Rebel (L'homme révolté) *and* The Myth of Sisyphus. *His plays are* Caligula, Cross Purpose, The Just Assassins *and* State of Siege *(a stage version of* The Plague*).* Exile and the Kingdom *is a collection of short stories.* The First Man *is a fascinating autobiographical sketch (childhood in Algiers), posthumously published.*

READ ON >

● *The Fall.*

▶ ▷Saul Bellow, *The Victim.* ▷ Hermann Hesse, *Rosshalde* ▷ William Golding, *The Spire;* Simone de Beauvoir, *The Mandarins;* Paul Bowles, *The Sheltering Sky;* ▷ Jean-Paul Sartre, *Nausea.*

READ ON A THEME: CANADA

▷ Margaret Atwood, *Surfacing*
  Marilyn Bowering, *Visible Worlds*
▷ Robertson Davies, *The Salterton Trilogy*
  Margaret Laurence, *A Jest of God*
▷ Brian Moore, *Black Robe*
▷ Alice Munro, *Friend of My Youth* (short stories)
▷ Mordecai Richler, *Solomon Gursky Was Here*
▷ Carol Shields, *Larry's Party*

CAREY, Peter (born 1943)
Australian novelist

A common theme of Australian writers, from ▷ Miles Franklin to ▷ Patrick White to ▷ Thomas Keneally, is the way discovering the vastness of the continent opens up psychological chasms in the souls of their leading characters. Carey follows this grand tradition, but instead of concentrating on Australian vistas, as most of these other writers do, he focuses on the inner torment and turmoil of his people, their precarious grasp on the condition of humanity. *Illywhacker* is the 'autobiography' of an outrageous boaster and liar, who has, it seems, personally supervised the entire history of white people in Australia. *Jack Maggs* (1997) skilfully mingles events copied from Dickens's life with a reworking of the plot of *Great Expectations* to create a new narrative that is both a powerful historical novel and a subtle examination of 'character' in life and in fiction. In *True History of the Kelly Gang* (2001) Carey returns to the 19th century to tackle the great Australian story, both 'true' and legendary, of the bushwhacker Ned Kelly. Told by Kelly himself, this is a dazzling recreation of the past.

☆ OSCAR AND LUCINDA (1988)
Oscar Hopkins is a freak of nature: a clumsy, obstinate Anglican clergyman with a genius for gambling. Lucinda Leplastrier is an heiress who buys a glassworks in the hope that it will be her ticket to equality with men. Sadly, for this is the 1850s, both are constricted by the manners and bigotries of their time. They end up in Sydney, planning to transport a glass-and-steel church deep into the Outback – a gamble as ludicrous and as pointless as anything else in their anguished, unsatisfied lives. They think that they are taking on the whole continent of Australia; in fact their battles are chiefly against themselves.

Carey's other novels are Bliss, The Tax Inspector *and* The Unusual Life of Tristan Smith. The Fat Man in History *is a collection of short stories.* The Big Bazoohley *is a Roald Dahl-ish children's book.*

READ ON

▶ to *Oscar and Lucinda*: Rupert Thomson, *Air and Fire*; Matthew Kneale, *English Passengers*.

▶ Equally powerful studies of self-exploration: ▷ Patrick White, *Voss*; ▷ Thomas Keneally, *The Playmaker*.

▶ to *True History of the Kelly Gang*: ▷ David Malouf, *The Conversations at Curlow Creek*; Desmond Barry, *The Chivalry of Crime* (Jesse James not Ned Kelly, Southern states of the US not Australia, but the same exploration of the dispossessed driven to crime).

READ ON A THEME: **THE CARIBBEAN**

Wilson Harris, *The Guyana Quartet*
▷ Rosamond Lehmann, *A Sea-Grape Tree*
Earl Lovelace, *The Wine of Astonishment*
Andrea Levy, *Fruit of the Lemon*
▷ Brian Moore, *No Other Life*
▷ Toni Morrison, *Tar Baby*
Shiva Naipaul, *The Chip-Chip Gatherers*
▷ V.S. Naipaul, *A Way in the World*
Caryl Phillips, *Cambridge*
▷ Jean Rhys, *Wide Sargasso Sea*
Marina Warner, *Indigo*

CARTER, Angela (1940–92)
British novelist and non-fiction writer

Carter's inspiration included fairy tales, Jung's theory of the collective unconscious, horror movies and the fantasies of such writers as ▷ Poe and ▷ Shelley.
Above all, she was concerned with female sexuality and with men's sexual
predations on women. Her early books range from Gothic reworkings of fairy tales
(*The Bloody Chamber*) to such surrealist nightmares as *The Passion of New Eve*
(see Read On). The novels begin with dream-images and spiral quickly into
fantasy. In the opening chapter of *The Magic Toyshop* (1967), for example, 15–
year-old Melanie walks in a garden at night in her mother's wedding dress – a
common, if none too reassuring dream. Soon afterwards, however, Melanie's
parents die, she is fostered by a mad toymaker-uncle, and the book climaxes
when she is forced to re-enact the myth of Leda and the Swan with a life-sized
puppet-swan. Later novels like *Nights at the Circus* (see below) and *Wise
Children* (1991) give full rein to Carter's gifts for the baroquely imagined, the
theatrical and the picaresque.

★☆ NIGHTS AT THE CIRCUS (1984)
Walser, a reporter, is investigating the claims of Fevvers, a winged trapeze artist
who may or may not be an angel disguised as a blowsy, turn-of-the-century
circus artiste. The story begins with wide-eyed accounts of Fevvers' early life in a
brothel, the object of strange and violent male lusts, and continues as she and
Walser tour Russia with Colonel Kearney's magic, surreal circus. At first *Nights at*

the Circus seems to be jollying up Carter's usual fascination for digging in the darker corners of society, and its gusto and wit continue to the end. But as the story proceeds, events become ever more sinister, and human endeavour is shown more and more to be a hopeless, grubby farce.

Carter's other novels are Shadow Dance, Several Perceptions, Heroes and Villains, Love, Wise Children *and* The Infernal Desire Machines of Dr Hoffman. The Sadeian Woman *is non-fiction, a study of the social and sexual potential of women.* Fireworks *and* American Ghosts and Old World Wonders *collect short stories (among her most disturbing works), and* Nothing Sacred *and* Expletives Deleted *collect essays and journalism.*

> READ ON

- ● *The Passion of New Eve.* **(In a near-future US where armies of blacks, feminists and pubescent children are waging guerrilla war, the young man Evelyn hides in the California desert, only to be kidnapped by devotees of the multi-breasted, all-engulfing Earth Mother, who rapes him, castrates him and remakes him as a woman, Eve).**
- ▶ **to Carter's work in general: D.M. Thomas,** *The White Hotel.* ▷ **Margaret Atwood,** *The Handmaid's Tale*; ▷ **Jeanette Winterson,** *Sexing the Cherry*; ▷ **Kate Atkinson,** *Human Croquet.*

CARVER, Raymond (1939–88)
US writer

Once described as 'America's laureate of the dispossessed', Raymond Carver wrote about ordinary-seeming people in the drab rooms, fly-blown diners and dusty streets of boring middle America. Nothing is happening, the people are leading mundane lives – preparing to go out, feeding a neighbour's cat, watching a quarrel in a car park – and yet there is an air of hovering, inescapable disaster. Carver describes atmosphere in brief, poetic phrases; his dialogue is like snippets of real, overheard conversation, tantalizingly incomplete; the effect is unsettling and satisfying, all at once. His collections are *Will You Please be Quiet, Please*; *What We Talk About When We Talk About Love*; *Where I'm Calling From*; *Cathedral* and *Elephant and Other Stories. Fires* and *No Heroics Please* contain poems, essays and other writings, as well as stories. Carver's poems, published in several volumes in his lifetime, are collected in one volume in *All of Us. Call if You Need Me* (2000) is a posthumous grab-bag of Carver material, including five stories never previously published, several that had never before been collected and all his non-fiction prose.

> READ ON

- ▶ **to contemporaries of Carver: Richard Ford,** *Rock Springs*; **Tobias Wolff,** *The Collected Stories*; **Andre Dubus,** *Finding a Girl in America.*
- ▶ **to classic short story writers whom Carver matches for intensity and precision:** ▷ **Anton Chekhov,** *Lady with a Lap Dog*; ▷ **Katherine Mansfield,** *In a German Pension*; **William Maxwell,** *All Days and Nights.*

CATHER, Willa (1876–1947)
US novelist

Most of Cather's books are set in the south-western US, and are about settlers (often European immigrants) coming to terms with the wilderness. But there is no Hollywood melodrama: her interests are in the contrast between civilized feelings and the wild natural environment, in psychological growth and change. In two characteristic books, *My Antonia* and *A Lost Lady*, the central female characters (the ones who change) are described by men who have watched them, and loved them, from a distance since childhood – a device which allowed Cather the objective, emotional distance from her characters which she preferred. This objectivity, and the elegance of her style, are two of the most enjoyable features of her books. Her sentences seem placid and unhurried: every event, every description seems to be given the same measured treatment. But nothing is extraneous. Every phrase has emotional or philosophical resonance, and after a few pages the reader is drawn into the narrative, hypnotized by nuance.

DEATH COMES FOR THE ARCHBISHOP (1927)
Based on true events, and on diaries and letters by real people, this novel tells of two French Catholic missionaries to New Mexico in the second half of the 19th century. The book is partly about landscape, and contains magnificent descriptions of the desert. But it is mainly concerned with relationships: between the two priests, friends for many years, between the humans and their animals (who have to carry them on long, lonely desert journeys from one Christian settlement to another), and between the missionaries' ancient European culture and the stripped-to-essentials, 'primitive' habits of life and mind of their New Mexican flock. The book's title is not a promise of high drama. It refers to a Holbein painting, and suggested to Cather the feeling of frozen movement, of life arrested at the instant of recording, which she found in paintings and tried to recapture in her prose.

Two of Cather's novels, The Song of the Lark *and* Lucy Gayheart, *are about young women torn between the claims of family life and an artistic, musical career. O* Pioneers!, *like* My Antonía, *is about foreign immigrants settling in the wilderness. The main character of* The Professor's House *is a successful academic who suddenly feels that he has failed, that lack of danger (emotional, intellectual or physical) has blighted his life. Other novels are* One of Ours *and* My Mortal Enemy. Obscure Destinies *is a collection of short stories.*

> READ ON

- *Shadows on the Rock* (a similarly quiet book about the impact of the North American wilderness on Europeans, this time 17th-century settlers in Quebec).
- ▶ Sarah Orne Jewett, *The Country of the Pointed Firs* (Jewett was an American writer of the previous generation to whom Cather paid particular tribute); ▷ Edith Wharton, *Ethan Frome*; William Maxwell, *Time Will Darken It*.

CHANDLER, Raymond (1888–1959)
US novelist

Born in the US, Chandler was brought to England as a boy and educated at Dulwich College (also the alma mater of ▷ P.G. Wodehouse). After a false start in England as a poet and literary journalist and war service in France, Chandler returned to the US. He became a successful executive in the oil industry until a fondness for the bottle resulted in unemployment. Broke and out of work, Chandler began writing stories for pulp magazines like *Black Mask*, treating violence, prostitution and betrayal in the cynical, hard-boiled style popular in films of the time. His ambition was to replace the kind of detective novels then fashionable (stories of bizarre crimes solved by wildly eccentric detectives, distantly modelled on Sherlock Holmes: see ▷ Christie; ▷ Sayers) with books about realistic crimes, investigated in a plausible way by a detective who would be ordinary, with recognisable human hopes, fears and reactions. Philip Marlowe (Chandler's private-eye hero) is an honest, conscientious man who sweats, cowers and lusts just like anyone else. He narrates the stories himself, in the wisecracking, deadpan style – 'The next morning was bright, clear and sunny. I woke up with a motorman's glove in my mouth, drank two cups of coffee and went through the morning papers' – that has become the target of a thousand parodies in the decades since Chandler first perfected it. Emphasizing atmosphere and character even more than plot – 'the ideal mystery is one you would read if the end was missing', he once remarked – Chandler's novels were among the first to alert more snobbish critics to the potential of genre fiction. They remain great works of American literature, as readable and enjoyable as when they were first published.

★☆ FAREWELL, MY LOVELY (1940)

Marlowe, as often, is drifting with nothing particular to do when he is picked up (literally, by the scruff of the neck) by a muscle-bound ex-convict called Moose Malloy. From this simple event, as ripples spread on a pond, the story grows to take in a priceless necklace, kidnapping, blackmail and murder – and at its heart, like the still centre of a whirlwind, Marlowe slouches from clue to clue, a martyr to his own curiosity, pushing open every door and investigating each alleyway even though he knows, from long experience, that painful or nasty surprises are all he'll find.

Chandler's Marlowe novels are The Big Sleep, Farewell My Lovely, The High Window, The Lady in the Lake, The Little Sister, The Long Goodbye *and* Playback. Killer in the Rain *is a collection of short stories.* Poodle Springs, *an unfinished Marlowe novel, was completed by Robert B. Parker in 1990.*

> READ ON ▷

- ● *The Big Sleep*; *The Lady in the Lake*.
- ▶ Robert B. Parker, *Perchance to Dream* (sequel). ▷ Dashiell Hammett, *The Maltese Falcon*; Ross MacDonald, *The Drowning Pool*; John D. Mcdonald, *The Deep Blue Goodbye*.

CHATWIN, Bruce (1940–89)
British novelist and travel writer

A journalist, Chatwin wrote precise, brisk prose – and it utterly belies the contents of his books. Neither fiction nor fact, they straddle the borders between dream and reality, reportage and philosophy. He was fascinated by nomads and the dispossessed, and inserted himself into his work as narrator, as rudderless and amazed as any of his characters. *In Patagonia*, ostensibly a travel book, is a magpie's nest of history, anecdote and self-revelation, set in a South America which seems to shimmer between fantasy and reality. *On the Black Hill*, ostensibly a novel, is a meditation on loneliness and the interaction between landscape and personality, set in the remote Welsh hills. Chatwin's masterpiece, *The Songlines* (1987), is a 'novel' about a white man, 'Bruce Chatwin', travelling in central Australia to investigate the Aboriginal 'songlines', the paths invisibly traced by the world's ancestors as they sang dream-reality into being. The book is raw with rage about both the whites ('caring people' and 'trash' alike) and the feckless, hopeless Aborigines – and most savage of all about its dogged, put-upon central character, a 1960s hippie floundering out of his depth and out of his time, lost in someone else's dream.

Chatwin's other novels are The Viceroy of Ouidah *and* Utz. What Am I Doing Here *is a fascinating collection of his journalism.*

READ ON ⟩

- *The Viceroy of Ouidah* (about a slave trader exporting 'black gold' from West Africa to Brazil).
- ▶ Keri Hulme, *The Bone People*. ▷ Chinua Achebe, *Things Fall Apart*; Carlos Fuentes, *The Old Gringo*.

CHEEVER, John (1912–82)
US novelist and short story writer

Most of Cheever's stories appeared in the *New Yorker* between 1945 and 1975. The majority of his characters are prosperous New England commuters. They have beautiful houses in tidy neighbourhoods, their children go to good schools, and they can afford European holidays (often in Italy). But they are walking wounded: their emotions may be intact, but their hearts and consciences have been sliced away. They lacerate one another with sexual affairs, rows, petty-minded gossip and dispiriting, single-minded malice. The reason is that they believe that they are living in the American Dream – and by the day, by the minute, they find that it is a mirage. Cheever narrates their empty lives in sleek, ironic prose: his dialogue is particularly good at suggesting overtones of menace or longing in commonplace remarks.

The Stories of John Cheever *collects all but a handful of Cheever's short works. Cheever's novels are* The Wapshot Chronicle, The Wapshot Scandal, Bullet Park, Oh What A Paradise it Seems *and* Falconer (*on an uncharacteristic subject: the rehabilitation of a murderer in a 'correctional facility'*).

READ ON ⟩

- Cheever's two Wapshot novels are set in the same world and among the same kind of bewildered characters as his stories. The Wapshot family, however, contains wonderful eccentrics, and the novels consequently spill into slapstick farce.
- ▶ to Cheever's novels: ▷ John Updike, *The Centaur*; Peter De Vries, *The Tunnel of Love*.

▶ to the stories: ▷ F. Scott Fitzgerald, *The Diamond as Big as the Ritz and Other Stories*.

CHEKHOV, Anton (1860–1904)
Russian short story writer and playwright

Chekhov paid his way through medical school by writing short comic articles for magazines; in his mid-twenties he began publishing more elaborate pieces, and by the time he was 40 (and turning from stories to plays) he was considered one of the finest of all Russian prose writers. Many of his stories are first-person monologues – he said that he was inspired by the sort of things people tell doctors during consultations, or penitents murmur at confession – and, like such monologues, they often reveal far more than the speaker intends. We hear symptoms, as it were, and from them diagnose a whole sick life. In other stories it is as if Chekhov were sitting beside us, drawing our attention to people moving about in the distance, and commenting in a quiet, compassionate way on their motives and feelings. Sympathetic detachment is the essence of his art: reading his stories (like watching his plays) is like looking through a window into other people's lives. The stories have been collected in a number of recent volumes including *The Lady with a Lap-Dog, The Fiancé and other stories, The Duel and other stories* and *The Kiss and other stories*

READ ON ▷

● of Chekhov's plays, the nearest in mood to his stories are *Uncle Vanya* and *The Seagull* (Michael Frayn's translations are recommended).
▶ ▷ Ivan Turgenev, *Sketches from a Hunter's Album*. ▷ Guy de Maupassant, *Selected Stories;* ▷ Katherine Mansfield, *In a German Pension;* ▷ Raymond Carver, *Where I'm Calling From* (Carver was a great admirer of Chekhov).

READ ON A THEME: CHILDREN

▷ Margaret Atwood, *Cat's Eye*
▷ Roddy Doyle, *Paddy Clarke Ha Ha Ha*
  Emma Freud, *Hideous Kinky*
▷ William Golding, *Lord of the Flies*
▷ L.P. Hartley, *Eustace and Hilda*
  Richard Hughes, *A High Wind in Jamaica*
  Nancy Mitford, *The Blessing*
▷ Marcel Proust, *Swann's Way* (Part One of *Remembrance of Things Past*)
▷ Mark Twain, *The Adventures of Tom Sawyer*

See also: Adolescence; Parents and Children; Teenagers

READ ON A THEME: CHINA AND HONG KONG

Pearl S. Buck, *The Good Earth*
Jung Chang, *Wild Swans*
James Clavell, *Taipan*

Wei Hui, *Shanghai Baby*
Timothy Mo, *An Insular Possession*
Wang Shuo, *Playing for Thrills*
Amy Tan, *The Joy Luck Club* (Chinese women's lives both in China and America)
▷ Paul Theroux, *Kowloon Tong*
Hong Ying, *Daughter of the River*

CHRISTIE, Agatha (1890–1976)
British novelist

Ingenuity is the essence of Christie's detective stories. She confined herself largely to two detectives, pompous Poirot and elderly, inquisitive Miss Marple. Nowadays, as well as her plots, it is the period detail of her books which fascinates: her English villages, spa hotels, 1930s cruise-ships and above all country houses are caught like flies in amber. She chronicles a vanished pre-Second-World-War, upper-middle-class Britain with an accuracy which is enhanced rather than diminished by the staginess of her characters and plots.

MURDER AT THE VICARAGE (1930)
This typical Miss Marple story is set in a picture-postcard English village riven by gossip and inhabited by as unlikely a collection of eccentrics as even Christie ever threw together. Everyone could be guilty of murder, and Miss Marple's investigation is so gently persistent, so self-effacingly efficient, that one trembles in case she ends up as victim rather than as sleuth.

MURDER IN MESOPOTAMIA (1936)
A nurse goes to look after the neurotic wife of an archaeologist on a dig, and is thrown into the middle of intrigue, suspicion, rancorous insult and finally, inevitably, murder. At the end of it all Poirot applies his 'little grey cells' to unearthing means, motive and opportunity as painstakingly as an archaeologist trowelling treasure.

Among the best known of Christie's 83 detective novels are The Murder of Roger Ackroyd, Ten Little Niggers/Ten Little Indians/Then There Were None, Murder on the Orient Express *and* The Crooked House. *She also wrote stage plays (including* The Mousetrap, *still breaking all records for longest West End run), an excellent Second-World-War espionage thriller (*N or M*), and six romantic novels under the pseudonym Mary Westmacott.*

> **READ ON**

- to *Murder at the Vicarage*: *A Murder is Announced*.
- to *Murder in Mesopotamia*: *Death on the Nile*.
▶ Patricia Wentworth, *Miss Silver Intervenes*; Dorothy Simpson, *Wake the Dead*; ▷ Ngaio Marsh, *Overture to Death*; ▷ Margery Allingham, *The Crime at Black Dudley*.

READ ON A THEME: CITIES: NEW WORLD

▷ Saul Bellow, *Herzog* (Chicago)
James Ellroy, *LA Confidential* (Los Angeles)

▷ Jay McInerney, *Bright Lights, Big City* (New York)
Armistead Maupin, *Tales of the City* (San Francisco)
▷ Mordecai Richler, *The Apprenticeship of Duddy Kravitz* (Montreal)
▷ Colm Tóibín, *The Story of the Night* (Buenos Aires)
▷ Edith Wharton, *The Age of Innocence* (New York)
▷ Tom Wolfe, *The Bonfire of the Vanities* (New York)

READ ON A THEME: CITIES: OLD WORLD

▷ Margery Allingham, *The Tiger in the Smoke* (London)
Louis Aragon, *Paris Peasant*
▷ Lawrence Durrell, *The Alexandria Quartet*
▷ Mrs Gaskell, *Mary Barton* (Manchester)
▷ Victor Hugo, *Nôtre Dame de Paris*
Ivan Klima, *My Golden Trades* (Prague)
▷ James Joyce, *Dubliners*
▷ Christopher Isherwood, *Goodbye to Berlin*

CLANCY, Tom (born 1947)
US novelist

For a generation of thriller writers the Cold War, with its superpower confrontation and its elaborate, deadly games of espionage and counter-espionage, provided superb plot material and Tom Clancy's first few books successfully mined this rich vein. *The Hunt for Red October* (1984), the story of a desperate attempt by a Russian frigate to defect to the West, made good use of Cold War rivalries and allowed Clancy to deploy his own knowledge of naval history and technology. In this first book, he also demonstrated his gift for gripping narrative. Yet, in the years after his bestselling debut, the potential in Cold War plots was clearly waning. The march of history was making them seem a little old-hat. Clancy saw this coming and, with a resourcefulness worthy of his ongoing character Jack Ryan, a CIA analyst who eventually becomes President, he turned his attention to other trouble spots of the world. *Clear and Present Danger* (1989) has Jack Ryan battling the drug barons of Colombia; *Patriot Games* (1987) pitches him into the turbulent waters of Irish politics; *The Sum of All Fears* (1991) imagines a nightmare scenario in which a nuclear weapon falls into the hands of Middle Eastern terrorists. Much is always made of Clancy's obsession with minute and careful description of the weaponry, hardware and gadgetry that fill his pages and his clear division of the world into goodies (Americans) and baddies (very nearly everybody else) as if these explained the success of his techno-thrillers with a male readership worldwide. In fact his readers respond to old-fashioned virtues of tight plotting and vivid characterization, mainstays of thriller writing since the days of Buchan and Childers, and the most important ingredients in Clancy's novels.

Tom Clancy's other novels include Red Storm Rising, The Cardinal of the Kremlin, Without Remorse, Debt of Honour, Executive Orders *and* The Bear and the Dragon. *In recent years he has given his name and an undisclosed (probably small) level of creative input to a series of stories set in the worlds of the Internet and virtual reality* (Net Force) *and to a series about the exploits of a shadowy government organization* (Op-Centre). *He has also written non-fiction on his favourite topics of naval and military technology.*

READ ON

- ● *The Bear and the Dragon* (President Jack Ryan spends 1,000 pages battling a succession of international crises).
- ▶ ▷ Frederick Forsyth, *The Fist of God*; Clive Cussler, *Deep Six*; Harold Coyle, *God's Children*; Campbell Armstrong, *Jigsaw*; Stephen Leather, *The Double Tap*.

CLARKE, Arthur C. (Charles) (born 1917)
British writer of novels, short stories and non-fiction

Apart from ▷ Asimov, Clarke is the best 'real' scientist among science fiction writers. His subject is space travel, and his 1940s and 1950s non-fiction books and articles predicted, in accurate detail, many things which have since happened, such as the invention of communications satellites, the first Moon landing and the development of laser space weaponry. He begins a fictional story with existing scientific fact or theory, and then extends it logically; even his wildest fantasies thus seem rooted in the possible. His main themes are the colonization from Earth of other planets and visits to Earth by explorers from distant galaxies. His stories bustle with the detail of space-travel and setting up home in alien environments, and he is particularly interested in the psychological stress on people faced with the unknown and with the relationship between human beings and high technology. These ideas outweigh sometimes wooden character drawing and creaky plots. A good story collection is *The Nine Billion Names of God*. Clarke's other novels include *Childhood's End*, *A Fall of Moondust* and *Imperial Earth*. *Astounding Days* is autobiography, excellent on why Clarke writes and how his career began.

RENDEZVOUS WITH RAMA (1973)
Like Clarke's story 'The Sentinel', which was the basis for Kubrick's film *2001: A Space Odyssey*, this novel is the story of man's contact with an enigmatic alien artefact. An enormous and seemingly abandoned spaceship drifts into our solar system. When humans explore Rama, they find their imaginations overwhelmed by its mystery and possible significance. The novel is a fine example of Clarke's capacity to evoke a sense of awe and to lead us to wonder about our own small place in the vastness of time and space.

READ ON

- ● *2001: A Space Odyssey; 2010: Odyssey Two; 2061: Odyssey Three, 3001, Rama* and *The Garden of Rama* (the latter two written with Gentry Lee).
- ▶ to *2001*: Algis Budrys, *Rogue Moon*; Robert Holdstock, *Earthwind*; Stanislaw Lem, *Solaris*.
- ▶ ▷ Jules Verne, *The First Men in the Moon*. ▷ H.G. Wells, *The War of the Worlds*; Greg Bear, *Eon;* Larry Niven, *Ringworld*.

READ ON A THEME: CLASSIC DETECTION

> Nicholas Blake, *The Beast Must Die*
> G.K. Chesterton, *The Innocence of Father Brown*
> Edmund Crispin, *Love Lies Bleeding*
> ▷ Michael Innes, *Death at the President's Lodging*
> ▷ P.D. James, *The Skull Beneath the Skin*
> ▷ Ngaio Marsh, *Surfeit of Lampreys*
> Gladys Mitchell, *Laurels are Poison*
> ▷ Dorothy L. Sayers, *Murder Must Advertise*
> Patricia Wentworth, *Latter End*

See also: Great (Classic) Detectives; Murder Most Mind-Boggling; Police Procedural; Private Eyes

---

COLETTE (Sidonie Gabrielle) (1873–1954)
French novelist

In the 1900s Colette's works were condemned as pornographic; in the 1970s she was claimed by the women's movement as one of the founders of feminism. The reason in each case is the same. Her themes are the awakening of sensual feelings in adolescence, the way in which young women first discover their sexual power, and the attempts by middle-aged people (of both sexes) to rejuvenate themselves by preying on innocence. Her stories are not explicitly sexual, but she writes in an impressionistic style in which sun, flowers, insects, animals and the textures of skin, grass and clothes blur into a kind of drowsy, erotic reverie, a counterpart to the awakening feelings of her characters. Adult experience is always just ahead – and every adult in Colette's books is a tragic figure, ineffectual or cynical. Youth, in the end, is the only worthwhile possession in life, and it is daily, hourly, squandered for experience. In *The Ripening Seed* (1923), for example, two adolescents, friends from childhood, feel a new tension within their relationship which is compounded by the seduction of the boy by an older woman.

The most substantial of Colette's works is the 'Claudine' series of novels, about a young girl growing up in the early years of the 20th century. Another pair of books, Chéri *and* The Last of Chéri, *is on a favourite theme, the corrupting effects of a young man's first sexual experience. Her other books, many based on her own experience and family, include* Sido, My Apprenticeship *and* The Tendrils of the Vine. *Her collected short stories were published in English in 1984.*

READ ON ⟩

● *A Lesson in Love* (*La naissance du jour*).
▶ Françoise Sagan, *Bonjour Tristesse*. Edna O'Brien, *The Country Girls* (and its sequels *The Lonely Girls* and the magnificent *Girls in Their Married Bliss*). David Garnett, *Aspects of Love*; ▷ Vladimir Nabokov, *Ada* and André Gide, *The Immoralist*, though their purposes and plot development are very different, catch the same sensual and poetic mood as Colette. ▷ Carson McCullers, *The Member of the Wedding* is a harsher view of the awakening of a young girl to adult feelings.

READ ON A THEME: COMEDY THRILLERS

▷ Eric Ambler, *Passage of Arms*
  Lawrence Block, *The Burglar Who Thought He Was Bogart*
  Richard Condon, *Prizzi's Honour*
  Janet Evanovich, *One for the Money*
▷ Carl Hiaasen, *Double Whammy*
  Greg Macdonald, *Fletch*
  Donald Westlake, *Don't Ask*

COMPTON-BURNETT, Ivy (1884–1969)
British novelist

After a single false start (*Dolores*, an imitation of ▷George Eliot, later disowned),
Compton-Burnett produced 19 comic novels in a uniquely bizarre, uncompromising style. Each book is set in a large late-Victorian or early-Edwardian
household, ruled by a tyrant (one of the parents or some elderly, inflexible
relative). Isolated by wealth from the outside world, the family members – often
grown-up, middle-aged children – bicker, snub and plot against one another,
powerless and embittered. There are family secrets to be revealed – incest,
murder, insanity – and no member of the household, neither family nor servants,
is a 'normal', unwarped human being. The books are written largely in a self-
consciously artificial dialogue, which fails to mask the appalling human cruelties
lurking beneath the surface. Compton-Burnett's detractors find her novels
unreadable; her fans think them hilarious and utterly unlike the work of any
other writer.

Compton-Burnett's novels are Pastors and Masters, Brothers and Sisters, Men
and Wives, More Women than Men, A House and its Head, Daughters and Sons,
A Family and a Fortune, Parents and Children, Elders and Betters, Manservant
and Maidservant, Two Worlds and their Ways, Darkness and Day, The Present
and the Past, Mother and Son, A Father and his Fate, A Heritage and its History,
The Mighty and their Fall, A God and his Gifts *and* The Last and the First.

| READ ON >

▶ **The uniqueness of Compton-Burnett's style means that no other writers' works are**
  truly similar. Stories of claustrophobic families, however, in artificial 'high styles'
  of their own and equally compulsive, are: Samuel Butler, *The Way of All Flesh* (a
  book which influenced Compton-Burnett herself); ▷ Edith Wharton, *The Age of*
  ***Innocence*; Jean Cocteau, *The Children of the Game* (*Les enfants terribles*). Some**
  of Compton-Burnett's self-consciously artificial dialogue has parallels in works by
  Ronald Firbank such as *Valmouth*.

CONRAD, Joseph (1857–1924)
Polish/British novelist

Born in Poland, Conrad ran away to sea at 17 and ended up a captain in the
merchant navy and a naturalized British subject. He retired from the sea at 37

and spent the rest of his life as a writer. There was at the time (1890s–1910s) a strong tradition of sea-stories, using the dangers and tensions of long voyages and the wonders of the worlds sailors visited as metaphors for human life. Most of this writing was straightforward adventure, with little subtlety; Conrad used its conventions for deeper literary ends. He was interested in 'driven' individuals, people whose psychology or circumstances force them to extreme behaviour, and the sea-story form exactly suited this idea. His books often begin as 'yarns', set in exotic locations and among the mixed (and mixed-up) human types who crew ocean-going ships. But before long psychology takes over, and the plot loses its straightforwardness and becomes an exploration of compulsion, obsession and neurosis.

★ HEART OF DARKNESS (FROM YOUTH, 1902)

This 120–page story begins as a 'yarn': Marlow, a sea captain, tells of a journey he once made up the Congo river to bring down a stranded steamer. He became fascinated by stories of an ivory merchant, a white man called Kurtz who lived deep in the jungle and was said to have supernatural powers. Marlow set out to find Kurtz, and the journey took him deeper and deeper into the heart not only of the 'Dark Continent', but into the darkness of the human soul. (Francis Ford Coppola's 1970s film *Apocalypse Now* updated this story to the Vietnam War, making points about US colonialism as savage as Conrad's denunciation of the ivory trade.)

Conrad's major novels are Lord Jim, The Nigger of the Narcissus, Nostromo, The Secret Agent *and* Under Western Eyes. *His short story collections (an excellent introduction to his work) are* Tales of Unrest, Youth, Typhoon, A Set of Six, 'Twixt Land and Sea, Within the Tides *and* Tales of Hearsay.

> READ ON

- *Typhoon* **(which deals with corruption and exploitation of a different kind, this time using as its metaphor a passenger steamer caught in a typhoon in the China Sea);** *The Secret Agent* **(about the conflict between innocence and corruption among a group of terrorists in 1900s London).**
- ▷ **Herman Melville,** *Billy Budd, Foretopman.* ▷ **Graham Greene,** *The Comedians;* **B. Traven,** *The Treasure of the Sierra Madre;* ▷ **Paul Theroux,** *The Mosquito Coast;* **Robert Edric,** *The Book of the Heathen* **(a modern novelist examines Conradian themes in the Conradian setting of 1890s Belgian Congo).**

COOKSON, Catherine (1906–98)
British novelist

'Catherine Cookson' was a pseudonym of Ann McMullen. Her books are warm-hearted romances about 'ordinary people' dealing with the 'ordinary' emotions of love and longing that affect us all . She set most of them in the north-east of England (Tyneside) where she was born, and showed how her characters coped with the harsh conditions of life in the area in the 19th century and the early decades of the 20th. She grouped many of her novels in series, for example the 'Mary Ann' books (beginning with *A Grand Man*) and the Mallen trilogy (*The Mallen Girl, The Mallen Litter* and *The Mallen Streak*). The heroine of *Tilly Trotter, Tilly Trotter Wed* and *Tilly Trotter Widowed* (a characteristic series, written in the

1960s) is a poor but spirited girl in 1930s County Durham who becomes the mistress of the owner of the 'big house', emigrates to America when he dies, and returns in middle age to find happiness at last in her beloved native country. *Kate Hannigan's Daughter*, published after her death, brought her remarkable career as perhaps the most popular British writer of her time to a fitting conclusion by being a sequel to *Kate Hannigan*, her very first novel, published more than fifty years earlier.

Cookson's other books include The Invisible Cord, The Gambling Man, The Black Candle, The Harrogate Secret, The Tinker's Girl, The Obsession, The Thursday Friend *and* A House Divided. *She also wrote as Catherine Marchant; titles include* Heritage of Folly, The Fen Tiger, The Mists of Memory, Miss Martha Mary Crawford *and* The Slow Awakening.

READ ON >

- **The House of Women (unusually, a modern story).**
- ► **Tessa Barclay, *Dayton and Daughter*; Emma Blair, *An Apple from Eden*; Josephine Cox, *Looking Back*; Sheelagh Kelly, *A Long Way from Heaven* (and others set in Victorian York); Pamela Oldfield, *All Our Tomorrows*; Mary Jane Staples, *Echoes of Yesterday* (and others in the series about the Adams family of Walworth).**

CORNWELL, Bernard (born 1944)
British novelist

Although he has published other series of historical fiction, Bernard Cornwell remains best known for the Sharpe books, set in the Napoleonic Wars and tracing the rise from the ranks of Richard Sharpe. Cornwell's fiction has the old-fashioned virtues of writers like ▷ C.S. Forester and ▷ John Buchan. His historical research is impeccable but unobtrusive. His capacity to sustain a suspenseful and exciting narrative and his gift for vivid description of military action are admirable. And his hero, flawed but likeable, retains the reader's sympathies. We want to know what will happen next to Sharpe and how he will deal with it. Modern readers demand a racier package than the readers of Forester and Buchan did, and Cornwell is willing enough to supply it, but essentially he is the inheritor of their tradition and the best contemporary exponent of it.

The Sharpe books cover the years 1799 to 1821. In chronological order (although not the order in which Cornwell wrote and published them), they are: Sharpe's Tiger, Sharpe's Triumph, Sharpe's Fortress, Sharpe's Trafalgar, Sharpe's Prey, Sharpe's Rifles, Sharpe's Eagle, Sharpe's Gold, Sharpe's Battle, Sharpe's Company, Sharpe's Sword, Sharpe's Enemy, Sharpe's Honour, Sharpe's Regiment, Sharpe's Siege, Sharpe's Revenge, Sharpe's Waterloo *and* Sharpe's Devil.

READ ON >

- **The Winter King (the first in a trilogy based on the Arthurian legends, the others being *Enemy of God* and *Excalibur*).**
- ► ▷ **Patrick O'Brian, *Master and Commander* (and the other Aubrey/Maturin books);**
  ▷ **C.S. Forester, *Mr. Midshipman Hornblower*; Allan Mallinson, *A Close Run Thing*.**

CORNWELL, Patricia (born 1952)
US writer

Each of Cornwell's thrillers begins with the discovery of a gruesomely mutilated body, which is then sent to Kay Scarpetta, Chief Medical Examiner of Richmond, Virginia. Scarpetta's post-mortem is the beginning of a spiral of serial killing, political machinations (she is not popular with corrupt official colleagues), personal involvement and nail-biting suspense. A favourite secondary character is her niece Lucy, a brilliant adolescent whose computer wizardry is equalled only by her social awkwardness. Since 1991 and the publication of *Post-Mortem*, the first of the Scarpetta books, Cornwell's combination of clinical and forensic expertise with tight plotting has made her books unputdownable.

POINT OF ORIGIN (1998)
Grisly murder comes once again to Scarpetta's home town of Richmond and once again Scarpetta's past returns to dog her. A farmhouse in Virginia has been destroyed in a fire and the remains of a body found there which reveal clear signs of brutal murder. Meanwhile Carrie Grethen, a killer who tangled with Scarpetta in *The Body Farm*, has escaped from a psychiatric hospital and is sending Kay cryptic messages threatening revenge.

READ ON >

● The other Scarpetta novels (best read in sequence, though self-contained) are *Post-Mortem, Body of Evidence, All That Remains, Cruel and Unusual, The Body Farm, From Potter's Field, Cause of Death, Unnatural Exposure, Black Notice, The Last Precinct. Hornet's Nest* and *Southern Cross* are non-Scarpetta novels.
▶ Jonathan Kellerman, *Over The Edge;* Carol O'Connell, *Mallory's Oracle*; Kathy Reichs, *Déjà Dead;* Lisa Scottoline, *Mistaken Identity.*

READ ON A THEME: COUNTRY HOUSES

▷Helen Dunmore, *A Spell in the Country*
▷ E.M. Forster, *Howards End*
Esther Freud, *Gaglow*
Henry Green, *Loving*
▷ Hermann Hesse, *Rosshalde*
▷ Evelyn Waugh, *Brideshead Revisited*
▷ Eudora Welty, *Delta Wedding*
▷ P.G. Wodehouse, *Summer Lightning*

See also: Dark Old Houses

COUPLAND, Douglas (born 1961)
Canadian novelist

Only a handful of writers get the chance to attach a lasting label to an entire generation. Gertrude Stein called the young people of the 1920s jazz era the 'Lost Generation' and the name stuck. ▷ Jack Kerouac (supposedly) coined the phrase 'Beat Generation' to describe his own group of boho drop-outs disillusioned with the materialism of 1950s America and instantly became, in the eyes of the media, the spokesman of youth. And Douglas Coupland, in calling his darkly ironic stories of three twentysomethings caught up in dead-end jobs in the service industry *Generation X* (1991), gave a name and a human face to a demographic trend. The dangers of naming a generation, as Kerouac cruelly and tragically found out, are that you never outgrow it; Coupland has recognized this and, in the ten years since *Generation X*, he has extended the range of his writing and produced a number of very different books. In *Microserfs* (1995) he turned his comic eye on the enclosed world of Silicon Valley programmers, trapped in a kind of perpetual adolescence. *Girlfriend in a Coma* (1998) uses an imaginative conceit to illuminate the compromises and limitations that life imposes on a group of high school friends. One of them, Karen, enters a coma in 1979 and only re-emerges twenty years later. An adolescent in the body of a woman approaching middle age, she is suddenly witness to the changes two decades have made to her friends. Her Rip Van Winkle-like astonishment at high-tech culture on the cusp of the millennium and her unjaded insights into the hollowness of the lives her friends are now leading are very well done. Less successful by far is the book's apocalyptic conclusion, but *Girlfriend in a Coma* is a clear sign of how much Coupland has matured as a writer since his generation-defining debut.

Douglas Coupland's other works of fiction are Shampoo Planet, Life After God, Polaroids from the Dead, Miss Wyoming *and* All Families Are Psychotic. *He has also written* City of Glass, *a guide to Vancouver, the city where he lives and where much of his fiction is set.*

> READ ON

● *Miss Wyoming.*
▶ ▷ William Gibson, *Virtual Light*; ▷ Jay McInerney, *Story of My Life*; Douglas Rushkoff, *The Ecstasy Club.*

CRACE, Jim (born 1940)
British writer

The settings of Crace's early books (*Arcadia, Continent*) are almost familiar: the forests, mountains, seas, villages and cities of our own real world. But they seem half-glimpsed, recognizable and strange all at once, like reality seen in dream. There is no history. Past and present exist in the same moment, the realities of medieval life and those of today blurring into one another. He is a prose poet, selecting just the aspects of life he needs, and letting the unsaid do as much work as what is there. *The Gift of Stones* (1988) is a recreation, remarkable because so understated and undemonstrative, of a Stone Age village and its inhabitants. In *Quarantine* (1997) he used his spare and beautiful prose to create his own memorable version of the Biblical story of Jesus's forty days in the wilderness. In *Being Dead* (1999) a middle-aged couple return to a beach where they first made love thirty years before and become the victims of a casual killer. Undiscovered, their bodies lie on the dunes and Crace charts, meticulously and dispassionately, their disintegration. In Crace's hands this is neither morbid nor voyeuristic but instead becomes a haunting and moving meditation on love, death and transience.

☆ ARCADIA (1992)

In a skyscraper tower above the ancient fruit and vegetable market lives Victor, the 80–year-old financier who began as a beggar in the streets below, and rose to be barrow-boy, stallholder, landlord and finally owner of all he surveys. From his eyrie above the stalls he plans change, plans to make a brave new world in the market – and only Rook, his impersonal personal assistant, and Anna, Rook's mistress, have any influence on what happens next. The book relates Victor's early life, tells what happens when he begins to remake his world, and shows us, in a blur of tiny details, a picture of society as bustling, as grotesque, as one of Brueghel's or Bosch's crowded scenes.

READ ON ▷

- *Continent, The Gift of Stones, Signals of Distress.*
- ▶ ▷ Italo Calvino, *The Baron in the Trees.* ▷ Vladimir Nabokov, *Ada.* ▷ William Golding, *The Inheritors.*

READ ON A THEME: CULTURE-CLASH

- ▷ Chinua Achebe, *Things Fall Apart*
- ▷ E.M. Forster, *A Passage to India*
- ▷ William Golding, *The Inheritors*
- ▷ Henry James, *The Europeans*
  Joseph Olshan, *A Warmer Season*
  Meera Syal, *Anita and Me*
- ▷ Evelyn Waugh, *The Loved One*

READ ON A THEME: CYBER FICTION

Richard Calder, *Malignos*
- ▷ William Gibson, *Neuromancer*
- ▷ Jeff Noon, *Vurt*
  Michael Marshall Smith, *Only Forward*
  Neal Stephenson, *Snow Crash*
  Bruce Sterling, *Holy Fire*
  Tricia Sullivan, *Dreaming in Smoke*
  Jack Womack, *Going, Going, Gone*

CRIME

Crime fiction began in 1841 with Edgar Allan Poe's story *The Murders in the Rue Morgue*, and its popularity has never waned. Stories concentrate either on events leading up to the crime or on detection. Some crime-centred books are darkly psychological, exploring the mind of the criminal compelled towards the crime. Others are 'caper' novels, showing the detailed planning and execution of the crime and concentrating on the relationships of everyone involved. Many detection-centred books are procedural, following the investigation of a crime step by meticulous step. Others centre on the character of the detective (an eccentric genius; a dogged cop with a complicated private life; a 'private eye' who is the guardian of morality and integrity in a corrupt world). In ninety-nine per cent of all crime fiction, from Arthur Conan Doyle's *The Hound of the Baskervilles* (1902) to the latest ▷ Sue Grafton or ▷ Ian Rankin, the crime is murder. In the first heyday of crime fiction (the 1930s) people favoured 'snobbery with violence' (as in the books of ▷ Dorothy L. Sayers) and 'locked room' mysteries (such as those of John Dickson Carr). Nowadays, in the second heyday, we prefer psychological thrillers (such as those of ▷ Barbara Vine), procedurals (often set in the past, or abroad) and private eye stories.

Block, Lawrence, *The Burglar Who Thought He Was Bogart*. Block has written a cherishable series of books about the amiable, witty burglar-cum-bookseller Bernie Rhodenbarr and this title, in which Bernie adopts the persona of Bogart, is one of the best.

Carr, John Dickson (1906–77), *The Blind Barber* (1933). Classic tale of beautiful women, international playboys, priceless jewels, stolen films, diplomatic incidents and murder, set on a transatlantic liner. Wonderful sense of period; one of the most rollicking of all 'locked room' mysteries.

▷ **Dexter, Colin (born 1930), *The Jewel that was Ours* (1991).** Opera-loving loner Morse and his assistant Lewis investigate murder among a group of Americans doing the Oxford Heritage Tour.

▷ **Dibdin, Michael (born 1947), *Cabal* (1992).** 1990s Roman policeman Aurelio Zen battles politicians, high society, the clergy and his own colleagues to unravel a cat's cradle of murder and secret-society intrigue in no less a location than the Vatican. Credible characters, a corkscrewing story, and an atmosphere you could swim in.

Ellroy, James, *The Black Dahlia* (1987). The first in Ellroy's powerful LA Quartet, this fictionalized account of a famous sex murder from the 1940s reveals Ellroy's mastery of period, dialogue and characterization and his dark, obsessive imagination.

Evanovich, Janet, *One for the Money* (1994). Stephanie Plum swaps a job as lingerie buyer for a career in bounty hunting in the first of Evanovich's madcap mixtures of screwball comedy and post-feminism.

Harvey, John, *Lonely Hearts* (1989). Jazz-loving, Nottingham-based Inspector Resnick investigates the murders of two women unlucky enough to meet a serial killer through the personal columns in fine example of British police procedural.

Hjorstberg, William, *Falling Angel* (1979). Cult classic, memorably filmed in 1987 as *Angel Heart* by Alan Parker, in which seedy, hardboiled hero Harry Angel homes in on some terrible truths. Trespassing rewardingly on other fiction genres (horror, fantasy), this is a crime novel like no other.

Lovesey, Peter (born 1936), *A Case of Spirits* (1975). Lovesey specializes in period detective stories. In this, 19th-century Sergeant Cribb investigates murder and spiritualism among the snobbish middle-class of suburban London.

Mitchell, Gladys (1901–83), *Laurels are Poison* (1942). Classic eccentric-detective tale, in which Mrs Lestrange Bradley, witch-like psychologist and sleuth, investigates murder of the warden of an all-women Teachers' Training College.

Parker, Robert B. (born 1932), *Looking for Rachel Wallace* (1980). Hardboiled private eye Spencer is hired to look after feminist writer on speaking tour. They hate each other on sight. Then Wallace is kidnapped, and Spencer has to find her.

Pelecanos, George, *Down by the River Where the Dead Men Go* (1998) Superboozer and PI Nick Stefanos awakes from a bender in a public park to find a body being dumped in the river nearby. In a novel filled with pop-culture references and 1980s hedonism, he pursues the killers.

Peters, Ellis (1913–1995), *One Corpse Too Many* (1979). Ellis Peters wrote a series about worldly-wise monk and herbalist Brother Cadfael in which cosy crime met the Middle Ages. TV has now given her books an even wider readership than before. This one, in which monks burying the dead from a battle find one more body than they bargained for, shows Cadfael at his most likeable.

▷ **Stout, Rex (1886–1975), *Too Many Cooks* (1938)**. Classic story in which fat, woman-hating, orchid-growing genius Nero Wolfe and his legman Archie Goodwin investigate murder at a conference for master-chefs at a West Virginia luxury hotel.

Also recommended: James Lee Burke, *Cadillac Jukebox*; Loren Estleman, *The Hours of the Virgin*; Dan Kavanagh, *Going to the Dogs*; H.R.F. Keating, *The Body in the Billiard Room*; John Milne, *Shadow Play*; ▷ Walter Mosley, *Devil in a Blue Dress*; James Sallis, *The Long-Legged Fly*; Josephine Tey, *The Daughter of Time*; Scott Turow, *Presumed Innocent*; Charles Willeford, *Miami Blues*; Robert Wilson, *A Small Crime in Lisbon*; Margaret Yorke, *No Medals for the Major*.

See also: Allingham, Chandler, Christie, Classic Detection, Dobyns, Grafton, Great (Classic) Detectives, Hammett, Higgins (George V.), Highsmith, Innes (Michael), Marsh, Murder Most Mind-boggling, Police Procedural, Private Eyes, Rendell, Simenon.

D

DAVIES, Robertson (1913–95)
Canadian novelist, journalist and playwright

The deceptively gentle, expansive tone of Davies's satires belies their extra-ordinary subject-matter: it is as if ▷Jane Austen had reworked ▷Rabelais. Davies's books are comedies of manners, many set in small university towns riven with gossip and pretension. *Tempest-tost* (1951) is about an amateur production of Shakespeare's *The Tempest* all but sabotaged by the unexpected, lacerating love of the middle-aged leading man for the girl who plays his daughter. *A Mixture of Frailties* (1958) describes the chain of bizarre events after a woman leaves money to educate a girl in the arts, unless and until the woman's son sires a male heir. The 'Deptford trilogy' (1970–75) begins with the throwing of a stone-filled snowball, and spirals out to cover three 20th-century lives, interlocking in a dazzling, bizarre mosaic, involving medieval (and modern) saints, big business, Houdini, Jungian analysis, touring freak-shows and a barnstorming company of travelling actors.

★☆ THE 'CORNISH' TRILOGY (1982)
The books in this trilogy, about members of the wealthy, eccentric Cornish family, are *The Rebel Angels, What's Bred in the Bone* and *The Lyre of Orpheus*. Hovering over the events, as puppeteers loom over marionettes, are guardian angels, devils and spirits of medieval mischief; we humans are not alone. Alternate chapters of *The Rebel Angels* are told by Father Darcourt, a professor of Biblical Greek at a small, Roman Catholic, Canadian university, and Maria Magdalene Theotoky, a research student. The university is a quiet place, dedicated to placid scholarship and barbed common-room gossip. But Ms Theotoky is researching Rabelais, and the plot suddenly erupts with priceless

manuscripts, bizarre lusts, devil worship, scatology, and a storm of passion and deceit against which no grove of academe could stand unbowed. *What's Bred in the Bone* is the life story of Francis Cornish, art expert, multi-millionaire, wartime spy and loner, whose search for himself, and for love, is hampered by his guardian devil Maimas. *The Lyre of Orpheus* tells of the recreation, in 20th-century Canadian academe, of a lost Arthurian opera by the devil-inspired 19th-century romantic composer E.T.A. Hoffman. The style in all three books is urbane, placid narrative, but the contents are sown with mines. If ▷ Jane Austen rules the tone of Davies's early trilogies, in this one ▷ Rabelais keeps blowing raspberries.

The books in the 'Deptford trilogy' are Fifth Business, The Manticore *and* World of Wonders. *Davies's other novels include* Murther and Walking Spirits, The Cunning Man *and a third trilogy, in a similarly urbane and hilarious vein, set in a small Ontario university town,* The Salterton Trilogy. The Diary of Samuel Marchbanks, The Table Talk of Samuel Marchbanks *and* Marchbanks' Almanac *are collections of humorous journalism. Davies had a great passion for theatre and the stage. His own plays include* A Jig for the Gipsy, Hunting Stuart *and the political satire* Question Time *and* Happy Alchemy *is a posthumous collection of his engaging, erudite writings on theatre.*

READ ON ▷

● *A Leaven of Malice.*
▶ to *The Rebel Angels*: ▷ David Lodge, *Small World*; ▷ Anthony Burgess, *Enderby's Dark Lady.*
▶ to *What's Bred in the Bone*: ▷ Thomas Mann, *The Confessions of Felix Krull.*
▶ to *The Lyre of Orpheus*: Randall Jarrell, *Pictures from an Institution*; D.J. Enright, *Academic Year.*
▶ to Davies's work in general: ▷ John Irving, *A Prayer for Owen Meany.*

DE BERNIÈRES, Louis (born 1954)
British novelist

Louis de Bernières spent some of his earlier career as a teacher in South America and his early novels are both set there and borrow many of the 'magic realist' qualities of the continent's great modern authors like García Márquez and Isabel Allende. *The War of Don Emmanuel's Nether Parts*, *Señor Vivo and the Coca Lord* and *The Troublesome Offspring of Cardinal Guzman* are the three volumes in a loosely-connected trilogy which takes place in an imaginary South American republic where farce, violence and sexual passion intermingle. Resuscitated conquistadors walk again, girls are transformed into magical cats, black jaguars are domesticated through a love of chocolate in books which, if they sometimes seem rather self-conscious amalgams of all the best-known characteristics of South American fiction, are never less than enjoyable. De Bernières's major success (sales in the millions, a movie based on the book) came, however, with *Captain Corelli's Mandolin* – a novel that is very traditional in its virtues. It has strong characterization, a powerfully evoked setting and a story of pathos and drama that told of individual lives caught up by the larger forces of history. In the Second World War the Greek island of Cephalonia is occupied by an Italian force led by the amiable and civilized Captain Antonio Corelli. More interested in music and his mandolin than he is in potential military glory, Corelli is a gentlemanly invader and embarks on an intense love affair with the local doctor's daughter, Pelagia. Yet, as the war goes on, its horrors draw ever closer to Cephalonia, the political and the personal become ever more difficult to disentangle and tragedy becomes ever more inevitable.

> READ ON

▶ to the earlier novels: ▷ Gabriel García Márquez, *One Hundred Years of Solitude*; ▷ Isabel Allende, *The House of the Spirits*; Laura Esquivel, *Like Water for Chocolate*.
▶ to *Captain Corelli's Mandolin*: ▷ Sebastian Faulks, *Charlotte Gray*.

READ ON A THEME: **DEEP SOUTH, USA**

James Lee Burke, *Cadillac Jukebox*
▷ William Faulkner, *Absalom, Absalom!*
Ellen Gilchrist, *Net of Jewels*
Harper Lee, *To Kill a Mockingbird*
▷ Carson McCullers, *The Ballad of the Sad Café*
▷ Margaret Mitchell, *Gone With the Wind*
Flannery O'Connor, *Wise Blood*
▷ Mark Twain, *The Adventures of Huckleberry Finn*
▷ Alice Walker, *The Color Purple*
Rebecca Wells, *Divine Secrets of the Ya-Ya Sisterhood*
▷ Eudora Welty, *Delta Wedding*
▷ Thomas Wolfe, *Look Homeward, Angel*
Richard Wright, *Uncle Tom's Children*

See also: Places; Small Town Life, USA

DEFOE, Daniel (1660–1731)
British novelist and non-fiction writer

A journalist, Defoe wrote over 500 essays, poems, political satires and other works, including a history of England, a handbook of good manners and a guide-book to Britain. In his sixties he began writing what he called 'romances': books which purported to be the autobiographies of people who had led unusual or adventurous lives (pirates, whores, treasure hunters) but which were really fiction and among the earliest English novels. Apart from his characters' proneness to theological and philosophical reflection (eminently skippable), his books lack the ponderousness of later 18th-century fiction. His fast-moving, simple prose and his journalist's talent for description give his work a freshness which belies its age.

★ ROBINSON CRUSOE (1719)
The germ of this story came from the autobiography of a real-life sailor, Alexander Selkirk, who was marooned on a deserted island in 1704. As often in his works,

Defoe was fascinated by the idea of the confrontation between civilization and barbarism, in this case by how a 'modern' European, filled with the knowledge and aspirations of the Age of Reason, might cope if all the trappings of civilization were stripped from him. Crusoe is allowed nothing but a few tools and other possessions saved from the shipwreck, and the resources of his own ingenuity. Later, after Crusoe has lived alone for 26 years, Defoe provides him with a companion, the 'savage' Friday, and so lets us see 'civilized' humanity through innocent, unsophisticated eyes.

Defoe's 'romances' include Moll Flanders *(set in the 18th-century criminal underworld),* The Life and Adventures of Mr Duncan Campbell *(whose hero is a deaf-and-dumb conjurer),* Captain Singleton *(whose hero is a pirate),* Memoirs of a Cavalier *and* Memoirs of Captain George Carleton *(whose heroes are swashbuckling soldiers-of-fortune), and – more serious –* A Journal of the Plague Year, *a day-by-day, first-person account of life during the Great Plague of London in 1664.*

| READ ON >

- ● *The Farther Adventures of Robinson Crusoe.*
- ▶ ▷ **Henry Fielding,** *Tom Jones.* ▷ **William Golding,** *Pincher Martin; Rites of Passage.* ▷ **Patrick White,** *Voss.* **Michel Tournier,** *The Other Friday* **and Jane Gardam,** *Crusoe's Daughter* **play fascinating games with** *Robinson Crusoe***'s themes and plot, Tournier by retelling the story from Friday's point of view, and Gardam by focusing on a reclusive girl fixated on** *Robinson Crusoe* **who makes it her chief emotional resource. C.S. Lewis's,** *Out of the Silent Planet* **is a similar novel of survival, set on the planet Mars, while J.M. Coetzee's** *Foe* **gives an alternative account of how** *Robinson Crusoe* **came to be written, and of the 'real' events which might have inspired it – Friday and Crusoe are the sole survivors from a wrecked slave ship.**

DEIGHTON, Len (born 1929)
British novelist

In the 1960s, fired by dislike of snobbish spy fantasies of the James Bond school, Deighton produced a series of books (beginning with *The Ipcress File*) showing spies as ordinary human beings, functionaries of a ridiculous and outdated bureaucracy in which requisitions for paper-clips could take precedence over analyses of the danger of nuclear war. He devised for them a documentary, 'dossier' technique, flooding the text with lists, letters, memoranda, meeting transcripts, diary entries and technical notes – and went on to use it in a series of devastatingly authentic-seeming novels on non-spy subjects. Although his material is fictional, it reads like fact, like the transcript of a TV documentary which shows us people's thoughts and feelings as meticulously as what they do and say.

BOMBER (1970)
In direct contrast to the stiff-upper-lip, jolly-good-show British war films of the 1950s, Deighton gives a blunt, detailed idea of what it was probably like to prepare for and make an RAF bombing raid in 1943. In this documentary novel he is particularly interested in the tensions between service and civilian per-

sonnel, the class divisions between officers and other ranks and the bumbling and paper-chasing which contrasted with, and sometimes jeopardized, the bravery of actual combat.

Deighton's spy novels include Funeral in Berlin, Horse Under Water, Spy Story, Mamista, City of Gold *and the trilogies* Berlin Game, Moscow Set, London Match *and* Spy Hook, Spy Line, Spy Sinker *and* Faith, Hope *and* Charity. Close-up *is a black satire on the film business.* Only When I Larf *is a comedy about confidence tricksters.* Violent Ward *is a sparky updating of the Marlowe, Lew Archer genre to 1990s L.A. His 'dossier' novels include* SS-GB, *a nightmarish vision of what might have happened if Britain had lost the Second World War and were now under Nazi rule.*

| READ ON ▷ |

▶ **to the spy stories:** ▷ **John Le Carré, *The Spy Who Came in from the Cold*; Adam Hall, *The Quiller Memorandum.***
▶ **to *Bomber*: Derek Robinson, *Piece of Cake.***
▶ **to *SS-GB*:** ▷ **Robert Harris, *Fatherland.***

DeLILLO, Don (born 1936)
US writer

Born to Italian immigrants in New York City, DeLillo studied at Fordham University in the Bronx before working in advertising. His first novel *Americana* appeared in 1971, and set the mould for his later work, in that it satirized, with acute perceptiveness and a laconic wit, a particular strand of American culture – in this case, the television industry. Subsequent subjects have included football in *Endzone* (where, by drawing a parallel with this game and nuclear warfare, he examined the violence implicit in much US culture); the music business in *Great Jones St* and *Running Dog*; Wall Street finance (and terrorism) in *Players*; academia in *White Noise*. *Libra* is a brilliant meditation on the Kennedy assassination and *Mao II* (1991) investigates the heavy price of fame and media attention for a reclusive author. This last novel was reported to be inspired by a photograph of J.D. Salinger, probably the most notorious post-war literary recluse, and DeLillo himself has been something of a literary hermit. For some years, little was heard of him and it looked as if *Mao II* might be his last book, but it was followed in 1997 by *Underworld.* A huge, sprawling epic, this, like *Libra*, was an immensely imaginative speculation based on actual historical events. In *Underworld* it is the Cold War that comes under DeLillo's penetrating gaze, specifically, the first nuclear bomb exploded by the USSR in the 1950s. Recalling *Endzone*, with its sly, playful teaming of sport and mass destruction, the book commences, in a typically bravura opening, with a scene at a baseball game when a figure in the crowds catches a ball hit by the batter. From there DeLillo takes the reader on a journey, backwards and forwards through time, across five decades of American life and culture in a panoramic book peopled by hundreds of characters, both real and fictional.

DeLillo's other work includes Ratner's Star, The Names *and* The Body Artist.

READ ON

▶ to *Libra*: ▷ Norman Mailer, *Oswald's Story*.
▶ to *Underworld*: ▷ Thomas Pynchon, *Vineland*; E.L. Doctorow, *Ragtime*.

READ ON A THEME: DEPRESSION AND PSYCHIATRY

Lisa Alther, *Other Women*
▷ Paul Bailey, *Peter Smart's Confessions*
▷ Doris Lessing, *The Golden Notebook*
Wendy Perriam, *Fifty-minute Hour*
▷ H.H. Richardson, *Maurice Guest*
▷ J.D. Salinger, *Franny and Zooey*
Paul Sayer, *The Comforts of Madness*
▷ Antonia White, *Beyond the Glass*

See also: Emotionally Ill at Ease; Madness; On the Edge of Sanity

---

DEXTER, Colin (born 1930)
British novelist

Since the days of Holmes and Watson there has been no surer ingredient of long-term success in detective fiction than an alliance between two apparently mismatched characters who are, in fact, devoted to one another. As the readers of his books know – and the millions who have watched the TV films – Colin Dexter created just such an alliance in the partnership of Chief Inspector Morse and Detective Sergeant Lewis of the Oxford police. Morse is grumpy, intellectual, fond of booze, opera and crosswords, and a bachelor. Lewis is stolid, reliable, diligent but slightly unimaginative. Together they form a classic genius/sidekick duo. The third constant in the Morse books is Oxford. The city of dreaming spires provides the ideal setting for the complicated crimes Morse and Lewis investigate. However, plot, particularly in the early books, is not sacrificed to character and place. Dexter is a one-time national crossword champion and his narrative twists and turns have the ingenuity of the most cryptic of crossword clues.

The other full-length Morse novels are: Last Bus to Woodstock, Last Seen Wearing, The Silent World of Nicholas Quinn, Service of All the Dead, The Dead of Jericho, The Riddle of the Third Mile, The Secret of Annexe 3, The Wench Is Dead, The Jewel That Was Ours, The Way Through the Woods, The Daughters of Cain, Death Is Now My Neighbour *and* The Remorseful Day. Morse's Greatest Mystery *is a collection of short stories, some about Morse, some not.*

READ ON

● *The Way Through the Woods*.
▶ ▷ Reginald Hill, *An Advancement of Learning*; John Harvey, *Easy Meat*; R.D. Wingfield, *A Touch of Frost* (one of a series that shares with Dexter's books TV success and a grumpy central character).

DIBDIN, Michael (born 1947)
British novelist

Dibdin's early novels, including one in which the Victorian poet Robert Browning plays amateur detective in Florence, are enjoyable mixtures of authentic crime fiction and pastiche. His finest creation, however, and one of the most appealing protagonists in contemporary crime writing, is Aurelio Zen, investigator for the Criminalpol section of the Italian Ministry of the Interior. Zen, unlike the one-dimensional ciphers of so much detective fiction, is a rounded and convincing character. Struggling to maintain what moral integrity he can amidst the labyrinthine bureaucracy and corruption of Italian society, he tries to unearth as much of the truth about the cases he is assigned as circumstances allow. Dibdin himself lived and worked in Italy for a number of years and the richness and unobtrusive detail of the Italian settings – Venice, Rome, the impoverished South – add to the pleasures of reading the novels. In addition to the Zen novels, Dibdin continues to write other books in which he cleverly manipulates the conventions of crime fiction to produce challenging and witty narratives.

CABAL (1992)
Cabal opens with startling suddenness as a man plummets to his death from the gallery in St. Peter's, Rome while a priest is celebrating mass. The man is a gambler, playboy and prominent Catholic aristocrat and the initial assumption is that he committed suicide. Zen is brought in by the Vatican police force to rubber stamp this verdict but soon concludes that the case is not that simple. The dead man was involved in dubious financial skulduggery and, as murder begins to seem the likeliest option, potential witnesses join the ranks of the dead. Caught between the Vatican and his own superiors, Zen suspects far-reaching conspiracies and secret organizations ruthlessly intent on covering up their misdeeds.

The other Zen novels (each one self-contained) are Ratking, Vendetta, Dead Lagoon, Cosi Fan Tutti, A Long Finish *and* Blood Rain. *Dibdin's other books include* The Last Sherlock Holmes Story, Dark Spectre, Dirty Tricks, The Tryst *and* Thanksgiving.

- ● *Dirty Tricks* ▶ to the Zen novels: Donna Leon, *The Death of Faith* (one of another crime series with an Italian setting and central character); Iain Pears, *Giotto's Hand*; ▷ Ian Rankin, *The Hanging Garden*; ▷ Reginald Hill, *Bones and Silence*.
- ▶ to *The Last Sherlock Holmes Story*; Julian Symons, *A Three-Pipe Problem*; Jamyang Norbu, *The Mandala of Sherlock Holmes*.
- ▶ to non-Zen crime stories: Nicci French, *Beneath the Skin*; ▷ Barbara Vine, *The House of Stairs*.

DICK, Philip K. (Kendred) (1928–82)
US novelist and short story writer

Dick used standard science fiction ideas – androids, alternative worlds, aliens – to write novels about the hinges between fantasy and reality, madness and sanity, paranoia and true perception. For a time in the 1960s, thanks to books like *The Three Stigmata of Palmer Eldritch* (1964), which deals with the effects of mind-altering drugs on our perception of reality – and with the nature of that perception – he had a huge cult following and he continues to be much admired, often by readers who otherwise read little science fiction. His characters often teeter on the brink of insanity, struggling to understand the world in which they feel trapped. In one classic novel, *Do Androids Dream of Electric Sheep?* (1968; later filmed as *Bladerunner*), their dilemma is entirely real, as they are not human beings at all but androids aspiring to humanity. Science fiction fans make high claims for Dick, and he is certainly a master of the genre. But his metaphorical transformation of well-worn ideas, and his bizarre humour, make him a pleasure not only for addicts, but for readers who would not normally cross the road to read science fiction.

THE MAN IN THE HIGH CASTLE (1962)
The rewriting of history is a standard idea in science fiction and, at first glance, *The Man in the High Castle* seems a standard example of the sub-genre of alternative history. The Axis powers have won the Second World War and the Japanese rule the US. Yet Dick's book soon reveals itself as far more complicated and subtle than a straightforward work of alternative history. It is an interlocking, intermeshing web of possible realities. Dick feeds the reader a heady cocktail of fascism, Taoism, the I Ching (which he used as an aid in plotting the book), individual schizophrenia and mass paranoia.

Dick's other novels include The Penultimate Truth, A Maze of Death, Eye in the Sky, Ubik, Martian Time-Slip, A Scanner Darkly *(about how the dual life of a future-Earth narcotics agent causes him to lose hold of his own identity), and* Time Out of Joint. Valis, *about what happens when an ancient, extra-terrestrial satellite beams directly into the hero's brain the news that reality ended in* AD 74, *is one of Dick's most challenging novels and draws on his own experiences of apparent contact with alien intelligences.*

READ ON >

- to *The Man in the High Castle*: *The Crack in Space*.
- to *Valis*: *Radio Free Albemuth; The Transmigration of Timothy Archer*.
- ▶ Other alternative history/science fiction: Norman Spinrad, *The Iron Dream*; Keith Roberts, *Pavane*.
- ▶ Drugs and altered perceptions: Brian Aldiss, *Barefoot in the Head*; ▷ Jeff Noon, *Vurt*; K.W. Jeter, *Dr Adder*; William S. Burroughs, *The Ticket That Exploded*.

DICKENS, Charles (1812–70)
British novelist

In his early 20s Dickens worked as a journalist, writing reports of law court proceedings and Parliamentary debates, and short essays on the life and manners of the time (later collected as *Sketches by Boz*). After the startling success of his first novel *Pickwick Papers*, when he was 25, he was able to make writing a full-time career and continued to be the most popular of Victorian novelists until his death. He composed large parts of his novels in dialogue, and was proud of his gift for showing character through speech alone; he also gave his minor characters (pot-boys, shop-customers, carters, oystermen, toddlers) turns of speech or physical eccentricities to make them instantly memorable. These are theatrical techniques and Dickens was renowned for his love of the theatre. The vividness of his depiction of character is combined with a sustained commentary on human nature and society: Dickens consistently savaged the humbug and petty-mindedness of the very middle classes who bought his books, and said that human happiness comes not from law, religion, politics or social structures but from gratuitous, individual acts of kindness. In his later books, notably *Great Expectations* and *Our Mutual Friend*, savagery predominated over sentimentality to an extent rivalled only by ▷ Zola.

★☆ DAVID COPPERFIELD (1849–50)

Dickens's own favourite among his novels, this tells the story (in the first person, as if an autobiography) of a boy growing up: his unhappy childhood and adolescence, his first jobs and first love affair, and the way he finally transmutes his experience into fiction and becomes a writer. As often in Dickens's books, subsidiary characters seem to steal the show: the grim Murdstones, the optimistic Micawbers, salt-of-the-earth Peggotty, feckless Steerforth and above all the viperish hypocrite Uriah Heep. But the book's chief interest is the developing character of Copperfield himself. Apparently passive, at other people's mercy, he learns and grows by each experience, maturing before our eyes.

Dickens's novels, in order of publication, are Pickwick Papers, Oliver Twist, Nicholas Nickleby, The Old Curiosity Shop, Barnaby Rudge, Martin Chuzzlewit, Dombey and Son, David Copperfield, Bleak House, Hard Times, Little Dorrit, A Tale of Two Cities, Great Expectations, Our Mutual Friend *and the unfinished* The Mystery of Edwin Drood. *His shorter works include* A Christmas Carol, A Child's History of England *and three collections of articles,* Sketches by Boz, American Notes *and* The Uncommercial Traveller.

> READ ON ▷

- *Nicholas Nickleby*; *Oliver Twist.*
- ▶ Novels of 'growing up', using a biographical framework to give a picture (documentary, satirical or both at once) of society: ▷ Henry Fielding, *Tom Jones*; ▷ W. Somerset Maugham, *Of Human Bondage*; ▷ Mark Twain, *The Adventures of Huckleberry Finn*; ▷ James Joyce, *Portrait of the Artist as a Young Man.*

DOBYNS, Stephen (born 1941)
US novelist

As a writer, Dobyns wears several hats. He has written a series of bizarre, baroque private-eye novels, each with 'Saratoga' in the title (*Saratoga Longshot, Saratoga Headhunter, Saratoga Snapper, Saratoga Bestiary, Saratoga Hexameter*): they are like a mixture of Ross MacDonald (for plot) and Chester Himes (for language). In other novels he revealed him as a master of a version of magic realism. These are set in South America, and are unpredictable, dreamlike stories of ordinary people whose lives are taken over by bizarre, surreal events. In *The Two Deaths of Señora Puccini* (1988), for example, guests persist in a sinister dinner party

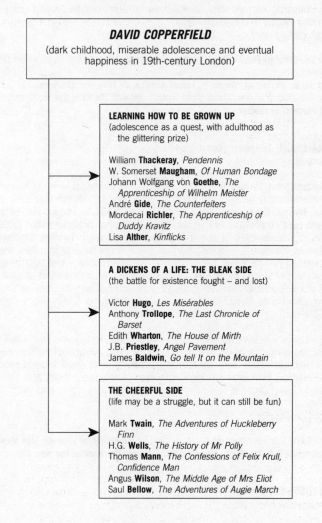

PATHWAYS

CHARLES DICKENS

DAVID COPPERFIELD
(dark childhood, miserable adolescence and eventual happiness in 19th-century London)

LEARNING HOW TO BE GROWN UP
(adolescence as a quest, with adulthood as the glittering prize)

William **Thackeray**, *Pendennis*
W. Somerset **Maugham**, *Of Human Bondage*
Johann Wolfgang von **Goethe**, *The Apprenticeship of Wilhelm Meister*
André **Gide**, *The Counterfeiters*
Mordecai **Richler**, *The Apprenticeship of Duddy Kravitz*
Lisa **Alther**, *Kinflicks*

A DICKENS OF A LIFE: THE BLEAK SIDE
(the battle for existence fought – and lost)

Victor **Hugo**, *Les Misérables*
Anthony **Trollope**, *The Last Chronicle of Barset*
Edith **Wharton**, *The House of Mirth*
J.B. **Priestley**, *Angel Pavement*
James **Baldwin**, *Go tell It on the Mountain*

THE CHEERFUL SIDE
(life may be a struggle, but it can still be fun)

Mark **Twain**, *The Adventures of Huckleberry Finn*
H.G. **Wells**, *The History of Mr Polly*
Thomas **Mann**, *The Confessions of Felix Krull, Confidence Man*
Angus **Wilson**, *The Middle Age of Mrs Eliot*
Saul **Bellow**, *The Adventures of Augie March*

while society degenerates into revolution and murder all round them. More recently books like *The Church of Dead Girls* (1997), in which the disappearance of three young girls triggers a small American town's descent into paranoia, and *Boy in the Water* (1999) have shown Dobyns to be capable of mixing the traditional thriller with precise social observation. Dobyns is also a poet and a critic.

Dobyns's other novels include Cold Dog Snap, The Wrestler's Cruel Study *and* The House on Alexandrine. *Poetry collections include* Black Dog, Red Dog, Cemetery Nights *and* Body Traffic.

READ ON ▷

▶ to the Saratoga books: Ross Thomas, *Briarpatch*; Loren D. Estleman, *Motor City Blue*.
▶ to the magic realist novels: ▷ Isabel Allende, *Of Love and Shadows*.
▶ to *The Church of Dead Girls*: Nicci French, *Beneath the Skin;* Val McDermid, *A Place of Execution*.

DONALDSON, Stephen (born 1947)
US novelist

Donaldson's major work, the 2600–page Thomas Covenant series (1977–84), is adventure-fantasy inspired by – and as good as – ▷Tolkien's *The Lord of the Rings*. Thomas Covenant, a leper, is transported to a distant country in the grip of the evil Lord Foul. He finds that his wedding ring is a powerful magic talisman, but is at first reluctant to use it because he believes himself psychologically tainted by his illness – in fact he wonders if the land and its plight are not fantasies of his own sick mind. The novels chart his spiritual agonizing, his recruitment of a band of helpers and followers, and his epic battles against Lord Foul. As well as the Thomas Covenant books, Donaldson has written the two-volume *Mordant's Need* (*The Mirror of her Dreams* and *A Man Rides Through*) and the science fiction *Gap* sequence of novels.

The Thomas Covenant books are Lord Foul's Bane, The Illearth War, The Power That Preserves, The Wounded Land, The One Tree, White Gold Wielder *and the brief* Gildenfire. *The* Gap *sequence consists of* The Real Story, Forbidden Knowledge, A Dark and Hungry God Arises, Chaos and Order *and* This Day All Gods Die. Daughter of Regals *and* Reave the Just *are collections of short stories.*

READ ON ▷

▶ ▷ David Eddings, *Pawn of Prophecy* (first of the Belgariad quintet); Jack Vance, *Lyonesse*; R.A. MacAvoy, *Damiano*; Gene Wolfe, *The Book of the New Sun*.

DOSTOEVSKY, Fyodor (1821–81)
Russian novelist

Dostoevsky admired ▷ Balzac and ▷ Dickens, and set out to describe Russian characters and society in a similar way, creating atmosphere by a series of vivid evocations (verbal snapshots) of everything from people's skin and clothes to the texture of furniture or the gleam of rain on cobblestones. His characters are a gallery of 'types', particularly strong on the destitute, the suffering and the inadequate. He was fascinated by people driven to extreme behaviour by despair or lack of external moral guidance. Raskolnikov, the central character of *Crime and Punishment*, makes himself a moral outsider by committing murder. Myshkin in *The Idiot* is so tormented by the thought of his own inadequacy that he becomes the imbecile he thinks he is. Every member of the Karamazov family (in *The Brothers Karamazov*) is morally tainted, and only the youngest, a novice monk, is able to wrestle with his own evil nature and win. If Dostoevsky had been a 20th-century writer his pessimistic view of human existence might have led him to surrealist black comedy (see ▷ Kafka); as it was, the psychological intensity of his books is closer to stage tragedy (*King Lear* or *Medea*, say) than to prose fiction, and has a similar all-engulfing power.

CRIME AND PUNISHMENT (1866)

Raskolnikov, a student, driven to neurotic frenzy by his powerlessness to change the injustice of the world, decides to demonstrate the freedom of his soul by a single gratuitous act: murder. Instead of being liberated, however, he is enslaved by his own guilt-feelings, and the book describes, in a remorseless and clinical way, the disintegration of his personality. The part of his 'conscience' is embodied in Inspector Petrovich, who harries him like a Fury from ancient myth, goading and cajoling him to admit his guilt and so to purge his soul.

Dostoevsky's other books include Notes from the House of the Dead (*based on his own prison-camp experiences: he was a political dissident*), Winter Notes on Summer Experiences (*a horrifying account of the degenerate Europe he found while visiting the London World Exhibition of 1862*), *and the novels* Notes from Underground, The Gambler *and* The Possessed.

> READ ON ▷

- ● *The Idiot*; *The Brothers Karamazov*.
- ▶ ▷ Victor Hugo, *Les misérables*; ▷ Nathaniel Hawthorne, *The Scarlet Letter*; ▷ Joseph Conrad, *Under Western Eyes*; ▷ Albert Camus, *The Fall* (*La chute*); ▷ Vladimir Nabokov, *Despair*.

READ ON A THEME: DOWN TO EARTH

(the implacability of nature)
   Stella Gibbons, *Cold Comfort Farm*
▷ Thomas Hardy, *The Woodlanders*
   Robert Morgan, *Gap Creek*
   Tim Pears, *In the Place of Fallen Leaves*
▷ Paul Theroux, *The Black House*
   Mary Webb, *Precious Bane*
▷ Fay Weldon, *The Heart of the Country*
▷ Edith Wharton, *Ethan Frome*

See also: The Rhythm of Nature

DOYLE, Arthur Conan (1859–1930)
British writer of novels, short stories and non-fiction

As a doctor with very few patients, Doyle began writing to improve his income. His main interest was military history, and he regarded his historical novels (e.g. *The White Company*, the story of a band of 14th-century knights-errant, or the Brigadier Gerard books, set during the Napoleonic Wars) as his best work. His Sherlock Holmes stories were meant as potboilers, and throughout his life he claimed to be embarrassed by their success. Famously, he attempted to finish Holmes off by sending him over the Reichenbach Falls in the clutches of his deadliest enemy, the criminal mastermind Professor Moriarty, but public pressure forced him to resurrect the cerebral, eccentric detective. The Holmes stories were published by *Strand Magazine* in the UK and by *Harper's* in the US; these papers also serialized Doyle's Professor Challenger novels (beginning with *The Lost World*), about a flamboyant scientific genius and explorer, a blend of the heroes of ▷ Verne and ▷ Rider Haggard.

☆ THE MEMOIRS OF SHERLOCK HOLMES (1893)
In each of the 11 stories in this collection, Holmes is presented with a problem which seems insoluble – at least so far as his friend and chronicler Dr Watson can see – and solves it by a mixture of dazzling deductive reasoning and melodramatic adventure. He is a master of disguise, an expert shot and boxer, a drug taker, a neurotic introvert, a plausible liar who uses every trick to trap his suspects – and Doyle's style has a single-mindedness, an obsessiveness, which perfectly suits both Holmes's character and the mysteries he is set to solve.

Doyle's Holmes books are the novels A Study in Scarlet, The Sign of Four, The Hound of the Baskervilles *and* The Valley of Fear, *and the short-story collections* The Adventures of Sherlock Holmes, The Return of Sherlock Holmes, His Last Bow *and* The Case Book of Sherlock Holmes. *The Challenger books include* The Poison Belt *and* The Land of Mist, *and Doyle's historical novels, apart from those mentioned, include* Micah Clarke *(set during the Monmouth Rebellion of 1685 and its bloody aftermath).*

READ ON ▷

● *The Case Book of Sherlock Holmes.*
▶ Nicholas Meyer, *The Seven-per-cent Solution* (one of the most convincing of many Holmes stories by others); G.K. Chesterton, *The Father Brown Stories;* John Dickson Carr, *The Emperor's Snuff Box.*

DOYLE, Roddy (born 1958)
Irish writer

The families in Doyle's early books (epitomized by the Rabittes of the Barrytown trilogy) are large, endlessly ambitious and totally useless. They live in Dublin, scraping a living on welfare (and by other less official activities), and always dreaming of the big time. The Barrytown trilogy consists of *The Commitments* (made into an exuberant film by Alan Parker), *The Snapper* and *The Van*. The 1993 Booker Prize-winning *Paddy Clarke Ha Ha Ha* is set in the same type of working class area of Dublin's northside as the Barrytown books and tells of the growing pains of its ten-year-old protagonist from his perspective. With *The Woman Who Walked Into Doors* (see below) Doyle indicated an ambition to extend his fictional range and this has been confirmed by his most recent novel *A Star Called Henry* (1999). This is the first of what is to be a trilogy re-examining the history of the Irish Republic through the eyes of Henry Smart. Born in the Dublin slums, Henry grows up quickly to play his part in the 1916 Easter Uprising (grittily and unromantically presented by Doyle) and to enter the violent politics of the Civil War years as a hard and unillusioned fighter.

THE WOMAN WHO WALKED INTO DOORS (1996)

Paula Spencer is looking back on seventeen years of marriage to a violent man. Her husband now dead (shot by police), she is an alcoholic consumed by self-hatred and the self-image imposed on her by the men in her life. Doyle provides unflinching insights into Paula's inner life and her struggles to regain dignity and self-worth. Often as funny as his earlier books (despite its stark subject-matter) *The Woman Who Walked Into Doors* is a remarkable feat of empathy and imagination.

READ ON ▷

▶ Patrick McCabe, *Breakfast on Pluto*; Jospeh O'Connor, *Cowboys and Indians*; Jeff Torrington, *Swing, Hammer, Swing* (for a working class Glasgow as exuberant as Doyle's working class Dublin).

DRABBLE, Margaret (born 1939)
British novelist and non-fiction writer

An admirer of ▷ Eliot and ▷ Bennett, Drabble has updated their fictional ideas to the present day. Her books are crammed with the detail of everyday lives – fetching children from school, making gravy, taking inter-city trains, washing tights – and are about 'ordinary' people: housewives, librarians, teachers, midwives. But Drabble, like Eliot and Bennett, is also interested in intellectual ideas, in describing the spirit of the times as well as their domestic detail. Her books centre on women's experience and tell us how middle-class girls of the late 1950s felt about their lives, how they went on in the 1960s to balance marriage, motherhood and careers, and how they coped in the 1970s, 1980s and 1990s with teenage children and rocky marriages. A.S. Byatt is Drabble's sister.

THE RADIANT WAY (1987)

The lives of three women of similar age (late 40s) and background (educated middle-class) are contrasted, in a brilliantly-evoked mid-1980s Britain. All were born in the north of England; Liz has moved south and made a career as a Harley Street psychiatrist; her sister has stayed at home to look after their senile mother; Alix and her husband, failing to make a success in London, are returning north to regenerate their lives. The characters' contrasting experiences, and their middle-aged views of the way their younger ambitions have worked out, match the political and social feelings Drabble sees as typical of Britain in the 1980s, when the young adults of the flower-power generation are just beginning to feel that life has passed them by. Their stories are continued in two sequels, *A Natural Curiosity* and *The Gates of Ivory*.

Drabble's novels include The Garrick Year, The Millstone, Jerusalem the Golden, The Waterfall, A Summer Bird-Cage, The Realms of Gold, The Ice Age, The Witch of Exmoor *and* The Peppered Moth. *She has also written biographies of Wordsworth and Bennett and has acted as general editor of* The Oxford Companion to English Literature.

READ ON ▷

● *The Garrick Year* (a moving study, set in the 1960s, of a woman trying to manage both marriage, to a rising actor, and the claims of her own career); *The Peppered Moth* (four generations of a family, from a young woman in an early 20th-century mining village trying to escape to a more fulfilling world to a granddaughter who has still not quite reached it.)
▶ Penelope Mortimer, *The Pumpkin Eater*; Deborah Moggach, *Close to Home*;
  ▷ Margaret Atwood, *The Edible Woman*; Joan Didion, *A Book of Common Prayer*; Mary Flanagan, *Trust*.
▶ Earlier books foreshadowing Drabble's concerns: ▷ George Eliot, *Middlemarch*; ▷ Arnold Bennett, *Hilda Lessways*; ▷ Virginia Woolf, *Mrs Dalloway*.

READ ON A THEME: DREAMING SPIRES

(books set in Cambridge and Oxford Universities)
▷ Max Beerbohm, *Zuleika Dobson*
▷ Barbara Pym, *Crampton Hodnett*
  Frederic Raphael, *The Glittering Prizes*
▷ Dorothy L. Sayers, *Gaudy Night*
▷ Tom Sharpe, *Porterhouse Blue*
▷ C.P. Snow, *The Masters*

See also: Groves of Academe; Higher (?) Education

DUMAS, Alexandre (1802–70)
French writer of novels, plays, short stories and non-fiction

In his 20s Dumas worked as a civil-service clerk; it was not until he was 29 that he was able to take up writing full-time. From then till his death, working with a team of assistants, he poured out over 250 plays, novels, essays, books on history, travel and cooking and no less than 22 volumes of memoirs. He was one of the most popular authors of his century, and the genre he specialized in, swashbuckling historical romance, has continued to enthrall many readers to the present day.

★☆ THE THREE MUSKETEERS (1844–5)
At the beginning of the 17th century d'Artagnan, a young country squire, goes to Paris to seek adventure. He makes friends with three of the King's musketeers (by the unusual method of challenging each of them to a duel on the same day) and the four become inseparable. D'Artagnan is accepted for

royal service, and the musketeers throw themselves into the political intrigues centring on weak King Louis, his unhappy queen and her arch-enemies Cardinal Richelieu and the seductive, treacherous Milady. The story involves stolen jewels, masquerades, bluff and double bluff, and the musketeers gallop the length and breadth of France, duelling, drinking, wenching and making a thousand skin-of-the-teeth escapes. Although the book's style is old-fashioned, its breathless plot, its good humour and above all the wise-cracking, bantering friendship between the four central characters, give it irresistible gusto. After a few dozen pages of acclimatization, it may prove hard to put it down.

Although Dumas was best-known – and is now best-remembered – for his Musketeers adventures, he wrote fine novels set in other periods, notably The Queen's Necklace *and* The Countess of Charny *(both of which take place during the French Revolution) and* The Count of Monte Cristo, *about a man falsely imprisoned for helping the defeated Napoleon, who escapes, discovers hidden treasure and proceeds to hunt down the people who betrayed him.*

> READ ON ▷

- Dumas continued the Musketeers' adventures in *Twenty Years After, The Vicomte of Bragelonne* and *The Man in the Iron Mask*.
- ▶ Old-fashioned swashbuckling stories: Rafael Sabatini, *Captain Blood*; Jeffery Farnol, *The Broad Highway*; Stanley J. Weyman, *Gentleman of France*; Baroness Orczy, *The Scarlet Pimpernel*.
- ▶ Today's versions of swash and buckle: ▷ George MacDonald Fraser, *Flashman*; ▷ Bernard Cornwell, *Sharpe's Regiment*; Allan Mallinson, *The Nizam's Daughters*; Bjorn Larsson, *Long John Silver*.

DU MAURIER, Daphne (1907–89)
British novelist and non-fiction writer

Although Du Maurier wrote novels and stories of many kinds, she is best known for a series of atmospheric romances set in the English West Country (Cornwall, Devon and Somerset) and drawing on the moorland landscape and seafaring associations of the area. In her best-loved book, ☆*Rebecca* (1938), a girl marries an enigmatic young widower and goes to be mistress of his large country house Manderley, only to find it haunted by the mystery of his first wife's death. Solving that mystery (against the wishes of the sinister house-keeper Mrs Danvers) is the only way to bring happiness to the young girl (who is unnamed) and peace to her tormented husband – and the search leads her into a psychological labyrinth as threatening as the corridors of the dark old house itself.

Du Maurier's romances include Jamaica Inn, My Cousin Rachel *and* Mary Anne. *Her other novels include* The King's General, The Parasites, The Glassblowers *and* The House on the Strand. The Birds and Other Stories *includes the short story that was the basis for Hitchcock's classic film.* Don't Look Now and Other Stories *includes the novella/short story that inspired the 1973 movie directed by Nicolas Roeg. Daphne Du Maurier also wrote plays, biographies (of her family,*

Branwell Brontë and Francis Drake) and an autobiography, The Shaping of a Writer/Myself When Young.

READ ON ▷

● *Frenchman's Creek* (**piracy and romance in Restoration Cornwall**).
▶ ▷ **Susan Hill,** *Mrs de Winter* (**sequel**)**; Philippa Gregory,** *The Favoured Child***; Barbara Erskine,** *House of Echoes* ▷ **Charlotte Brontë,** *Jane Eyre.* ▷ **Susan Howatch,** *Penmarric.*

DUNMORE, Helen (born 1952)
British poet, novelist and short story writer

Helen Dunmore's fiction explores, in prose of a strong, lyrical sensuousness that reflects her gifts as a poet, the seductive charms and potential betrayals of intense love affairs. Her characters often harbour dark secrets or transgressive desires which threaten the stability of everyday life. Past events continue to echo in the present and to re-emerge, often to devastating effect. In *Talking to the Dead* (1996) Nina arrives at her sister's home to provide help after a difficult childbirth but is drawn into an affair with her brother-in-law. The relationship grows more obsessive, her sister retreats further into a private world and Nina finds disturbing memories of childhood and the death of a brother returning with new force. Set in Edwardian England, *A Spell of Winter* (1995) borrows elements of Gothic melodrama and the most sinister of fairy tales in its story of a family that has been traumatized by the desertion of a mother. The father has been driven into an asylum and the two children, living in isolation in an eerily described country home, have found comfort in an incestuous relationship. *With Your Crooked Heart* (1999) adds dimension and depth to the cliché of the eternal triangle in its story of the stifling interrelationship of Louise with her husband Paul and his younger, charming, irresponsible brother. The settings of Dunmore's novels are various but all share the same sense of the enabling power and threatening danger of erotic love.

Helen Dunmore's other novels are Zennor in Darkness, Burning Bright, Your Blue-Eyed Boy *and* The Siege. Love of Fat Men *and* Ice Cream *are collections of short stories. She has also written several volumes of poetry and a number of books for children.*

READ ON ▷

● *The Siege* (**a love affair set against the larger backdrop of the siege of Leningrad**).
▶ ▷ **Barbara Vine,** *The House of Stairs***; Alison Fell,** *Mer de Glace***; Linda Grant,** *The Cast Iron Shore***; Nicci French,** *Killing Me Softly.*

DUNNETT, Dorothy (born 1923)
British writer

Dunnett worked as a civil servant until the 1950s, and then began a double career as portrait painter and novelist. She is best known for two enormous historical sagas, swashbuckling romances set in the European High Renaissance, a time of intellectual explosions in religion, politics, the arts, war and business. Her 'Lymond' books begin with Scottish border quarrels, and then spread out to England, France, Malta and beyond. The 'House of Niccolò' series, centring on a handsome, mysterious Scots-Belgian merchant, travels all over Europe, the Mediterranean, and into Asia as far as the Towers of Trebizond. Dunnett's other books include *King Hereafter*, a novel about the historical Macbeth, king of Scotland.

The 'Lymond' books, in order, are The Game of Kings, Queen's Play, The Disorderly Knights, Pawn in Frankincense, The Ringed Castle *and* Checkmate. *The 'House of Niccolo' books are* Niccolò Rising, The Spring of the Ram, Race of Scorpions, Scales of Gold, The Unicorn Hunt, To Lie With Lions *and* Gemini.

> READ ON >

▶ **Reay Tannahill, *The World, the Flesh and the Devil*; Sharon Penman, *The Sunne in Splendour* (a novel of Richard III); Nigel Tranter, *Macbeth the King*.**

DURRELL, Lawrence (1912–90)
British writer of novels, poems and non-fiction

Durrell lived most of his life out of Britain: in Greece, Egypt and France. As well as fiction, he wrote poetry and half a dozen non-fiction books about Greek islands: they are among his most enjoyable work, allowing scope for the impressionistic descriptions of landscape and character and the ruminations on love and life which sometimes clog his novels. In his fiction, he used experimental forms, constantly varying each story's structure and standpoint; this sets up a dialogue between writer and reader, a feeling of collaboration, which is one of the most exhilarating aspects of his work.

☆ THE ALEXANDRIA QUARTET (1957–60)
Each book in the quartet, *Justine, Balthazar, Mountolive* and *Clea*, tells us part of the story: they give different viewpoints of the same events, and it is not till the end that every motive, every action, every twist of character becomes clear. The people are a group of friends and lovers, English, Greek and Egyptian, living in the turmoil of late-1930s Alexandria. At the centre is Darley, a teacher and would-be writer who observes events, partakes, but cannot explain. A main 'character' is the city of Alexandria itself. Durrell/Darley pretends to be giving accurate pictures of its souks, bars, palaces, brothels and crumbling embassies, but it is a dream city, a fantasy land where reality is subjective and events are only what you make of them.

As well as The Alexandria Quartet, *his novels include* The Black Book, The Dark Labyrinth/Cefalù *and the five-novel 'Avignon quincunx',* Monsieur, Livia, Constance, Sebastian *and* Quinx. *Durrell's* Collected Poems *have also been published, while* Antrobus Complete *is a collection of satirical short stories about life in the diplomatic service. His island books include* Prospero's Cell (*about Corfu, also the subject of his brother Gerald's* My Family and Other Animals), Reflections on a Marine Venus *(about Rhodes) and* Bitter Lemons (*about Cyprus).*

READ ON ▷

● *Tunc* and *Numquam* (a pair of Siamese-twin novels) are similarly dreamlike, setting bizarre events and characters in a blur of countries and climaxing magnificently, if unexpectedly, under the dome of St Paul's Cathedral, London.

▶ ▷ Olivia Manning, *The Balkan Trilogy*; *The Levant Trilogy*.

E

ECO, Umberto (born 1932)
Italian novelist

Before publishing his first novel in Italian in his late forties, Eco had carved out a substantial career for himself as an academic and was a well-known figure in the Italian intellectual and cultural world. Beginning as a medievalist with a particular interest in Thomas Aquinas, Eco moved into the emerging field of semiotics and became the first professor of the subject at one of Europe's oldest universities, Bologna. *The Name of the Rose* (see below) was an enormous success, selling millions of copies worldwide, and Eco was launched on a parallel career as a novelist. He has published only three further novels, however, one not yet translated into English. *Foucault's Pendulum* (1989) is a huge, sprawling narrative which uses crackpot conspiracy theories, particularly about the Knights Templar, as the starting point for a story of murder, esoterica and the mysteries of belief and reality. In *The Island of The Day Before* (1995) a 17th-century Italian nobleman is shipwrecked and finds refuge on another, apparently abandoned ship. As he explores the ship and begins to realize that he is not alone on it, Eco's tale opens out into another dazzling display of erudition and imagination.

THE NAME OF THE ROSE (1983)
The framework of Eco's first novel is a murder mystery. A 14th-century monk, William of Baskerville, using methods of deduction which anticipate those of Sherlock Holmes, solves seven murders in the monastery he happens to be visiting. On this simple frame Eco weaves a wonderful tapestry of philosophy, intellectual jokes, extraordinary lore about monasticism, alchemy and religious belief. Although *The Name of the Rose* tweaks and stimulates the intellect, it is

anything but hard to read – largely due to Eco's beautifully clear prose and to his affection for even the tiniest detail of medieval life.

> READ ON ▷

▶ ▷ Lawrence Norfolk, *The Pope's Rhinoceros;* ▷ John Barth, *The Sot-Weed Factor;* ▷ William Golding, *The Spire;* ▷ Hermann Hesse, *The Glass Bead Game;* Richard Zimler, *The Last Kabbalist of Lisbon.*

EDDINGS, David (born 1931)
US novelist

After one modern adventure story, *High Hunt,* Eddings concentrated on fantasy. His best-known work is the 'Belgariad quintet' (1982–4), a ▷ Tolkien-influenced saga of good and evil, magic and mysticism – but laced, unlike *The Lord of the Rings,* with a strong sense of the absurd. The books in the series are *Pawn of Prophecy, Queen of Sorcery, Magician's Gambit, Castle of Wizardry* and *Enchanter's Endgame.* A second series (the 'Mallorean' quintet, beginning with *Guardians of the West*) tells further adventures of his hero Garion, who begins as a scullion, graduates to be sorcerer's apprentice and ends up as a fully-fledged wizard.

> READ ON ▷

▶ Alan Dean Foster, *Spellsinger;* Piers Anthony, *A Spell for Chameleon;* T.H. White, *The Once and Future King;* ▷ J.R.R. Tolkien, *The Lord of the Rings.*

READ ON A THEME: EGYPT

(Ancient)
    Paul Doherty, *The Mask of Ra*
    Christian Jacq, *Son of Light*
▷ Norman Mailer, *Ancient Evenings*
▷ Wilbur Smith, *River God*
    Mika Waltari, *Sinuhe the Egyptian*

(Modern)
▷ Lawrence Durrell, *Justine*
▷ Naguib Mahfouz, *Palace Walk*
▷ Olivia Manning, *The Levant Trilogy*
    Michael Pearce, *The Mamur Zapt and the Spoils of Egypt*
    Robert Solé, *The Photographer's Wife*
    Ahdaf Soueif, *The Map of Love*

READ ON A THEME: THE ELDERLY

▷ Kingsley Amis, *Ending Up*
▷ Honoré de Balzac, *Old Goriot*
▷ Julian Barnes, *Staring at the Sun*
    Jenny Diski, *Happily Ever After*

ELIOT, George (1819–80)
British novelist

'George Eliot' was the pen-name of Marian Evans, a farm manager's daughter. She grew up in the stifling provincial pieties of middle-class Victorian England, but after her father's death became an atheist and freethinker, travelled abroad and set up home in London. She was at the heart of the liberal intellectual circles of her time: a supporter of Darwin, an admirer of ▷William Morris and other early socialists. A similar receptivity to new ideas and disdain for convention mark her novels. They deal with the kind of moral issues (such as whether a 'good life' can be lived without religion, or if sexual happiness is essential to a successful marriage) which were rarely discussed in polite Victorian company and were even less common in literature. At the same time her books teem with realistic detail of provincial society, minutely observed. The combination of exact documentation of behaviour and character with unashamed discussion of ideas normally left unspoken was a heady one: she was one of the most widely read authors of her day.

★☆ MIDDLEMARCH (1871–2)
Two people try to break free from the petty-minded boredom of the English provincial town of Middlemarch. Dorothea Brooke marries because of intellectual infatuation, only to find that her husband (an elderly scholar) is a domestic tyrant. Tertius Lydgate, a doctor struggling to introduce new medical ideas in a society which is deeply suspicious of them, marries for love, only to find that his wife's brainless following of fashion destroys his bank balance, his self-confidence and his social position.

Apart from Romola, *set in 15th-century Florence, all Eliot's novels have 19th-century English locations and characters. Her first book,* Scenes of Clerical Life, *contains three mid-length stories; it and the short novel* Silas Marner *(about a free-thinking country weaver tormented for his beliefs and for a crime he did not commit) are the most accessible of all her works. Her full-length novels are* Adam Bede, The Mill on the Floss, Felix Holt, Middlemarch *and* Daniel Deronda.

> READ ON

- **The Mill on the Floss** (about a brother and sister who are idyllically happy together as children, grow apart in adult life, and are finally, tragically reunited).
- ▶ Matching Eliot's concern for the individual stifled by society: ▷ Gustave Flaubert, *Madame Bovary*; ▷Mrs Gaskell, *North and South*; ▷ Thomas Hardy, *Jude the Obscure*; Benjamin Disraeli, *Sybil*; ▷ Arnold Bennett, *Anna of the Five Towns*.
- ▶ 20th-century books combining social observation with 'issues' in an Eliotish way, though their styles are entirely different: ▷Margaret Drabble, *The Millstone*; Winifred Holtby, *South Riding*.

ELLIS, Bret Easton (born 1964)
US novelist

Controversy has raged over Bret Easton Ellis's novels, particularly *American Psycho* (see below) and there are diametrically opposed views of the blank tones his narrators employ to describe even the most viscerally violent and disturbing events. Are we reading the work of a deadpan satirist, revealing the moral shallowness of the age, or that of a voyeuristic misogynist? Ellis's most severe critics underestimate the extent to which his style is consciously crafted and overestimate the extent to which writer and fictional narrator must be identified. From his first novel (*Less Than Zero*, published in 1985 when he was 21) Ellis has shown his interest in people who are sleepwalking, morally and emotionally, through life and the narrator of *American Psycho* is a clear descendant of the spaced-out, over-indulged teenagers of that first book.

AMERICAN PSYCHO (1991)
Patrick Bateman is good-looking, intelligent and earns colossal sums of money working on Wall Street. His life, which he describes in careful detail, relentlessly namechecking the designer label clothing and accessories that help create the persona he presents to the world, appears to be an embodiment of the American Dream. Yet Bateman's inner life, and secret world, is one of appalling moral depravity. He mutilates and murders young women, acts which he describes with the same cool precision he applies to his wardrobe and toilette. *American Psycho* is a very disturbing book, graphic in its descriptions of violence and bodily dismemberment, and is not to be recommended to the squeamish or those in search of light reading. Ellis is not, however, writing violent pornography. His intent is to paint a portrait of moral nullity in the midst of material plenty, of a man who finds no meaning in life save conspicuous consumption and his own monstrous acts and desires. There is humour of the blackest kind in the disparity between Bateman as he appears to others and his terrible hidden world but, ultimately, this is a serious study of moral blankness.

Bret Easton Ellis's other books include *The Rules of Attraction*, *Glamorama* and *The Informers*.

> READ ON

▶ **to the fiction in general:** ▷ Jay McInerney, *Bright Lights, Big City*; ▷ Douglas Coupland, *Generation X*; Chuck Palahniuk, *Fight Club*.

▶ **to *American Psycho*:** Dennis Cooper, *Frisk* (another exploration of death, desire and sadism, not for the squeamish); Jason Starr, *Cold Caller*; Poppy Z. Brite, *Exquisite Corpse* (a horror novel about necrophiliac serial killers, even more extreme than *American Psycho*, but admired by some as a portrayal of contemporary decadence).

READ ON A THEME: EMOTIONALLY ILL-AT-EASE

▷ Anita Brookner, *Look at Me*
  Anita Desai, *Baumgartner's Bombay*
▷ George Eliot, *Middlemarch*
▷ Gustave Flaubert, *Madame Bovary*

▷ **E.M. Forster,** *Howard's End*
  Elizabeth Jolley, *Milk and Honey*
▷ **Rosamond Lehmann,** *The Ballad and the Source*
  Mary McCarthy, *The Company She Keeps*
▷ **John Updike,** *Marry Me*

See also: **Battling with Life; Perplexed by Life**

F

FARMER, Philip José (born 1918)
US novelist

Since his emergence as a major writer of science fiction in the 1950s, Farmer has been one of the great iconoclasts of the genre, eager to give to it a psychological and sexual maturity it previously lacked. His best-known work is the 'Riverworld' series (1972–80; the individual titles are *To Your Scattered Bodies Go*; *The Fabulous Riverboat*; *The Dark Design*; *The Magic Labyrinth*; *Gods of Riverworld*). Riverworld is a planet on which every human being ever born, from the dawn of history to beyond the present day, has been granted a second life and the chance of moral self-reformation. Historic personalities from Jesus to Goering, Mark Twain to Bad King John explore the potential of this unexpected afterlife. Farmer has also written pastiches and parodies of other writers' characters and mythologies (including Edgar Rice Burroughs's Tarzan) which often reveal surprising depths unexplored by the original authors.

Farmer's other books include three separate novels dealing with the pull between love and sex: Flesh, The Lovers *and* A Feast Unknown, Night of Light *(about religious experience), and the dazzling short story collection* The Book of Philip José Farmer.

READ ON ▷

● *Tarzan Alive, Time's Last Gift, Lord of the Trees.*
▶ to *To Your Scattered Bodies Go* and other *Riverworld* books: Brian Aldiss, *Hothouse*; ▷ Michael Moorcock, *The Dancers at the End of Time*, Jack Vance, *The Dying Earth.*
▶ to *Flesh* and themes of sex and gender: ▷ J.G. Ballard, *Crash*; ▷ Ursula Le Guin, *The Left Hand of Darkness*; ▷ Michael Moorcock, *The Final Programme*; Joanna Russ, *The Female Man.*

FARRELL, J.G. (James Gordon) (1935–79)
British novelist

After three contemporary novels, including *The Lung* (1965, based on his own experience), about the onset of polio, Farrell took all his themes from history. *Troubles* (1970), set in Ireland after the First World War, is a barbed account of the Irish freedom struggle against the English, and draws uncomfortable parallels with the present-day situation in Northern Ireland. *The Siege of Krishnapur* (1973), equally vitriolic and farcical – its tone is close at times to ▷ Heller's *Catch-22* – is set in 1850s India, during the so-called 'Mutiny'. *The Singapore Grip* (1978) is a blockbuster about the Japanese capture of Malaysia in the Second World War – for Farrell, the beginning of Britain's eclipse as a global power. Taken together, the three books are an indictment of Britain's attitude towards its empire: not so much thuggishness as boneheaded indifference, the unconcern of those who never imagine that others might resent their rule.

READ ON ▷

▶ to *Troubles*: Liam O'Flaherty, *The Informer*; Bernard MacLaverty, *Cal.*
▶ to *The Siege of Krishnapur*: John Masters, *Nightrunners of Bengal*; Giles Foden, *Ladysmith.*
▶ to *The Singapore Grip*: ▷ J.G. Ballard, *Empire of the Sun*; Timothy Mo, *An Insular Possession.*

FAULKNER, William (1897–1962)
US novelist and short story writer

Faulkner's work deals obsessively with a single theme: the moral degeneracy of the US Deep South. His characters are the descendants of the cotton barons of the time before the Civil War, and of the slaves who worked for them. The whites live in crumbling mansions, dress in finery handed down from previous generations and bolster their sagging self-esteem with snobbery, racism and drink. The blacks either fawn, as if slavery had never been abolished, or seethe in decaying slums on the edge of town. The air itself seems tainted: despair, lust, introversion and murder clog people's minds. It is a society without hope or comfort, and Faulkner describes it in a series of moral horror stories, compulsive and merciless.

THE SOUND AND THE FURY (1929)

The novel's theme is how moral decadence overwhelms two generations of the white Compson family. We see a brother and sister, Caddy and Quentin, growing up as bright, happy adolescents, full of hope for the future, only to fall victims to the family taint and spiral into incest, nymphomania and suicide. One of their brothers, Jason, a morose bully, succeeds his father as head of the family and becomes a miser and a tyrant; their other brother Benjy has a mental age of two. In the second half of the book we see the corruption threatening to engulf Caddy's and Quentin's incestuous daughter, and her attempts to break free from the family curse. Large sections of the book are told as first-person narratives, by Caddy, Jason, Quentin and – eerily, a *tour de force* of writing, demanding concentration in the reader – the retarded Benjy. A final strand of claustrophobia is added by the Compsons' negro servants: watching, always present, like the chorus of a particularly fraught Greek tragedy.

Faulkner's short stories are in two fat volumes, Collected Stories *and* Uncollected Stories. *His main Southern novels, a series set in the imaginary Yoknapatawpha County, Mississippi, are* Sartoris, Absalom, Absalom!, The Unvanquished *and the trilogy* The Hamlet, The Town *and* The Mansion. *His other books include* Intruder in the Dust, Light in August, The Reivers, Sanctuary *and two books in experimental styles,* As I Lay Dying *and* Requiem for a Nun.

> READ ON

- *Light in August* (a woman searches for the father of her unborn child and a man struggles to assert his divided identity in a society riven by racism); *Intruder in the Dust* (an adolescent awakens to adult responsibilities as he strives to repay a debt to an elderly black man accused of murder).
- ▶ Good Deep South follow-ups: ▷ Carson McCullers, *The Ballad of the Sad Café*; William Styron, *Lie Down in Darkness*; Harper Lee, *To Kill a Mockingbird*; Tennessee Williams, *Short Stories*.
- ▶ Good follow-ups on the theme of the degenerate, collapsing family: ▷ Thomas Mann, *Buddenbrooks*; Giuseppe Tomaso di Lampedusa, *The Leopard*; ▷ Ivy Compton-Burnett, *Mother and Son*.
- ▶ Good stylistic follow-ups: ▷ James Joyce, *Ulysses*; ▷ Virginia Woolf, *To the Lighthouse*; ▷ Thomas Pynchon, *Gravity's Rainbow*.

FAULKS, Sebastian (born 1953)
British novelist

There are writers (nearly all men) who write with knowledge of, even enthusiasm for, war, the technology of warfare and the comradeship of men in battle. There are writers (mostly women) who are precisely observant of the subtlest nuances of the ebb and flow of romantic relationships. Other writers (men and women) are skilled at the evocation of place. Sebastian Faulks is an unusual writer in that he writes with equal power about love, war and landscape. His finest novel to date is *Birdsong* (see below). Before *Birdsong* Faulks had written two novels, *The Girl at the Lion d'Or* (an atmospheric story of a woman in a small French provincial town in the 1930s, still carrying the weight of the past on her shoulders) and *A Fool's Alphabet*. Since the resounding commercial and critical success of *Birdsong* he has published *Charlotte Gray* (about a young woman journeying into occupied France in the Second World War in search of her lover and involving herself in the work of the Resistance) and *On Green Dolphin Street* (2001), set in Kennedy-era Washington.

BIRDSONG (1993)

In 1910 a young Englishman, Stephen Wraysford, arrives in Amiens to stay with the Azaire family. Soon he is embarked upon an intense, convention-defying affair with Madame Azaire and, when it is discovered, the two leave together. The affair does not last and Stephen is left a cold and empty man by its failure, uncaring of what his future might be. History and politics decree that his future is to be the trenches of the Great War where he becomes an officer. Taking part in Ypres, the Somme and many of the major actions of the war, Stephen watches men die horribly all around him and discovers in himself a surprising, steely determination to survive. As the northern France he knew before the war becomes a quagmire and a slaughterhouse, his past relationship with Madame Azaire resurfaces in an unexpected and disturbing way. No précis of *Birdsong* can do justice to the power of Faulks's writing both in its evocation of the overwhelming love affair and in its descriptions of the claustrophobia and terror of the trenches and battle. Imagining the unimaginable, Faulks creates a remarkable novel of individuals trapped in the coils of history.

Sebastian Faulks has also written The Fatal Englishman, *a non-fiction study of three talented and self-destructive men (Christopher Wood, Richard Hillary and Jeremy Wolfenden) whom Faulks sees as representative of their respective generations. He has also edited* The Vintage Book of War Stories.

> READ ON

● *Charlotte Gray*.
▶ ▷ Pat Barker, *Regeneration* (and its successors *The Eye in the Door* and *The Ghost Road*); ▷ Louis de Bernières, *Captain Corelli's Mandolin*; Andrew Greig, *That Summer*.

FIELDING, Henry (1707–54)
British novelist and playwright

Fielding's first successes were with satirical stage comedies: they included *Rape upon Rape* (a farce) and *The Tragedy of Tom Thumb* (a parody of melodramatic tragedy). But his plays were too political for the authorities, who closed them down. He qualified as a magistrate and set up the Bow Street Runners, ancestors of the modern police force. He continued to write, but now turned to prose fiction, announcing that he meant to write an English equivalent of *Don Quixote*. His books are comic life-stories, following charming young people in a series of escapades as they journey from country house to inn, from farmyard to theatre box, from law court to bedroom, gathering experience and outwitting would-be predators at every step. Fielding's novels are long and leisurely: it is as if he is taking a stroll through English society, high and low, and everything he sees or hears reminds him of an anecdote, genial, unhurried and preposterous.

★☆ TOM JONES (1749)

Tom Jones is a foundling brought up by kindly Squire Allworthy. He is a personable, amorous young man, and his immorality finally makes Allworthy send him into the world to seek his fortune. The novel tells Tom's adventures, in and out of bed, as he wanders through England enjoying life as it comes, torn by the thought of his true love Sophia Western, but still ready to be seduced by every pretty girl he meets. The story is told in short chapters, like extended anecdotes, and Fielding keeps breaking off to address the reader directly, telling jokes, pointing morals and commenting on the life and manners of the time.

Fielding's other novels are Joseph Andrews *and* Amelia. A Journey from This World to the Next *and* The Life and Death of Jonathan Wild the Great *are short, savage satires: the second, for example, treats a notorious, real-life thief as if he were an epic hero.* Journal of a Voyage to Lisbon *is a fascinating travel diary about crossing the Bay of Biscay in a leaky, storm-tossed ship.*

> READ ON

- *Joseph Andrews* (a parody of the heroine-in-moral-danger novels of ▷ Samuel Richardson: the story of a young man so beautiful that every woman he meets longs to entice him into bed).
- ▶ Other picaresque adventures: Miguel de Cervantes Saavedra, *Don Quixote*; ▷ Laurence Sterne, *Tristram Shandy*.
- ▶ Later books in a similarly relaxed, discursive vein: ▷ H.G. Wells, *Kipps*; ▷ Thomas Mann, *Confessions of Felix Krull*; ▷ Saul Bellow, *The Adventures of Augie March*.

READ ON A THEME: THE FILM BUSINESS

    Dirk Bogarde, *West of Sunset*
    Charles Bukowski, *Hollywood*
▷ Len Deighton, *Close Up*
    John Gregory Dunne, *Playland*
▷ F. Scott Fitzgerald, *The Last Tycoon*
▷ Elmore Leonard, *Get Shorty*
    Frederic Raphael, *California Time*
    Theodore Roszak, *Flicker*
    Budd Schulberg, *What Makes Sammy Run?*
    Terry Southern, *Blue Movie*
▷ Nathanael West, *The Day of the Locust*

FISCHER, Tibor (born 1959)
British novelist

Don't Read This Book If You're Stupid is the self-consciously defiant title of a collection of short stories published by Tibor Fischer in 2000. It is a health warning that could be attached to all of Fischer's books. He really doesn't like stupidity. Most of us get annoyed or mildly irritated by the petty, everyday stupidities of ordinary life. Fischer gets outraged. He has the 'savage indignation' of the great satirists and his books are scathing, witty indictments of our follies. *The Thought Gang* (1994) is a dazzling display of linguistic and intellectual fireworks which tells the unlikely story of an out-of-work philosopher joining forces with a one-armed robber in a crime spree through France. Peppered with epigrams, puns and stylistic inventions, it is one of the funniest and most imaginative novels of the last twenty years. *The Collector Collector* is a darker and more misanthropic book but almost equally original. Its 'narrator' is an ancient Sumerian bowl, a clay vessel somehow made sentient and marked by a uniformly poor view of the human clay that has possessed it over the centuries. The narrative alternates between stories from 4000 years of human lust, greed and hypocrisy (as observed by the bowl) and a modern story of sexual and financial treacheries centred on the bowl's current owner.

> READ ON

- *Under the Frog* (Fischer's first novel, a black comedy about two members of a travelling basketball team in 1950s Hungary).
- ▷ Will Self, *Great Apes*; Jonathan Coe, *What a Carve Up!*; ▷ John Lanchester, *The Debt to Pleasure*.

FITZGERALD, F. (Francis) **Scott** (1896–1940)
US novelist and short story writer

In the US of the 1920s the earnestness which had been needed to win the First World War was replaced by giddy exhilaration. Jazz, bootleg liquor, drugs and sex seemed to be not merely pleasures, but symbols of a new, liberated age – and the fact that that age was clearly doomed, that the dancing would end in tears, gave every party, every spending-spree, an edge of extra excitement, as if people were roller-skating on the brink of the abyss. Rich, handsome, athletic and talented, Fitzgerald not only wrote about this doomed high society, but was one of its leaders. In the 1930s, when the inevitable reckoning came – the Great Depression was paralleled in Fitzgerald's life by his wife's madness and his own alcoholism and bankruptcy – his books not unnaturally turned sour and sad. But his 1920s stories and novels told the legend of the 'jazz age' with such glittering force that it is easy, now, to believe that all Americans, and not just a few thousand sophisticates, lived like that.

☆ THE GREAT GATSBY (1925)
In a millionaire community on Long Island, the enigmatic bachelor Gatsby gives huge all-night parties at his mansion, orgies of dancing, drugs and sex, the season's most fashionable events. His fascinated neighbour, the book's narrator Nick Carraway, makes friends with him and begins unravelling the secrets of his personality. Carraway's intervention triggers revelations about Gatsby's criminal past, and a love affair between Gatsby and the wife of a wealthy oaf, Tom Buchanan; these in turn lead to further tragedy. At the end of the book Carraway sits alone outside Gatsby's deserted house, reflecting on the emptiness of the lives he has just described.

Fitzgerald's 1920s novels include This Side of Paradise, The Beautiful and Damned *and* The Great Gatsby. Tender is the Night, *bitterly autobiographical, describes the life of an alcoholic doctor and his insane wife on the French Riviera, and the unfinished* The Last Tycoon *is a satire on the Hollywood for which he wrote rubbish to earn money in his last desperate months of life.* Tales of the Jazz Age *and* Taps at Reveille *are collections of short stories.*

> READ ON

- *The Beautiful and Damned* (about the doomed marriage of two bright young things, leaders of Jazz Age society, a book displaying fierce irony for today's readers given what we know of the eventual decay in Fitzgerald's own marriage).
- ▶ ▷ Evelyn Waugh, *Vile Bodies*: ▷ Anthony Powell, *Afternoon Men*; Anita Loos, *Gentlemen Prefer Blondes.* ▷ Martin Amis, *Success* applies Fitzgerald's tone of hopeless, cynical black farce to a much later 'doomed' generation: our own.

FITZGERALD, Penelope (1916–2000)
British writer

Fitzgerald published her first novel, *The Golden Child*, in 1977 when she was 61, won the Booker Prize two years later with *Offshore*, and went on to publish seven more novels. Each is different in period, setting and characters, but all have the same wry style, the same feeling that Fitzgerald is a detached but not uninvolved spectator of the miseries and follies of her people, and the same 'hint of the sublime' (in one reviewer's florid praise). She shares these qualities with ▷Jane Austen, and if Austen were writing today this is exactly the kind of barbed, wise prose she might produce. Two typical Fitzgerald books are *At Freddie's* (1982) set in a Covent Garden stage school for precocious brats in the 1960s, and *The Gate of Angels* (1990) about a young academic in a 1912 all-male college coming to terms with the torments of 'the mind-body problem' – that is, reconciling the Apollonian quest for truth with the Dionysian urge for emotional experience, not least of sex.

Fitzgerald's other novels include The Bookshop, Human Voices, The Beginning of Spring *and* The Blue Flower *(a haunting recreation of life and love in the circle of the German Romantic poet Novalis).* The Means of Escape *is a collection of short stories. She also wrote prize-winning biographies:* Edward Burne-Jones, The Knox Brothers *(one of whom, E.V. Knox of* Punch, *was her father) and* Charlotte Mew and her Friends.

> READ ON

- *Innocence* (set in Italy after the Second World War; about the problems and difficulties of trying to make other people happy).
- ▶ ▷ Beryl Bainbridge, *Every Man for Himself*; ▷ Rose Tremain, *Music and Silence;* ▷ Anne Tyler, *Morgan's Passing.*

FLAUBERT, Gustave (1821–80)
French novelist

Many of Flaubert's contemporary writers – even such 'realists' as ▷ Balzac and ▷ Dickens – believed that 'fiction' involved larger-than-life characters, events or emotions. Flaubert's ambition, by contrast, was to hold up a mirror to ordinary people in humdrum situations, to take the boring events of commonplace lives and make them interesting. He also avoided heightened language, wit, irony and the other devices novelists used to enliven their narrative. He worked to make his prose evenly-paced and unobtrusive, taking its tensions and climaxes from the flow of events themselves. In modern times, similar techniques have been used in 'fly-on-the-wall' TV documentaries, where a camera-crew records unscripted scenes from daily life – and if nothing else, these programmes have shown just how tempestuous and extraordinary everyday lives can be.

★☆ MADAME BOVARY (1857)

Emma, a romantic and foolish young woman, dreams of being swept away on clouds of ecstasy, either by a handsome lover or into the arms of the Church. She marries a small-town doctor and finds the routine of provincial life stifling and unfulfilling. She tries to bring excitement into her life by flirting, and is gradually trapped in pathetic and grubby love affairs, stealing from her husband to pay for her ever more eccentric whims. In the end, destroyed by her inability to live up to her own dreams, she kills herself – and everyone else's life goes on as if she had never existed.

Flaubert's novels of ordinary French life are Madame Bovary, Sentimental Education (L'Éducation sentimentale) *and the unfinished* Bouvard and Pécuchet. Salammbô *applies the same techniques to a story of the Carthage of Hannibal's time, to bizarre effect, as if an archaeological treatise had been jumbled up with the script for a Hollywood epic film.* The Temptation of St Anthony *seeks to describe all the temptations, of flesh, spirit and will, which might assail a devout Roman Catholic;* Three Stories *contains 'A Simple Heart', one of the most moving of all Flaubert's works.*

> READ ON >

- *Sentimental Education* (about a young man who tries, like Emma Bovary, to spice his boring life with grand passions, and fails. A secondary strand in the book is the political situation leading up to the 1848 revolution – something as busy and sterile, in Flaubert's opinion, as his hero's attempts to find meaning in existence).
- ▶ ▷ Italo Svevo, *A Life*; ▷ Arnold Bennett, *Hilda Lessways*; ▷ Joseph Heller, *Something Happened*; ▷ Elizabeth Taylor, *A Wreath of Roses*; ▷ Iris Murdoch, *Under the Net.* ▷ R.K. Narayan, *The English Teacher*, though set in a society (provincial India) and a period (the 1950s) remote from *Madame Bovary*, and less than a quarter as long, magnificently matches Flaubert's insight into the way that the joys and sorrows of small lives, no less than large, can tear the heart.

FLEMING, Ian (1908–64)
British novelist

Fleming's James Bond books are like comic strips for adults: Bond is a super-hero who saves the world from spectacularly nasty, psychopathic master-criminals. Bond wins through by a mixture of supreme physical prowess and late-Edwardian one-upmanship somewhat bizarre in the 1960s setting. Adult tastes are catered for less by psychological insight or intellectual depth than by frequent sex scenes (Bond, as well as everything else, is a super-stud) and by laconic, hardboiled wit. In everything but plot – over-the-top technology, larky dialogue, high-gloss violence – the Bond films give the exact flavour of Fleming's books.

The Bond novels include Goldfinger, Moonraker, Thunderball, From Russia With Love, Diamonds are Forever, Dr No, On Her Majesty's Secret Service, You Only Live Twice *and* The Man With the Golden Gun. Octopussy *is a collection of short stories.*

READ ON ▷

● *From Russia With Love.*
▶ In the 1960s, until ▷ Len Deighton and ▷ John Le Carré took the spy-story in a different direction, there were a million Bond imitations and spoofs, of which some of the jolliest are by John Gardner, Fleming's official successor as chronicler of Bond. (A good example of Gardner at his best is *Scorpius*.) Peter O'Donnell's *Modesty Blaise* all but out-Flemings Fleming, with the added zest that the super-sexed superspy is a woman.
▶ More recent follow-ups: ▷ Robert Ludlum, *The Matarese Circle*.

FOLLETT, Ken (born 1949)
British novelist

Most of Follett's novels are fast-action thrillers, many with industrial espionage or wartime themes. These include *The Bear Raid* (about stock market espionage), *Storm Island/The Key to Rebecca* (a fight for survival on an uninhabited island during the Second World War), *The Man from St Petersburg* (Russian communist arrives in Britain with a murder mission) and *Code to Zero* (a man wakes with no memory of his earlier life and gradually becomes aware that his amnesia is mysteriously linked with American-Russian space rivalry). *The Pillars of the Earth* (1989) is an equally powerful saga of betrayal and derring-do, set in medieval times. *A Dangerous Fortune* (1993) is a fast-paced Victorian melodrama.

READ ON ▷

▶ ▷ Jack Higgins, *A Game for Heroes*; ▷ Frederick Forsyth, *The Fist of God*; ▷ Robert Ludlum, *The Bourne Identity*.

FORD, Ford Madox (1873–1939)
British novelist and non-fiction writer

Although Ford produced books of all kinds, from biographies to historical novels (*The Fifth Queen*, a Tudor trilogy), he is best remembered for *Parade's End* and *The Good Soldier. The Good Soldier* (1915) is a ▷ Jamesian story about two couples who meet in a German hotel and become emotionally and sexually entwined, with devastating results for both themselves and the innocent young ward of one of them. The four novels of *Parade's End* (1924–8) tell how a country landowner, a young man rooted in the social and moral attitudes of the past, is forced by experience (as an officer in the First World War and as a reluctant participant in the freer sexual atmosphere of the post-war years) to slough off the skin of Victorian morality and come to terms, a dozen years later than everyone else, with 20th-century values.

READ ON >

▶ Vita Sackville-West, *The Edwardians*. Isabel Colegate, *The Shooting Party*. ▷ C.P. Snow, *Strangers and Brothers*. ▷ Kazuo Ishiguro, *An Artist of the Floating World* (setting the 'coming-to-terms' theme in post-war Japan).

FORESTER, C.S. (Cecil Scott) (1899–1966)
British novelist

Forester is best known for his 'Hornblower' novels, about a career officer in the British navy of Nelson's time. The books are rich in the detail of life on wooden fighting ships, and the historical background is meticulous. Forester however gives Hornblower 20th-century sensibilities (he is for example sickened by floggings and horrified by the brutality of war) which both flesh him out as a character and draw the reader into the story. The Hornblower series has overshadowed Forester's other books, which include two superb novels set during the Napoleonic Wars (*Death to the French*; *The Gun*), the psychological crime stories *Payment Deferred* and *Plain Murder*, and the comedy-thriller *The African Queen*, memorably filmed in the 1950s with Katharine Hepburn and Humphrey Bogart.

The core of the Hornblower series is a trilogy of books (The Happy Return, Flying Colours, Ship of the Line) *often published together as* Captain Horatio Hornblower. *Other books in the series fill in details of Hornblower's career, tracing his adventures over a quarter of a century. Typical titles are* Mr Midshipman Hornblower, Hornblower and the Atropos, Hornblower in the West Indies *and* Lord Hornblower.

READ ON >

● *The African Queen* (about a prissy missionary and a rough-diamond ship's captain who take a leaky old boat full of dynamite downriver in World War I Africa to blow up an enemy convoy – and fall in love on the way).
▶ to the Hornblower books: ▷ Patrick O'Brian, the Jack Aubrey stories, beginning with *Master and Commander*; ▷ Bernard Cornwell, *Sharpe's Honour* (one of a series about an army officer at the time of the Peninsular War); Alexander Kent, *Richard Bolitho, Midshipman*.

FORSTER, E.M. (Edward Morgan) (1879–1970)
British novelist

All Forster's novels were written in the 1900s (though *A Passage to India* was not published until 1924), and all are concerned with the crippling emotional reticence he considered typical of the Edwardian age. (Many were filmed in the 1980s and 1990s, with huge success.) Outwardly extrovert and competent, the Edwardians (Forster thought) were afraid of intimacy. They replaced it with 'manners', and often even members of the same family, even husbands and wives, were inhibited from showing towards each other the kind of genuine feelings they revealed towards God, the flag or their pampered pets. Forster's plots all turn on the disastrous results of emotional inexperience, of people blundering about in each other's sensibilities. In *Where Angels Fear to Tread* an Edwardian family's inability to believe that an Italian can have true paternal feelings for his baby leads to a doomed expedition to Italy to kidnap the child. In *Howards End* a note from one friend to another, confessing love (in fact one snatched kiss in a garden) leads to a hurricane of emotional misunderstanding and disapproval which involves a dozen people and three generations. The central character in *The Longest Journey* tries to 'connect' emotionally with his newly-discovered, no-good step-brother, and in the process destroys first his marriage and then himself. Forster, himself an emotional introvert (a self-deprecating homosexual), offers no solutions. But few writers have better described the problem: his intuition for emotional nuance and his compelling characterization (especially of women), give his books fascination despite their narrow focus.

★ A PASSAGE TO INDIA (1924)

Adela Quested leaves for India to get to know her fiancé Ronny before she marries him. Her openness of manner, and especially the way she treats Indians as equals, offends the stuffy British community. For her part, she is overwhelmed by India, and her stupefaction leads her to a moment of mental confusion during which she accuses an Indian friend, Dr Aziz, of molesting her on a visit to the Malabar Caves. In court, oppressed by the certainty of the English that Aziz must be guilty, she reruns the events at Malabar in her mind, and suddenly recants. Her behaviour has, however, made apparent the unbridgeable gulf between Indians and English under the Raj, not to mention the lack of communication between 'free spirits' such as herself and her more hidebound contemporaries.

Forster's other fiction includes the novel Maurice *(about a homosexual friendship; written in the 1910s but not published until the 1970s) and three collections of short stories,* Celestial Omnibus, The Eternal Moment *and* The Life to Come.

> **READ ON**

- *A Room With a View* (about the emotional awakening of a naive English girl visiting Italy for the first time and realizing that there is a real world beyond Edwardian English convention).
- ▶ to *A Passage to India*: ▷ Ruth Prawer Jhabvala, *Heat and Dust*; Paul Scott, *The Raj Quartet*; M.M. Kaye, *The Far Pavilions*.
- ▶ to Forster's work in general: ▷ Henry James, *The Wings of the Dove*; ▷ Marcel Proust, *Within a Budding Grove* (Part Two of *Remembrance of Things Past*); ▷ L.P. Hartley, *The Go-Between*;

FORSTER, Margaret (born 1938)
British novelist

The film of Forster's novel, *Georgy Girl*, was one of the most characteristic British movies of the 1960s and the book was Forster's first major success. Its heroine (a perfectly ordinary girl desperate to sample the 'Swinging Sixties' before they, or her own youth, disappeared) was a neat alternative to other, more bubble-headed, fictional heroines of the time. Forster is outstanding at showing slow change in people's characters: the coming of maturity, the growth of wisdom, processes of human warmth or misery. Many of her best-known novels (for example *Marital Rites, Private Papers* and *Mother Can You Hear Me?*, all published in the 1980s), are about people trapped in relationships, who find an escape not because of outside events, but through their developing awareness of their own potential. Her style is patient, meticulous and absorbing.

☆ LADY'S MAID (1990)

Elizabeth Wilson, a shy country girl, goes to 1850s London to become lady's maid to Elizabeth Barrett, a brilliant intellect trapped in the body of a feeble invalid. We see, from Wilson's point of view, the development of their relationship, as Barrett is warmed by Wilson's understated robustness of character, and Wilson learns from Barrett that she herself is a person, with a brain and character worth consideration. Then Robert Browning courts and marries Barrett, and the relationship, the mutual dependency between mistress and maid (or is it by now friend and friend?) is forever changed.

Forster's other novels include The Travels of Maudie Tipstaff, Have the Men Had Enough, Mother's Boys *and* The Memory Box. *In the last few years she has published two remarkable and revealing volumes about her own family and North of England background,* Hidden Lives *and* Precious Lives. *She has also written biographies of Elizabeth Barrett Browning,* ▷ *Daphne Du Maurier, Bonnie Prince Charlie, eight 'pioneering women' (*Significant Sisters*) and an 'autobiography' of* ▷ *William Thackeray.*

> READ ON ⟩

● *Private Papers*; *The Battle for Christabel.*
▶ ▷ Margaret Drabble, *The Garrick Year*; ▷ Anne Tyler, *Morgan's Passing*; Elizabeth Jolley, *Miss Peabody's Inheritance*; Nina Bawden, *Afternoon of a Good Woman.*

FORSYTH, Frederick (born 1938)
British novelist

Forsyth worked as a BBC reporter and a war correspondent, and his thrillers are as immediate and waffle-free as good news stories. They often include real people and events; only the hair-trigger tension of his plots makes actuality look tame. In *The Odessa File* (1972), for example, a journalist covering the hunt for a war criminal uncovers a Nazi arms-smuggling conspiracy to help Arab terrorists in Israel. The details are fiction, but the story is as fresh as this morning's news.

Forsyth's novels are The Day of the Jackal, The Devil's Alternative, The Fourth Protocol, The Dogs of War, The Negotiator, The Fist of God *and* Icon. The Shepherd *is a short novel;* The Deceiver *contains four linked stories;* No Comebacks *is a collection of short stories.*

> READ ON ⟩

▶ Gerald Seymour, *The Heart of Danger* ▷ Jack Higgins, *The Eagle Has Landed*; ▷ Ian Fleming, *From Russia With Love.*

FOWLES, John (born 1926)
British novelist

Fowles worked as a teacher (of modern languages), until the success of *The Collector* (1963) made it possible for him to write full-time. His main themes are obsession and delusion. The deranged hero of *The Collector* 'collects' a pretty girl as one might a butterfly. The heroes of *Daniel Martin* (1977) and *Mantissa* (1983) are authors deserted by the Muse, one a screenwriter corrupted by success, the other a novelist undergoing creative therapy at the hands (and other parts) of a seductive, feminist goddess. *A Maggot* (1985), set in the 18th century, reworks a real-life murder investigation to take in erotic obsession, witchcraft, religious mania and flying saucers. Fowles further blurs the boundary between 'truth' and 'fiction' by using experimental techniques. He shifts between past and present, makes authorial asides and comments, and gives us two, three or half a dozen alternative versions of the same events. As with ▷ Durrell, this experimentalism is coupled with ornate prose (sometimes in brilliant imitation of 18th- and 19th-century styles); few modern best-selling writers offer such a packed experience.

☆ THE FRENCH LIEUTENANT'S WOMAN (1969)

The book's heart is a straightforward 19th-century story about the obsessive love between a rich man and an outcast, the 'French Lieutenant's Woman' of the title. They meet in the seaside town of Lyme Regis; their affair scandalizes society; she runs away; he pursues her. Fowles's prose, likewise, is for much of the time straightforward and solid in the 19th-century manner. But he also plays games with the reader. He keeps interrupting the story to tell us things about Lyme Regis (home of Mary Anning the fossil-collector), Darwin, Freudian psychology and the social customs of Victorian London. He claims that he has no idea what will happen next, that this is the characters' story, not his. He supplies alternative endings, so that we can choose our own. These devices give the book an unexpectedness in marked contrast to its sober 19th-century heart – it is as if someone reading us ▷ Eliot or ▷ Thackeray kept breaking off to perform conjuring tricks. The book was filmed in the 1980s, starring Meryl Streep and Jeremy Irons, and with a mesmeric script by Harold Pinter.

Apart from novels, Fowles has published a story collection, The Ebony Tower, The Aristos, *a set of philosophical meditations and* Wormholes, *a collection of non-fiction pieces.*

> READ ON ▷

- ● *The Magus* (revised version recommended), about a man trying obsessively to find out if what he thinks he experiences is real or fantasy. Much of it involves magic and takes place on a mysterious Greek island – or seems to, for our perception of 'truth' and 'fiction' is as shifting as the character's.
- ▶ to *The French Lieutenant's Woman*: ▷ John Barth, *The Sot-Weed Factor*; John Berger, *G*; ▷ William Golding, *Rites of Passage*.
- ▶ to *The Magus*: ▷ Lawrence Durrell, *The Dark Labyrinth/Cefalù*; D.M. Thomas, *The White Hotel*.

FRANCIS, Dick (born 1920)
British novelist

Authenticity is a priceless commodity in crime fiction and thriller writing. Pick up any Dick Francis novel and it is immediately apparent that he knows the world of racing inside out and is familiar with the characters who people it. It is this authenticity (and his ability to fashion a tightly-constructed plot) that has kept him a bestselling writer for nearly forty years. Francis was champion jockey in 1953/4 and was riding the Queen Mother's horse Devon Loch in the 1956 Grand National when it fell so mysteriously with victory in sight. In a later fall Francis was badly injured and forced to give up riding. He turned to journalism and, in 1962, published his first novel *Dead Cert*. Many others have followed, all of them providing that first-hand knowledge of the racing game which fans so much enjoy.

Dick Francis's other novels include For Kicks, Blood Sport, Bonecrack, High Stakes, Reflex, Bolt, The Edge, Comeback, Wild Horses, Come to Grief, To the Hilt, 10lb Penalty, Second Wind *and* Shattered.

READ ON >

● *Bonecrack, Hot Money.*
▶ John Francome, *Lifeline*; ▷ Stephen Dobyns, *Saratoga Fleshpot* (racing crime with a US setting); Richard Pitman, *Hunted*.

FRANKLIN, Miles (1879–1954)
Australian novelist

'Miles Franklin' was one of the pseudonyms of Stella Miles Franklin. She wrote optimistic tales of pioneer farming life in Australia in a cheerful, bustling style; her novels are like literary patchwork quilts. Under the name Miles Franklin she is best-known for *My Brilliant Career* (1901), its sequel *My Career Goes Bung* (1946) – the story of a breathlessly enthusiastic adolescent, Sybylla Melvyn, as she learns about life, the arts and love on outback farms and in the big city – and *All That Swagger* (1936), a more serious panorama of outback life. Under a second pseudonym, 'Brent of Bin Bin', Franklin published six lighter novels on the same lines, 'snapshots of ordinary life' modelled on the writings of ▷ Mark Twain. Their titles are *Up the Country, Ten Creeks Run, Back to Bool Bool, Cockatoos, Prelude to Waking*, and *Gentlemen at Gyang Gyang*. One editor (Carmen Callil) called her an 'unsophisticated genius', prone to 'ebullient out-pourings'; the description is exact.

READ ON >

▶ ▷ Mark Twain, *The Adventures of Tom Sawyer*; Laura Ingalls Wilder, *The Little House on the Prairie*; ▷ Christina Stead, *For Love Alone* (another story of the emotional awakening of a young Australian woman but very different in style).

FRASER, George MacDonald (born 1925)
British writer

Fraser wrote the screenplays for the Richard Lester films *The Three Musketeers, The Four Musketeers, The Return of the Musketeers* and for the larky Bond film *Octopussy*. In literature, he had the brilliant idea of taking Flashman, the bully from the 19th-century boarding-school novel *Tom Brown's Schooldays* and recording his further adventures throughout a long life. In the original book he was just an adolescent thug; in Fraser's hands he becomes sexy, sly and, although an irredeemable coward and cad, an unlikely hero of the British empire. He progresses through the ranks of the British army, and plays his part in such events as the Indian Mutiny, the Charge of the Light Brigade, the Crimean War and Little Big Horn. There are a dozen books, all told in the voice of Flashman himself, and all are equally enjoyable. Typical is *Flashman and the Angel of the Lord* (1995), in which Flashman gets mixed up with the American anti-slavery campaign and its Harper's Ferry hero John Brown (the man whose soul, in the song, goes 'marchin' on').

The Flashman books are, in order of publication, Flashman, Royal Flash, Flash for Freedom, Flashman at the Charge, Flashman in the Great Game, Flashman's Lady, Flashman and the Redskins, Flashman and the Dragon, Flashman and the Mountain of Light, Flashman and the Angel of the Lord *and* Flashman and the Tiger.

> READ ON

- **The Candlemass Road** (non-Flashman: a swashbuckling novel set on the bandit-ridden Scots-English borders at the time of Mary Queen of Scots).
- ▶ ▷ Bernard Cornwell, **Sharpe's Honour** (Peninsular War; serious) Allan Mallinson, **A Close-Run Thing** ▷ J.G. Farrell, **The Siege of Krishnapur**.

READ ON A THEME: FRIENDS (?) AND NEIGHBOURS

(gossip; bitchiness; one-upmanship)
- ▷ E.F. Benson, *Mapp and Lucia*
  Amanda Craig, *A Vicious Circle*
  Peter De Vries, *The Mackerel Plaza*
- ▷ Mrs Gaskell, *Cranford*
  Tama Janowitz, *A Certain Age*
  Sinclair Lewis, *Main Street*
- ▷ Barbara Pym, *A Glass of Blessings*
- ▷ John Updike, *Couples*

See also: The Human Comedy

READ ON A THEME: FUTURE SOCIETIES

- ▷ Margaret Atwood, *The Handmaid's Tale*
- ▷ Iain M. Banks, *Consider Phlebas*
- ▷ Angela Carter, *The Passion of New Eve*
- ▷ Philip K. Dick, *The Man in the High Castle*
- ▷ Robert Graves, *Seven Days in New Crete*
- ▷ Russell Hoban, *Riddley Walker*
- ▷ Aldous Huxley, *Brave New World*
  Walter M. Miller, *A Canticle for Leibowitz*
- ▷ William Morris, *News from Nowhere*
- ▷ George Orwell, *1984*
- ▷ John Wyndham, *The Chrysalids*

See also: Fantasy Societies

G

GALSWORTHY, John (1867–1933)
British novelist and playwright

In the 1960s an adaptation of Galsworthy's *The Forsyte Saga* was the most popular British TV series ever shown until then. It spawned a thousand imitations – series and books about rich families quarrelling over multi-million–pound businesses and living wretched private lives have become a genre in themselves. Some critics say that this is unfair to Galsworthy, who was regarded as a heavyweight writer in his day (of plays as well as novels). But although he intended his first Forsyte book (*The Man of Property*) as a serious novel, as soon as the Forsytes became popular he quite happily extended it into a saga, adding another dozen novels and short stories.

THE FORSYTE SAGA (1922)
This contains three novels and two short stories. Its subject is the way money-making and commercial endeavour atrophy the emotions. Three generations of Forsytes are morally tainted by their family's business success, in particular Soames and his unhappy wife Irene. Every boardroom victory is balanced by a bedroom defeat; children inherit not only wealth, but the poisoned character which goes with it. There is more than a whiff of Victorian moralizing about it all: in Galsworthy the bad always end unhappily (and so do the good). But unlike many later family-business sagas, his books offer three-dimensional characters, and he is particularly good at showing the ebb and flow of relationships between the sexes. *To Let*, the third volume of the saga, a Romeo and Juliet story with a devastating final twist, is a fine example of this and is one of Galsworthy's most satisfying books.

Apart from the Forsyte books (two trilogies – The Forsyte Saga*;* A Modern Comedy *– and the short-story collections* Four Forsyte Stories *and* On Forsyte Change*), Galsworthy's novels include* The Island Pharisee, Fraternity *and the trilogy* End of the Chapter*, a saga about the Charwell Family (cousins of the Forsytes).*

> READ ON

- ● *A Modern Comedy.*
- ▶ ▷ Anthony Trollope, *Can You Forgive Her?* (and its sequels: the 'Palliser' family saga). ▷ Thomas Mann, *Buddenbrooks* (an equally withering account of the decline of a powerful mercantile family). ▷ C.P. Snow, *The Conscience of the Rich* (a moving study of the son of a family dynasty at odds with his parents).

GARLAND, Alex (born 1970)
British novelist

Even before Leonardo DiCaprio bestowed some of his superstar magic on *The Beach* (1996) by appearing in the movie version of it, Alex Garland's novel had become an iconic book for a certain generation of readers. The great achievement of Garland's novel is that it combines a dark and dramatic adventure story, thought-provoking ideas about our need to search out faraway utopias and contemporary concerns about the environmental impact of Western tourism in one highly readable package. And it possesses an instant appeal to all those many thousands of young people who, every year, set out on the backpacking trail to Asia. The central character of the novel, Richard, hears of an idyllic beach community near Thailand from a half-crazed Vietnam vet who later commits suicide. He and two others set off in search of the Beach but soon discover, when they eventually reach it, that they have brought a serpent to this particular Eden. Garland's very different second novel, *The Tesseract* (1998), more ▷ Graham Greene or ▷ Paul Theroux than Generation X, is an ingeniously constructed book in which three dark stories of life in contemporary Manila intermesh.

> **READ ON**

▶ Esther Freud, *Hideous Kinky*; ▷ Douglas Coupland, *Generation X*; Simon Lewis, *Go*; William Sutcliffe, *Are You Experienced?*.

GASKELL, Mrs (Elizabeth Cleghorn) (1810–65)
British novelist

For a century after her death, Gaskell was chiefly remembered for a biography of her friend ▷ Charlotte Brontë, and for *Cranford* (1853), a gently malicious book about middle-class life in a provincial town. (It reads like a collaboration between ▷ Austen and ▷ Trollope, without being quite as good as either.) But she was actually a novelist of a far tougher kind. She was a friend of ▷ Dickens and ▷ Eliot, and shared their interest in social themes, particularly the way men treat women and the plight of the urban poor. She lived in Manchester, and wrote pungently about life among the 'dark Satanic mills' (as Blake had called them) which her southern readers had until then imagined were figments of the revolutionary imagination. Her novels were discussed in Parliament and led to social reform, a result which greatly pleased her. They survive today less as social documents than as powerful stories of people struggling against their environment or the indifference of others.

MARY BARTON (1848)
Mary's father is a mill-hand employed by the unfeeling Henry Carson. He is also a staunch fighter for workers' rights. When the mill-owners ignore their workers' requests for better treatment, the men decide to murder Carson as a warning to his class, and nominate Barton to fire the gun. Mary's beloved Jem Wilson is arrested for the crime, and Mary has to face the agony of proving his innocence by incriminating her father.

Gaskell's novels Ruth, Cousin Phyllis *and* Wives and Daughters *concern the relationship between the sexes.* Sylvia's Lovers, *an unsmiling tale set in 18th-*

century Whitby, is about a man snatched by the press gang. Mary Barton *and*
North and South *are about class war.* Lois the Witch, *a long short story, is set
during the Salem witch-hunts of the 17th century.*

READ ON ▷

- *North and South* (in which a southern minister goes to preach God's word in a
  northern mill town, and his wife and daughter become involved in the class
  struggle – a concern greatly complicated when the daughter falls in love with a
  mill-owner's son).
- ▷ Charlotte Brontë, *Shirley.* ▷ Charles Dickens, *Hard Times.* ▷ Émile Zola,
  Germinal. ▷ Arnold Bennett, *Clayhanger.* ▷ D.H. Lawrence, *Sons and Lovers.*
  Lewis Grassic Gibbon, *A Scots Quair* (partly in dialect, but comprehensible) is a
  saga of three generations coping with harsh conditions, on West Highland crofts
  and in industrial Glasgow during the 1920s General Strike.

READ ON A THEME: GAY/LESBIAN FICTION

- ▷ James Baldwin, *Giovanni's Room*
  Djuna Barnes, *Nightwood*
  Emma Donoghue, *Stir Fry*
  Radclyffe Hall, *The Well of Loneliness*
- ▷ Alan Hollinghurst, *The Swimming Pool Library*
  David Leavitt, *The Lost Language of Cranes*
  Adam Mars Jones, *Monopolies of Loss*
- ▷ Colm Tóibín, *The Story of the Night*
  Edmund White, *A Boy's Own Story*
  Christopher Whyte, *The Gay Decameron*
- ▷ Jeanette Winterson, *Oranges Are Not the Only Fruit*

GIBSON, William (born 1948)
US novelist

In the history of science fiction there has been a handful of books which have
re-defined the genre for a new generation of readers. One of these is William
Gibson's *Neuromancer* (1984). Gibson is often dubbed the father of 'cyberpunk' but critics do not always agree on what a definition of 'cyberpunk' might
be. In truth, what Gibson did was what the best science fiction writers have
always done. He took contemporary scientific and technological developments,
seized upon potential implications and projected them imaginatively into the
future. In the case of *Neuromancer*, and the books which followed it in a
loosely-connected trilogy, *Count Zero* and *Mona Lisa Overdrive*, it was computer technology and the newly developing internet. In his books since the
trilogy, Gibson has turned his attention to other subjects. In *Virtual Light* and
Idoru, with its emphasis on the blankness of media celebrity, he has shown
another quality of the best science fiction writers. While ostensibly writing
fantasies of the future, he is using the freedom the genre gives him to reflect,
obliquely, the realities of modern society.

NEUROMANCER (1984)

The time is the mid-21st century. Case, once a master hacker able to project his consciousness into cyberspace (a term Gibson invented), is now a low-life addict in the massive urban sprawl of Japan. He is given a chance to redeem himself when a group of shadowy corporate conspirators offers him the means to regain the buzz that travelling cyberspace provided. The plot of *Neuromancer* is clichéd enough, familiar from dozens of thrillers, but what give the book its strength are the enormous energy of Gibson's imaginative construction of the world in which his anti-hero operates and the originality of the language he uses. In prose that deftly combines streetwise slang and techno-vocabulary (often his own inventions) he describes a nightmarish future in which personal relationships have been irrevocably compromised by materialism and hope lies in release from the meat of the body into the exhilarating ether of cyberspace.

> READ ON

● *Idoru.*
▶ Neal Stephenson, *Snow Crash*; Bruce Sterling, *Heavy Weather*; Tricia Sullivan, *Someone to Watch Over Me.*

GIDE, André (1861–1951)
French novelist, poet and non-fiction writer

In Plato's dialogues, Socrates tries to reach the core of a philosophical argument by elimination: each wrong assumption, each false trail is considered and rejected until what is left is 'truth'. Gide admired Plato – his favourite among his own works was *Corydon*, a set of four Platonic dialogues discussing homosexuality – and he used Socrates's methods in his fiction. His heroes seek the truth about themselves, the core of their being, and they do it by considering and rejecting all religious, social, sexual and intellectual conventions. Sometimes a quest results in the happiness of self-knowledge, but often the young men – Gide was not over-interested in young women – find, when they reach the core of themselves, that there is nothing there at all. Many of Gide's contemporaries found his moral stripteases shocking and he was condemned as a pornographer; nowadays the most striking thing about his books is their spare, limpid style, which makes even more startling the things they say.

THE IMMORALIST (1902)

Michel, a young intellectual, nearly dies of tuberculosis, and his brush with death changes his character. He rejects his former convention-ridden life in favour of living each moment for itself, of doing exactly what he pleases. As his personality flowers, that of his beloved wife begins to wither, leaving him to agonize over whether his actions have led to psychic liberation or to a surrender to selfishness.

Gide's other fiction includes Strait is the Gate (La porte étroite), The Vatican Cellars, Isabelle, The Pastoral Symphony (La Symphonie pastorale) *and* The Counterfeiters. *His non-fiction works on similar themes include* If it Die (Si le grain ne meurt), Et nunc manet in te/Madeleine *and* Journals.

READ ON

- *Strait is the Gate*; *The Pastoral Symphony*. *The Vatican Cellars* is a more extrovert romp involving murder, the kidnapping of the Pope and a frantic chase across Europe. *The Counterfeiters* is about a group of secondary schoolboys in Paris, their adolescent friendships and the adults who initiate them into grown-up life.
- ▶ to Gide's short, philosophical books: ▷ Hermann Hesse, *Peter Camenzind*; Joris-Karl Huysmans, *Against Nature*; Frederick Rolfe, *The Desire and Pursuit of the Whole*; ▷ Aldous Huxley, *Eyeless in Gaza*.
- ▶ to *The Counterfeiters*: ▷ Colette, *A Lesson in Love*; ▷ Marcel Proust, *Cities of the Plain* (Part Four of *Remembrance of Things Past*).
- ▶ More modern books on Gidean themes: ▷ Iris Murdoch, *The Flight from the Enchanter*; ▷ Ian McEwan, *The Comfort of Strangers*; ▷ Alan Hollinghurst, *The Swimming Pool Library*.

GOETHE, Johann Wolfgang von (1749–1832)
German writer of novels, poems, plays and non-fiction

As well as being a writer, Goethe was a politician, lawyer, theatre manager, philosopher and scientist. His genius expressed itself in restless intellectual energy: he never heard an idea without wanting to develop it. In his writing, he took the nearest convenient form – Shakespearean or Greek tragedy, letters, biography – and crammed it with philosophical and political reflections, discussions and suggestions. During his lifetime he was regarded as an innovator, forming European thought; with hindsight he seems rather to have caught ideas in the air – humanism, romanticism, political libertarianism – expanded them and given them wide circulation.

THE SORROWS OF YOUNG WERTHER (1774)
Werther is a melancholic artist out of tune with the times and with himself. Through a series of letters he tells the story of his growing, indeed obsessive, love for Lotte who is engaged to another man, Albert. All Werther's attempts to distract himself from the pain his love causes him prove ineffectual and eventually he kills himself with Albert's pistol. One of the earliest works to announce the arrival of the new spirit of romanticism, Goethe's book was astonishingly successful throughout Europe. Young men dressed like Werther and memorized long parts of the novel; copycat suicides were recorded.

Goethe is best-known for his poetry, and for such plays as Egmont, Iphigenia in Tauris, Götz von Berlichingen/Ironhand *and* Faust. *Apart from* The Sorrows of Young Werther, *his novels are* Wilhelm Meister *and* Elective Affinities.

READ ON

- *Elective Affinities* is a heartless, amoral book (anticipating ▷ André Gide) about a married couple each of whom has a love-affair.
- ▶ to Wilhelm Meister: Miguel de Cervantes Saavedra, *Don Quixote* ▷ Thomas Mann, *The Magic Mountain*.
- ▶ to *Elective Affinities*: ▷ George Eliot, *Daniel Deronda*; ▷ Christina Stead, *The Man Who Loved Children*.
- ▶ to *The Sorrows of Young Werther*: ▷ Hermann Hesse, *Gertrud*.

GOGOL, Nikolai Vasilevich (1809–52)
Russian writer of novels, short stories and plays

The despair which seems to hover over much Russian fiction was replaced in Gogol by hilarity: he was a 20th-century surrealist ahead of his time, a forerunner of ▷ Kafka and Ionesco. His best-known work, the stage farce *The Government Inspector*, is about a confidence trickster mistaken for a high official by a village of pompous fools. In one of his stories a nose takes on a malign, satirical life independent of its owner's will; in another a man saves for years to buy a new coat, only to be mugged and robbed the first time he wears it. Gogol's preferred form was the short story: he was terrified of writer's block. He struggled for a dozen years to finish his one long book, *Dead Souls*, and in 1852, convinced by a religious adviser that the second (unpublished) half of the book was 'sinful' and that if he went on writing he would go to hell, he burned the manuscript and fasted until he died.

★ DEAD SOULS (1842)
In 19th-century Russia landowners estimated their wealth not only by the acres they owned, but also by the number of their serfs, or slaves. Chichikov, a confidence trickster, realizes that serfs who die between official censuses are not legally dead until the next census, and so still count as property. He travels the length and breadth of Russia, buying 'dead souls' from landowners, and becomes – on paper at least – one of the wealthiest men in the country. Gogol uses this simple story as the basis for a set of farcical character studies: he saw the book as a portrait-gallery of contemporary Russia, and filled it with short, self-contained comic episodes. He also wrote, with ironical pointedness, that Chichikov's journey stands for the journey of every human being through life: we move on, never sure of what is coming next, relieved each time that whatever it was we did, we got away with it.

Gogol's most surreal short stories are 'Diary of a Madman', 'Nevski Prospekt', 'The Portrait', 'The Nose' *and* 'The Overcoat'. *His collections* Evenings on a Farm, Mirgorod *and* Arabesques *are more farce than surrealism, short sketches about tongue-tied suitors, credulous peasants and feather-headed, pretty girls.*

> READ ON

▶ Gogol's sinister brilliance is matched in the short stories of ▷ Franz Kafka, Saki and Roald Dahl; his gentler comic stories are like ▷ Anton Chekhov's.
▶ Good follow-ups to *Dead Souls*: Ivan Goncharov, *Oblomov* (about a man so alienated from the world that he decides to spend the rest of his life in bed); ▷ Franz Kafka, *America*; ▷ Jaroslav Hašek, *The Good Soldier Svejk*; Bernard Malamud, *The Fixer*; Miguel de Cervantes, *Don Quixote*.

GOLDING, William (1911–93)
British novelist

Golding worked in the theatre and served in the Royal Navy in World War II. He worked as a schoolmaster until *Lord of the Flies* brought him international fame in 1954. The story of that book (about choirboys reverting to savagery after being marooned on a desert island) is typical of all his work: an exploration of the dark side of human nature. He believed that homo sapiens is corrupt, that we destroy more than we create, that we are devilish without redemption. But instead of baldly stating this philosophy, he dressed it in allegories of the most unusual and fantastical kind. He pictured the devil engulfing not only choirboys on an island, but also (in other novels) a drowning sailor, a tribe of neanderthal people, the dean of a medieval cathedral, a boy growing up in 1960s Britain, and a group of 18th-century people sailing towards Australia. He evoked each of these situations with absolute conviction: few writers were better at suggesting the feel, taste, smell and sound of things, the texture of experience.

THE SPIRE (1964)

Inspired by a vision, medieval Dean Jocelin commissions for his cathedral a 400–foot spire. He intends it as proof of human aspirations towards God; his enemies see it as a symbol of vanity, the devil's work; the master-builder points out that as the cathedral's foundations are inadequate, the tower will bring the whole building crashing down. Jocelin overrides all objections, the work proceeds – Golding gives fascinating, vertigo-inducing detail of medieval building techniques – and the higher the spire rises the more people are destroyed. In the end the struggle between God and the devil takes over Jocelin's own self. In truly medieval manner, his brain and body become a battleground, and the issue moves from the tower to questions of his own moral integrity and saintliness.

Golding's novels are Lord of the Flies, Pincher Martin, Free Fall, The Spire, The Pyramid, Darkness Visible, *the trilogy about an ill-assorted cargo of passengers on a voyage to 18th-century Australia* (Rites of Passage, Close Quarters *and* Fire Down Below), The Paper Men *and the unfinished* The Double Tongue *(fictional 'memoirs' of a sybil at ancient Delphi).* The Scorpion God *is a collection of three long stories, one based on his stage comedy* The Brass Butterfly, *about a crazy inventor trying to interest a decadent Roman ruler of Egypt in steam power.*

> READ ON ▷

- ● *The Inheritors* (a brilliantly imagined story of the coming of *homo sapiens*, seen from the standpoint of the gentle ape-people they exterminate).
- ▶ to *The Spire*: Peter Benson, *Odo's Hanging* (about the clash between Bishop Odo, commissioning a wall-hanging to commemorate the accession of William the Conqueror, and Tuvold, the genius-craftsman who wants to do things *his* way).
  ▷ Hermann Hesse, *Narziss and Goldmund* (which parallels both the good/evil theme and the medieval craft-background of *The Spire*); ▷ John Barth, *Giles Goatboy*; ▷ Umberto Eco, *The Name of the Rose*.
- ▶ to *Lord of the Flies*: Marianne Wiggins, *John Dollar*; Richard Hughes, *A High Wind in Jamaica*.
- ▶ to the Australian trilogy: ▷ Barry Unsworth, *Sacred Hunger*; ▷ Thomas Keneally, *The Playmaker*.

READ ON A THEME: GOOD AND EVIL

(the devil at large)
   Mikhail Bulgakov, *The Master and Margharita*
▷ John Fowles, *A Maggot*
▷ Stephen King, *Carrie*

▷ **Doris Lessing**, *The Fifth Child*
▷ **Ian McEwan**, *The Comfort of Strangers*
▷ **I.B. Singer**, *Satan in Goray*
▷ **John Updike**, *The Witches of Eastwick*
▷ **Fay Weldon**, *The Life and Loves of a She-Devil*

See also: Something Nasty . . .

GORDIMER, Nadine (born 1923)

South African novelist and short story writer

Gordimer makes life in South Africa (and especially among the tormented liberal whites who are her main characters) an objective background for subjective choice. Her concerns are the diversity of human nature, and the way our moral and psychological personality is revealed in what we do. She also, magnificently, evokes the vastness and beauty of Africa. Like other South African writers (Alan Paton, Laurens van der Post, ▷ André Brink) she gives the continent a kind of mystical identity; its indigenous inhabitants understand this completely, but it gives the incoming whites (who can only dimly perceive it) an unsettling sense of their own inadequacy, as if they are made second-class citizens not by other people's laws but by the very place they live in.

A SPORT OF NATURE (1987)

From adolescence rich, white Hillela is dominated by politics and sex, and combines the two: sex is a source of power, politics give orgasmic satisfaction. She is attracted by, and attracts, powerful men of all professions and races – and progressively moves out of the orbit of whites to a leading position in the black revolutionary movement. The book ends with the success of the revolution, the establishment of majority rule – and with doubts sown in the reader's mind about Hillela herself. Has she really identified as wholly with the blacks as she hoped, or does she remain the 'sport of nature', or freak, of the book's title?

Gordimer's other novels are The Lying Days, A World of Strangers, Occasion for Loving, The Late Bourgeois World, A Guest of Honour, Burger's Daughter, The Conservationist, July's People, My Son's Story, None to Accompany Me *and* The House Gun. *Her short story collections include* Not For Publication, Livingstone's Companion, A Soldier's Embrace, Why Haven't You Written? *and* Jump. The Essential Gesture *and* Living in Hope and History *contain sharp, thoughtful essays*.

> READ ON

● *The House Gun* (a study of a liberal-minded but politically uncommitted couple forced into a confrontation with social violence when their son is accused of murder).

▶ ▷ André Brink, *Rumours of Rain* (about redneck Afrikaanerdom); J.M. Coetzee, *In the Heart of the Country*. Alan Paton, *Cry, the Beloved Country* (a moving book about the harmony between ancient Zulu culture and the land, and the discord brought by invading whites; it is mirrored, from a different country and a different point of view, by ▷ Chinua Achebe, *Things Fall Apart*).

PATHWAYS

WILLIAM GOLDING

LORD OF THE FLIES
(choirboys lost on a desert island
revert to Satanic evil, humanity's dark side)

THE DEVIL
(Takes many forms, and can't be resisted –
or can he?)

Fay **Weldon**, *The Heart of England*
John **Updike**, *The Witches of Eastwick*
James **Blish**, *Black Easter*
Robertson **Davies**, *The Rebel Angels* (first
book of the 'Cornish' trilogy)

SURVIVING
(shipwreck or desertion, the door to new
adventure)

Daniel **Defoe**, *Robinson Crusoe*
Jonathan **Swift**, *Gulliver's Travels*
James Vance **Marshall**, *Walkabout*
Jim **Crace**, *Signals of Distress*

EVIL AND CHILDREN
(childish innocence an ideal vessel for evil –
and sometimes, the children themselves
are not so innocent)

Susan **Hill**, *I'm the King of the Castle*
Stephen **King**, *Carrie*
John **Wyndham**, *The Midwich Cuckoos*
Henry **James**, *The Turn of the Screw*
Richard **Hughes**, *A High Wind in Jamaica*

THE WILDERNESS
(surviving the most inhospitable areas on
Earth)

Patrick **White**, *Voss*
Joseph **Conrad**, *Heart of Darkness*
Brian **Moore**, *Black Robe*
Paul **Theroux**, *The Mosquito Coast*

GORKY, Maxim (1868–1936)
Russian writer of novels, short stories and plays

Gorky (a pseudonym meaning 'bitter') was left to fend for himself at the age of eight, and spent his childhood as a barge-hand, washer-up, thief, beggar, tramp and journalist. This 'apprenticeship', as he called it, affected the style and content of his writing. He saw himself as a colleague and heir of ▷ Dostoevsky and ▷ Tolstoy, and aimed to write the same kind of panoramic, allegorical works as theirs. But whereas their world was that of landowners and the bourgeoisie, his was one of serfs, vagabonds, criminals and other members of what he called society's 'lower depths'. He despised the middle class, and wrote with contempt of their dependence on money, gentility and religion, the very forces which were destroying them. His preoccupations led him to friendship with Lenin, and to enthusiastic support for the 1917 revolution. Many of his post-1917 books are grandiose and propagandist, and his revolutionary sympathies have diminished his reputation in the West. But his early work places him squarely in the company of the great 19th-century writers he admired.

Gorky is known for plays (such as The Lower Depths *and* Smug Citizens*) as well as for prose fiction. His novels include* Mother, Foma Gordeev, The Artamonov Affair, The Life of Klim Samgin *and the post-revolutionary tetralogy* Bystander, The Magnet, Other Fires *and* The Spectre. *His short stories have been collected in single volume editions. His best-known work, in or out of Russia, is the autobiographical trilogy* My Childhood, My Apprenticeship *and* My Universities.

READ ON ▷

- ● *My Childhood* (the first volume of Gorky's autobiography, a scalding account of his life as a young boy living with a tyrannical grandfather and storytelling grandmother and of his initiation into the terrifying world of adult labour and suffering).
- ▶ ▷ Fyodor Dostoevsky, *The Gambler* (a harsh account of aristocratic folly and obsession in Tsarist Russia, the kind of decadence Gorky vociferously denounced); Jean Genet, *Querelle of Brest* (the story of a boy's brutal upbringing among criminals and gangsters in France between the two world wars).

GRAFTON, Sue (born 1940)
US writer

Ever since ▷ Sara Paretsky's V.I. Warshawski led the way in the early 1980s, female private eyes have been forging forward. One of the best is Kinsey Millhone, who stars in a series of books by Sue Grafton. Each title begins with a letter of the alphabet (*A is for Alibi*, 1986, *B is for Burglar*, 1987, *C is for Corpse*, 1988, and so on). Millhone is a splendid loner and the cases she undertakes are as marvellously tangled as any addict of the genre could demand. As one critic said, this is a series to kill for.

The other Millhone books so far published are D is for Deadbeat, E is for Evidence, F is for Fugitive, G is for Gumshoe, H is for Homicide, I is for Innocent, J is for Judgement, K is for Killer, L is for Lawless, M is for Malice, N is for Noose, O is for Outlaw *and* P is for Peril.

READ ON ▷

▶ Linda Barnes, *Snapshot*; Val McDermid, *Crack Down*; Karen Kijewski, *Katwalk*;
▷ Sara Paretsky, *Toxic Shock*; Janet Evanovich, *One for the Money*.

GRASS, Günter (born 1927)
German writer of novels, plays and non-fiction

In his twenties Grass worked as a graphic artist, stage designer and jazz musician; he took up writing full-time only after his novel *The Tin Drum* was a best-seller, when he was 32. Politics are the main subject of his books: he grapples with what has happened in Germany over the last half-century, and what is happening now. He uses a framework of absurdity, blending real events with wild black fantasy, collapsing history (so that time is like a well from which you draw not systematically but at random), and making his characters allegorical figures like the people in cartoons. The leading character in *The Tin Drum* (1959), for example, symbolizing the German people, is a child who chooses to stop growing at the age of three, and who spends 40 years banging a toy drum and giggling as the procession of Nazism and post-war reconstruction passes by. For Grass, the human condition is 'absurd': not only ridiculous but morally and philosophically out of focus. His books offer no solutions, but they point out the problems with enormous, malicious glee.

★☆ THE FLOUNDER (1977)
The wife and husband from a Grimm fairy-tale move through the entire history of the human race, popping up in this period or that, playing each role by the conventions of its time, and endlessly, affably arguing about gender dominance. They are aided or hindered by a talking fish from the same fairy-tale: it takes now her side, now his. Finally the fish is ordered to defend itself before a late 20th-century feminist tribunal, and the whole male/female business is thrashed out in a hearing as preposterous as the trial in *Alice in Wonderland*. The fact that this book is about sexual rather than German politics makes it one of Grass's most accessible novels to non-German readers, and it is also wonderfully enlivened with puns, poems, satires and recipes.

Grass's other novels include the 'Danzig trilogy' (The Tin Drum, Cat and Mouse *and* Dog Years), From the Diary of a Snail, Cat and Mouse, The Meeting at Telgte, Headbirths, The Rat *and* The Call of the Toad. *His most recent work translated into English,* My Century (1999), *is a collection of linked stories, each one appropriate to a particular year of the 20th century.*

READ ON ▷

● *The Tin Drum* is the most accessible of the Danzig novels, and although its theme (Nazism) gives it a harsher tone than *The Flounder*, it is equally hilarious and bizarre.
▶ Other books similarly reinventing the human race, tossing all human knowledge and invention into a single fantastic melting-pot: ▷ Thornton Wilder, *The Eighth Day*; ▷ Kurt Vonnegut, *Galápagos*; ▷ J.G. Ballard, *The Unlimited Dream Company*; ▷ Jeanette Winterson, *The Passion*.

GRAVES, Robert (1895–1985)
British novelist, poet and non-fiction writer

Graves's main interests were myth and poetry. He wrote a best-selling version of the Greek myths, a controversial account of the Bible stories as myth, and *The White Goddess* (1948–52), a study of poetic inspiration. Throughout his life he composed poetry (much of it autobiographical), and his love poems in particular are much admired. He claimed that his novels were potboilers, written to finance 'real' work, but their quality and craftsmanship belie this description. Most are historical, reimagining characters of the past – from the author of the *Odyssey* to Jesus – as people with markedly 20th-century sensibilities, able to view the events of their own lives, as it were, with hindsight. His books are like psychological documentaries, as if we are looking directly into his characters' minds.

★☆ I, CLAUDIUS (1934)
This novel and its sequel *Claudius the God* purport to be the autobiography of the fourth Roman emperor. A spastic and an epileptic, he is regarded by everyone as a fool and ignored; he thus survives the myriad political and dynastic intrigues of the first 50 years of the Roman empire, the reigns of his three dangerous predecessors. He is finally made emperor himself, in a palace coup – and proceeds to rule with a blend of wisdom, guile and ruthlessness which he describes with fascinated relish. The story ends – typically for Graves – with a real document, an account by a Roman satirist of the 'Pumpkinification of Claudius', the arrival of the stammering, limping fool of an emperor in Olympus, home of the gods and of his own terrifying, deified relatives.

Graves's other novels include Count Belisarius *(set in 6th-century Byzantium),* Sergeant Lamb of the Ninth *and* Proceed, Sergeant Lamb *(about the American War of Independence),* Wife to Mr Milton *(set in Puritan England, and written in a brilliant pastiche of 17th-century prose),* Homer's Daughter *(set in prehistoric Greece), and* King Jesus *(about the life and death of Christ).* Seven Days in New Crete *is an urbane future-fantasy, and* Goodbye to All That *is autobiography, moving from a tormented account of Graves's time as an officer in the First World War to malicious glimpses of Oxford life and the literary London of the 1920s.*

READ ON

▶ to *I, Claudius*: David Wishart, *I, Virgil* (about the Roman Civil War, Caesar's assassination, Antony and Cleopatra, the rise of Augustus – a kind of 'prequel' to *I, Claudius*); ▷ Mary Renault, *The King Must Die*; ▷ Marguerite Yourcenar, *Memoirs of Hadrian*; Naomi Mitchison, *The Corn King and the Spring Queen*; Allan Massie, *Tiberius*.

▶ Books of similar gusto, on non-classical subjects: Frederick Rolfe, *Hadrian the Seventh* (about a waspish inadequate who is elected Pope); Augusto Roa Bastos, *I, The Supreme* (the 'autobiography' of a deranged 19th-century Paraguayan dictator); ▷ Gore Vidal, *Kalki* (about an insane Vietnam veteran who imagines himself Kalki, the Hindu god whose coming will end the present cycle of human existence).

GRAY, Alasdair (born 1934)
British writer

Founding father of the renaissance of Scottish literature in the last twenty years, Alasdair Gray has demonstrated his erudition, playful wit and skill as an illustrator and designer in a series of books that have ranged from gothic fantasy to dark eroticism. Gray loves all aspects of the writing, reading and making of books. His own are packed with allusion and parody, arcane snippets of literary knowledge, experiments with form and style. He jumps into the midst of his own fiction to offer justifications for the developments in it. He starts novels with 'Book 3', includes a 'Prologue' after 100 pages and then moves on to 'Book 1'. He takes literary and sub-literary genres like science fiction and pornography and plays unexpected games with readers' expectations of what they will offer. Gray is involved closely with the design of his works and, like a modern version of a medieval illuminator, he scatters his illustrations through his text. Even errata slips provide food for Gray's comic imagination. 'This erratum slip has been placed in this book in error' reads one sandwiched between the pages of one of his books. Gray has published a number of excellent books in the last twenty years. *Poor Things* (1992), an imaginative Victorian pastiche which tells of the creation of a kind of female Frankenstein's monster in 19th-century Glasgow, deservedly won the Guardian Fiction Prize when it first appeared. *A History Maker* (1994), set in a 23rd-century world where war has become an elaborate board-game, is Gray's extremely idiosyncratic but enjoyable version of a science fiction novel. However, Alasdair Gray's major achievement, the book that gave a new confidence to Scottish literature, remains *Lanark* (1981). Moving between the two worlds of 1950s Glasgow, where Duncan Thaw struggles to find love and fulfil his artistic vision, and the strange city of Unthank where the dead Thaw is reincarnated as Lanark, the book is an imaginative *tour de force*, a place where fantasy and realism collide to startling effect.

> [!NOTE] READ ON

- *Poor Things*.
- ▷ James Kelman, *How Late It Was, How Late*; Jeff Torrington, *Swing, Hammer, Swing*; Flann O'Brien, *At Swim Two-Birds* (for the same mixture of erudition and playfulness); ▷ Jorge Luis Borges's stories with very different settings but a similar love for the arcana and byways of literature.

READ ON A THEME: GREAT (Classic) DETECTIVES

John Dickson Carr, *Death Watch* (Gideon Fell)
▷ Agatha Christie, *Murder on the Orient Express* (Hercule Poirot)
▷ A. Conan Doyle, *The Hound of the Baskervilles* (Sherlock Holmes)
▷ Michael Innes, *Hamlet, Revenge!* (Inspector Appleby)
▷ Ngaio Marsh, *Death and the Dancing Footman* (Chief Inspector Roderick Alleyn)
▷ Dorothy L. Sayers, *The Nine Tailors* (Lord Peter Wimsey)
▷ Georges Simenon, *Maigret and the Headless Corpse*
▷ Rex Stout, *Murder by the Book* (Nero Wolfe)

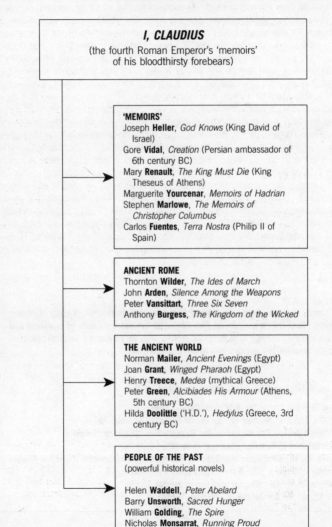

PATHWAYS

ROBERT GRAVES

I, CLAUDIUS
(the fourth Roman Emperor's 'memoirs'
of his bloodthirsty forebears)

'MEMOIRS'
Joseph **Heller**, *God Knows* (King David of
    Israel)
Gore **Vidal**, *Creation* (Persian ambassador of
    6th century BC)
Mary **Renault**, *The King Must Die* (King
    Theseus of Athens)
Marguerite **Yourcenar**, *Memoirs of Hadrian*
Stephen **Marlowe**, *The Memoirs of
    Christopher Columbus*
Carlos **Fuentes**, *Terra Nostra* (Philip II of
    Spain)

ANCIENT ROME
Thornton **Wilder**, *The Ides of March*
John **Arden**, *Silence Among the Weapons*
Peter **Vansittart**, *Three Six Seven*
Anthony **Burgess**, *The Kingdom of the Wicked*

THE ANCIENT WORLD
Norman **Mailer**, *Ancient Evenings* (Egypt)
Joan **Grant**, *Winged Pharaoh* (Egypt)
Henry **Treece**, *Medea* (mythical Greece)
Peter **Green**, *Alcibiades His Armour* (Athens,
    5th century BC)
Hilda **Doolittle** ('H.D.'), *Hedylus* (Greece, 3rd
    century BC)

PEOPLE OF THE PAST
(powerful historical novels)

Helen **Waddell**, *Peter Abelard*
Barry **Unsworth**, *Sacred Hunger*
William **Golding**, *The Spire*
Nicholas **Monsarrat**, *Running Proud*

GREENE, Graham (1904–91)
British writer of novels, plays and non-fiction

In the 1930s Greene wrote several thrillers influenced by ▷ Buchan and by action films of the time: they include *Stamboul Train* (set on the Orient Express), *A Gun for Sale/This Gun for Hire* (about the manhunt for a political assassin) and *The Confidential Agent* (about left-wing politics in a right-wing state). This work culminated in atmospheric film-scripts, of which the best (later novelized) was *The Third Man*. But thrillers – and, later, comedies such as *Our Man in Havana, Travels With My Aunt* and *Monsignor Quixote* – always took second place, at least in Greene's own estimation, to his Catholic novels. These are all concerned with people tormented by their own moral failure and by the longing for God's forgiveness. The settings are often the tropics; the political situations are unstable; the heroes are second-rank functionaries despised by their superiors. Two novels, *Brighton Rock* (1938, about a petty criminal in 1930s Brighton) and *The Human Factor* (1978, about the minor-public-school loyalties and betrayals of the British Intelligence Services), set similar searches for grace in a soulless, down-at-heel Britain. Despite the Catholic overtones of these books, which non-believers may find unconvincing, Greene's plots are fascinating, and his evocation of character and place is marvellous.

★ THE HEART OF THE MATTER (1948)
Scobie, Captain of Police in a God-forsaken African colony during the Second World War, is a decent, honest man. His wife Louise, tormented by memories of their dead daughter and by her own isolation from the rest of the British community, begs him to send her away to South Africa – and because of a mixture of pity for her misery and anguish at his inability to make her happy, he breaks police rules and borrows money from a suspected diamond-smuggler. From that lapse onwards, everything Scobie does ends in disaster, and there is nothing he can do but watch himself, appalled but helpless, as he plunges remorselessly towards damnation.

Greene's other novels include The End of the Affair, The Quiet American, A Burnt-out Case, The Comedians, The Honorary Consul, Doctor Fischer of Geneva *and* The Captain and the Enemy. *His short stories (many of them 'comedies of the sexual life', as he called them) are collected in* Twenty-one Stories, May We Borrow Your Husband? *and* The Last Word. *He also wrote travel books and plays and a fascinating book intended as a 'substitute for autobiography',* A World of My Own, *recounting his dreams.*

READ ON ▷

- *The Power and the Glory* (a lacerating story, set in Mexico during a left-wing revolution, about a drunken, self-hating priest who struggles against his own fear and the persecution of the revolutionaries to take God to the peasants).
▶ 'Psychic thrillers', similarly showing people driven to the edge of breakdown and beyond, by circumstances, their surroundings or consciousness of their own moral failings: ▷ Malcolm Lowry, *Under the Volcano*; ▷ Joseph Conrad, *Nostromo*; B. Traven, *The Treasure of the Sierra Madre*.

GRISHAM, John (born 1955)
US writer

Before turning to fiction, Grisham practised law and he has become the most successful writer of the 'legal thriller' genre in which lawyers play central roles and the intricacies of the law often provide the fuel for the plot. His first novel, *A Time to Kill* (1989), with its story of a lawyer defending a black father who has killed his daughter's rapists, had many of what would be later recognized as the classic ingredients of a Grisham plot. But it was with his second book *The Firm* (1990) that Grisham really hit his stride and propelled himself into the bestseller ranks. The central character is a brilliant and ambitious young lawyer who joins a prominent law firm and gradually discovers that it is a front for the Mafia, working solely for the benefit of organized crime. The novel follows his attempts to break free of the dangerous web in which the firm has entangled him. Grisham cranks up the tension with great skill and the legal details are neatly dovetailed into a plot that twists and turns with satisfying suspense. For many of his fans this remains Grisham's best book but he has followed it with a number of other thrillers that are almost equally engrossing. In *The Client* (1992) a senator has been the victim of a mafia hitman and a small boy is the only person who knows the identity of the killer. He becomes the innocent centre of a legal battle. In *The Brethren* (1999) three judges, imprisoned for assorted crimes, concoct a blackmail plot which goes disastrously astray when they pick the wrong man to blackmail. *A Painted House* (2001), Grisham's most recent book, shows a desire to get away from the courtroom and is a nostalgic story of a boy growing up in the rural Midwest in the 1950s. His change of pace and style will have surprised many of his readers although it is safe to assume that this does not mean we have seen the last of Grisham's expertly-crafted legal thrillers.

Grisham's other novels are The Partner, The Pelican Brief, The Runaway Jury, The Testament, The Rainmaker, The Street Lawyer *and* The Chamber.

> READ ON

- ● *The Runaway Jury.*
- ▶ Scott Turow, *Presumed Innocent*; James Patterson, *Along Came a Spider*; Michael Crichton, *Rising Sun*; Steve Martini, *The Attorney*.

READ ON A THEME: GROVES OF ACADEME

- ▷ Kingsley Amis, *Lucky Jim*
- ▷ Margaret Atwood, *The Robber Bride*
- ▷ A.S. Byatt, *Possession*
- ▷ Penelope Fitzgerald, *The Gate of Angels*
- ▷ David Lodge, *Changing Places*
  Mary McCarthy, *The Groves of Academe*

See also: Dreaming Spires; Higher (?) Education

GUTERSON, David (born 1956)
US novelist

By combining elements of both courtroom drama and murder mystery with an evocative recreation of a particular community caught at a particular moment in its history, David Guterson produced one of the most satisfying bestsellers of the 1990s. *Snow Falling on Cedars* (1994) is set on an island off the Pacific Northwest coast of America in the 1950s. A fisherman has been murdered on his boat and a man stands accused of the murder in the dock of the courtroom. The man is Kabuo Miyamoto, one of the large Japanese community on the island. Watching the proceedings is Ishmael Chambers, owner of the local newspaper, a lonely man whose only love has been for a woman who refused him and later became Miyamoto's wife. As the trial moves forward, with the inherent tension that courtroom dramas in fiction and film so often possess, the story also moves back in time to Chambers's failed love affair, to the war and the racial tensions it released on the island. Piece by piece, Guterson builds up his picture of an entire community, living precariously in a harsh landscape that the novel brilliantly evokes. And he does so while both maintaining the reader's interest in the 'whodunnit' elements of his plot and exploring a drama of clashing cultures and values. For any novelist it would be a major achievement. For a first novelist it is remarkable.

Guterson has also written a collection of short stories, The Country Ahead of Us, the Country Behind *and a second novel,* East of the Mountains *(about a terminally ill man who sets out on a journey into the mountains which becomes a journey into his own past).*

READ ON >

▶ Amy Tan, *The Joy Luck Club*; ▷ Annie Proulx, *The Shipping News*; Charles Frazier, *Cold Mountain*; Arthur Golden, *Memoirs of a Geisha*.

H

HAGGARD, H. Rider (Henry) *(1856–1925)*
British novelist

Haggard's novels are adventure fantasies set in wildly exotic locations: the geysers and glaciers of Iceland (*Erik Bright-eyes*), the South American jungle (*Montezuma's Daughter*) or – most commonly of all – Darkest Africa, a continent of the imagination as fabulous as the setting of Sinbad's adventures in *The Arabian Nights*. (He knew what he was writing about: in his 20s he was a colonial administrator in the Transvaal.) In ☆*King Solomon's Mines* (1885), Haggard's best-known book, Allan Quatermain leads a safari in search of the fabulous treasure beyond Africa's Solomon Mountains, a treasure which has already claimed a thousand lives. Desert heat, jungle, hostile warrior-tribes and ice-caves in the mountains must all be faced, to say nothing of black magic, cannibalism and the guile and treachery of members of Quatermain's own party. Hokum? The best.

> READ ON

- *She*; *Allan Quatermain*; *Ayesha*; *The Return of She*.
  ▷ John Buchan, *Prester John*; ▷ Jules Verne, *Around the World in 80 Days*;
  ▷ Wilbur Smith, *A Falcon Flies*.

HAMMETT, Dashiell (1894–1961)
US writer of novels, short stories and screenplays

A former private detective, Hammett wrote stories and serials for pulp magazines, and later became a Hollywood scriptwriter. He perfected the 'private eye' story, in which kidnappings, thefts and murders are investigated by laconic, wisecracking individuals who are always just on the side of the angels and just one step ahead of the police. His best-known detectives are Sam Spade (made famous by Humphrey Bogart), the urbane Nick Charles (made famous in William Powell's 'Thin Man' films) and the Continental Op. Hammett's novels are *The Dain Curse, Red Harvest, The Maltese Falcon, The Glass Key* and *The Thin Man*; his story-collections include *The Continental Op* and *The Big Knockover and other Stories*.

> READ ON

▶ ▷ Raymond Chandler, *The Lady in the Lake*; James M. Cain, *Double Indemnity*; Ross Macdonald, *The Drowning Pool*; Jim Thompson, *The Killer Inside Me*.

HARDY, Thomas (1840–1928)
British novelist and poet

As a young man Hardy worked as an ecclesiastical architect, sketching and surveying country churches. This work intensified his love of the old ways of the countryside, patterns of life and customs which dated from feudal times. This is the background to his novels (which are all set in south-western England, the ancient kingdom of Wessex). He describes the minutiae of farming and village life with the exactness of a museum curator, and his characters' habits of mind are rooted in the ebb and flow of the seasons, in the unending cycle of tending for their animals and caring for the land. Life is unhurried but inexorable: Hardy's people are owned by their environment. They are also subject to a range of violent passions and emotions – Hardy thought of human beings as the playthings of destiny, struggling against the indifferent and inexplicable forces of nature and fate – and the placid continuum of existence is the setting for such irrational psychological forces as jealousy, intolerance and revenge. Hardy's bleakness and pessimism were much criticized, and in 1895 he gave up novels to concentrate on poetry.

FAR FROM THE MADDING CROWD (1874)
The shepherd Gabriel Oak works for Bathsheba Everdene, and loves her. Bathsheba's head is turned by dashing Sergeant Troy, who marries her and then deserts her, letting her believe that he is dead. Bathsheba now agrees to marry Boldwood, a yeoman farmer, unimaginative and dull, who has secretly loved her for years. Then Troy comes back and claims his wife – provoking a crisis and the resolution of the uneasy relationship between Oak and Bathsheba which has simmered all this time.

Hardy's other novels include Under the Greenwood Tree, A Pair of Blue Eyes, The Return of the Native, The Trumpet Major, The Mayor of Casterbridge, The Woodlanders, Tess of the D'Urbervilles *and* Jude the Obscure. *He wrote an epic drama set during the Napoleonic Wars*, The Dynasts, *and several books of poetry including* Satires of Circumstance, Moments of Vision *and* Winter Words.

> READ ON

- ● *The Mayor of Casterbridge* (Michael Henchard rises to become rich and respected but his past returns to bring him down); *Tess of the D'Urbervilles*.
- ▶ Books on similar themes, in a similar style: ▷ George Eliot, *Adam Bede*; ▷ Mrs Gaskell, *Ruth*; ▷ Edith Wharton, *Ethan Frome*; ▷ Melvyn Bragg, *The Hired Man*.
- ▶ Further away in period or manner or setting, but equally atmospheric: ▷ John Fowles, *The French Lieutenant's Woman*; Sigrid Undset, *Kristin Lavransdatter*; Halldor Laxness, *Independent People*.

HARRIS, Robert (born 1957)
British writer

In his fiction Robert Harris shows all the best qualities of the fine political journalist he once was. He is exact in description, his eye for the telling detail which illuminates a scene is acute and his prose is precise but relaxed. The result is that his books have a plausibility that is sustained even when the plot is based on imaginative speculation. 'What if?', he asks and then provides an answer that convinces because it is rooted in everyday realities. Many writers, most of them working in the science fiction genre, have written alternative histories in which the Nazis won the Second World War. None has produced a portrait of what that alternative reality might have been like that matches the one Harris provides in *Fatherland* (1992). And he succeeds precisely because he rejects sweeping, generalized conjecture in favour of closely observed, mundane details. Within a short time we are immersed in Berlin 1964 as preparations begin to celebrate Hitler's 75th birthday. This is the day-to-day world of Kripo detective Xavier March and it rapidly becomes ours. The puzzling murder of a figure from the wartime past disturbs March's world. As he takes his investigation into territory his superiors would rather avoid, he edges towards truths about the Nazi world that we know but March doesn't.

Robert Harris's other novels are Enigma *(set in the Second World War code-breaking centre at Bletchley) and* Archangel. *He has also written several works of non-fiction including* Selling Hitler, *the very funny and scarcely credible story of the forged Hitler diaries of the 1980s.*

READ ON ▷

- *Archangel* (centres on the search for a missing archive of Stalin's papers).
- ▶ ▷ Len Deighton, *SS-GB*; ▷ Eric Ambler, *The Mask of Dimitrios*; ▷ Frederick Forsyth, *The Odessa File*; Philip Kerr, *A Philosophical Investigation*; Alan Furst, *The World at Night*.

HARRISON, Harry (born 1925)
US novelist and short story writer

Although Harrison has written serious science fiction (e.g. the fast-moving adventure series *Deathworld I, Deathworld II* and *Deathworld III*), he is best-known for farce, and especially for his books about The Stainless Steel Rat. In a future where technology has made crime all but redundant, James Bolivar di Griz, the Stainless Steel Rat, is a spectacular exception to the rule. He sees himself as a public benefactor, keeping the police on their toes, giving employment to insurance clerks and bringing colour and excitement to TV newscasts. In the first book of the series, *The Stainless Steel Rat*, the galactic police decide that the only way to cope with him is to recruit him and send him to catch the lovely interplanetary criminal Angelina.

The Stainless Steel Rat books include The Stainless Steel Rat's Revenge, The Stainless Steel Rat Saves the World, The Stainless Steel Rat Wants You! *and* The Stainless Steel Rat for President. *Harrison's other novels include* Bill, the Galactic Hero, Planet of the Damned, Star Smashers of the Galaxy Rangers, *and the more serious* Make Room, Make Room! *and* Mechanismo.

READ ON

● *Make Room! Make Room!* (the basis for the film *Soylent Green*, this is set in a dark future of overpopulation and food shortages and follows one day in the life of an NYPD detective as he attempts to solve the mystery of a murder).
▶ to Harrison's comedies: ▷ Kurt Vonnegut,*The Sirens of Titan*; Robert Rankin, *The Sprouts of Brentford*; Robert Sheckley, *The Status Civilization*; John Sladek, *The Reproductive System*.
▶ to *Make Room, Make Room!*: ▷ J.G. Ballard, *The Drought*; David Brin, *Earth*; John Brunner, *Stand on Zanzibar*.

HARTLEY, L.P. (Leslie Poles) (1895–1972)
British novelist and short story writer

An admirer of ▷ James and ▷ E.M. Forster, Hartley wrote a dozen decorous, restrained novels about emotional deprivation and the way childhood experience shadows a person's whole existence. His best-known books are the 'Eustace and Hilda' trilogy (*The Shrimp and the Anemone, The Sixth Heaven* and *Eustace and Hilda*, 1944–7), about a brother and sister whose emotional interdependence, innocent-seeming when they are children, blights their later lives, and ☆ *The Go-Between* (1953), about a boy on holiday during an idyllic Edwardian summer. Carrying messages between two doomed lovers (the daughter of the 'big house' and a tenant farmer), he is emotionally crippled by the passions he senses but hardly understands.

READ ON

● *The Hireling*.
▶ ▷ Henry James, *What Maisie Knew*; ▷ Anita Brookner, *Hôtel du Lac*; ▷ Elizabeth Bowen, *The Death of the Heart*; Jane Gardam, *A Long Way from Verona*; Philip Larkin, *Jill*.

HAŠEK, Jaroslav (1883–1923)
Czech novelist and journalist

Hašek spent most of his youth as a dropout and a half-baked political activist (for which, for six months, he was imprisoned by the Russians as a spy). He served, reluctantly, in the First World War, was invalided out and returned to the journalistic career he had begun before the war. This career was as unpredictable as most other things in Hašek's boozy, disorganized life. He worked on an anarchist paper but was sacked for stealing the office bicycle. For a while he edited a magazine called *Animal World* but was again shown the door when it was discovered that he had been inventing animals about which to write. Hašek's masterpiece, the 700–page comic novel ★☆*The Good Soldier Svejk*, makes hilarious use of all his early experiences. Svejk is the town drunk, a dog-catcher, who is conscripted into the Austrian army as the lowliest of privates. A moon-faced, brainless lump, he obeys every fatuous order and follows every regulation to the letter. The book follows his farcical army career, during which he rises to the dizzy heights of chaplain's batman, takes part in the First World War and sees the first skirmishes of the Russian revolution. He understands nothing of what is going on: food, drink and staying out of trouble are all that interest him. Hašek uses Svejk's blankness like a mirror, showing up officers, politicians and bureaucrats for the fools they are.

All earlier English translations of The Good Soldier Svejk *were outclassed by Cecil Parrott's, written in the 1970s. Parrott also published a selection of Hašek's journalism and shorter works,* The Red Commissar.

> READ ON

▶ ▷ François Rabelais's *Gargantua* is the nearest match for Hašek's farcical gusto, and Von Grimmelshausen, *Simplex Simplicissimus* is about a Middle Ages precursor of Svejk. Of more modern books, Eric Linklater's *Private Angelo* is a genial satire on the Second World War; Thomas Berger's *Reinhart in Love* is a similarly light-hearted novel about a Svejkish US 'little man'. ▷ Thomas Mann's *The Confessions of Felix Krull, Confidence Man*, about a confidence trickster travelling the spas and luxury hotels of Europe in the 1900s, though it lacks Hašek's devastating view of war and politics, exactly parallels his wide-eyed, amiable style. ▷ Joseph Heller, *Catch-22* (a hilarious black-farce 'take' on all Hašek's themes).

HAWTHORNE, NATHANIEL (1804–1864)
US novelist

A member of a long-established New England family, Hawthorne was born in Salem, Massachusetts. Salem was, of course, the town in which the notorious witch-trials of the 17th century had taken place and Hawthorne was a direct descendant of one of the judges in the trial. Much of his work is concerned with his heritage of New England Puritanism. Many of his novels and stories struggle to understand the combination of personal moral rectitude with ferocious and pitiless intolerance of others that characterized both his ancestors and many of his contemporaries. Hawthorne wrote and published fiction throughout his adult life but his greatest achievements belong to an extraordinary burst of creativity in the late 1840s and early 1850s, which saw the publication of *The Scarlet Letter, The House of the Seven Gables* and *The Blithedale Romance*. Hawthorne's gifts can also be seen in many of his short stories, particularly 'Young Goodman Brown' (good and evil battling it out again in New England), 'The Maypole of Merry Mount' and 'Rappaccini's Daughter'.

★ THE SCARLET LETTER (1850)
This study of intolerance and humbug is set among the first Puritan settlers in the US. Hester Prynne has spent two years in Boston, waiting for her elderly husband to join her from England. In the meantime she has borne a love-child, Pearl, and the Puritans pillory her and brand her as an adulteress, making her wear the scarlet letter 'A' embroidered on her clothes. Her husband arrives, discovers that her secret lover is a minister of the church, and mercilessly persecutes him for refusing to admit his guilt. Hester's husband and lover pursue their enmity to the end; they ignore Hester herself, who in the meantime lives an unobtrusive but truly Christian life helping the neighbours who once mistreated her.

READ ON >

- *The House of the Seven Gables* (a similarly remorseless novel about a New England family cursed for generations because of their forebears' persecution of an innocent man for witchcraft); *The Blithedale Romance* (a satire, based on Hawthorne's own experience, about life in a Massachusetts utopian community).
- ▶ ▷ Aldous Huxley, *The Devils of Loudon* (about an outbreak of hysteria and demonic possession in a 16th-century French village); ▷ I.B. Singer, *Satan in Goray* (set in a medieval community of Polish Jews harassed by pogroms and torn apart by the appearance of a false Messiah); ▷ Edgar Allan Poe, *Tales of Mystery and Imagination*.

HEINLEIN, Robert (1907–88)
US novelist

Heinlein's 1930s and 1940s writings were a bridge between early science fiction (▷ Verne and ▷ Wells) and the present day. They are straightforward stories of space-travel and the colonization of distant planets, and much of their detail has been overtaken by events. In the 1960s his novel *Stranger in a Strange Land* had a cult following, because it seemed to be advocating a mystical union of humankind brought about by flower-power, free love and hallucinatory drugs. His 1970s and 1980s books range from the serious *I Will Fear No Evil* to the ironical farce *Job*, akin to the bleakly hilarious fantasies of ▷ Joseph Heller and ▷ Kurt Vonnegut. Heinlein's work, especially gung-ho space-war classics like *Starship Troopers* (1959), has been condemned as excessively right wing but there is no doubting Heinlein's imaginative range. His best-known books, the heart of his achievement, are a series of independent but linked novels about Lazarus Long, a man who has the ability to live forever, and who ends up as a kind of universal patriarch; everyone in existence is one of his descendants. Heinlein explores the personal and social problems of such a person, stirring in exotic and fascinating plot-ideas. In *Time Enough to Love* (1973), for example, Lazarus Long, bored with life and contemplating suicide, is distracted by being allowed to try the forbidden experience of time travel. He goes back to 1917, fights in the First World War, meets himself as a six-year-old and falls in love with his own mother.Other books including Lazarus Long are *Methuselah's Children, The Number of the Beast* and *The Cat Who Walks Through Walls*.

READ ON >

- *Job* (a Bible-inspired story of a human being tormented by a practical-joking, malicious God and finally befriended by the Devil).
- ▶ ▷ Philip José Farmer, *Ringworld*; ▷ Isaac Asimov, *Foundation*; Orson Scott Card, *Ender's Game*; Ray Bradbury, *The Martian Chronicles*.

HELLER, Joseph (1923–1999)
US novelist

Throughout the 1950s, the escalation of the nuclear-arms race produced in many people a feeling of desperate impotence. Faced with imminent apocalypse, the only possible option seemed to be hysterical, cynical laughter. By the early 1960s this mood was common in plays, comedians' routines, cartoons and satirical magazines, and Heller's first novel *Catch-22* expressed it perfectly. On the surface a wild farce about airmen in the Second World War, it shows human beings as both trapped in a detestable destiny and paradoxically liberated, by the absence of hope or choice, to do exactly as they please, to turn reality into fantasy. *Catch-22* was such an enormous critical and popular success that its shadow fell over the rest of Heller's career. As he once sardonically remarked, 'People say that, in the last thirty years, I haven't written a novel as good as *Catch-22*. True, but, then, nor has anyone else.' In fact, several of Heller's later novels are comic masterpieces in their own right

★☆ CATCH-22 (1961)

A group of US bomber pilots is stationed on a Mediterranean island during the Second World War. Every time a man thinks he has flown his quota of bombing-missions, high command doubles the number. There is no escape, and the reason is Catch-22: if you're sane enough to ask to be grounded because what you're doing is crazy, you're sane enough to fly. For all its bleak philosophy, *Catch-22* is brilliantly funny, particularly in its deadpan reporting of the lunatic, gung-ho US top brass, of Milo Minderbinder's extension to infinity of the rules of free-market enterprise (profiteering on everything from eggs to his comrades' lives), and of such pitiful victims of destiny as Major Major Major Major, a man haunted by his name.

Heller's other novels are Something Happened, Good as Gold, God Knows *and* Picture This. No Laughing Matter *is non-fiction, a blackly funny account of Heller's recovery from near-fatal illness.* Now and Then *is a memoir of growing up in Coney Island and of service in the US Air Force during the Second World War.*

> READ ON

- ● *Closing Time* is a sequel to *Catch-22*, in which Yossarian and his ex-comrades are facing old age, despair and death in the hell that is 1990s capitalist New York. Two other Heller novels centre on characters who are trapped. *Something Happened* shows a man in thrall to the routine and ordinariness of his life; in *God Knows* the Old Testament King David is shackled by knowledge of the world's whole future history, and by his relationship with a wisecracking, cynical and unhelpful God. ('Where does it say nice?' asks God. 'Where does it say I have to be nice?').
- ▶ ▷ Jaroslav Hašek, *The Good Soldier Svejk*. ▷ Philip Roth, *Portnoy's Complaint*; ▷ John Kennedy Toole, *A Confederacy of Dunces*.

HEMINGWAY, Ernest (1898–1961)
US novelist and short story writer

Few great writers provoke such love/hate reactions as Hemingway: it seems impossible to read him without judging him. The reason is that although he wrote some of the most evocative, persuasive prose of the century – as direct and compelling as the best journalism – many people find his subject-matter and philosophy of life repellent. He believed that creatures, including human beings,

PATHWAYS

JOSEPH HELLER

CATCH-22
(the lunacy of war, seen in a USAF base on a fantasy
Mediterranean island during the Second World War)

THE CRAZINESS OF COMMAND
(you'll laugh till you die)

Richard **Hooker**, *M*A*S*H*
Kurt **Vonnegut**, *Slaughterhouse Five*
Thomas **Pynchon**, *Gravity's Rainbow*
Jaroslav **Hašek**, *The Good Soldier Svejk*
 (– and sometimes you won't even laugh)
Herman **Wouk**, *The Caine Mutiny*
Peter **George**, *Red Alert*

WAR KILLS OUR YOUNG MEN
(war at the sharp end: brutal, unglorious, and
  pointless)

Mario Vargas **Llosa**, *The City and the Dogs/
  The Time of the Hero*
Stephen **Crane**, *The Red Badge of Courage*
Erich Maria **Remarque**, *All Quiet on the
  Western Front*
Len **Deighton**, *Bomber*
Norman **Mailer**, *The Naked and the Dead*
Neville **Shute**, *Landfall*

THE WORLD GONE MAD
(laugh or cry, we live in an insane asylum)

Andrew **Sinclair**, *Gog*
Günter **Grass**, *The Tin Drum*
Richard **Condon**, *Mile High*
Jerzy **Kosinski**, *Being There*
Terry **Southern**, *Candy*

are at their noblest when fighting for survival, and his novels and stories are therefore about boxing, big-game hunting, deep-sea fishing, bull-fighting and above all war. Hemingway himself realized that his macho philosophy belonged more to the Middle Ages than the 20th century, and most of his books are tinged with failure. His heroes rarely succeed in 'proving' themselves, their wars are futile, the emphasis is on pain, despair and death. But the dream remains, and is Hemingway's own dream. He spent his leisure time in exactly the activities he describes – precise details of how to fight bulls, hunt big game, box or fish are what he does best – and in 1961, feeling too old and sick to continue, he shot himself.

★ A FAREWELL TO ARMS (1929)

A US ambulance driver in Italy during the First World War is wounded and taken to hospital, where he falls in love with an English nurse. While he convalesces the couple are deliriously happy, but then he is commanded back to the front. She tells him that she is pregnant, and they decide that their only course is 'a farewell to arms', escaping from the war to neutral Switzerland.

Hemingway's other novels are The Torrents of Spring, The Sun Also Rises/Fiesta *(which includes a superb description of bull-running during the festival at Pamplona)*, The Green Hills of Africa, To Have and Have Not, For Whom the Bell Tolls *(set during the Spanish civil war)*, Across the River and Into the Trees *and* The Old Man and the Sea. *Several unrevised, unfinished books were published posthumously: most famous is* Islands in the Stream, *most recent is* True at First Light. *His short story collections include* In Our Time, Men Without Women *and* Winner Take Nothing. Death in the Afternoon *combines non-fiction descriptions of bullfighting with short stories on the same subject.* A Moveable Feast *is his memoir of happy days as a young, would-be writer in Paris in the early 1920s.*

> **READ ON**

- ● *The Old Man and the Sea* describes a duel to the death between the old Cuban fisherman Santiago and a gigantic marlin, the biggest fish he has ever tried to catch in his life. The book is short, and concentrates on Santiago, struggling not only with the marlin but his own failing powers, and kept going only by determination and a lifetime's skill.
- ▶ ▷ Graham Greene, *The Power and the Glory*; ▷ Norman Mailer, *The Naked and the Dead*; ▷ George Orwell, *Homage to Catalonia*; ▷ Jack London, *The Sea-wolf*.

HERBERT, Frank (1920–86)
US novelist

Herbert's work is dominated by the 2000–page (6–novel) ★☆ 'Dune' series (1965–85), a science fiction epic whose scope and complexity dwarf all rivals. Dune is a desert planet, inhabited by gigantic sand-worms which produce mélange, a substance which inhibits aging and gives knowledge of the past and future. The saga (each of whose novels is self-contained) tells how Paul Atreides inherits Dune, has to win it from his enemies and then colonize it. It describes the 'greening' of a planet where water is the most precious of all commodities, and recounts the wars between the Atreides family and other interests (especially the powerful Bene Gesserit sisterhood, which is dedicated to harnessing the pure power of thought and so dispensing with science and technology). The books are partly a swaggering multi-generation saga, the apotheosis of space-opera, and partly a detailed and moving account of the inter-relationship between the colonists and their planet.

The first Dune trilogy is Dune, Dune Messiah *and* Children of Dune; *the second is* God Emperor of Dune, Heretics of Dune *and* Chapterhouse of Dune. *Herbert's many other books include* The Dragon in the Sea, The Whipping Star, The Dosadi Experiment, The Green Brain *and* The Santaroga Barrier.

READ ON

▶ to *Dune*: Brian Aldiss, *Helliconia Spring* and its sequels; ▷ Anne McCaffrey, *Dragonflight*; ▷ Robert Silverberg, *Majipoor Chronicles*; Jack Vance, *Big Planet*.
▶ to *God Emperor of Dune*: Alfred Bester, *The Stars My Destination*; ▷ Philip José Farmer, *Jesus on Mars*; Roger Zelazny, *Lord of Light*; Kim Stanley Robinson, *A Memory of Whiteness*.

HESSE, Hermann (1877–1962)
German/Swiss novelist and non-fiction writer

A poet and mystic, Hesse was influenced by Jung's ideas of the unconscious and the collective unconscious, and later by Buddhist philosophy. His most famous mystical novel, *The Glass Bead Game/Magister Ludi* (*Das Glasperlenspiel*), is about a future utopia where all questions about life, morality and personality are covered by a monastic philosophical system centred on a zen-like game involving coloured beads and an abacus. Hesse's reputation for gentle, philosophical woolliness has obscured his true worth. His novels before *The Glass Bead Game* are spare, moving accounts of how people in psychological turmoil reach peace with themselves, either through their own efforts or with the help of friends and loved ones. He is something of a special taste, but few writers' works so reward their devotees.

★☆ ROSSHALDE (1914)
Veraguth, a world-renowned painter, is suffering creative block. His marriage is breaking down, and he and his wife stay together out of love for Rosshalde, their beautiful country estate, and devotion to their young son, Pierre. Veraguth's problems seem beyond cure – until unexpected tragedy forces him to come to terms with himself, and so to find peace at last.

Hesse's major novels are Gertrud, Peter Camenzind, Under the Wheel/The Prodigy, Siddhartha *(about Buddha),* Steppenwolf, Narziss and Goldmund *and* The Glass Bead Game. *He also published shorter, more mystical fiction (*Knulp; Klingsor's Last Summer*), poetry, short stories, essays and letters.*

READ ON

● *Gertrud* (the story of a tragic love-triangle between a girl and two young men who are close friends). *Steppenwolf* and *Narziss and Goldmund* are both about the divided self. In *Steppenwolf* a hopeless, middle-aged recluse is 'brought back' by the spiritual energy of three young people who may be dream-figures from his subconscious. In *Narziss and Goldmund* (set in medieval Europe) the conflict between flesh and spirit is symbolized by the two main characters, close friends, one carnal, one spiritual.

▶ to *Rosshalde*: ▷ André Gide, *The Pastoral Symphony*.

▶ to Hesse's work in general: ▷ Heinrich Böll, *The Clown*; ▷ Kazuo Ishiguro, *An Artist of the Floating World*.

HIAASEN, Carl (born 1953)
US journalist and novelist

Carl Hiaasen knows the world of which he writes with such black relish in his comedy thrillers. Born and raised in Florida, the setting for his books, he has worked as a journalist investigating the kinds of corruption and chicanery that provide the fuel on which his plots run. Hiaasen's novels have the suspense and mystery of the best crime fiction but it is safe to assume that what readers remember of them are the manic, comic energy, the grotesque villains (and, often, even more grotesque heroes) and the writer's ability to focus on one seemingly trivial incident, spinning out its consequences to logical but bizarre lengths. Only in a Hiaasen novel is a hit-man a seven-foot tall Amish man. Only in a Hiaasen novel does a deranged bad guy spend the second half of the book with a dead dog's rotting head firmly embedded by the teeth in his forearm. And only a Hiaasen plot can begin with the theft of blue-tongued mango voles from the Kingdom of Thrills in Key Largo and escalate into an insane confrontation between environmentalists and a mobster-developer that results in the total destruction of the Kingdom. As P.J. O'Rourke once pointed out (correctly), 'Reading Hiaasen will do more to damage the Florida tourist trade than anything except an actual visit to Florida'.

TOURIST SEASON (1986)
A band of anti-tourist terrorists is on the loose in Florida, led by a rogue newspaperman appalled by the destruction of the state's natural beauty and resources. The head of Miami's Chamber of Commerce has been found dead with a toy rubber alligator lodged in his throat. More murders follow. Another reporter turned private eye is given the job of tracking down the terrorists, a job that soon turns into one of Hiaasen's characteristic excursions along the wilder highways and byways of the Sunshine State. And beneath the mayhem, violence and dark farce, the author's serious environmental concerns are apparent.

Hiaasen's other novels are Double Whammy, Skin Tight, Native Tongue, Strip Tease, Stormy Weather, Lucky You *and* Sick Puppy. *He has also written three novels with William Montalbano* (Powder Burns, Trap Line *and* A Death in China), *less anarchic than his solo fiction.*

READ ON ▷

● *Sick Puppy.*

▶ Lawrence Shames, *Sunburn*; Dave Barry, *Big Trouble*; Charles Willeford, *The*

Shark-Infested Custard; Doug J. Swanson, *Dreamboat*; Charles Higson, *King of the Ants* (for an English version of Hiaasen's mix of grotesquerie, violence and comedy).

HIGGINS, George V. (1939–2000)
US writer

Working as a lawyer (including several years as assistant DA for Massachusetts) gave Higgins an insight not just into crime, but into the mind of criminals and those politicians and businessmen who do exactly as they please without ever actually turning crooked. His books use the crime-novel formula and are exciting reading, with superbly convincing dialogue and deadpan wit. But they also dissect and discuss the state of the late-20th-century US, with its problems of drugs, poverty, racism and moral bankruptcy. These are crime stories not just to pass the time but to make you think.

Higgins's novels include the trilogy The Friends of Eddie Coyle, The Digger's Game *and* Defending Billy Ryan, *and the self-standing books* Cogan's Trade, The Outlaws, Impostors, Trust, Wonderful Years, Wonderful Years, A Change of Gravity *and the last book completed before his death,* At End of Day. The Sins of the Fathers *collects short stories.*

> READ ON

▶ John Gregory Dunne, *True Confessions*; ▷ Elmore Leonard, *City Primeval;* Richard Price, *Clockers.*

HIGGINS, Jack (born 1929)
British novelist

'Jack Higgins' is one of the pseudonyms of Henry Patterson, who also writes thrillers as Martin Fallon, James Graham, Hugh Marlow and Harry Patterson. The Higgins books are pacy, violent and full of character. They include *The Last Place God Made, The Eagle Has Landed* (about a plot to assassinate Churchill during the Second World War), *The Dark Side of the Street, A Season in Hell* (ex-SAS officer takes revenge on drug barons who have killed two apparently harmless addicts), *The Violent Enemy, Day of Reckoning* and *Edge of Danger* (most recently published of a number of books featuring British intelligence agent and assassin Sean Dillon).

> READ ON

● *The Eagle Has Flown* (sequel to *The Eagle Has Landed*); *Thunder Point.*
▶ ▷ Len Deighton, *Berlin Game*; Alexander Fullerton, *Regenesis*; Colin Forbes, *Terminal*; Gerald Seymour, *Kingfisher*; Andy McNab, *Crisis Four.*

READ ON A THEME: HIGH ADVENTURE

▷ Tom Clancy, *Patriot Games*
▷ Alexandre Dumas, *The Three Musketeers*
▷ H. Rider Haggard, *King Solomon's Mines*

▷ Anthony Hope, *The Prisoner of Zenda*
Stephen Hunter, *A Time to Hunt*
Rafael Sabatini, *Captain Blood*
▷ Wilbur Smith, *Birds of Prey*
B. Traven, *The Treasure of the Sierra Madre*

See also: Action Thrillers; Spies and Double Agents; Terrorists/Freedom Fighters

READ ON A THEME: HIGHER (?) EDUCATION

▷ Malcolm Bradbury, *The History Man*
▷ Robertson Davies, *The Rebel Angels*
▷ J.P. Donleavy, *The Ginger Man*
Richard Gordon, *Doctor in the House*
Howard Jacobson, *Coming from Behind*
Randall Jarrell, *Pictures from an Institution*
▷ Alison Lurie, *The War Between the Tates*
▷ Tom Sharpe, *Wilt*

See also: Dreaming Spires; Groves of Academe

HIGHSMITH, Patricia (1921–95)
US novelist and short-story writer

Except for *The People Who Knock on the Door* (1982, about the disintegration of an 'ordinary' US family, whose father becomes a born-again Christian) High-smith's books are chiefly psychological thrillers. They show the planning and commission of horribly convincing, 'everyday' crimes, and the way murder erodes the murderer's moral identity. Few writers screw tension so tight in such functional, unemotional prose. Highsmith's most chilling insight is how close the criminally insane can be to people just like ourselves.

RIPLEY'S GAME (1974)
Ripley, who appears in several Highsmith books, is a charming American psychopath who lives in France. In this book, out of boredom, he sets up circumstances to snare an entirely innocent man into committing murder. But the murder victim is a mafia boss, and soon assassins begin to hunt down both Ripley and his dupe. The plot is exciting, but Highsmith's main concern is the comparison between Ripley's icy amorality and the conscience-racked flailings of the man he corrupts.

Other Ripley books are The Talented Mr Ripley, Ripley Under Ground, The Boy Who Followed Ripley *and* Ripley Under Water. *Highsmith's other novels include* Strangers on a Train, The Two Faces of January, The Storyteller/A Suspension of Mercy, The Tremor of Forgery, Edith's Diary, Found in the Street, Small G: a Summer Idyll *and* The Price of Salt/Carol. The Snailwatch-er/Eleven, The Animal-lover's Book of Beastly Murder, The Black House,

Mermaids on the Golf Course *and* Tales of Natural and Unnatural Catastrophes *contain short stories.*

READ ON ▷

- the central character of *The Glass Cell* (a typical non-Ripley book) is a man released from prison after six years during which his character has been brutalized and his moral integrity destroyed. Tormented by the possibility of his wife's unfaithfulness, he sets out to discover the truth.

▶ Julian Symons, *The Man Who Killed Himself*; ▷ Barbara Vine, *A Fatal Inversion;* ▷ P.D. James, *The Skull Beneath the Skin*; ▷ Minette Walters, *The Echo.*

HILL, Reginald (born 1936)
British novelist

In his first novel, *A Clubbable Woman* (1970), Hill introduced the two characters who have been central to his books ever since – the aggressive, slobbish but shrewd Superintendent Dalziel and the eager, sensitive Inspector Pascoe. Each successive book has expanded our knowledge of the pair and shown Hill's increasingly confident use of humour, deft characterization and ingenious plotting to tell traditional crime stories in a contemporary setting. To many readers Reginald Hill is now the best crime writer in Britain.

ON BEULAH HEIGHT (1998)
During a hot summer a village re-emerges from the reservoir which had covered it 15 years earlier. At the time the villagers were evacuated three girls were missing and so too was the man suspected of abducting them. Now he seems to have returned, another girl is missing and Dalziel is obliged to face once again the most demanding and puzzling of cases from his past. Hill produces a crime story of satisfying complexity and depth which also manages, unpretentiously, to say something about the power of the past to haunt the present.

Hill's other books include *An Advancement of Learning, A Fairly Dangerous Thing, A Very Good Hater, Bones and Silence,* the cheekily-named *Another Death in Venice*, the superbly comic *Pictures of Perfection, Arms and the Women* and *Dialogues of the Dead.* Under his own name he has written several novels about a Luton-based private investigator, Joe Sixsmith and has also published fiction under the pseudonyms Dick Morland, Patrick Ruell and Charles Underhill.

READ ON ▷

▶ Val McDermid, *A Place of Execution*; ▷ Colin Dexter, *Death Is Now My Neighbour*; ▷ Ian Rankin, *The Falls.*

HILL, Susan (born 1942)
British writer

Apart from *Mrs de Winter* (a 1993 sequel to ▷Du Maurier's *Rebecca*) and two 'classic' ghost stories, *The Woman in Black* and *The Mist in the Mirror*, all Hill's

HISTORICAL NOVELS

For a writer, setting novels in the past is seductive. If you write about the present, readers know as much as you do – and judge you by what they know. But if you write about the past, you are often their main source of information. All you have to do is convince. Some writers stun their readers with research, showing every detail of clothes, food, manners and turns of phrase, and keeping strictly to such facts as are known. This kind of 'documentary' historical novel used to be more popular than any other, and there can be few great names or historical events which have not been used: the range is from Caesar's assassination (in Thornton Wilder's *The Ides of March*) to the domestic life of Elizabeth Barrett Browning (in Margaret Forster's *Lady's Maid*), from Columbus's career (in Stephen Marlowe's *The Memoirs of Christopher Columbus*) to Scott's last Polar expedition (in Beryl Bainbridge's *The Birthday Boys*). The second kind of novel puts the 'great' aside, and concentrates on ordinary people's lives. These books are, so to speak, 'true' novels which are given extra depth and colour by their setting in the past, by the way they show recognizable relationships, family life, hopes and fears in a context of historical events. This kind of historical novel, nowadays more popular than the other, ranges from 'literary' books (such as Barry Unsworth's *Sacred Hunger*, set on an 18th-century slave-ship) to crime novels (Ellis Peters's 'Brother Cadfael' series, set in 12th-century Shrewsbury and Lindsey Davies's 'Falco' novels, set in the Roman Empire of Vespasian, for example) and romances and family sagas such as Sheelagh Kelly's series set in the slums of Victorian York.

Carr, Caleb, *The Alienist* (1994). Pioneer psychiatrist (or alienist) teams up with unlikely group of social misfits to track down a serial killer in 1900 New York. Superbly researched and evocative book which combines for the reader the pleasures of historical and crime fiction.

Edric, Robert, *The Book of the Heathen* (2000). Conrad's *Heart of Darkness* revisited in a story set in a remote English trading station in the Belgian Congo where a white man is to be tried for the inexplicable killing of a black child.

▷ **Graves, Robert (1895–1985), *Wife to Mr Milton* (1943).** In Puritan London in the mid-17th century, Mary Powell tells the story of her marriage to the poet and political secretary John Milton. Good on period detail, especially domestic; outstanding on the problems of being married to a morose, irascible genius who regards you not as a fellow human being but as a chattel.

McCullough, Colleen, *The First Man in Rome* (1990). In Republican Rome Marius and Sulla vie for political power in the first of a sequence of novels which bring the ancient world to life with a vividness rarely seen since the work of Mary Renault.

Miller, Andrew, *Ingenious Pain* (1997). In the 18th century James Dyer, a freak of nature who is impervious to pain, embarks on a journey through Europe that will finally introduce him to suffering and humanity.

▷ **Moore, Brian (born 1921), *Black Robe* (1985)**. In the mid-17th century, a Jesuit missionary is captured by North American Indians.

▷ **Renault, Mary (1905–83), *The Mask of Apollo* (1966)**. Niko, a Greek actor of the 4th century BC, is used as a go-between by politicians trying to organize a political coup in Sicily. Complicated private life; fascinating theatre detail (Niko is a true luvvie); aromatic sense of sunny, blood-soaked ancient Greece.

▷ **Roberts, Michèle (born 1949), *The Wild Girl* (1984)**. The events of the Gospels, from a startlingly new point of view: that of Mary Magdalene.

▷ **Rogers, Jane (born 1952), *Mr Wroe's Virgins* (1992)**. Hell-fire preacher and prophet in 1820s Nottingham demands seven virgins to 'serve' him.

Edward Rutherfurd, *London* (1997). Episodic but compelling, this book unfolds the history of England's capital through the lives of ordinary people down the centuries.

▷ **Seth, Vikram (born 1952), *A Suitable Boy* (1993)**. Panoramic story of four families in 1950s India, just after independence from Britain. High hopes; bitter politics; fascinating clash of cultures; tragic, comic family life.

Shaara, Michael (1928–1988) *The Killer Angels* (1974). Pulitzer Prize-winning novel about the Battle of Gettysburg. Brings the reality of American Civil War battlefields home like no fiction since Crane's *The Red Badge of Courage*.

▷ **White, Patrick (1912–90), *A Fringe of Leaves* (1976)**. In the 1840s, an Englishwoman returning home is shipwrecked on the Queensland coast, is rescued by Aborigines – and the resulting culture-clash makes her re-examine her entire life and values.

▷ **Winterson, Jeanette (born 1959), *The Passion* (1987)**. Surreal fantasy spinning off from the story of the peasant boy who became Napoleon's cook.

Richard Zimler, *The Last Kabbalist of Lisbon* (1998). A renowned scholar is murdered during an anti-Jewish pogrom in early 16th-century Lisbon and his nephew devotes himself to finding the killer.

Also recommended: Ivo Andric, *The Bridge Over the Drina*; Thomas Berger, *Little Big Man*; Melvyn Bragg, *Credo*; Anthony Burgess, *The Kingdom of the Wicked*; Angela Carter, *Nights at the Circus*; Douglas Galbraith, *The Rising Sun*; Matthew Kneale, *Sweet Thames*; Ross Leckie, *Hannibal*; Hilary Mantel, *The Giant O'Brien*; Lawrence Norfolk, *Lemprière's Dictionary*; William Watson, *The Last of the Templars*.

See also: Carey, Dunnett, Eco, Farrell, Fowles, Fraser, Keneally, Other Peoples, Other Times, Tolstoy, Unsworth.

novels are about emotional relationships. Often, the relationship is predatory: one partner (spouse, friend, lover or acquaintance) can only survive by engulfing the other, and the process is agonizing and deliberate. The exceptions are *In the Springtime of the Year* (1974), in which a young woman devastated by the death of her husband is rescued from despair by the tranquil daily round of country life, and *Air and Angels* (1992), a moving story of the love in Edwardian times of a lonely, middle-aged bachelor for a 15-year-old girl.

☆ I'M THE KING OF THE CASTLE (1970)

Mr Hooper, a lonely widower, invites Mrs Kingshaw to be housekeeper of his large old mansion. He hopes that his ten-year-old son and her son will become friends. But the boy Hooper resents young Kingshaw's invasion of his psychological territory, and torments him. The psychopathic child, possessed by the devil, was a familiar figure in 1970s fiction (and in films made from it, such as the 'Omen' series); Hill turns the same subject into art.

Hill's other novels include Strange Meeting, The Bird of Night *and* The Service of the Clouds. The Albatross *is a novella and* A Bit of Singing and Dancing *contains short stories.* The Magic Apple Tree *and* Family *are autobiographical. She has also written radio plays and many children's books.*

> **READ ON**

- **The Bird of Night** (about a manic-depressive artist and the friend who tries to help him).
- ▶ to *I'm the King of the Castle*: ▷ Henry James, *The Turn of the Screw*; ▷ John Wyndham, *Chocky*; ▷ William Golding, *Lord of the Flies*.
- ▶ to *In the Springtime of the Year*: ▷ Penelope Lively, *Perfect Happiness*.
- ▶ to *Air and Angels*: ▷ Penelope Fitzgerald, *The Gate of Angels*.

READ ON A THEME: HISTORICAL ADVENTURE

Peter Carter, *The Black Lamp*
▷ Bernard Cornwell, *Sharpe's Regiment*
▷ C.S. Forester, *Mr Midshipman Hornblower*
Bjorn Larsson, *Long John Silver*
▷ George Macdonald Fraser, *Flashman*
▷ Homer, *Odyssey*
Derek Robinson, *Goshawk Squadron*
▷ R.L. Stevenson, *Kidnapped*

See also: Action Thrillers; High Adventure; Spies and Double Agents

HOBAN, Russell (born 1925)
US/British novelist

Hoban first made his name with children's books and with *Turtle Diary* (1976), a novel about two lonely people drawn together by their ambition to return the turtles from the London Zoo to the sea. In the quarter of a century since *Turtle Diary*, Hoban has published a number of idiosyncratic and highly imaginative novels. Each one is different from Hoban's other works and all of them are largely unlike anything else being published in English. *Pilgermann* is told by a narrator who is, literally, a ghost writer, a phantasm of waves and particles, which remembers its time on earth – the 11th century – but can also range in time through the centuries to the present day. In *Angelica's Grotto* an ageing art historian, trying to deal with the mutinies of his mind and body, finds himself drawn into new sexual territory by a pornographic website.

RIDDLEY WALKER (1980)
This is a future-fantasy, set in England generations after the nuclear holocaust. The society is primitive – making fire is still a problem, never mind organizing the rule of law – and the survivors are haunted by memories of the time before the bomb. Rags of old culture, technology and morality flap in their minds, as inexplicable and as powerful as myth. Their language, similarly – the one the book is written in – is shredded, reconstituted English: words coalesce, grammar has collapsed, new metaphors sprout like weeds. Although this style is difficult at first, it becomes perfectly comprehensible after a few pages, and before long the broken, patched-together words begin to seem like poetry, as Riddley, the story-teller, struggles to find ways to describe the pictures inside his mind.

READ ON ▷

- ● *The Lion of Boaz-Jachin and Jachin-Boaz, The Medusa Frequency, Amaryllis Night and Day.*
- ▶ to *Riddley Walker*: Walter Miller Jr., *A Canticle for Leibowitz*; ▷ Anthony Burgess, *A Clockwork Orange.*
- ▶ to the imaginative realms of Hoban's fiction in general: ▷ William Golding, *Pincher Martin*; ▷ Italo Calvino, *Invisible Cities.*

HØEG, Peter (born 1957)
Danish novelist

The author biography on the English editions of Peter Høeg's books proclaims a more adventurous life than most desk-bound writers can claim. He has been, at different times, a dancer, an actor, a fencer, a sailor and a mountaineer. His fiction has shown a similar variety, an unwillingness to be pinned down by the restrictions of genre and the conventional pigeon-holes into which novelists are so regularly placed. *Miss Smilla's Feeling for Snow* (see below) is a thriller of great intelligence and depth. *Borderliners* is the story of three emotionally troubled children, trapped inside the Danish care system, who attempt to escape an experimental school and its oppressive, time-regulated regime. Mixing realism and allegory, it manages to be both a moving and compelling story and an exploration of the cramping ways in which Time holds us all. *The Woman and The Ape* also takes the reader into the realms of fable and allegory but the story could hardly be more different, telling as it does of the unlikely but liberating love affair between the dipsomaniac wife of a zoologist and an ape, significantly more intelligent than the human characters, called Erasmus.

MISS SMILLA'S FEELING FOR SNOW (1993)

A small boy has apparently fallen to his death from an apartment block in a snowbound Copenhagen. The police are satisfied it is an accident but the boy's neighbour is Smilla Jesperson, half-Danish, half-Inuit, who has an uncanny ability to read the stories that tracks in the snow can tell. And the story the boy's tracks tell suggests murder. In pursuit of the truth about the death, Smilla is led into realms of corruption, double-dealing and death, and she is forced to board a ship heading into dark waters off the coast of her native Greenland. *Miss Smilla's Feeling for Snow* is an exceptional book. It is a thriller of great pace and invention with all the precise interest in technical detail, the way things work, the mechanics of machinery that can be found in, say, ▷ Frederick Forsyth. It has a central character of remarkable originality. Smilla, self-sufficient and resourceful, a high-flying academic from an unusual family background who has become a sharp-tongued acerbic misfit in Copenhagen, is an unforgettable heroine.

Peter Høeg has also written The History of Danish Dreams *and a collection of stories* Tales of the Night, *which all take place, in different parts of the world, on the same night in 1929.*

> READ ON

● *The Woman and the Ape.*
▶ Kirstin Ekman, *Blackwater*; ▷ David Guterson, *Snow Falling on Cedars.*

HOLLINGHURST, Alan (born 1954)
British writer

Hollinghurst, who worked for many years on the *Times Literary Supplement*, gained immediate acclaim as a novelist with the publication in 1988 of *The Swimming-Pool Library*. Centred on the relationship between a rich, cultured and promiscuous aristo and an ageing gay roué, it was an unembarrassedly open and very funny exploration of gay life, sex and love in pre-AIDS Britain. Hollinghurst's most recent novel *The Spell* tells the story, half-farcical, half-sad, of the entangled sex lives of four very different men.

THE FOLDING STAR (1994)

Edward, ill-at-ease with himself, his life and his age (a prematurely middle-aged 33) goes to teach English in an unnamed Belgian city, and falls in love with one of his pupils. Unable to declare his feelings or have them returned, he drifts in a kind of psychic no-man's-land, a fog of unsatisfactory relationships, one-night stands and desperate attempts to find and make some step which will end his confusion and define his life. At the same time, he is drawn into the world of a painter from the first half of the 20th century, whose obsessive love for a young model seems to have mirrored Edward's feelings for his pupil and whose paintings echo the psychic swirl inside Edward's own head. A death occurs, and Edward goes briefly home to England – and to memories of an earlier, unsatisfying, love affair – before the novel moves to its bleak conclusion. *The Folding Star* makes bilious comedy out of the narrator's obsessions and his attempts to immerse himself in the Flemish gay scene. But long after you finish the book, Edward's predicament stays in the mind – and it is not homosexuality, not sexuality, but the emptiness created and endlessly renewed by the need for love.

READ ON

- ● *The Swimming-Pool Library*.
- ▶ Edmund White, *A Boy's Own Story*; Neil Bartlett, *Mr. Clive and Mr. Page*; David Leavitt, *While England Sleeps*.

HOMER (*c* 9th century BC)
Greek epic poet

Although Homer's ★☆ *Odyssey* was composed to be declaimed, section by section, at royal feasts, the depths of its character-drawing and its psychological perception transcend such fragmented performances: in a good prose translation (such as E.V. Rieu's), it is as complex and fascinating as any modern novel. Its plot, taken from Greek myth, recounts Odysseus's supernatural adventures on his way home from the Trojan War and his epic battle with the suitors who have plagued his wife Penelope during his absence. But it is also the story of Odysseus' own development, of the way his experiences mould and mature his personality. Each of his encounters – with the flesh-eating giant Polyphemus, the Lotus-eaters, the Sirens, the seductress Calypso, Circe, Nausicaa – changes him, teaches him more about himself, until he is ready to prove himself to his enemies, his people and his patient wife. The *Iliad*, similarly, uses the framework of myth (the quarrel between Achilles and Hector during the Trojan War) to discuss such themes as ambition, pride, courage, the place of destiny in human lives and the glory and futility of war.

READ ON

- ▶ ▷ Robert Graves, *Homer's Daughter* (a fantasy about the events leading up to the composition of the *Odyssey*); ▷ Mary Renault, *The King Must Die*; Henry Treece, *Electra*.
- ▶ Books using Homeric style or themes: Virgil, *Aeneid*; Petronius, *Satyricon* (a parody of the *Odyssey* set among the prostitutes, hermaphrodites, fake prophets and pimps of a fantasy ancient Rome); Miguel de Cervantes, *Don Quixote*; ▷ Leo Tolstoy, *War and Peace*. The themes and structure of the *Odyssey* inspired ▷ James Joyce, *Ulysses*.

HOPE, Anthony (1863–1933)
British novelist

In *The Prisoner of Zenda* (1894) Hope invented the 'Ruritanian' adventure-story, a colourful escapist yarn set in some fantasy foreign kingdom. Rudolf Rassendyl, an upper-class Englishman on holiday in the middle European country of Ruritania, is astonished to find that he is an exact double of the king, and even more surprised when the king is kidnapped just before his coronation, and Rassendyl is asked to impersonate him. As the story proceeds, the kidnappers (the king's ambitious brother and his henchman Rupert of Hentzau, the finest swordsman in Ruritania) try to foil the coronation-plans, and Rassendyl (who has meanwhile fallen in love with Flavia, the future queen) breaks into Zenda Castle to rescue the imprisoned king. The novel has been filmed a dozen times, and has inspired one of the cinema's favourite clichés: two men, one debonair, one saturnine, duelling up and down the steps of an ancient castle, slicing candles in half, parrying thrusts with three-legged stools and matching each rapier-thrust with a dazzling shaft of wit.

READ ON

● *Rupert of Hentzau* (the sequel)
▶ John Spurling, *After Zenda* (sequel); Rafael Sabatini, *Captain Blood*; ▷ A. Conan Doyle, *The White Company*; ▷ George MacDonald Fraser, *Royal Flash* (arch-cad Flashman finds himself in uncannily similar situation to Rudolf Rassendyll); P.C. Wren, *Beau Geste*.

HORNBY, Nick (born 1957)
British writer

No one in the last twenty years has been as successful as Nick Hornby at portraying the emotional confusions and immaturities of a certain kind of white middle-class male. His more severe critics may complain that Hornby restricts himself to a narrow field that he has, by now, fairly thoroughly ploughed but his wit and insight into masculine failings and self-doubt are undeniable. Hornby's first book, *Fever Pitch* (1992), an autobiographical account of his obsession with football in general, and Arsenal FC in particular, was a bestseller. It allowed a whole generation of white-collar football fans to emerge from the closet in which they had been hiding and proclaim from the rooftops their love of the beautiful game. His first two novels cover similar territory and do so in the same relaxed, easy and (often) very funny prose that marked *Fever Pitch*. *High Fidelity* (1995) has as its central character a thirtysomething record-store owner whose emotional life is a mess. Shying away from commitment, he hides his feelings behind relentless list-making ('my desert-island, all-time, top five most memorable split-ups in chronological order') and a superbly-organized record collection. The book is an engaging chronicle of his slow, unwilling progression to something halfway resembling adult emotions. *About a Boy* (1998) records the life of Will Lightman, clinging to cool in North London and living off royalties from a jingle his father wrote decades earlier. Pretending to single fatherhood as a means of ingratiating himself with desirable single mothers, Will meets Fiona and, more importantly, her son Marcus. The terminally unhip Marcus latches on to Will who finds himself, at first very unwillingly, cast in the role of father figure that he has been play-acting. Two boys together (one 12, the other 36), Marcus and Will begin to learn about emotional competence.

READ ON

● *How to Be Good* (in his third novel Hornby takes the ambitious step of choosing to narrate the story in a woman's voice).
▶ Tony Parsons, *Man and Boy*; Tim Lott, *White City Blue*; William Sutcliffe, *The Love Hexagon* (twentysomethings having much the same relationship problems as Hornby's thirtysomethings).

HOWATCH, Susan (born 1940)
British novelist

Susan Howatch's earlier novels, all huge bestsellers, were family sagas, filled with dramas and romances and stretching across generations. *Penmarric* (1971) followed the fortunes of a Cornish family from the 19th century through to the Second World War. Since the late 1980s her novels have been largely stories of spiritual upheaval and emotional crises amongst Church of England clergy, often set in the fictional West Country town or Starbridge. This might seem unpromising material for enjoyable fiction but Howatch's gift for memorable characterization and her genuine interest in the religious temperament, demonstrated when she endowed a chair in theology at Cambridge University, combine to produce books as gripping as her earlier work. *Glittering Images* (1987), in which scandal and corruption bubble beneath respectable surfaces, is a good example of her ecclesiastical fiction.

READ ON

- *Glamorous Powers*, *Ultimate Risks* (further volumes in the Church of England series).
- ▶ to the Penmarric novels: Winston Graham's Poldark novels.
- ▶ to the ecclesiastical fiction: ▷ Anthony Trollope, *The Warden* (the Church of England in a previous century); ▷ Joanna Trollope, *The Rector's Wife*.

HUGO, Victor (1802–85)
French novelist, poet and playwright

Although Hugo was principally a poet and dramatist, he is also remembered for his panoramic historical novels. *Nôtre Dame de Paris* (1831), set in medieval times, is about the beautiful foundling Esmeralda, the men who try to seduce her, and the deformed Quasimodo, bell-ringer at Nôtre Dame cathedral, who loves her. The book's detail of Parisian low-life is matched in *Les misérables* (1862) about a noble-hearted convict and the corrupt policeman who persecutes him. Hugo's novels are long and prone to philosophizing, but they make up for it by the energy of their plots, the melodramatic attraction of their characters – not for nothing is the Hunchback of Nôtre Dame a Hollywood favourite – and the extraordinary feeling they give that every event, every story, is just one glimpse of the teeming anthill of human life.

READ ON

- ▶ to *Nôtre Dame de Paris*: ▷ Alessandro Manzoni, *The Betrothed* (*I promessi sposi*).
- ▶ to *Les misérables*: Heinrich Mann, *The Blue Angel/Small Town Tyrant*.
- ▶ to *The Toilers of the Sea*: ▷ Charles Dickens, *Hard Times*.
- ▶ to *Ninety-three*: ▷ Alexandr Solzhenitsyn, *August, 1914*.
- ▶ to the more swaggering elements of Hugo's style: Lew Wallace, *Ben Hur*; ▷ Alexandre Dumas, *The Man in the Iron Mask*; Mika Waltari, *Sinuhe the Egyptian*.

READ ON A THEME: THE HUMAN COMEDY

▷ Jane Austen, *Pride and Prejudice*
▷ John Cheever, *The Wapshot Chronicle*

▷ David Lodge, *The British Museum is Falling Down*
▷ Alison Lurie, *Real People*
  Armistead Maupin, *Tales of the City*
▷ Barbara Pym, *A Glass of Blessings*
▷ William Thackeray, *Vanity Fair*
▷ Barbara Trapido, *Brother of the More Famous Jack*
▷ Anne Tyler, *The Accidental Tourist*
▷ H.G. Wells, *Tono-Bungay*

See also: Dreaming Spires; Friends (?) and Neighbours; Groves of Academe; Higher (?) Education

---

HUXLEY, Aldous (1894–1963)
British novelist and non-fiction writer

Huxley's early books were glittering satires on 1920s intellectual and upper-class life, accounts of preposterous conversations at country-house costume parties and in such unlikely meeting-places as publishers' offices or the Egyptian Room at the British Museum. His characters are intelligent, creative, fascinating and empty; haunted by the pointlessness of existence, they pass their time flirting, gossiping, swapping philosophical ideas and planning trivial alarms and excursions. In the 1930s, beginning with *Brave New World*, he changed his approach. Instead of focusing his satire on a single section of British society, he turned on the human race at large and wrote a series of increasingly bitter books demolishing all our ambitions to make a better society by science, philosophy, religion, socialism or (in the late 1950s, at the germination-stage of flower-power) hallucinatory drugs. His books are a witty, cold dazzle of ideas; enjoyable as you read them, they leave an acid aftertaste.

BRAVE NEW WORLD (1932)
In a soulless future world, genetic engineering programmes people from birth for their status in society, and removes all aggressive or unproductive instincts. Individuality, creativity and personality are sacrificed in the causes of material prosperity, good health and freedom from anxiety. Only a small group of 'savages' – people like us – survives, in a community in New Mexico, and one of them escapes and is brought into the 'real world', with tragic results. As in all his novels, Huxley tells this tale soberly and without comment: the flatness of his prose brilliantly intensifies the horror of what he is saying. Nothing truly terrible happens – and that is the most terrifying thing of all.

In chronological order, Huxley's novels are Crome Yellow, Antic Hay, Those Barren Leaves, Point Counter Point, Brave New World, Eyeless in Gaza, After Many a Summer, Time Must Have a Stop, Ape and Essence, The Genius and the Goddess *and* Island. Limbo, Mortal Coils, The Little Mexican, Two or Three Graces *and* Brief Candles *are collections of short stories.*

> READ ON

● *Ape and Essence* (about a California-dwelling group of survivors from the nuclear holocaust, primitives visited by a horror-struck scientist from New Zealand).

▶ to Huxley's social satires: ▷ F. Scott Fitzgerald, *The Beautiful and Damned* (from the 1920s); ▷ Anthony Powell, *Venusberg* (from the 1930s); ▷ Martin Amis, *Money* (from the 1980s).

▶ to *Ape and Essence*: ▷ Paul Theroux, *O-Zone*.

▶ to Huxley's later books: Frederick Pohl and C.M. Kornbluth, *The Space Merchants*; ▷ L.P. Hartley, *Facial Justice*; Michael Frayn, *Sweet Dreams*.

I

READ ON A THEME: INDIA

▷ **J.G. Farrell,** *The Siege of Krishnapur*
▷ **E.M. Forster,** *A Passage to India*
▷ **Ruth Prawer Jhabvala,** *Heat and Dust*
▷ **Rudyard Kipling,** *Kim*
   Rohinton Mistry, *A Fine Balance*
▷ **R.K. Narayan,** *The Vendor of Sweets*
   Arundhati Roy, *The God of Small Things*
▷ **Salman Rushdie,** *Midnight's Children*
▷ **Vikram Seth,** *A Suitable Boy*

INNES, Hammond (1913–98)
British novelist

Innes wrote tough action thrillers, often with a background of the services, mining, oil drilling or seafaring. One of his major interests, reflected in many books, is the balance between human beings and the natural environment. His books include *Wreckers Must Breathe/Trapped*, *The Blue Ice*, *Maddon's Rock/ Gale Warning*, *Campbell's Kingdom*, *The Mary Deare/The Wreck of the Mary Deare*, *Atlantic Fury*, *Solomon's Seal* and *Medusa* (1989). Innes also wrote thrillers under the name 'Ralph Hammond' (*Isle of Strangers/Island of Peril*; *Saracen's Gold/Cruise of Danger*).

>>> READ ON

● *Levkas Man.*
▶ ▷ **Alistair Maclean,** *When Eight Bells Toll.*

INNES, Michael (1906–95)
British novelist

'Michael Innes' was the pseudonym of J.I.M. Stewart, a leading writer from the Golden Age of English detective fiction. His novels set bizarre puzzles in the unhurried world of Oxford colleges, English country houses and fine-art auction rooms in the 1930s–1950s. Exquisitely educated people cheat, lie and kill without ruffling a hair and with a well-turned quotation always on their lips. The books are snobbish, urbane and thrilling; good sample titles are *Death at the President's Lodging*, *Hamlet, Revenge!*, *The Journeying Boy*, *Operation Pax/*

Paper Thunderbolt and *The Daffodil Affair*. Under his real name, J.I.M. Stewart also wrote novels about mistaken identity, bizarre legacies and genteel love-affairs: typical is the 'Oxford quintet' *The Gaudy, Young Patullo, A Memorial Service, The Madonna of the Astrolabe* and *Full Term*.

> READ ON >

▶ to the detective stories: Edmund Crispin, *The Moving Toyshop;* Gladys Mitchell, *Laurels are Poison*; Michael Gilbert, *Smallbone Deceased.*
▶ to Stewart's novels: ▷ C.P Snow, *The Masters;* ▷ Anthony Powell, *What's Become of Waring?*

READ ON A THEME: IRELAND

▷ Maeve Binchy, *Echoes*
▷ Roddy Doyle, *The Van*
▷ J.G. Farrell, *Troubles*
  Dermot Healy, *A Goat's Song*
▷ James Joyce, *Portrait of the Artist as a Young Man*
  Molly Keane, *Good Behaviour*
  John McGahern, *Amongst Women*
  Patrick McGinley, *The Trick of the Ga Bolga*
▷ Edna O'Brien, *The Country Girls*
  Flann O'Brien, *At Swim-Two-Birds*
  James Plunkett, *Strumpet City*
  E. Somerville and Martin Ross, *The Irish RM*
▷ Colm Tóibín, *The Blackwater Lightship*
▷ William Trevor, *Mrs Eckdorff in O'Neill's Hotel*

IRVING, John (born 1942)
US novelist

Irving's novels are surreal black comedies, except that nothing that happens in them is unbelievable. His tales may lose nothing in the telling, but they are always plausible. The hero of *The World According to Garp* (1978) is a writer whose terror of death leads him to imagine appalling catastrophes for his loved ones – only to have even more, unimagined horrors actually occur. The family in *The Hotel New Hampshire* (1986) turns a derelict girls' school into a hotel (complete with dancing bear), and later, when business falls off, moves to Austria where the hotels are smaller, the bears are cleverer, and terrorists are threatening to take over the Vienna Opera. In his most recent novel, *The Fourth Hand* (2001) a philandering journalist has his hand eaten by a lion live on TV and falls in love with the widow of the man whose hand is used by surgeons to replace his own. Irving, in his deadpan way, constantly implies – and who can deny it? – that there is nothing eccentric here, that he is recording the bizarreness of life itself.

☆ THE CIDER HOUSE RULES (1985)
Homer Wells, brought up in a rural Maine orphanage and abortion clinic run by the saintly ether-addict Dr Larch, struggles against his destiny, which is to become a

gynaecologist and take his mentor's place. He runs away, becomes the manager of a cider farm, falls in love with his best friend's wife and lives a life of confused obscurity – but he constantly feels the pull back to the clinic and to Melony, a homicidal feminist who hero-worships him and is waiting her chance to murder him.

Irving's other novels include The Water-Method Man *and* The 158–Pound Marriage.

READ ON ⊳

- *A Prayer for Owen Meany* (about the friendship of two boys, one of whom (Owen Meany) is a charming freak gifted with second sight and the ability to transform other people's lives). *A Son of the Circus*, dedicated 'to Salman', marries Irving's usual preoccupations to a Rushdiesque Indian setting, with results which bewilder some readers and make others claim it as his finest book so far.
- ▶ to *The Cider House Rules*: ▷ Robertson Davies, *What's Bred in the Bone*.
- ▶ to Irving's work in general: ▷ Salman Rushdie, *Midnight's Children*; ▷ Thomas Pynchon, *The Crying of Lot 49*; ▷ Don DeLillo, *White Noise*.

ISHERWOOD, Christopher (1904–86)
British/US writer of novels, screenplays and non-fiction

Isherwood was one of the Thirties generation of writers of which the most conspicuous member was W.H. Auden. In 1939, in company with Auden, he moved to the US and eventually settled in California where he worked as a teacher and Hollywood screenwriter. In the 1940s he became a follower of the Hindu mystic Swami Prabhavananda and several of his non-fiction works are on the subject of the Vedanta. His novels and stories are all based on personal experience. The best known (*Mr Norris Changes Trains/The Last of Mr Norris*, 1935; *Goodbye to Berlin,* 1939; *The Berlin Stories*, 1946) are set in 1930s Berlin, a seedy, decadent city haunted by the German defeat in the First World War and by the gathering power of Nazism. They are first-person stories, told by a naive young language teacher amused, perplexed and vaguely terrified by the human tragi-comedy he reports. They have been filmed, made into a stage-play (*I Am a Camera*) and a hit musical (*Cabaret*).

READ ON ⊳

- *All the Conspirators, The Memorial*.
- ▶ to the Berlin novels: Klaus Mann, *Mephisto*; Alexander Döblin, *Berlin Alexanderplatz*.

ISHIGURO, Kazuo (born 1954)
Japanese/British novelist

Ishiguro was educated in England and writes in English. His first two books are gentle, poetic studies of the effects on present-day Japanese of earlier 20th-century events. The central character of *A Pale View of Hills* (1982), a middle-aged woman living in England is driven by her daughter's suicide to a prolonged reverie about her own childhood in Nagasaki, and her attempt to rebuild her life and her emotional relationships after the city's atomic destruction in 1945. Oni, the elderly protagonist of *An Artist of the Floating World* (1986), was a prominent propagandist for Japanese militarism in the 1930s; now, in his own 60s, he has to come to terms with the collapse of his professional life, his ostracism by younger colleagues, and the way his own children's moral values, typical of the new Japan, seem to deny everything he ever believed in or affirmed. More recently Ishiguro's fiction has become more expansive, although it has remained no less ambiguous and enigmatic. *The Unconsoled* (1995) is a long, Kafkaesque account of the psychological disintegration of a famous concert pianist. *When We Were Orphans* (2000) tells the story of a famous detective from the 1930s who returns to Shanghai, where he grew up, in order to try and solve the mysteries surrounding his own parents. Playing cleverly with the conventions of mystery fiction, Ishiguro creates a book that is both a richly rewarding narrative and a subtle study of the way we all re-make our pasts.

THE REMAINS OF THE DAY (1989)

Ishiguro's Booker-prize winning novel is a powerful study of emotional desiccation. Told in the first person by the humourless and pernickety English butler Stevens, it cleverly reveals the self-deceptions and moral cowardice of its narrator. Looking back on a life which has been busily self-important (his master was at the centre of dubious pro-appeasement negotiations in the late 1930s) Stevens cannot acknowledge that he has denied himself true human contact and the opportunity for emotional growth. His inability to deal with his attraction to the housekeeper Miss Kenton is only the most obvious example of personal failures which, somewhere beneath the cold formality of his prose, Stevens himself sadly, and movingly, half-recognizes.

$\boxed{\text{READ ON}}$ $>$

▶ ▷ R.K. Narayan, *The English Teacher/Grateful to Life and Death*. ▷ Graham Greene, *The Quiet American*; ▷ Ian McEwan, *Black Dogs*.

READ ON A THEME: ISRAEL

Lynne Reid Banks, *Children at the Gate*
Lionel Davidson, *A Long Way to Shiloh*
Linda Grant, *When I Lived in Modern Times*
David Grossman, *The Yellow Wind*
▷ John Le Carré, *The Little Drummer Girl*
Amos Oz, *Black Box*
Leon Uris, *Exodus*

J

JAMES, Henry (1843–1916)
US/British novelist and short story writer

As well as novels, James wrote plays, essays, travel books, literary criticism and a dozen volumes of short stories. In his fiction he returned again and again to the same theme: the conflict between decadence and innocence. James identified decadence with the 'old culture' of Europe, and innocence with the late 19th-century US; his books often depict visitors from one continent experiencing and coming to terms with the other. Because he was not religious – he was brought up as a rationalist – the moral struggle of his plots is usually less between overt 'good' and 'evil' than between different standards and manners, and he also liked to tease out every strand of meaning in a situation, to explain and theorize about his characters' motives and the possible outcome of each choice they make. Untangling this, especially in his last three, most intricately stylized novels (*The Wings of the Dove, The Ambassadors* and *The Golden Bowl*), is one of the chief pleasures of his work.

★ THE WINGS OF THE DOVE (1902)
Kate Croy lives with her snobbish aunt, who plans to make a 'great' marriage for her. But Kate is secretly engaged to a penniless journalist, Merton Densher. Millie Theale, a young, rich American, visits Kate's aunt to be introduced to London society, and becomes Kate's friend. Millie is frail, and it is soon apparent that she is dying. She goes to Venice, where she welcomes all her friends in a decaying palazzo on the Grand Canal. Kate persuades Merton to try and comfort Millie's last months by pretending that he loves her. Kate hopes that Millie will then leave money to Merton which will enable them to marry. So everyone will be happy. But another of Millie's suitors, the unprincipled Lord Mark, tells Millie of Merton's and Kate's secret engagement – a revelation which brings tragedy to all three principal characters.

James's other novels include Daisy Miller, Portrait of a Lady, Washington Square, The Bostonians, The Spoils of Poynton *and* The Tragic Muse. *Of his 100 short stories and novellas, the best known are* The Turn of the Screw *(about two children haunted by a sinister dead couple),* The Real Thing *and* The Lesson of the Master.

> READ ON

- *Portrait of a Lady* (about the moral and social consequences of a young American's decision to settle in England and Italy); *The Ambassadors* (a long, ironical novel about how Europe changes a group of Americans, young and middle-aged, rich and poor, friends and strangers).

▶ ▷ Marcel Proust, *Swann's Way* (Part One of *Remembrance of Things Past*); ▷ E.M. Forster, *A Room with a View*; ▷ Edith Wharton, *The Reef*; ▷ Muriel Spark, *The Mandelbaum Gate*; ▷ Stendhal, *Scarlet and Black*; ▷ Elizabeth Bowen, *Eva Trout*.

JAMES, P.D. (Phyllis Dorothy) (born 1920)
British novelist

Although James is often described as the 'Queen of Crime', ▷ Agatha Christie's heir, she is more like a cross between ▷ Sayers and ▷ Highsmith. The crimes in her books are brutal, are committed by deranged, psychopathic people, and are described in chilling, unblinking prose, as objective as a forensic report. Her principal detective, Adam Dalgliesh, is a poet and aesthete, combining brilliant detective instincts with a liberal conscience and a dandyish distaste for what he does. Although the books at first seem long and leisurely, James racks tension inexorably tighter until her dénouement: not a cosy Christieish explanation round the library fire, but a scene of pathological, cathartic violence.

A TASTE FOR DEATH (1986)
A lonely spinster, taking flowers to decorate her local church, finds the throat-cut corpses of a tramp, Harry Mack, and a prominent Tory MP, Sir Paul Berowne. Berowne has been the subject of recent slanderous accusations, and Dalgliesh's investigation must begin by deciding whether he was murdered or committed suicide after killing Mack. The story gradually sucks in various members of Berowne's large and mutually hostile family, his servants and his mistress – and as well as showing us this, and describing the police work in exact, unhurried detail, the book also concerns itself with the lives and preoccupations of Dalgliesh's assistants, especially Inspector Kate Miskin, the newest member of the team.

James's other novels are Cover Her Face, A Mind to Murder, Death of an Expert Witness, Unnatural Causes, Shroud for a Nightingale, An Unsuitable Job for a Woman *(which introduces James's female private investigator, Cordelia Gray),* The Black Tower, Innocent Blood, The Skull Beneath the Skin, Original Sin, Devices and Desires, A Certain Justice *and* Death in Holy Orders. Children of Men *is set in England in 2021, when there are no children and there is therefore no future.* Time to Be in Earnest *is a memoir.*

> **READ ON**

▶ ▷ Ngaio Marsh, *Surfeit of Lampreys*; ▷ Margery Allingham, *The Tiger in the Smoke*; ▷ Ruth Rendell, *A Sleeping Life*; ▷ Colin Dexter, *The Way Through the Woods*.

READ ON A THEME: JAPAN

Alan Brown, *Audrey Hepburn's Neck*
James Clavell, *Shogun*
Shusako Endo, *Silence*
Arthur Golden, *Memoirs of a Geisha*
▷ Kazuo Ishiguro, *An Artist of the Floating World*

Yukio Mishima, *Confessions of a Mask*
Haruki Murakami, *The Wind-Up Bird Chronicle*
Murasaki Shikibu, *The Tale of Genji*

JEROME, Jerome K. (Klapka) (1859–1927)
British novelist and journalist

Jerome, an actor, wrote humorous pieces while waiting to go on stage; after the success of ★☆ *Three Men in a Boat* in 1889 he became a full-time writer. *Three Men in a Boat* is the story of a boating holiday on the Thames undertaken by three London clerks (to say nothing of the dog). The book's deadpan humour – what Jerome calls its 'hopeless and incurable veracity' – depends on magnifying life's small problems (such as opening a tin without a tin-opener, or being in the same house as a courting couple without embarrassing them) to epic proportions, and on losing no opportunity for reflections on life, liberty, the pursuit of happiness, and the heroes' invincible conviction that middle-class Victorian young Britons, such as themselves, are the goal to which all human evolution has been progressing.

> READ ON

● *Three Men on the Bummel*; *My Life and Times* (autobiography).
▶ George and Weedon Grossmith, *The Diary of a Nobody*; ▷ Max Beerbohm, *Zuleika Dobson*; W.E. Bowman, *The Ascent of Rum Doodle*; H.F. Ellis, *The Papers of A.J. Wentworth, BA*.

JHABVALA, Ruth Prawer (born 1927)
British novelist and screenwriter

In a series of placid, gently ironical novels and screenplays (beginning with *Shakespeare Wallah* (1965) for the Merchant-Ivory partnership), Jhabvala has become a main European chronicler of India since the Raj. She is less interested in public events than in emotions, and particularly in the interface between two mutually uncomprehending cultures, Indian and European. In her best-known book, *Heat and Dust* (1975, filmed 1983), a young Englishwoman visits modern India to find out about her aunt's unhappy love affair there 60 years before. The story cuts between the two periods, contrasting the modern character's apparently sophisticated racial and cultural awareness with the aunt's naivety and immaturity, and making points about attitudes (of Indians towards the English and vice versa) both during the Raj and in our own day.

Jhabvala's novels include Esmond in India, The Householder, Get Ready for Battle, A Backward Glance, Three Continents, Shards of Memory, Poet and Dancer *(set in New York) and* In Search of Love and Beauty *(set in the US, and influenced by her experience scripting* ▷Henry James's The Europeans *for Merchant-Ivory).* Like Birds Like Fishes, A Stronger Climate, An Experience of India, Out of India, How I Became a Holy Mother *and* East into Upper East *are collections of short stories.*

READ ON >

● *Esmond in India*.

▶ ▷ E.M. Forster, *A Passage to India*; Paul Scott, *Staying On*; Rabindranath Tagore, *The Home and the World*; Anita Desai, *Games at Twilight* (short stories).

JONG, Erica (born 1942)
US novelist and poet

Jong is chiefly famous for four rollercoaster novels satirizing the 1970s–1990s obsession with sex. The first three novels are the autobiography of Isadora Wing. In *Fear of Flying* (1974), having abandoned her husband for a lover, she spends her time cock-hunting. The Holy Grail, she tells us, is the 'zipless fuck', sex without commitment – and she searches for it in locker-rooms, on trains and planes, on beaches, in hotel rooms and wherever else multiple orgasms beckon. At the end of the book, disillusioned, she returns to her husband. *How To Save Your Own Life* (1978), *Parachutes and Kisses* (1984) and *Any Woman's Blues* (1990; Isadora's own novel framed by commentary from a feminist critic) are the three follow-up novels. The novels sold on explicit sex, outspoken in its day. Now that the excitement of that is wearing off, their wit and sharp critique of First World obsession with 'lifestyle' (as opposed to life) are what catch the mind.

Serenissima is a fantasy about a woman transported back in time to 16th-century Venice, where she has an affair with an English playwright and poet who later immortalizes her as the 'Dark Lady'. Inventing Memory tells a multi-generational story of mothers and daughters searching for identity in a male-dominated world. Fear of Fifty is a funny, acerbic 'midlife' memoir.

READ ON >

▶ Lisa Alther, *Kinflicks*; Marilyn French, *The Women's Room*; ▷ Margaret Atwood, *Wilderness Tips* (not so sexy, but just as scathing).

READ ON A THEME: JOURNALISM

   Colin Bateman, *Divorcing Jack*
▷ Heinrich Böll, *The Lost Honour of Katharina Blum*
   Michael Frayn, *Towards the End of the Morning*
   George Gissing, *New Grub Street*
▷ Jay McInerney, *Model Behaviour*
▷ William Thackeray, *Pendennis*
▷ Evelyn Waugh, *Scoop*

JOYCE, James (1882–1941)
Irish novelist and short story writer

Although Joyce exiled himself from his native land as a young man, he never left the Ireland of his memory: his work is a ceaseless exploration of Irish scenery, education, history, religion, habits of thought and patterns of daily life. His early writings – the short stories in *Dubliners* (1914) and the novel ★☆*A Portrait of the Artist as a Young Man* (1915), based on his own school and university life – are stylistically straightforward. They are also notable for precise evocation of sensation and atmosphere. By giving a mosaic of tiny impressions (the feel of wooden desks in a schoolroom, the taste of mud on a rugby field, the smell of gas lamps in student digs) Joyce builds up a detailed picture which is both factually and emotionally compelling. (▷Proust used a similar idea in the childhood sections of *Remembrance of Things Past.*) In his two long novels, *Ulysses* (1922) and *Finnegans Wake* (1939), Joyce developed this mosaic structure further: *Ulysses* relates the events of a single day, *Finnegans Wake* a man's thoughts and dreams during a single night. Parts of these books are stream-of-consciousness monologues, a tumble of apparently unrelated sentences threading a path through the maze of one person's mind. Joyce often seems to be collapsing language itself: syntax splits apart; words blur into one another; each page is a kaleidoscope of puns, parodies, half-quotations, snatches of song and snippets from half a dozen languages. Some people find this style unreadable; for others it is endlessly rewarding, a mesmeric impression of the jumble of thought itself.

★ ULYSSES (1922)

The book follows two people, Leopold Bloom and Stephen Dedalus, from dawn to midnight on a single day in Dublin in 1904. At one level what they do is ordinary: they shave, go to the privy, eat, drink, argue in bars, go to a funeral, borrow money, flirt with girls on a beach, visit Dublin's red-light area. But Joyce also shows us their thoughts, the fragmentary responses and impressions evoked by each real incident. The book ends with a 60–page 'interior monologue', the inconsequential, erotic reverie of Bloom's wife Molly as she lies beside him, drifting into sleep.

Joyce's works are Dubliners; Portrait of the Artist as a Young Man *(based on an earlier, unfinished novel,* Stephen Hero, *which has also been published);* Ulysses; Finnegans Wake; Chamber Music *and* Pomes Penyeach *(poetry).*

READ ON ▷

▶ Ralph Ellison, *Invisible Man*; ▷ Malcolm Lowry, *Under the Volcano*; ▷Thomas Wolfe, *Look Homeward, Angel*; ▷ Virginia Woolf, *Mrs Dalloway.* ▷ John Kennedy Toole, *A Confederacy of Dunces* is a kind of comic *Ulysses*, set in New Orleans, and both Joyce's experimental writing and the whole concept of Irishness are spectacularly sent up in Flann O'Brien's *At Swim-Two-Birds.*

PATHWAYS

JAMES JOYCE

ULYSSES
(journey of self-discovery on a single Dublin day in 1904)

'JOYCEAN' NOVELS
(big, experimental, all-encompassing)

John **Barth**, *Giles Goat-boy*
Alexander **Theroux**, *D'Arconville's Cat*
Salman **Rushdie**, *Midnight's Children*
Italo **Svevo**, *The Confessions of Zeno*
Joyce **Cary**, *The Horse's Mouth*
John Kennedy **Toole**, *A Confederacy of Dunces*
Laurence **Sterne**, *Tristram Shandy*
Anthony **Burgess**, *Earthly Powers*
Robertson **Davies**, *What's Bred in the Bone*

CITIES
(where we live is what we are)

Saul **Bellow**, *Humboldt's Gift* (Chicago)
J.D. **Salinger**, *The Catcher in the Rye* (New York)
Lawrence **Durrell**, *The Alexandria Quartet*
Eleanor **Dark**, *Waterway* (Sydney)
James **Plunkett**, *Strumpet City* (Dublin)

IRELAND
Molly **Keane**, *Good Behaviour*
Roddy **Doyle**, *The Snapper*
William **Trevor**, *Mrs Eckdorff in O'Neill's Hotel*
J.P. **Donleavy**, *The Ginger Man*
Flann **O'Brien**, *At Swim-Two-Birds*

SELF-DISCOVERY
Virginia **Woolf**, *Mrs Dalloway*
Marcel **Proust**, *The Guermantes Way* (Part Three of Remembrance of Things Past)
Iris **Murdoch**, *The Sandcastle*
John **Fowles**, *The Magus*

K

KAFKA, Franz (1883–1924)
Czech novelist and short story writer

In the 1920s and 1930s people regarded Kafka as an unsmiling neurotic who depicted the human condition as a bureaucratic hell without explanation or compassion: 'Kafkaesque' was a synonym for 'nightmarish'. Kafka, by contrast, always regarded himself as a humorist, in the line of such surrealist East European jokers as ▷Gogol. Each of his novels and stories develops a single idea to ludicrous, logical-illogical extremes. In 'Metamorphosis' a man has to cope with the fact that he has turned into a gigantic beetle overnight. The prison-camp commander of 'In the Penal Colony' is so eager to show off a newly-invented punishment-machine that he turns it on himself. In 'The Burrow' a creature designs a defence-system of underground tunnels so complex and so perfect that it becomes the whole meaning of existence: it engulfs its own creator. The central figure of The Trial (Der Prozess) is arrested one morning although he has done nothing wrong, spends the book trying to discover the charges against him, and is finally executed without explanation. It is easy to treat such tales as psychological or political allegories. But it is also possible to read them as jokes, grimly funny anecdotes invented just for the hell of it. Perhaps keeping his face straight was Kafka's best trick of all.

★☆ THE CASTLE (DER SCHLOSS) (1926)
An ordinary, unremarkable man, K, arrives in a strange town to take up the post of Land Surveyor. He finds that no one is expecting him, that the town and the castle which dominates it are a labyrinthine bureaucracy where everyone is responsible only for passing the buck to someone else, and each favour done, each door opened, leads only to more confusion. K's efforts to reach the heart of the mystery, to be given some official confirmation of his existence, are doomed, hilarious and have the logic not of reality but of a very bad dream indeed.

Kafka's novels are The Trial, The Castle and America. His short stories have been published in one-volume collected editions and in shorter collections such as Metamorphosis and Other Stories and The Great Wall of China and Other Short Works. Kafka's correspondence with the two women with whom he conducted complicated and soul-searching relationships gives fascinating insights into this most enigmatic of writers and has been published as Letters to Felice and Letters to Milena.

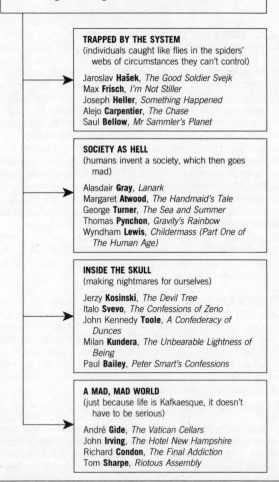

PATHWAYS

FRANZ KAFKA

THE TRIAL
(Josef K. is arrested and forced to fight – for his life – against charges which he is never told)

TRAPPED BY THE SYSTEM
(individuals caught like flies in the spiders' webs of circumstances they can't control)

Jaroslav **Hašek**, *The Good Soldier Svejk*
Max **Frisch**, *I'm Not Stiller*
Joseph **Heller**, *Something Happened*
Alejo **Carpentier**, *The Chase*
Saul **Bellow**, *Mr Sammler's Planet*

SOCIETY AS HELL
(humans invent a society, which then goes mad)

Alasdair **Gray**, *Lanark*
Margaret **Atwood**, *The Handmaid's Tale*
George **Turner**, *The Sea and Summer*
Thomas **Pynchon**, *Gravity's Rainbow*
Wyndham **Lewis**, *Childermass (Part One of The Human Age)*

INSIDE THE SKULL
(making nightmares for ourselves)

Jerzy **Kosinski**, *The Devil Tree*
Italo **Svevo**, *The Confessions of Zeno*
John Kennedy **Toole**, *A Confederacy of Dunces*
Milan **Kundera**, *The Unbearable Lightness of Being*
Paul **Bailey**, *Peter Smart's Confessions*

A MAD, MAD WORLD
(just because life is Kafkaesque, it doesn't have to be serious)

André **Gide**, *The Vatican Cellars*
John **Irving**, *The Hotel New Hampshire*
Richard **Condon**, *The Final Addiction*
Tom **Sharpe**, *Riotous Assembly*

READ ON ▷

- *The Trial*; *America* (the story of a naive young German who goes to the US thinking that its streets are paved with gold, and goes on believing it despite being cheated and betrayed by everyone he meets).
- ▶ Echoing Kafka's dark humour: ▷ Jaroslav Hašek, *The Good Soldier Svejk*; ▷ Joseph Heller, *Catch-22*; ▷ Nathanael West, *The Dream Life of Balso Snell*; Joe Orton, *Head to Toe*.
- ▶ Echoing the idea of a 'Kafkaesque', nightmare society: Rex Warner, *The Aerodrome*; ▷ Alasdair Gray, *Lanark*; ▷ George Orwell, *1984*.

KAVANAGH, Dan: see BARNES, Julian

KENEALLY, Thomas (born 1935)
Australian novelist and playwright

Although Keneally has written books on many subjects, including the partly-autobiographical *Three Cheers for the Paraclete* (1968), about a young Roman Catholic losing his faith, he is best-known for 'faction': powerful fictional treatments of the issues and personalities behind real events. His books are set at decisive moments in the history of peoples or continents – and Keneally gets under the skin of the participants, showing how great events happen for what are usually far smaller and more personal reasons (a quarrel; a cold in the head) than the awareness of grand political or strategic trends which historians would suggest. He is not, however, a 'historical' novelist, simply telling stories about the past. His concentration on issues gives his stories universal resonance: we are constantly shown the relevance of the events he describes to our present-day situation or attitudes. His books include *The Chant of Jimmie Blacksmith* (1971, about racial confrontation in 19th-century Australia), *Confederates* (1979, about Stonewall Jackson's campaigns in the American civil war) and *The Playmaker* (1987). His most recent novel, *Bettany's Book* (2000), ranges confidently from rural New South Wales in the 19th century to the story of a modern woman working for a charity in war-ravaged Sudan.

☆ SCHINDLER'S ARK (1982)
Schindler is a bragging, boozing opportunist who makes a fortune in Poland during the Second World War German occupation, buying up the businesses of dispossessed Jews. We read about his black-market deals, his backslapping relationship with the authorities, his parties and his mistresses – and gradually discover that his lifestyle is a façade, that his true activity is saving thousands of Jews from the gas chambers. The novel is also known as *Schindler's List*, after the Steven Spielberg movie of the same name.

READ ON ▷

- *The Playmaker* (in which convicts transported to 18th-century New South Wales, under the guidance of a confused, would-be liberal army lieutenant, rehearse and perform – of all things – Farquhar's Restoration comedy *The Recruiting Officer*).
- ▶ Jane Rogers, *Promised Lands*; ▷ Peter Carey, *True History of the Kelly Gang*; ▷ William Boyd, *An Ice-Cream War*; William Styron, *Sophie's Choice*.

PATHWAYS

THOMAS KENEALLY

THE PLAYMAKER
(1780s English officer guides convicts in Australia
through production of a Restoration comedy)

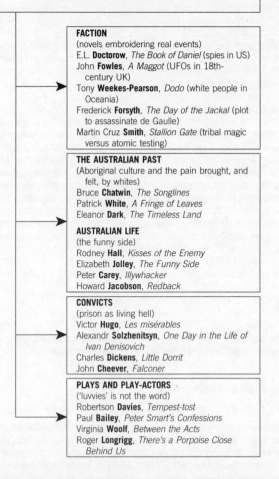

FACTION
(novels embroidering real events)
E.L. **Doctorow**, *The Book of Daniel* (spies in US)
John **Fowles**, *A Maggot* (UFOs in 18th-
  century UK)
Tony **Weekes-Pearson**, *Dodo* (white people in
  Oceania)
Frederick **Forsyth**, *The Day of the Jackal* (plot
  to assassinate de Gaulle)
Martin Cruz **Smith**, *Stallion Gate* (tribal magic
  versus atomic testing)

THE AUSTRALIAN PAST
(Aboriginal culture and the pain brought, and
  felt, by whites)
Bruce **Chatwin**, *The Songlines*
Patrick **White**, *A Fringe of Leaves*
Eleanor **Dark**, *The Timeless Land*

AUSTRALIAN LIFE
(the funny side)
Rodney **Hall**, *Kisses of the Enemy*
Elizabeth **Jolley**, *The Funny Side*
Peter **Carey**, *Illywhacker*
Howard **Jacobson**, *Redback*

CONVICTS
(prison as living hell)
Victor **Hugo**, *Les misérables*
Alexandr **Solzhenitsyn**, *One Day in the Life of
  Ivan Denisovich*
Charles **Dickens**, *Little Dorrit*
John **Cheever**, *Falconer*

PLAYS AND PLAY-ACTORS
('luvvies' is not the word)
Robertson **Davies**, *Tempest-tost*
Paul **Bailey**, *Peter Smart's Confessions*
Virginia **Woolf**, *Between the Acts*
Roger **Longrigg**, *There's a Porpoise Close
  Behind Us*

KENNEDY, A.L. (born 1965)
British novelist and short story writer

Other, usually male, writers in the recent renaissance of Scottish fiction have achieved more attention and been more regularly in the media spotlight but none has as strong and individual a voice as A.L. Kennedy. She writes of outsiders and grotesques, people who find it difficult or even undesirable to connect with others, people who march to the beat of very different drums and she does so in an edgy, blackly comic language. In her early short stories, published in *Night Geometry and the Garscadden Trains* and *Now That You're Back*, she had already found a distinctive voice. This has only become clearer, stronger and more confident in the novels that have followed. *Everything You Need* (1999) is a complex novel set largely on a small island which is a retreat for writers. The book centres on the developing relationship between Nathan Staples, a self-tormenting, self-obsessed middle-aged novelist and the young would-be writer Mary. Nathan knows Mary to be the daughter he has not seen since she was a small child. Mary does not know that the older mentor and teacher, for whom she has such ambivalent feelings, is her father. Through the relationship, Kennedy deals with difficult issues of love, pain and loss and the process of finding appropriate words to describe them.

SO I AM GLAD (1995)
So I Am Glad is a kind of bizarre, contemporary fairy-tale for grown-ups. Jennifer Wilson, the narrator, is a radio announcer whose unhappy upbringing has led her to close down communication with others. She has chosen isolation and she works hard to maintain it and to keep buried the emotions, 'moles' she calls them, which are at work under the surface. Into her life comes a strange roommate (is he fantasy or is he real?) who claims to be, and perhaps is, the ghost of Cyrano de Bergerac. The moles within Jennifer begin to stir and can no longer be ignored. A brief outline of *So I Am Glad* is sufficient to indicate the weirdness of Kennedy's imagination but can do little to demonstrate the power of the prose, its unique combination of grotesquerie, humour and poignancy. Only an actual reading of the book can do that.

A.L. Kennedy's other books are Original Bliss, Looking for the Possible Dance *and the non-fiction* On Bullfighting.

> **READ ON**

● *Original Bliss.*
▶ To her novels: ▷ Alasdair Gray, *Lanark*; Alan Warner, *The Sopranos*.
▶ To her short stories: ▷ Ian McEwan, *First Love, Last Rites*.

KEROUAC, Jack (1922–1969)
US novelist

Born in Lowell, Massachusetts, Kerouac was from a French-Canadian family and only learned English at primary school, a fact that must have contributed to the lifelong feeling of being an outsider that is so evident in his fiction. After a period in the US Merchant Marines and in the Navy Kerouac returned to Columbia University (which he had attended before his naval service) where he met a student named Allen Ginsberg. Ginsberg introduced him to a disparate group of like-minded spirits, united in little save an aversion to post-war America, and to the man who was to become his 'muse', Neal Cassady. *On the Road* (1957) is, and always will be, the archetypal Kerouac novel. This ground-breaking book was written (and re-written) between 1948 and 1956. The story of Sal Paradise (Kerouac) and Dean Moriarty (Cassady) and their trans-coastal odysseys in an assortment of beat up jalopies, fuelled on benzedrine, marijuana, wine and a hunger for kicks, is a tremendous, joy-filled paean to life and freedom amid the arid sterility of post-war America. A huge success, the book gave Kerouac the permanent label as leader of the 'Beat Generation'. Although it is generally agreed that he invented the term, playing on an association of 'beat', as in 'worn out', with a shortening of 'beatitude', it was a title he never wanted. He has been revered by generations of would-be hipsters ever since, but Kerouac may well have been not so much a rebel as a rather weak-willed misfit who remained the outsider he felt he was as a child. Yet, in *On the Road* and (fitfully) in other works, he created a self-mythology and a prose style that have been culturally influential for nearly fifty years.

Kerouac's other novels include Big Sur, Doctor Sax, The Subterraneans, Visions of Cody *and* Vanity of Duluoz. Lonesome Traveller *is a collection of meditations and essays triggered by his travels;* Satori in Paris *is his account of a journey to France.* Pomes All Sizes *is a collection of his poetry.*

READ ON >

- ● *The Dharma Bums* (beats and bohemians in San Francisco waver between asceticism and excess).
- ▶ ▷ Thomas Wolfe, *Look Homeward, Angel* (fictionalized autobiographical odyssey from an earlier US generation); William Burroughs, *Junky*; John Clellon Holmes, *Go*; Herbert Huncke, *The Herbert Huncke Reader*.

KING, STEPHEN (born 1946)
US novelist

Stephen King is one of the most popular novelists in the world and there can be few people who have not encountered his work in some form, either on the printed page or in one of the innumerable film and TV adaptations of his books. He is categorized, by those who like to place writers in categories, as a horror writer but this label may well alienate some readers who would actually relish his fiction. King's strengths do not lie in the descriptions of blood, viscera and violence that characterize other horror writers (although his books are not for the squeamish or easily distressed). His great gift is for writing about ordinary, everyday fears and emotions in extraordinary ways. His first great success, *Carrie* (1974), describes an adolescent girl, bullied and tormented at school, who discovers telekinetic powers which she turns on her tormentors. But the power of the book comes not so much from the supernatural trappings of the story but from the precision with which King describes small-town nastiness and from the way he taps into everybody's fear of being an outsider, not one of the gang. The pages of *Bag of Bones* (1998) are packed with gory ghosts and visitors from other worlds but the book is concerned with love, lost and found, mourning and recovery from grief as much as with haunting and horror. In the mammoth, 1,000-pages plus *It* (1986) the small Maine town of Derry is terrorized by the return of a supernatural killer. Seven friends who, as teenagers, experienced the horror of the first murderous spree return to confront the renewed nightmare. King ruthlessly dissects small town life and gives to Derry a realism that is undermined and compromised by the horror. Who knows what lurks beneath the surface of the ordinary? That is the question King repeatedly asks in his fiction and he has provided some gripping and wildly imaginative answers in his string of bestsellers.

King's other novels include Salem's Lot, The Shining, The Stand, Pet Sematary, Misery, The Tommyknockers, Dolores Claiborne, Rose Madder *and* Dreamcatcher. The Dark Tower *is a series of four books (so far) which chronicles the adventures of the 'Gunslinger' in a bleak world parallel to ours.* The Green Mile *is a six-part sequence of short novels, set on the death row of a penitentiary in the 1930s. Short story collections include* Night Shift, Nightmares and Dreamscapes *and* Hearts in Atlantis. *King has also written fiction under the pseudonym Richard Bachman and collaborated with fellow horror novelist Peter Straub on* The Talisman. *On Writing combines recollections of King's own development as a writer with practical advice to budding novelists.*

READ ON >

- ● *Misery, Pet Sematary.*
- ▶ Peter Straub, *Ghost Story*; James Herbert, *Sepulchre*; Dean Koontz, *Darkness Comes*; Clive Barker, *The Damnation Game*; Mark Z. Danielewski, *House of Leaves* (a dazzling combination of horror motifs and post-modern playfulness).

KINGSOLVER, Barbara (born 1955)
US novelist

Like the great 19th-century novelists, Barbara Kingsolver believes that fiction has a duty to engage with the real world. Her books are, in the best sense of the word, old-fashioned in that they grapple with political, social and moral issues. Where Victorian writers like Dickens, Eliot and Disraeli gave fictional form to debates about an England divided between the two nations of rich and poor, Kingsolver tackles contemporary concerns about colonialism, the rift between the developed and underdeveloped worlds and man's impact on the natural environment. And she does so in narratives that grip the reader with their imaginative depth and powerful characters. Her most ambitious book, *The Poisonwood Bible* (see below) is set in the Congo as it emerges from colonial rule. The setting for her other fiction is small town rural America. In *The Bean Trees* (1988) Marietta Greer flees the small town in Kentucky in which she grew up, changes her name to 'Taylor' and forges a new sense of family and identity with a small Cherokee child, abandoned to her care, and with other outsiders and refugees from personal and political trauma. The story is continued in *Pigs in Heaven* (1993) in which the child becomes the focus of a legal battle between Taylor (her new mother), and the Native American community from which she comes. Kingsolver is alert to the moral complexities of the conflict and offers no easy solutions.

☆ **THE POISONWOOD BIBLE (1999)**
The Poisonwood Bible is, by some way, Barbara Kingsolver's most ambitious novel to date. Nathan Price, a narrow-minded Christian evangelist, arrives with his family in the Belgian Congo to serve as a missionary to African people to whom his message means little. The year is 1959 and great changes are on hand in the country but the messianic Price is as blind to these as he is to the real needs of his family and the people he has volunteered to 'save'. The narrative moves inexorably towards personal tragedy set amidst the wider tragedy of a new nation still in thrall to the forces of economic imperialism. The story is told in the very different voices of Price's wife and his four daughters – pouting would-be prom queen Rachel, Leah (at first her father's greatest supporter but soon his fiercest critic), her twin sister Adah who suffers from hemiplegia but has her own idiosyncratic perspective on events, and the five-year old Ruth May. Acute in its psychological and political insight, rich in its evocation of a natural world indifferent to the cares and ambitions of individuals, *The Poisonwood Bible* is a very powerful and resonant novel.

Barbara Kingsolver's other books include Animal Dreams, Prodigal Summer, Homeland *(a collection of short stories) and* High Tide in Tucson *(a volume of essays and non-fiction writings).*

> **READ ON**

▶ ▷ Jane Smiley, *A Thousand Acres*; Louise Erdrich, *Love Medicine*; Ronan Bennett, *The Catastrophist* (another narrative set in Zaire; politically acute although very different from *The Poisonwood Bible* in its aims).

KIPLING, Rudyard (1865–1936)
British short story writer and poet

Kipling learned his craft working for English-language newspapers in India in the 1880s. He wrote reports, stories and poems about the British soldiers and administrators, their servants and the snake-charmers, fortune-tellers and other characters of the towns they lived in. Later, during the Boer War, he worked as a correspondent in South Africa, where he was a friend of Cecil Rhodes. Under the circumstances, it would have been hard for him not to reflect the imperialist attitudes of his age, first sunny confidence and then the jingoistic panic which overtook it in late Victorian times. But he is a more rewarding writer than this suggests. His sympathies were always with subordinates – with private soldiers rather than generals, servants rather than employers, children rather than adults. He wrote well about all three: his stories for and about children, in particular, are magnificent. Something like half of each collection – most books contain both stories and poems – is nowadays hard to take, not least where he writes in baby-talk (as in the *Just-So Stories*, O best-beloved) or uses funny spellings to evoke Cockney or Irish speech. But every archness is balanced by a gem of insight or sensitivity. In this, too, he was characteristic of his time.

KIM (1901)
This episodic novel is the story of a British orphan brought up as a beggar in Lahore, who becomes first the disciple of a wandering Buddhist monk and then an agent of the British secret service. He travels throughout India, and Kipling

uses his adventures as a framework for descriptions of everyday scenes and characters, of 'such a river of life as nowhere else exists in the world'.

Kipling's collections include Barrack-room Ballads, The Seven Seas *and* The Years Between *(verse)*, Soldiers Three *(stories), and the mixed prose-and-verse collections* Many Inventions, Traffics and Discoveries, A Diversity of Creatures *and* Captains Courageous, *and his children's books include the* Just-So Stories, The Jungle Book, Puck of Pook's Hill *and the public-school yarn* Stalky and Co. Something of Myself *is a guarded autobiography.*

READ ON

- *Plain Tales from the Hills, Debits and Credits.*
- ▶ to Kipling's stories about children: ▷ Katherine Mansfield, *Bliss and Other Stories.*
- ▶ to his stories about colonial adults: many of W. Somerset Maugham's short stories, collected in several volumes, deal with the English at large in the empire.
- ▶ John Masters, *Nightrunners of Bengal* and ▷ J.G. Farrell, *The Siege of Krishnapur,* about the 1857 Indian 'Mutiny', match Kipling's insight into the heyday of the Raj. Paul Scott, *The Raj Quartet.*

L

LANCHESTER, John (born 1962)
British novelist

Lanchester has published only two novels but they have both been major achievements and, in very different ways, remarkable exercises in style and story-telling. *The Debt to Pleasure* begins with the narrator's archly ironic statement, 'This is not a conventional cookbook.' What follows is not a conventional first novel. Constructed around a sequence of menus, the book begins as an apparent memoir of its narrator, gourmet and aesthete Tarquin Winot, centred on his love and knowledge of food and cooking. Self-consciously erudite and civilized, Tarquin seems, at first, a harmless food snob with a fondness for heavy irony, arcane information and baroquely extravagant language. As the book progresses, however, Lanchester slowly and subtly allows his narrator to reveal a monstrous egotism lurking beneath the surface. By the time we reach the last pages we know we are in the company of a man whose selfishness and self-obsession have led to terrible deeds. Lanchester's second novel, *Mr. Phillips*, could hardly have a more different central character. Mr. Phillips is an accountant, just made redundant, who has not yet had the courage to tell his wife of his dismissal. Setting out as if for work, he spends his day idly wandering London, musing on life and sex and death and the humdrum occurrences that have made up his own existence. Written in a deliberately flat prose that is the reverse of Tarquin Winot's verbal acrobatics, *Mr. Phillips* risks being as dull as his nondescript hero must appear to passers-by. Lanchester's triumph is that he succeeds in making his commuter-everyman a touching and comic character, an embodiment of our own ordinary failures, compromises and small pleasures. In the two contrasting figures of Winot, the amoral hedonist and Mr. Phillips, the downsized suburbanite, Lanchester has created two of the most memorable characters in recent English fiction.

> **READ ON**

▶ to *The Debt to Pleasure*: ▷ Vladimir Nabokov, *Lolita*; Alain de Botton, *The Romantic Movement*; ▷ Tibor Fischer, *The Collector Collector*.
▶ to *Mr. Phillips*: ▷ Virginia Woolf, *Mrs. Dalloway* (different in style and period but also the thoughts of an ordinary person at large in London).

READ ON A THEME: LARGER THAN LIFE

▷ Peter Carey, *Illywhacker*
▷ Angela Carter, *Nights at the Circus*
▷ Robertson Davies, *What's Bred in the Bone*

Howard Jacobson, *Redback*
Robert Nye, *Falstaff*
Petronius, *Satyricon*
▷ François Rabelais, *Gargantua*
▷ Laurence Sterne, *Tristram Shandy*

LAWRENCE, D.H. (David Herbert) (1885–1930)
British writer of novels, short stories, plays and poems

For 80 years Lawrence's radicalism outraged as many people as it enthralled. He thought that every matter of concern to human beings, and moral and ethical issues in particular, could be settled by rational discussion, if people would only be honest about themselves. His novels deal with such matters as female emancipation, the class struggle, atheism, sexual liberation and pacifism – not explicitly but as part of an ongoing advocacy of nakedness, of people at their best when stripped of inhibition and convention. Lawrence regarded his plain speaking as a way of shedding light in dark corners, a return to the innocence of the Garden of Eden; his enemies thought it shocking. Nowadays, when his rawness seems less threatening, his books stand up not only for moral earnestness – they read at times like humourless, non-religious sermons – but for their acute presentation of people and society in turmoil, of attitudes to life which the Second World War and the nuclear age have made seem unimaginably remote.

★ SONS AND LOVERS (1913)
Paul Morel is the son of ill-matched parents, an ex-school-teacher and an illiterate, alcoholic miner. Morel's mother is determined to help her son escape from the physical grind and intellectual atrophy of pit-village life and fulfil his ambition to be a painter. Her love for him is, however, a force for darkness not liberation. It inhibits both his self-discovery and his relationship with other people (especially the young farm-girl Miriam, who encourages his artistic ambitions), and it is only when he breaks free of his mother – a protracted, agonizing process, a second birth – that he is able to fulfil the destiny she has planned for him.

Lawrence's other novels include The Rainbow *and its sequel* Women in Love, Aaron's Rod, Kangaroo, The Plumed Serpent *and* Lady Chatterley's Lover. *He also published poems, travel books (e.g.* Sea *and* Sardinia; Mornings in Mexico), *plays, books on history and literature, and collections of short stories (e.g.* England, My England; The Woman Who Rode Away).

> **READ ON**

● *The Rainbow.*
▶ ▷ George Eliot, *Middlemarch*; ▷ Thomas Hardy, *Jude the Obscure* (especially close to *Women in Love* in its treatment of tensions between the sexes); David Storey, *Radcliffe*; ▷ Melvyn Bragg, *The Maid of Buttermere*; ▷ Thomas Wolfe, *Look Homeward, Angel*; Henry Roth, *Call It Sleep*; and ▷ James Baldwin, *Go Tell it on the Mountain* all deal with Lawrentian themes in very different settings. Elaine Feinstein, *Lady Chatterley's Confession* is a sequel to – and a more searching novel than – *Lady Chatterley's Lover.*

LE CARRÉ, John (born 1931)
British novelist

For over a century, writers from ▷ Verne to ▷ Fleming depicted espionage as a swashbuckling, Robin Hood activity with clear rules, absolute moral standards and a penchant for flamboyance. But in the 1960s this view changed. The Cuban missile crisis all but led to world annihilation; the Berlin Wall was built; a series of well-publicised defections revealed that spies were secretive, unremarkable men, morally hesitant and trapped by their own profession. Betrayal, not derring-do, was their stock-in-trade; east, west, north, south, they were as indistinguishable as civil service clerks. This is the atmosphere of Le Carré's books. His characters are not James Bonds, swaggering forth to smash conspiracies of global domination; in dark back streets and rainy woods they nibble away at one another's loyalties, hardly even certain of their own. It is a world of remorseless moral erosion, and Le Carré chillingly shows how it functions for itself, inward-looking and self-perpetuating, with minimal relevance to real life. The end of the Cold War, which triggered creative collapse in lesser writers, led him to turn back to the other, Greeneish, Amblerish peaks of the genre, and to update them magnificently. In *The Night Manager* (1993) the focus is moral exhaustion, not in political life, but in late-20th-century society in general, and an international drugs-for-arms scandal in particular.

☆ A PERFECT SPY (1986)
Magnus Pym, the best of all agents, has gone missing, and Jack Brotherhood is desperately trying to track him down. Pym is in fact holed up in a tatty English seaside resort, writing his memoirs, and trying to discover his lost integrity as a human being. As the memoirs near completion, the hunt closes in . . .

Le Carré's other spy-books are The Spy Who Came in from the Cold, The Looking Glass War, A Small Town in Germany, Our Game, The Russia House, *and the four 'Smiley' books (*Tinker Tailor Soldier Spy, The Honourable Schoolboy, Smiley's People *and* The Secret Pilgrim*). His other books are the detective stories* Call for the Dead *and* A Murder of Quality, The Naive and Sentimental Lover, The Little Drummer Girl, The Tailor of Panama, Single & Single *and* The Constant Gardener (*a devastating fictional indictment of the activities of large pharmaceutical companies in Africa*).

> READ ON >

- **The Russia House, The Constant Gardener.**
- ▶ to the spy stories: ▷ Eric Ambler, *Judgement on Deltchev*; ▷ Graham Greene, *The Human Factor*; ▷ Len Deighton, *Berlin Match* (and its follow-ups, *Mexico Set* and *London Match*).
- ▶ to *The Naive and Sentimental Lover*: ▷ John Fowles, *Daniel Martin*.
- ▶ to *The Little Drummer Girl*: ▷ Doris Lessing, *The Good Terrorist*.

LE GUIN, Ursula (born 1929)
US novelist

Le Guin made her name writing space opera (the 'League of All Worlds' series), and the prize-winning 'Earthsea Quartet', originally aimed at children but one of

LETTERS AND DIARIES

Fewer people write letters and diaries than did so even twenty years ago but for centuries they were favourite forms of literature. Readers turned to them to find the writer's unguarded, private thoughts. Sometimes these were what they got – intimate documents meant only for personal use. In other cases, they got ideas selected and polished with the full intention of publication. (Politicians' diaries and letters, with the notable exception of Alan Clark's *Diaries*, are seldom 'private' documents.) The books selected here therefore contain some of the grandest, as well as the most revealing, of all literature.

Boswell, James, *London Journal* In the 18th century Boswell arrives in London as a young man in search of women, wine and the celebrities of the day and records his adventures with endearing honesty. Self-reproach and vows to lead a better life are swiftly followed by further debauches.

Chesterfield, Lord (1694–1773), *Letters to His Son* (1774). Written to teach the young man the thoughts and manners of a gentleman. Politics, etiquette, religion, morals, the way of the world – each beautifully written letter is a glimpse into the 18th-century mind.

Clark, Alan, *Diaries* (1993). Arch-cad of the Tory party reveals the gossip, bitchiness and backbiting of politics while also chronicling, with rueful, witty self-awareness, his own shortcomings and sexual escapades. Will be read long after most political memoirs have entered a decent oblivion.

Coward, Noel, *Diaries* Coward demonstrates his talent to amuse, and his own inner doubts and self-questionings, in his 20th-century diaries. The beautiful and the famous and the notorious flit through its pages.

Crèvecoeur, St John de (1735–1813), *Letters from an American Farmer* (1782). Crèvecoeur, an English army officer, settled as a farmer in New York State, and wrote these letters describing American frontier life before the Revolution. A classic.

Davies, Russell (ed), *The Diaries of Kenneth Williams* (1993). In the 'Carry On' films, on TV and on radio, Williams slipped into one outrageous character after another – and hated himself for doing so. In real life he was obsessive, lonely, bitchy and miserable. The broken-hearted clown is a showbiz cliché, but Williams's life gives it hypnotic, tragic power.

Frank, Anne (1929–45), *The Diary of Anne Frank* (1947). Frank's own heart-rending account of how she and her family hid from the Nazis in an attic – and of what it's like to spend one's formative years in such circumstances.

Goncourt, Edmond de (1822–96) and Jules de (1830–70), *The Goncourt Journal* (1887–96). The Goncourts were at the hub of the Paris chattering class – actors, painters, writers, politicians, society folk – in the so-called Belle Époque, and wrote these gossipy, malicious journals up each night.

Kilvert, Francis (1840–79), *Kilvert's Diary* (1938–40). Kilvert was a parson in rural Wales, and his *Diary* gives unsentimental pictures of country life 125 years ago.

Klemperer, Victor, *Diaries 1933–1945* Astonishing and moving record of a Jew who survived the war, although still living in Germany throughout it.

Marchand, Leslie (ed), *Byron: Selected Letters and Journals* Byron's character revealed in all its complexity in letters and journals that sometimes read as if they were written yesterday instead of in the early 19th century.

Pepys, Samuel (1633–1703), *Diary* (1825). Not written for publication – it was even in code – Pepys's *Diary* tells of life in Restoration London, and of its happy, hard-working (and hard-playing) author. Shortened version advised, at least for first sampling.

Plath, Sylvia (1932–1963), *Letters Home* A moving mixture of domestic incident and despairing soul-searching in the letters Plath wrote, largely to her mother. Knowledge of the future, which we have but she doesn't, adds to the poignancy.

▷ **Waugh, Evelyn (1903–1966), *Letters*** Waugh's bilious wit and jaundiced view of the world and the people in it emerge entertainingly in his letters.

Also recommended: Kingsley Amis, *Letters*; Elizabeth Barrett and Robert Browning, *Letters, 1845–46*; Fanny Burney, *Diary*; John Evelyn, *The Diary of John Evelyn*; James Joyce, *Collected Letters*; Joe Orton, *Diaries*; Pliny the Younger, *Letters*; Oscar Wilde, *Letters*; Dorothy Wordsworth, *The Alfoxden and Grasmere Journals*.

the great works of 20th-century fantasy-writing. Le Guin uses alternative-world fantasy to discuss social, ecological and political themes. Although many of her books are still technically science fiction, set in the future and on other planets, she also lets people from the past and the present break through into magical kingdoms whose values and customs are ironical variations on our own. This happens literally in *Threshold* (1980): a supermarket checkout operator crosses the freeway into a wood, finds himself in another realm with its own time and its own reality, and meets and falls in love with a girl, another escapee from reality. The hero of *Malafrena* (1980) becomes a revolutionary leader in an alternative world in which the political ferment of post-Napoleonic Europe is blended with the religious outlook of Germany in Luther's time and with psychological and ecological concerns of the late 20th century. *Always Coming Home* (1985) is set among a pastoral tribe living peaceful, Zen-like lives in a far-future California.

THE DISPOSSESSED (1974)

The Dispossessed, 'an ambiguous utopia' as its subtitle calls it, tells the story of the different societies founded by humans on the verdant planet Urras and its barren moon Anarres. Anarres's society is a peaceful anarchy whose inhabitants have no possessions, live without laws and do not use the words 'I', 'Me' and 'Mine'; Urras is a capitalist meritocracy. Shevek, a mathematical genius from Anarres, travels to Urras where he is feted as a success but is alienated by the class-ridden society of the planet. His involvement with a revolution on Urras is the backdrop to his theoretical mathematics which will ultimately lead to the invention of the Ansible, a device that will allow instantaneous contact with other planets, no matter how distant. But will Shevek let the materialistic society of Urras control and exploit the potential of the Ansible?

Le Guin's other novels include Rocannon's World, Planet of Exile, City of Illusions, The Lathe of Heaven *and* The Left Hand of Darkness. The Wind's Twelve Quarters *and* Orsinian Tales *are collections of short stories.* The Earthsea Quartet *is* A Wizard of Earthsea, The Tombs of Atuan *and* The Farthest Shore *and* Tehanu.

> READ ON

● *The Left Hand of Darkness.*
▶ to *The Dispossessed*: ▷ Margaret Atwood, *The Handmaid's Tale.*

LEHMANN, Rosamond (1901–90)
British novelist

The ideas behind Lehmann's novels were strengthened by reading Jung and by psychic research after her daughter's death in the 1950s. She believed that we are not alone, that each person is part of a greater whole: the experience and knowledge of all human beings who have ever existed. We can enter into that experience, make use of it, during the rites of passage from one stage of existence to another – birth, adolescence, marriage, death – when the subconscious is particularly receptive. Lehmann's heroines are people on the brink of self-discovery; they are either innocents or victims of life, and the novels describe, in a lucid way far removed from the exoticism and mysticism of their events, how self-knowledge is achieved and how it changes the heroine's life, for bad or good.

THE BALLAD AND THE SOURCE (1944)

Ten-year-old Rebecca, picking bluebells in the garden of the old house beside the churchyard, is invited inside by the owner, Mrs Jardine, who knew Rebecca's grandmother and becomes Rebecca's friend. Rebecca listens enthralled to Mrs Jardine's tales of 'the old days' – and the more terrible the stories (they are accounts of passion, adultery, betrayal and hatred in Mrs Jardine's own young life), the more Rebecca is ensnared. Mrs Jardine is not so much like a witch casting a spell – though this is how Rebecca's alarmed mother sees her – as a sibyl from the remote past, revealing the true nature of human emotional existence.

Lehmann's other novels are Dusty Answer, Invitation to the Waltz *and its sequel* The Weather in the Streets, The Echoing Grove *and* A Sea-Grape Tree. The Gipsy's Baby *collects short stories, and* The Swan in the Evening *is an auto-biographical memoir centring on her reactions to her daughter's death.*

> READ ON

- In *A Sea-Grape Tree* (the sequel to *The Ballad and the Source*), Rebecca, now grown-up and betrayed by men exactly as Mrs. Jardine had been, goes to a Caribbean island to sort out her life and is affected not only by the people she meets there but by spirit-visitors from her past, including Mrs Jardine herself.
- ▷ Rose Macaulay, *The World My Wilderness.* ▷ Iris Murdoch, *The Philosopher's Pupil.* ▷ Virginia Woolf, *Mrs. Dalloway.* ▷ Alison Lurie, *Imaginary Friends*; Jane Gardam, *Crusoe's Daughter.*

LEONARD, ELMORE (born 1925)
US novelist

In the last ten years Elmore Leonard has become one of Hollywood's favourite novelists and perhaps the hippest of all American crime writers. Quentin Tarantino's film *Jackie Brown* was based on Leonard's novel *Rum Punch.* One of the roles which returned John Travolta to star status was that of Chili Palmer, the movie-loving gangster in the film version of Leonard's *Get Shorty.* And literary critics love Leonard's books, too. Even Martin Amis, often a difficult reader to please, described *Get Shorty* as a masterpiece. Leonard's status as America's most widely admired crime writer has been hard-won. He has been writing fiction since the 1950s. His earliest books were Westerns (the 1967 Paul Newman film *Hombre* is based on a Leonard novel) but, when he turned to crime writing, he found a home for his finest gifts as a writer. Leonard writes the kind of dialogue that other writers would kill to achieve. His fast, funny stories – filled with low-life, weirdos and bad-assed villains – display a talent for expertly drawn action and a mastery of wisecracking and street-smart language that mark Leonard out as a king of crime writing.

Elmore Leonard's novels include The Big Bounce, City Primeval, Freaky Deaky, Glitz, Gold Coast, Killshot, La Brava, Out of Sight, Pronto, Split Images, Stick *and* Bandits

> READ ON

- *Be Cool* (Chili Palmer applies his particular talents to the music industry); *Cuba Libre* (not a crime novel but historical fiction set in Cuba as the Spanish-American War of 1898 is about to start).

▶ ▷ Carl Hiaasen, *Double Whammy*; Robert B. Parker, *Night Passage*; James Ellroy, *L.A. Confidential*; Richard Stark, *The Hunter*.

LESSING, Doris (born 1919)
British novelist and non-fiction writer

Lessing was brought up in Rhodesia (now Zimbabwe), but her involvement in progressive politics made it an uncomfortable place to live, and she moved to London in 1949. In the same year she published her first novel, *The Grass is Singing*, about relationships between the races, and followed it in 1952 with the semi-autobiographical *Martha Quest*, the first in a five-book series (the other volumes, published over the next 17 years, are *A Proper Marriage, A Ripple from the Storm, Landlocked* and *The Four-gated City*). The sequence took her heroine from girlhood to marriage in white Rhodesia, from political virginity to radical activism, from Africa to London, from youth to age. Martha becomes a feminist; she samples and rejects the 'Swinging Sixties'; she tries religion and mysticism; she watches, and reports on, the last hours of the human race as we writhe towards the apocalypse. The books are in a straightforward 'as-told-to' style: they have the power of documentary as much as fiction. Two other Lessing novels, *The Golden Notebook* (1962, about an unhappy writer coming to terms with herself as a person and with her place in a male-dominated society) and *Briefing for a Descent into Hell* (1971, about nervous breakdown), have similar intensity. Lessing's (Jungian) psychological interests, and her fascination with Sufi mysticism, influence much of her other work, especially the five-volume sequence 'Canopus in Argus' (1979–83), which uses a science fiction format to explore ideas not so much of outer as of inner space, the alternative realities inside the mind.

The 'Canopus in Argus' novels are Shikasta; The Marriage Between Zones Three, Four and Five; The Sirian Experiments; The Making of the Representatives for Planet 8 *and* Documents Relating to the Sentimental Agents in the Volyen Empire. *The more recent* Mara and Dann *is also a visionary fiction set in the future. Lessing's other novels include* Memoirs of a Survivor, The Summer before the Dark, The Good Terrorist, Love, Again, The Fifth Child *and* Ben, in the World. *Her short stories are collected in such volumes as* The Habit of Loving, A Man and Two Women, African Stories *and* London Observed.

> READ ON

▶ to *Canopus in Argus*: Olaf Stapledon, *Last and First Men*.
▶ to Lessing's work in general: Margaret Laurence, *A Jest of God*; ▷ Patrick White, *The Solid Mandala*; ▷ Margaret Drabble, *Jerusalem the Golden*; ▷ Nadine Gordimer, *July's People*; Simone de Beauvoir, *She Came to Stay*; ▷ H.H. Richardson, *The Fortunes of Richard Mahony*.

LEWIS, Wyndham (1882–1957)
British writer and artist

Lewis spent his life outraging the bourgeoisie, first as a wild avant-garde artist and then as a fiercely opinionated essayist on art and politics, a member of Mosley's

British fascist party and an outspoken Hitler-supporter. His novels were prancing satires in the manner of ▷ Huxley or ▷ Waugh. *Tarr* (1918) and *The Apes of God* (1930) send up art-snobs and the dealers and phoney artists who prey on them. *The Revenge for Love* (1937) is about society people playing at politics but understanding nothing of a real tragedy (the Spanish Civil War) going on under their noses. The hero of *Self-condemned* (1954), a middle-aged professor tired of European life, retreats to a Canadian hotel, only to find it fuller of frauds and fools than the world he has left. Lewis's most stinging satire is the trilogy *The Human Age* (1928–55). It is about Armageddon, and shows the Day of Judgement not in lofty Christian terms but as a dusty, sweaty carnival, human beings prancing or shuffling to their doom at the whim of a cackling, deformed Showman – the gatekeeper of eternity is not St Peter but Mr Punch.

> **READ ON** >

▶ ▷ **Aldous Huxley, *Antic Hay*; Joyce Cary, *The Horse's Mouth*; ▷ Patrick White, *The Twyborn Affair*.**

LIVELY, Penelope (born 1933)
British writer

As well as for adults, Lively writes for children, and at least two of those books, *The Ghost of Thomas Kempe* and *A Stitch in Time*, are modern classics. Her adult novels share the same qualities – they are crisply written, strong on character and atmosphere, and have dazzlingly life-like dialogue. She is particularly good at evoking the emotional 'feel' of a place and of its history, showing how these impinge on her characters – and the places and characters range widely, from the Oxfordshire village of *Judgement Day* (1980), wracked over fund-raising for its historic (and slightly disreputable) church or the crumbling stately home of *Next to Nature, Art* (1982), whose owner is trying to revitalize it as an Arts Centre, to the terrorist-threatened, age-old African state of *Cleopatra's Sister* (1993). She works the convincing trick of lulling us by making us think the dilemmas and characters of her people are as familiar as our own – and then springing at least one major, sinister surprise.

MOON TIGER (1987)
Dying in hospital, Claudia Hampton reviews her whole past life, and in particular the wartime affair with a doomed young soldier in Egypt which both liberated her emotions and then (after his death) dried up her character even as it roused her to take up history, the profession at which she became so dauntingly successful.

Lively's other adult novels include The Road to Lichfield, According to Mark, Passing On *and* Heat Wave. *Her short story collections include* Pack of Cards *and* Beyond the Blue Mountains. *Her children's novels include* The Wild Hunt of Hagworthy *and* Fanny and the Monsters. Oleander Jacaranda *is a wonderfully evocative account of growing up in Egypt in the 1930s and 1940s.*

> **READ ON** >

● *City of the Mind.*
▷ **Anita Brookner, *A Closed Eye*; ▷ Susan Hill, *In the Springtime of the Year*; ▷ Joanna Trollope, *The Choir*.**

LODGE, David (born 1935)
British novelist

In the 1960s Lodge wrote half a dozen tragi-comic novels about young people perplexed by the pull between their Catholic upbringing and the urge of the 'Swinging Sixties'; the funniest is *The British Museum is Falling Down*. In the 1970s he began to write campus comedies, many set in an imaginary Midlands university, Rummidge. These include *Changing Places* (in which an innocent Rummidge lecturer changes places for a year with brash, oversexed Maurice Zapp of Euphoria State University, USA), *Small World* (about a young man pursuing a beautiful girl at a succession of ludicrous academic conferences) and *Nice Work* (1988; in which an uptight feminist lecturer and a chauvinist captain of industry are set to 'shadow' each other for a year). *Therapy* (1995) combines satire on modern literary preoccupations (such as writing unperformable screen-plays or being a TV pundit) with a bleak account of a middle-aged man discovering what existentialist angst is all about. *Thinks* (2000) records the developing relationship of a middle-aged novelist and a media don set in familiar Lodge territory.

Lodge's other novels include Ginger, You're Barmy, How Far Can You Go? *and* Paradise News. *He has also written academic books, chiefly on the writing of fiction and on structuralism.*

READ ON ▷

▶ to the campus comedies: ▷ Malcolm Bradbury, *The History Man*; Howard Jacobson, *Coming From Behind*; Mary McCarthy, *The Groves of Academe*.

READ ON A THEME: LONDON
▷ Peter Ackroyd, *The House of Doctor Dee*
  Jake Arnott, *The Long Firm*
  Alexander Baron, *Low Life*
▷ Peter Carey, *Jack Maggs*
  Justin Cartwright, *Look at it This Way*
  Esther Freud, *Peerless Flats*
  Anthony Frewin, *London Blues*
  Patrick Hamilton, *Hangover Square*
  Hanif Kureishi, *The Buddha of Suburbia*
  Colin McInnes, *Absolute Beginners*
▷ Michael Moorcock, *Mother London*
▷ J.B. Priestley, *Angel Pavement*
▷ Iain Sinclair, *Downriver*
  Nigel Williams, *They Came from SW19*

LONDON, Jack (1879–1916)
US novelist, short story and non-fiction writer

In his teens London worked as a docker, a seal-hunter, an oyster pirate (stealing from other fishermen's oyster-beds) and a customs officer; he also tramped across the US and took part in the Klondike Gold Rush. At 19 he settled down to writing, aiming to produce 1000 words a day, and began turning out he-man articles and short stories, heavy on adventure and light on character. His human beings (most of them fur-trappers, gold-miners or fishermen) take a two-fisted approach to life. Brutality rules, and survival is only guaranteed until someone stronger or brighter comes along. However blinkered London's view of life – he managed, at the same time, to be a fervent socialist and a fascist convinced that fair-haired, blue-eyed Aryans were the master-race – he wrote of it with breath-taking, blood-hammering effectiveness. His descriptions of fights, and of men battling against enormous natural hazards, set a model which many tough-guy writers have imitated, but none surpassed.

THE CALL OF THE WILD (1903)

Buck, a St Bernard dog, is stolen from his home in California and taken to the Klondike as a sledge-dog. He passes from owner to owner, each more brutal than the last, until he finds kindness at the hands of John Thornton. But Thornton is killed, Buck's last link with human beings is broken and he escapes to the wild and becomes the leader of a pack of wild dogs.

London's novels include Before Adam *(about the prehistoric ancestors of homo sapiens),* The Sea-wolf *(a ▷Conradian account of the struggle between a brutal sea-captain and the city couple he kidnaps) and* The Iron Heel *(a story of the future, recounting the struggle of a group of urban guerrillas to overthrow a dictatorship which has overrun Chicago).* John Barleycorn *is an autobiographical novel about a writer battling alcoholism.* The People of the Abyss *is a powerful study of East End London in the early years of the 20th century, based on London's own experience of living briefly in the city.*

> READ ON

- ● *White Fang* (a mirror-image of *The Call of the Wild*: the story of a wild dog drawn to the human race, who is betrayed and ill-treated by every owner – the description of his life as a fighting-dog is particularly harrowing – until he ends up at last with a master he can trust).
- ▶ to *The Call of the Wild*: Richard Adams, *The Plague Dogs*; Romain Gary, *White Dog*.
- ▶ to London's books about humans: ▷ Ernest Hemingway, *The Old Man and the Sea*, *To Have and Have Not*; ▷ Joseph Conrad, *Typhoon*.

LOWRY, Malcolm (1909–57)
British novelist

Lowry began drinking at Cambridge, and by the time he was 20 he was irretrievably addicted. He spent the rest of his life bumming across the world, in rehabilitation clinics, or in self-imposed isolation while he struggled to turn his experiences into fiction. He had published *Ultramarine* in 1933 soon after leaving Cambridge but the only other novel published during his lifetime – it took him 20 years to write it – was *Under the Volcano* (1947). This tells of the last two days in the life of an alcoholic British consul in revolution-torn Mexico, and intertwines memory, dream and reality in the manner of ▷Joyce's *Ulysses*. His posthumous novels are *Lunar Caustic*, set in a 'drying-out' clinic in New York, and *Dark as the*

Grave Wherein my Friend is Laid, about a boozy, doom-ridden tour of Mexico. *Hear Us, O Lord, From Heaven Thy Dwelling Place* is a collection of shorter pieces.

READ ON ▷

▷ Joseph Conrad, *Heart of Darkness*; ▷ F. Scott Fitzgerald, *Tender is the Night*; ▷ Fyodor Dostoevsky, *The Idiot*; ▷ Lawrence Durrell, *The Black Book*; ▷ Ernest Hemingway, *Islands in the Stream*.

LUDLUM, Robert (born 1927)
US novelist

Ludlum also writes as Jonathan Ryder *(The Cry of the Halidon*; *The Rhineman Exchange)*. His thrillers (many based on real-life incidents) are suspenseful, tough-talking and racy: they include *The Scarlatti Inheritance*, *The Gemini Contenders*, *The Matarese Circle*, *The Osterman Weekend*, *The Parsifal Mosaic*, *Road to Gandolfo* (and its sequel *The Road to Omaha*), *The Icarus Agenda*, *The Cry of the Halidon*, and *The Apocalypse Watch*. *The Prometheus Deception* (2001), in which a retired American agent discovers unpleasant truths about the covert organization for which he worked and is forced by the CIA to emerge from retirement to investigate, is a recent example of Ludlum's continuing ability to deliver the kind of goods his many fans want.

READ ON ▷

● *Trevayne, The Cry of the Halidon*.
▷ Tom Clancy, *Clear and Present Danger*; ▷ John Grisham, *The Brethren*; ▷ Wilbur Smith, *The Sunbird*.

LURIE, Alison
US novelist

The people in Lurie's novels are all terribly nice: well educated, well off, well dressed, liberal and compassionate. Their lives are like placid pools – and into each of them Lurie drops the acid of discontent (usually something to do with sex) and invites us to smile as the water seethes. Her funniest books are set on university campuses: *Love and Friendship* (1962) is about two people trapped in an affair (and what everyone else thinks about it); *The War Between the Tates* shows the gradual collapse of a 'perfect' marriage under threat from a combination of adultery and student politics. The people of *Imaginary Friends* are participants in or investigators of a bizarre religious cult. The narrator of *Only Children* is a child who reports on the sexual imbroglios of the adults around her with a wide-eyed gravity which arises less from innocence than from a precocious understanding not only of what is going on but of the sort of butter-won't-melt-in-*my*-mouth cuteness adults expect from little girls.

FOREIGN AFFAIRS (1984)
Three Americans are visiting England: Vinnie, a 54–year-old professor, Fred, a hunky young academic, and Chuck, a middle-aged, none-too-bright business-

man on a package tour. The novel shows Vinnie's attempts to bring into the two men's lives the same kind of decorous, unflustered order she herself enjoys – and the way her own values crumple under the strain of real emotion.

Lurie's other novels are Real People, Love and Friendship, Nowhere City (*a serious book about a woman trying to cope with unfocused psychological panic*), The Truth About Lorin Jones (*about a woman writing the biography of a painter, whose life becomes totally entangled with the facts and emotions she is researching*) *and* The Last Resort. Women and Ghosts *is a collection of supernatural stories.*

READ ON ▷

● *The War Between the Tates*.
▶ ▷ Anita Brookner, *Look at Me*; ▷ Carol Shields, *Larry's Party*; ▷ Anne Tyler, *Ladder of Years*; Alice Thomas Ellis, *The Birds of the Air*; Gail Godwin, *The Good Husband*.

M

MACAULAY, Rose (1881–1958)
British novelist

In the 1920s Macaulay wrote deadpan satires (*Potterism, Crewe Train, Told by an Idiot*). In the 1930s she began to concentrate on the sympathetic side of her art, writing about people (young girls especially) who are racked by the need to choose between the life of the mind and that of the flesh: their intellectual or spiritual ambitions are ambushed by sexual infatuation. *They Were Defeated* (1932) is set in 17th-century Puritan England and tells the ultimately tragic story of a young woman torn between her first sexual affair and the heady religious and intellectual atmosphere of Cambridge. The Second World War, and a succession of private misfortunes, made Macaulay give up novel-writing for a dozen years, but she returned triumphantly in her mid-seventies with *The World My Wilderness* (about a confused girl trying to discover her psychological identity after the Second World War) and a riotous, malicious romp about love (sacred and profane), *The Towers of Trebizond*.

Macaulay's other novels include (from the 1920s) Dangerous Ages, Orphan Island, Keeping Up Appearances and Staying with Relations, and (from the 1930s) I Would be Private and No Man's Wit. She also wrote poetry, essays on literature and religion, and a book combining travel, archaeology and autobiography, The Pleasure of Ruins.

> READ ON

- ● *The Towers of Trebizond*.
- ▶ To the satires: Compton Mackenzie, *Vestal Fire*; Nancy Mitford, *Love in a Cold Climate*; ▷ Muriel Spark, *The Ballad of Peckham Rye*.
- ▶ To *They Were Defeated*: ▷ Robert Graves, *Wife to Mr Milton*.
- ▶ to Macaulay's work in general: ▷ Willa Cather, *The Song of the Lark*; ▷ Elizabeth Bowen, *The Death of the Heart*; ▷ A.S. Byatt, *The Virgin in the Garden*; Elizabeth Jolley, *The Sugar Mother*.

McCAFFREY, Anne (born 1926)
US novelist

Although McCaffrey has written novels, romances, a thriller and books on music and cookery, she is best-known for science fiction (often, e.g. in *The Crystal Singer*, with a musical background) and fantasy. Her most substantial work is the 'Pern' sequence of novels. Pern is a distant, medieval world where the élite ride and telepathically control – or are controlled by – dragons; the dragons are the only beings which can destroy Thread, a devastating space-virus which would otherwise engulf all other life. The series details the fragile balance of society on Pern, and in particular the symbiosis – by turns comic, tragic and movingly poetic – between humans and dragons on which all life depends.

The Pern books (self-contained but linked) include Dragonflight, Dragonquest, The White Dragon, Dragonsong, Dragonsinger, Dragondrums, Moreta, The Dolphins of Pern, The Renegades of Pern, The Masterharper of Pern *and* The Skies of Pern. *McCaffrey's other science fiction books include* The Ship Who Sang, Restoree, Dinosaur Planet, Damia, Damia's Children. *She has also written the 'Catteni' sequence which consists of* Freedom's Landing, Freedom's Choice *and* Freedom's Challenge *and the 'Talent' series of* To Ride Pegasus, Pegasus in Flight *and* Pegasus in Space.

> READ ON ▷

- ● *The Crystal Singer; Restoree* (about a girl who finds herself transported to an unknown body on another planet).
- ▶ Piers Anthony, *Vicinity Cluster;* ▷ Robert Heinlein, *Glory Road;.* ▷ Ursula Le Guin, *The Word for World is Forest;* Tom de Haan, *The Child of Good Fortune.*

McCARTHY, Cormac (born 1933)
US novelist

Cormac McCarthy's portrayal of America is on a canvas that's dark and stained with blood. Celebrated primarily for his acclaimed Border Trilogy, comprising *All the Pretty Horses* (1992), *The Crossing* (1994) and *Cities of the Plain* (1997), he has written five other novels, each one a powerful example of his stark and sombre vision. *The Orchard Keeper* (1965), a tale of rural Tennessee and the violence that pervades a small community, set the course for the rest of his oeuvre. His next two books, *Outer Dark*, a story of illegitimacy, infanticide and incest, and *Child of God*, with its central character, Lester Ballard, a serial killer and necrophiliac who secretes the corpses of his victims in a cave, continued to reveal McCarthy's obsession with the dark nightmares of American life. *Suttree* (1979) is a substantial and densely written book, which McCarthy worked at (on and off) for twenty years. Suttree abandons his middle-class life and family to live in a decaying houseboat on a stygian river and hang out with thieves, drunks and a whole gallery of grotesque outcasts. The torpor of his existence on the rancid river is punctuated by outbursts of appalling violence and a doomed, traumatic love affair. The book resembles some kind of black parody of ▷ Steinbeck's *Tortilla Flat*. After being awarded the prestigious MacArthur Fellowship in 1981 (presiding over the judges was Saul Bellow who praised McCarthy's 'life-giving and death-dealing sentences'), he had time and freedom to concentrate on his next book. This was *Blood Meridian, or the Evening Redness in the West* (1985), which many consider his masterpiece. The American West is utterly divested of any kind of mythology or heroism and depicted as an inferno. The book's two central characters are 'the kid', an orphan with no name but 'a taste for mindless violence', and a figure known as 'the judge', a shrewd, cunning psychopath who is to this sun-scorched domain what Melville's Captain Ahab is to the endless ocean. The cheapness of life envisaged in this hellish world was noted by a critic who calculated that, on average, there was a murder every fifth page. Although the Border Trilogy confirmed McCarthy's status commercially, *Blood Meridian* remains his key work, an extraordinary portrait of an apocalypse that destroys all, taking no prisoners save the reader, captured by McCarthy's rich and mesmeric prose.

READ ON ▷

▶ ▷ William Faulkner, *Light in August*; ▷ Herman Melville, *Moby Dick*; Flannery O'Connor; *Wise Blood*; Ron Hansen, *Desperadoes*.

McCULLERS, Carson (1917–53)
US novelist

Reading McCullers sometimes seems like visiting a freak-show: her characters are repulsive but fascinating, macabre misfits set down in America's Deep South. The hero of *The Heart is a Lonely Hunter* (1940) is a deaf-mute, distracted by his inability to communicate either his sensitivity or his generosity of spirit. The awkward, ugly heroine of *The Ballad of the Sad Café* (1951) runs a haven in the Georgia swamps for tramps, lunatics and other social misfits – and her world is shattered when she falls in love with a malign homosexual dwarf. *Reflections in a Golden Eye* (1941) describes boredom and sexual obsession among the wives in a wartime army camp. *Clock Without Hands* is about racism. Only in one book, *The Member of the Wedding*, does McCullers transcend her more nightmarish imaginings. Her heroine is a young adolescent in a household bustling with preparations for a wedding: fascinated but totally ignorant about what is going on: she feels as locked out of 'real' (i.e. adult) society as the freaks and emotional cripples of McCullers's other books.

READ ON ▷

▶ to *The Member of the Wedding*: ▷ Eudora Welty, *Delta Wedding*; ▷ Katherine Anne Porter, *The Leaning Tower* (short stories).
▶ to McCullers's books in general: Flannery O'Connor, *Wise Blood*; ▷ William Faulkner, *Intruder in the Dust*; Elizabeth McCracken, *The Giant's House*.

McEWAN, Ian (born 1948).
British novelist and short story writer

McEwan began his career writing short stories and short novels in which, in precise and glacially cool prose, he led his readers towards hidden horrors and terrible revelations. What, for example, is the secret of *The Cement Garden* (1978), which only the children know? What unimaginable violence is to end the dreamlike trip to Venice recounted in *The Comfort of Strangers* (1981)? Later novels are just as tense, but the characters are more sympathetic, the atmosphere is less claustrophobic and human warmth and humour leaven the pain. *The Child in Time* (1987) is a superb book about a young couple devastated when their baby is stolen. *The Innocent* (1990) combines Cold War thriller (1950s vintage), love story and psychological-horror story. *Black Dogs* (1992) is about a man researching the life of his wife's parents ('borrowing them', so to speak, since his own parents died when he was young), and in particular trying to find out what was the horror (the Black Dogs of the title) they found on their honeymoon trip to France just after World War II. McEwan's most recent fiction has included a short but potent morality tale of love, death and deception (*Amsterdam*), and the story of a man whose comfortable middle-class life is arbitrarily disrupted by the obsessions and delusions of another man (*Enduring Love*).

McEwan's other books include First Love, Last Rites *and* In Between the Sheets *(short stories) and* The Imitation Game *(a psychological thriller about the code-breakers in post-World War II Bletchley).* The Daydreamer *is a children's/adult's fantasy about a middle-aged MP catapulted back in time to his 1950s,* 'Just William'*-style childhood.*

READ ON >

▶ ▷ Barbara Vine, *A Fatal Inversion*; David Cook, *Crying Out Loud*; ▷ Beryl Bainbridge, *A Quiet Life*; ▷ Martin Amis, *London Fields*.

McGRATH, Patrick (born 1950)
British novelist

The word most frequently associated with the fiction of Patrick McGrath is 'grotesque'. Indeed one of his earlier novels, in which a cerebrally damaged lord of the manor watches in mute, enraged impotence as his new butler assumes control of his wife and home, was actually called *The Grotesque*. McGrath was born in London and lived near Broadmoor Mental Hospital where his father was the medical superintendent for many years, autobiographical facts that are often cited as the ultimate source of his grim and Gothic sensibility. Certainly one of his best novels, *Asylum* (see below), the story of a forensic psychiatrist at a well known psychiatric institution, was directly influenced by his father's experiences. Two more novels followed: *Spider* (1990) and *Dr. Haggard's Disease* (1992), a tale of sexual obsession (a recurring theme in McGrath's work), set in the medical profession in a superbly evoked 1930's England, just before the outbreak of the war. *Martha Peake* (2000), McGrath's latest novel, is historical fiction set in eighteenth century London and America.

ASYLUM (1997)
Asylum once again dwells on sexual obsession, this time between the wife of a psychiatrist and one of her husband's patients. A beautiful and intelligent woman, Stella Raphael forms a destructive relationship with Edgar Stark, a mentally ill patient under the care of her husband Max; this is told by Peter Cleave, another psychiatrist, who knows the Raphaels well. McGrath is fond of using unreliable narrators, however, and Cleave, with his tale of Stella's terrible compulsion to love the decidedly dangerous Stark, is no exception.

READ ON >

▶ ▷ Ian McEwan, *The Cement Garden*; Patrick McCabe, *The Dead School*; Bradford Morrow, *Giovanni's Gift*.

McINERNEY, Jay (born 1955)
US novelist

Like a latter-day version of his hero F. Scott Fitzgerald, McInerney exploded onto the American literary scene with his first novel, *Bright Lights, Big City* (1984), a slick, hilarious, semi-autobiographical tale of life in the Big Apple. The book's nameless narrator is fuelled by 'Bolivian Marching Powder', married to a beautiful model and just about holding down a cool job. Naturally, everything falls apart and McInerney chronicles the social and personal meltdown with detached wit and epigrammatic prose. The novel's success launched a 'bratpack' of similarly hip and cynical young novelists, including ▷ Bret Easton Ellis, Tama Janowitz and Madison Smartt Bell. What distinguishes McInerney from his contemporaries is a solid gold wit that goes well beyond hip phrasemaking. Most of his other books have dealt with similar characters – Manhattanites in high jinks – and those that have attempted to break the mould have not been amongst his most successful. (*Ransom* (1986) is set around a group of expatriate young Americans in Japan and the backpack trail around India and Nepal and McInerney, like his characters, seems far from home.) *The Story of My Life* (1988) returns to New York and the often very funny sex and drug-filled social lives of another bunch of gilded youth – this time, women. *Brightness Falls* (1992) is an amusing and mostly effective satire on both the publishing world and the shark pool of high finance, low cunning and hostile takeover bids that is Wall Street. *Model Behaviour* (1998) explored, in a harder, more brittle manner, the same territory as the first novel.

McInerney's other books include The Last of the Savages, How It Ended *(a collection of shorter fiction) and* Bacchus and Me *(a collection of magazine columns on wine)*

> READ ON ▷

● *Model Behaviour.*
▶ ▷ **Bret Easton Ellis, *The Rules of Attraction*; ▷ F.Scott Fitzgerald, *The Great Gatsby*; Tama Janowitz, *Slaves of New York*; Ted Heller, *Slab Rat* (blistering satire on glitzy New York magazine world by Joseph Heller's son); David Handler, *The Man Who Would Be F. Scott Fitzgerald* (an amusing crime novel set in the New York literary scene which namechecks McInerney and the rest of the 'bratpack').**

MacLEAN, Alistair (1922–87)
Scots/Swiss novelist

By the nature of their business, thriller-writers tend to come and go, dating as fast as last year's news. Popular fiction all too rapidly becomes unpopular fiction. MacLean is one of the few thriller-writers whose works have lasted. Most are set in wartime, and describe deeds of great daring or endurance. War, however, is merely the reason for the events: what counts in the stories is suspense, heroism and lantern-jawed grit. Typical stories are *The Guns of Navarone* (1957), about the rescue of 1200 British soldiers from a small Greek island under the noses of German guns in the Second World War, and *Ice*

Station Zebra (1963), about a submarine sent to recover secret Cold War data from a Russian spy-satellite which has crashed and become trapped beneath the Arctic ice.

READ ON >

- *Breakheart Pass, Where Eagles Dare, Fear Is the Key.*
- ▶ Nicholas Monsarrat, *The Cruel Sea;* ▷ Hammond Innes, *Maddon's Rock/Gale Warning;* ▷ Wilbur Smith, *Hungry Is The Sea.*

READ ON A THEME: **MADNESS**

▷ Margaret Forster, *The Bride of Lowther Fell*
   Janet Frame, *Faces in the Water*
   Charlotte Perkins Gilman, *The Yellow Wallpaper*
   Lesley Glaister, *The Private Parts of Women*
▷ Susan Hill, *The Bird of Night*
   Ken Kesey, *One Flew Over the Cuckoo's Nest*
   Sylvia Plath, *The Bell Jar*
▷ Jean Rhys, *Good Morning, Midnight*
▷ Evelyn Waugh, *The Ordeal of Gilbert Pinfold*

See also: Depression and Psychiatry; On the Edge of Sanity

MAHFOUZ, Naguib (born 1912)
Egyptian novelist

Modern Arabic literature is little known in the West, and the loss is ours. Mahfouz is a Nobel-prize-winning novelist, known worldwide for his *Cairo Trilogy* (1956–7). This is a panorama of life in the city during the first half of the 20th century, and includes not only a family saga to rival ▷ Singer's *The Family Moskat* or ▷ Naipaul's *A House for Mr Biswas*, but also atmospheric studies of slum life, political satire and an absorbing description of a society trying to struggle free from centuries of religious and social stagnation into the modern, rational, democratic age. Mahfouz's style is leisurely, but the trilogy's span is enormous and repays time taken to get into it. The individual volumes are *Palace Walk, Palace of Desire* and *Sugar Street*.

READ ON >

- *Children of the Alley, Midaq Alley, The Harafish.*
- ▶ Ahdaf Soueif, *The Map of Love*; Nawal el Sadaawi, *God Dies by the Nile*; Robert Solé, *Birds of Passage.*

MAILER, Norman (born 1923)
US writer

As well as novels, Mailer has published both non-fiction (e.g. *Oswald's Tale*, an epic search for the truth behind Lee Harvey Oswald and the Kennedy assassination) and 'faction', a blend of real events and fiction (e.g. *The Executioner's Song*, 1979, an examination of the character and crimes of the murderer Gary Gilmore). Most of his novels are set in the present day, and deal with a single theme: maleness. He regards violence and competitiveness as essential components of masculinity, related to sexual potency – and claims, further, that capitalist society will only succeed if it models itself on the aggressive, cocky male. The world being what it is, Mailer is often forced – like ▷ Hemingway before him – to describe the failure of these macho fantasies, and because so many of his books are about the failure of the American Dream, despair gives his writing its stinging and continuing relevance. *The Naked and the Dead* (1948) is about the brutalization of a group of bewildered young airmen in the Second World War. In *Why Are We in Vietnam?* (1967), a savage Hemingway parody, a man takes his son on a bear-hunt as an 18th-birthday celebration, and this quintessential US manhood-ritual is linked, in a devastating final paragraph, with the mindless, gung-ho crowing of the gook-slaughtering US army in Vietnam, into which the boy will be drafted now that he is adult. *An American Dream* (1965), an equally pungent satire, shows a man at the end of his tether who commits murder and then tries to cudgel from his increasingly insane mind the reason why his country should have conditioned him to kill, why someone else's violent death should be the outcome of the American Dream.

ANCIENT EVENINGS (1983)
Pharaoh Rameses IX of Egypt, perplexed by his failure as a ruler, asks his minister Menenhetet to think back to a former existence as charioteer to the great warrior pharaoh Rameses II, and to explain the secrets of Rameses's success. Menenhetet's account is the bulk of the book, a dazzling description of a society dependent on belief in magic and on a (not unconnected) view of its own powers of rejuvenation, of constantly being able to deconstruct and reconstruct its past.

A good sampler of Mailer's work is Advertisements for Myself, *an anthology of his early writings with a fascinating autobiographical commentary. His other novels include* Barbary Shore, The Deer Park, *the thriller* Tough Guys Don't Dance, *the blockbusting* Harlot's Ghost, *an epic about the CIA, and* The Gospel According to the Son, *a curiously mild take on the New Testament.*

> READ ON ⟩

▶ to Mailer's contemporary fiction: ▷ **Ernest Hemingway,** *For Whom the Bell Tolls*; ▷ **Don DeLillo,** *Underworld*; **Henri de Montherlant,** *The Bullfighters*; **Robert Stone,** *Dog Soldiers*; **William Styron,** *The Long March.*
▶ to *Ancient Evenings*: **L.P. Myers,** *The Near and the Far*; ▷ **Thomas Mann,** *Joseph and His Brothers.*

MALOUF, David (born 1934)
Australian novelist and poet

Malouf has written novels set in a variety of historical and geographic settings (*An Imaginary Life*, for example, describes the exile of the Roman poet Ovid) but his most successful fiction explores, in prose of a rich and poetic range, the history of his native Australia. *Remembering Babylon* (1993) is set in Queensland in the 19th century and tells the story of Gemmy, who suddenly appears out of the bush at the edge of a small white settlement. Gemmy is himself white but, after a shipwreck, he has spent sixteen years living with the Aborigines. All the white characters in the novel are alternately fascinated and appalled by Gemmy's ambiguous status, the position he holds poised between two, for them, mutually exclusive categories, white and black. Gemmy may be white but his years with the Aborigines have marked him. He hardly remembers any English and his sense of self and the natural world belong to his adopted people. As the novel progresses and Gemmy moves towards the realisation that, to save himself, he must return once more to the bush, one can only admire the skill and subtlety with which Malouf unfolds his story. *The Conversations at Curlow Creek* (1996) is also set in the 19th century. The date is 1827 and the novel takes the shape of the night-long conversation between Carney, an Irish bushranger who is to be hanged in the morning, and Adair, the police officer who is overseeing the hanging. As they talk the narrative moves back and forth in time through their memories as the forces that have shaped them both become clearer and connections are established between the criminal and the man deputed to punish him.

David Malouf's other novels include Fly Away, Peter, The Great World, Child's Play, Harland's Half Acre *and* Johnno. Dream Stuff *is a collection of short stories;* 12 Edmonstone Street *an idiosyncratic autobiography. Malouf has also published volumes of his poetry.*

> READ ON

▶ **to *An Imaginary Life*: Christoph Ransmayr, *The Last World*.**
▶ **to the novels set in Australia's past: ▷ Thomas Keneally, *The Chant of Jimmie Blacksmith*; ▷ Patrick White, *Voss*; ▷ Peter Carey, *True History of the Kelly Gang*.**

MANN, Thomas (1875–1955)
German novelist and non-fiction writer

Although Mann was not a political writer, the themes of his work reflect northern European politics of the last 100 years. His first great novel, *Buddenbrooks* (1901), shows the decline of a powerful German industrial family over three decades – and although it is superficially a Forsyte-like family saga, its strength comes from the persistent impression that the Buddenbrooks are characteristic of the decadent 'old Germany' as a whole. The hero of *The Magic Mountain* (1924) spends much of the book learning about Europe's moral, artistic and philosophical heritage – and then goes to fight in the First World War. In *Joseph and His Brothers* (1933–43), based on the Bible and written under the shadow of Nazism, Joseph, the figure symbolizing progress, is a plausible rogue, a Hitler-figure, and his brothers, symbolizing barbarism, are as gullible as they are honest. The composer-hero of *Doctor Faustus* (1947) can unlock his creativity only by entering ever deeper into the morass of his own mind, and by accepting that to be 'ordinary' is to opt not for cultural calm but for chaos. The con-man central character of *The Confessions of Felix Krull, Confidence Man* (1954), Mann's only comic novel, preys on the expectations of those who still believe in the old rules of religion, society and politics.

★ THE MAGIC MOUNTAIN (DER ZAUBERBERG) (1924)

Castorp, a rich, unimaginative young man, spends seven years in a Swiss tuberculosis sanatorium. The sanatorium is full of endlessly talkative intellectuals, who educate Castorp in music, philosophy, art and literature. The book shows him growing in both knowledge and moral stature, until at last he is cured both of tuberculosis and of the greater disease (in Mann's eyes) of ignorant complacency. As the novel ends, however, he strides out to fight in the First World War – and Mann invites us, in the light of hindsight, to ponder his probable fate and that of the European culture he has so laboriously acquired.

Mann's shorter works include Mario the Magician *(about demonic possession),* Death in Venice *(Tod in Venedig; about a writer galvanized by longing for a beautiful boy),* Lotte in Weimar *(a historical novel about the young ▷Goethe), and* The Holy Sinner *(a beautiful – and poker-faced, despite the ridiculousness of its events – retelling of a medieval religious legend involving incest, communion with angels and magical transformations).*

> READ ON

- *Buddenbrooks*; *The Confessions of Felix Krull, Confidence Man.*
- ▶ to *The Magic Mountain*: ▷ Johann Wolfgang von Goethe, *The Apprenticeship of Wilhelm Meister*; Robert Musil, *The Man Without Qualities.*
- ▶ to *Buddenbrooks*: ▷ I.B. Singer, *The Family Moskat*; ▷ Honoré de Balzac, *Cousin Bette.*
- ▶ to *Joseph and His Brothers*: ▷ Gustave Flaubert, *Salammbô.*

MANNING, Olivia (1908–80)
British novelist

Manning is best known for the 6–novel sequence, *Fortunes of War* (*The Balkan Trilogy*, 1960–65 and *The Levant Trilogy*, 1977–80, memorably filmed for TV with Kenneth Branagh and Emma Thompson). The central characters, Guy and Harriet Pringle, are English expatriates during the early years of the Second World War. They settle in Bucharest, where Guy teaches English; then, as the Axis powers advance, they move to Athens and from there to Cairo, where they 'hole up' during the desert campaign of 1942. Like the rest of Manning's characters, English, Middle Eastern or European, the Pringles dwell on the fringes, not at the centre, of great events; their lives are bounded by bread-shortages, electricity-cuts and squabbles over status. The civilization which bred them is collapsing, and they are themselves symbols of its decadence: they are effete and powerless, able only to run before events. Nonetheless, Harriet's character does contain the seeds of change. When she marries Guy she is an unawakened personality, a genteel 1930s 'English rose'. Events draw from her emotional and intellectual strength she didn't know she possessed – and the effects are to alienate the rest of the stuffy British community and to put stress on her marriage to the honourable but unimaginative Guy. At first sight Manning seems to be offering no more than a series of artless anecdotes about the muddle and horror of life in exotic cities engulfed by war. It is not until the mosaic is complete that her underlying scheme becomes apparent: the description of a whole culture in a state of unwished-for, panic-stricken change.

The novels in The Balkan Trilogy *are* The Great Fortune, The Spoilt City *and* Friends and Heroes; *those in* The Levant Trilogy *are* The Danger Tree, The Battle Lost and Won *and* The Sum of Things. *Manning's other novels include* School for Love, The Doves of Venus, *and* The Rain Forest. Growing Up *and* A Romantic Hero *are collections of short stories.*

READ ON >

▶ ▷ **Elizabeth Bowen, *The Heat of the Day*; Jennifer Johnston, *The Captains and the Kings*; Isabel Colegate, *The Shooting Party*; ▷ Evelyn Waugh, *Sword of Honour* (trilogy comprising *Men at Arms*, *Officers and Gentlemen* and *Unconditional Surrender*).**

MANSFIELD, Katherine (1888–1923)
New Zealand short story writer

Mansfield went to London at 14, and spent the rest of her life in Europe. When she wrote of New Zealand it was either with childhood nostalgia (for example in 'Prelude' and 'At the Bay') or with distaste for the lives its adults led in the outback ('Ole Underwood'; 'The Woman at the Store') or in dingily genteel suburbs ('Her First Ball'; 'How Pearl Button was Kidnapped'). She admired ▷ Chekhov's stories, and sought to write the same kind of innocent-seeming anecdotes distilling single moments of human folly or aspiration. Her characters are often shallow, silly and desperate people: an unemployable film-extra ('Pictures'), a snobbish mother and her unmarried daughters ('The Garden-Party'), a hen-pecked singing-teacher ('Mr Reginald Peacock's Day'), expatriates on the continent ('The Man Without a Temperament'; 'Je ne parle pas français'). She polished and refined her prose, often spending months on a single story – and the feeling of craftsmanship in her work, of slightly self-conscious artistry, greatly enhances the impression she seeks to give, that tragedies are not diminished because the lives they affect are small.

Mansfield's story collections are In a German Pension, Bliss, The Garden-Party and Other Stories, The Dove's Nest *and* Something Childish. *Her* Journals *give fascinating glimpses both of her character and of the events and conversations which she drew on in her work.*

READ ON >

▶ ▷ **Anton Chekhov, *The Lady With the Lap-Dog and Other Stories*; ▷ John Cheever, *Collected Stories*; Jean Stafford, *Collected Stories*; ▷ V.S. Pritchett, *Collected Stories*.**

MANTEL, Hilary (born 1952)
British writer

Mantel is a varied writer. Her earlier novels, with the exception of *Eight Months on Ghazzah Street* (1988), an account of women's life in Saudi Arabia, are surrealist black farces. Her characters are obsessive, pathetic people trapped in situations which drive them over the edge of sanity and give them crazy, terrifying strength. What they do is grotesque and awful but we pity them. In *Vacant Possession* (1986) Muriel Axon, whose intelligence seems to have been stunned by the terrible events of her childhood and adolescence, is released from a mental hospital. With devastating logic she sets to work to 'haunt' the places and people she remembers. More recently Mantel has turned to historical fiction, either in the relatively conventional form of *A Place of Greater Safety* (1992), a story of the leaders of the French Revolution, or in the shape of oblique, suggestive narratives such as *The Giant O'Brien* (1999).

> READ ON

● *Fludd; The Giant O'Brien.*
▶ ▷ Bernice Rubens, *Our Father*; ▷ Muriel Spark, *The Abbess of Crewe*, ▷ Beryl Bainbridge, *Master Georgie* ; Alice Thomas Ellis, *The 27th Kingdom*.

READ ON A THEME: **MANY GENERATIONS**

▷ Isabel Allende, *The House of the Spirits*
▷ Kate Atkinson, *Behind the Scenes at the Museum*
▷ Gabriel García Márquez, *One Hundred Years of Solitude*
  Elizabeth Jane Howard, *The Light Years*
▷ Thomas Mann, *Buddenbrooks*
  Tim Pears, *In a Land of Plenty*
  Rosamunde Pilcher, *The Shell Seekers*
▷ I.B. Singer, *The Family Moskat*

See also: All-engulfing Families; Eccentric Families

MANZONI, Alessandro (1785–1873)
Italian writer

Manzoni was Italy's leading 19th-century poet, playwright and novelist, a writer of the stature of ▷ Goethe or ▷ Tolstoy. His one novel, ★ *The Betrothed* (*I promessi sposi*, 1842), is ranked with Tolstoy's *War and Peace* both as imaginative fiction and as a study of a whole society from top to bottom. The heart of the story is a series of somewhat operatic events surrounding the engagement, in 17th-century Lombardy, of two young peasants. Their innocent plans create ripples of involvement which draw in landowners (good and bad), priests (saintly and venal), village gossips, gipsies, children and the aged – an entire society, revealed in magnificent, poet's prose.

> READ ON

▶ Eucleides da Cunha, *Revolution in the Badlands* (a similarly panoramic view of a whole society, this time that of Brazil, town and country, during an uprising); Sigrid Undset, *Kristin Lavransdatter* (set among the peasants and landowners of medieval Norway); ▷ Boris Pasternak, *Doctor Zhivago* (matching Manzoni's counterpointing of private and public affairs).

PATHWAYS

GABRIEL GARCÍA MÁRQUEZ

ONE HUNDRED YEARS OF SOLITUDE
(many-generation saga of the Buendia family)

MANY GENERATIONS

Isabel **Allende**, *House of the Spirits*
I.B. **Singer**, *The Family Moskat*
Michèle **Roberts**, *Flesh and Blood*
Thomas **Mann**, *Buddenbrooks*

PLACES
(locations so powerful, so engulfing, that they
    affect the characters almost like living
    things)

Paul **Theroux**, *The Mosquito Coast*
Patrick **White**, *A Fringe of Leaves*
V.S. **Naipaul**, *A House for Mr Biswas*
Robertson **Davies**, *The Cornish Trilogy*
    (beginning with *Rebel Angels)*
Kurt **Vonnegut**, *Galàpagos*

GROWN-UP FAIRY TALES

Angela **Carter**, *Nights at the Circus*
Peter **Carey**, *Oscar and Lucinda*
R.K. **Narayan**, *The Maneater of Malgudi*

SOUTH AMERICA
(in fiction, at least, the magic-realist continent
    to end them all)

Mario Vargas **Llosa**, *The Storyteller*
Alejo **Carpentier**, *The Chase*
Stephen **Dobyns**, *After Shocks/Near Escapes*
Carlos **Fuentes**, *The Old Gringo*
Augusto Roa **Bastos**, *I, The Supreme*

MÁRQUEZ, Gabriel García (born 1928)
Colombian novelist and short story writer

In Márquez's invented South American town of Macondo, a place isolated from the outside world, 'magic realism' rules: there is no distinction between magic and reality. At one level life is perfectly ordinary: people are born, grow up, work, cook, feud and gossip. But there is a second, irrational and surrealist plane to ordinary existence. The Macondans (unless they murder each other for reasons of politics, sex or family honour) live for 100, 150, 200 years. Although they are as innocent of 'real' knowledge as children – they think ice miraculous and they are amazed to hear that the world is round – they know the secrets of alchemy, converse with ghosts, remember Cortez or Drake as 'uncles'. Macondo is a rough-and-tumble Eden, a paradise where instinct rules and nothing is impossible – and Márquez spends his time either describing its enchantment or detailing the savage results when people from the outside world (jackbooted generals; con-men; lawyers; bishops) break through to 'civilize' it. For Márquez, Macondo stands for the whole of South America, and his stories are barbed political allegories. But he seldom lets this overwhelm the books. Instead of hectoring, he opens his eyes wide, puts his tongue in his cheek and tells us wonders.

★☆ ONE HUNDRED YEARS OF SOLITUDE (1967)
As Colonel Aureliano Buendia faces the firing squad, the whole history of his family flashes before his eyes. They begin as poor peasants in a one-roomed hut on the edge of a swamp. They proliferate like tendrils on a vine: Aureliano himself has 17 sons, all called Aureliano. The family members absorb knowledge, people and property until they and Macondo seem indissoluble. Finally, led by Aureliano senior, they defend the old, innocent values against invasion by a government which wants to impose the same laws in Macondo as everywhere else, and the dynasty disappears from reality, living on only in fantasy, as a memory of how human beings were before the whole world changed.

Márquez's other novels are No One Writes to the Colonel, In Evil Hour, Chronicle of a Death Foretold, The Autumn of the Patriarch *(the stream-of-consciousness monologue of a dying dictator),* Love in the Time of Cholera *(a mesmeric love-story spanning 60 years),* The General in His Labyrinth *(about the last days of Simón Bolívar) and* Of Love and Other Demons *(about an 18th-century priest and the 'mad' girl he falls in love with). His short story collections include* Leaf-storm and Other Stories, Strange Pilgrims *and* Innocent Erendira and Other Stories. *His non-fiction includes* The Fragrance of Guavas *(conversations with a fellow Colombian novelist),* News of a Kidnapping *(about the Colombian drugs wars and their effects on ordinary Colombians) and* The Story of a Shipwrecked Sailor.

READ ON ⟩

● *Love in the Time of Cholera.*
▶ ▷ Salman Rushdie, *Shame*; ▷ Isabel Allende, *The House of the Spirits*; Carlos Fuentes, *Terra Nostra*; ▷ Mario Vargas Llosa, *The Storyteller*; Machado de Assis, *Epitaph of a Small Winner* (19th-century Brazilian novel which is the grandfather of all Latin American 'magic realism').

MARSH, Ngaio (1899–1982)
New Zealand novelist

Few writers used 'classic' detective-story ingredients as magnificently as Marsh. Her murder methods are ingenious and unexpected. Her locations are fascinating: backstage (and onstage) at theatres; during a village-hall concert; in the shearing-shed of a sheep-farm; at a top-level diplomatic reception. Her characters are exotic and her detection is scrupulously fair, with every clue appearing to the reader at the same time as to Alleyn, Marsh's urbane and hawk-eyed sleuth. Above all, her books move at a furious pace, fuelled by her effervescent glee at the follies of humankind. Typical examples are *Artists in Crime* (1938), in which a life-model meets an unfortunate end, *Enter a Murderer* (a 1935 novel about a blackmailing actor done to death on stage) and *A Man Lay Dead* (1934), about a weekend house party in which a murder game becomes all too real.

Marsh continued to publish until the early 1970s and her other books include Hand in Glove, Died in the Wool, Clutch of Constables, Vintage Murder, Spinsters in Jeopardy, Surfeit of Lampreys, Black as He's Painted *and* Death in Ecstasy. Black Beech and Honeydew *is an autobiography, especially interesting on her childhood and her fascination with theatre.*

> READ ON

- *Overture to Death*; *Surfeit of Lampreys*.
- ▷ **Margery Allingham, *The Beckoning Lady*; Caroline Graham, *The Killings at Badger's Drift*; Martha Grimes, *The Man With a Load of Mischief*; ▷ Dorothy L. Sayers, *The Unpleasantness at the Bellona Club*.**

MAUGHAM, W. (William) Somerset (1874–1965)
British writer of novels, short stories and plays

A tireless traveller (especially in the Far East), Maugham wrote hundreds of short stories based on anecdotes he heard or scenes he observed en route. Many of them were later filmed: 'Rain', for example (about a missionary on a cruise-liner in Samoa struggling to reform a prostitute, and losing his own soul in the process), was made half a dozen times. Maugham's novels used true experience in a similar way, shaping it and drawing out its meaning but keeping close to real events. *Liza of Lambeth* (1897) is about a London slum girl tormented by her neighbours for conceiving a bastard child. *Of Human Bondage* (1915) is the story of an orphan, bullied at school because he has a club foot, who struggles to find happiness as an adult, is ravaged by love for a worthless woman, and settles at last to become a country doctor. The stockbroker hero of *The Moon and Sixpence* (1919) gives up career, wife and family to become a painter in the South Seas, as Gauguin did. *Cakes and Ale* (1930) is an acid satire about the 1930s London literary world; Maugham avoided libel suits only by claiming that every writer it pilloried was just another aspect of himself.

Maugham's other novels include The Trembling of a Leaf, The Casuarina Tree, The Razor's Edge *and* Catalina. *His* Complete Short Stories and Collected Plays *(from 1907–32 he wrote two dozen successful plays, mainly comedies) were published in the 1950s.* A Writer's Notebook *and* The Summing Up *give fascinating insights into the balance between his life and work.*

READ ON ▷

▶ to *Liza of Lambeth*: Arthur Morrison, *A Child of the Jago*.
▶ to *Of Human Bondage*: ▷ C.P. Snow, *Strangers and Brothers*.
▶ to *The Moon and Sixpence*: Joyce Cary, *The Horse's Mouth*.
▶ to *Cakes and Ale*: ▷ Rose Macaulay, *Crewe Train*; ▷ J.B. Priestley, *The Image Men*.
▶ to the short stories: ▷ Guy de Maupassant, *Boule de Suif*; ▷ R.L. Stevenson, *Island Nights' Entertainment*; ▷ Rudyard Kipling, *Wee Willie Winkie*; ▷ Paul Theroux, *World's End*.

MAUPASSANT, Guy de (1850–93)
French writer

De Maupassant's stories – over 300, from two-page sketches to full-length novels – have a scalpel ability to cut through pretension, hope, emotion and pretence to the bones of human experience. His best-known work is the long short story *Boule de Suif* (1880). A group of people are travelling across France in a stage-coach; they include Boule de Suif, a prostitute. The rest of the passengers despise her, but she gradually wins them over by her friendliness and humanity. Then the coach is held up by an army officer, who demands sex from her to let it continue. The other passengers beg her to agree – and when the journey continues, they reject her once more. The plot belongs to late 19th-century 'realism', but the way de Maupassant tells it, unsparingly, simply and apparently without inserting any authorial point of view, makes the story and the characters unforgettable.

READ ON ▷

▶ The stories of ▷ Anton Chekhov, ▷ Gustave Flaubert and ▷ V.S. Pritchett.

MAURIAC, François (1885–1970)
French novelist

Mauriac's books, all set among rich families in the Bordeaux wine country at the start of the 20th century, are based on Roman Catholic doctrines of guilt and repentance. They show people tormented by conscience (often quite justified: his characters include murderers, embezzlers, adulterers and family tyrants). Some are never challenged; others are outcasts, reviled by neighbours and relatives as unpleasant as they are themselves. A few repent, and the move from moral darkness to light irradiates their souls. The quest for redemption is, however, always left to the individual: no one is saved against his or her own will. Despite the religious starting point of Mauriac's books, they are anything but churchy: they are psychological case-studies rather than religious tracts. Like ancient Greek tragedy, his work can seem remorselessly gloomy – and it has a similar hypnotic power.

★ THE NEST OF VIPERS (LE NOEUD DE VIPÈRES) (1932)

The book is the confession of a dying man, trying to explain to his grown-up children how his wife's infidelity, many years before, shrivelled his soul and led him to hate both her and them. For 30 years he has plotted to rob them of their inheritance, taking pleasure in the prospect of their distress when he dies and leaves them penniless. Then his wife unexpectedly dies, and he begins a reassessment of his moral situation and a painful process of rehabilitation.

Mauriac's other novels include Thérèse Desqueyroux *(a chilly investigation of the mind of a woman who has poisoned her husband),* Genetrix, The Desert of Love *and* The Woman of the Pharisees *(about religious bigotry, and the way the middle-aged resent the young).*

READ ON >

▶ Georges Bernanos, *The Diary of a Country Priest;*▷ Carson McCullers, *Reflections in a Golden Eye;* ▷ Graham Greene, *Brighton Rock;* Theodore Dreiser, *Sister Carrie;* Julien Green, *The Dark Journey.*

MELVILLE, Herman (1819–91)
US novelist

As a teenager, Melville educated himself by reading the Bible, Shakespeare, Milton and Sir Thomas Browne. He served at sea until he was 23, and later worked as a customs officer. His books take their style from the grand literature he read, and their stories from his own seafaring adventures or from travellers' tales. Many of his novels are long, and read at times as if Genesis or Job had been revised to include whaling, smuggling, shipwreck and naval war. But their epic thought and style easily match the magnificence of the books which influenced him.

★ MOBY-DICK (1851)

Moby Dick is a huge sperm whale, and the novel tells of Captain Ahab's obsessive attempts to hunt it down and kill it. Melville's whaling-lore is extensive, his action-scenes are breathtaking, and he gives an unforgettable picture of Ahab: lonely, driven, daunting as an Old Testament patriarch, a fitting adversary for the monster he has vowed to kill.

Melville's other novels include Typee *and* Omoo*, based on his own experiences after being shipwrecked among cannibals in Polynesia;* Redburn: His First Voyage*;* White-jacket, or The World in a Man-o'-War*; the bitter satire* The Confidence Man *and* Billy Budd*, the story of an inarticulate young sailor who kills a sadistic petty officer. Two short works, of very different styles but both equally haunting, are* Bartleby, the Scrivener*, about a scrivener (copyist) who one day refuses to participate any longer in life, and* Benito Cereno*, a story centred on a mysterious slave ship.*

READ ON >

▶ ▷ Nathaniel Hawthorne, *The Scarlet Letter;* ▷ Victor Hugo, *Toilers of the Sea;* ▷ Joseph Conrad, *The Nigger of the Narcissus.*

▶ novels about dark obsessions of other kinds: ▷ Thomas Mann, *Doctor Faustus*; ▷ Norman Mailer, *An American Dream*; ▷ John Fowles, *The Collector*.

READ ON A THEME: THE MIDDLE AGES

▷ Italo Calvino, *Our Ancestors*
▷ Umberto Eco, *The Name of the Rose*
  John Fuller, *Flying to Nowhere*
▷ William Golding, *The Spire*
▷ Victor Hugo, *Nôtre Dame de Paris*
▷ Thomas Mann, *The Holy Sinner*
  Rosalind Miles, *Guinevere: Queen of the Summer Country* (first of an Arthurian trilogy)
  Ellis Peters, *A Morbid Taste for Bones*
▷ Barry Unsworth, *Morality Play*
  Helen Waddell, *Peter Abelard*

See also: Other Peoples, Other Times; Renaissance Europe

MITCHELL, Margaret (1900–49)
US novelist

☆ *Gone with the Wind*, Mitchell's only book (published in 1936; filmed three years later with Clark Gable and Vivien Leigh) was aptly described in its day as 'the greatest love story ever told'. In Atlanta, Georgia, at the outbreak of the 1860s American Civil War, Scarlett O'Hara falls in love with Ashley Wilkes, the foppish son of a neighbouring plantation owner. But he marries someone else, and she is heartbroken. She pours her love into her family's beautiful house and plantation, Tara. But as the Civil War proceeds, the South loses, Atlanta is burned, and to keep Tara Scarlett is forced to marry other men, including the cynical, rakish Rhett Butler. All fails, Tara is plundered, the devastation of war mirrors the suffering in Scarlett's heart – and when she tells Rhett of her hopeless love for Ashley, Rhett leaves her (with a blunt 'Frankly, my dear, I don't give a damn'). Now, too late, she realizes that he (Rhett) was the man she loved all the time.

> READ ON

▶ Alexandra Ripley, *Scarlett* (authorized sequel, published in 1991) ▷ Boris Pasternak, *Doctor Zhivago*; ▷ Daphne Du Maurier, *Rebecca*; Colleen McCullough, *The Thorn Birds*; M.M. Kaye, *The Far Pavilions*.

READ ON A THEME: MONEY

▷ Martin Amis, *Money*
  Po Bronson, *Bombardiers*
  Linda Davies, *Into the Fire*
▷ John Galsworthy, *The Forsyte Saga*
▷ Jay McInerney, *Brightness Falls*
▷ Christina Stead, *House of All Nations*
▷ Tom Wolfe, *The Bonfire of the Vanities*

MOORCOCK, Michael (born 1939)
British novelist

In the 1960s Moorcock edited the science fiction magazine *New Worlds*, pioneering and encouraging 'new wave' writing, which attempted to give science fiction a new social and political relevance to the time. Moorcock's own 'new wave' work is at its peak in his Jerry Cornelius books (e.g. *The English Assassin*; *The Final Programme*), which are less straightforward novels than firework displays of ideas, magical mystery tours round one man's overheated brain. In later books Moorcock returned to a more sober style, still crammed with ideas but much easier to read. Many of his novels offer alternative versions of the present (*Warlord of the Air*, for example, imagines a 20th century where the First World War never happened and the old 19th-century empires, British, Austrian, Russian and German, are still jockeying for power). Others (*Gloriana*; *The Jewel in the Skull*) are satires about societies which are dark and decadent perversions of our own. All of Moorcock's work, however, is interlinked at some level, a reflection of 'the multiverse' he has imagined, the interconnected, parallel universes through which his characters travel. Jerry Cornelius, Elric of Melnibone (doomed albino prince of a dying race in some of Moorcock's best sword-and-sorcery titles), Corum, Hawkmoon, Von Bek and others are all avatars of the Eternal Champion, Moorcock's Hero With a Thousand Faces.

Many of Moorcock's novels are grouped in series: The Chronicles of the Black Sword, The High History of the Runestaff, The Chronicles of Castle Brass, The Books of Corum, The History of the Eternal Champion. Byzantium Endures, The Laughter of Carthage *and* Jerusalem Commands *are three epic novels which follow the scheming Colonel Pyat through the story, real and imagined, of the twentieth century.* Mother London *and* King of the City *are non-science fiction novels, dazzling recreations of London lives past and present.*

> READ ON

- *Behold the Man* (time traveller arrives in Judaea at the time of Christ), *The Dancers at the End of Time*.
- ▶ to *Mother London*: ▷ Iain Sinclair, *Downriver*; Maureen Duffy, *Capital*.
- ▷ to other New Wave SF writers: Brian Aldiss, *Galaxies Like Grains of Sand*; ▷ J.G. Ballard, *The Terminal Beach*.

MOORE, Brian (1921–99)
Irish/Canadian novelist

Moore's novels explore personal anguish and unease in a similar way to ▷Graham Greene's, though his characters are quite different. He is particularly good at describing feelings of rootlessness and sexual longing in lonely women (*The Lonely Passion of Judith Hearne*; *The Great Victorian Collection*; *The Doctor's Wife*; *The Temptation of Eileen Hughes*), and the torments of firm Roman Catholic believers in threatening situations (*Catholics*; *I am Mary Dunne*; *Black Robe*).

THE COLOUR OF BLOOD (1987)
Cardinal Bem, head of the Church in an unnamed eastern European communist state, survives an assassination attempt only to be taken into 'protective custody'.

He must escape, to make a vital speech at a forthcoming religious celebration – and the book concerns his attempts to shed his physical identity in order to evade police checks, while maintaining the blazing religious and political certainty by which he has always lived his life.

Moore's other novels include Cold Heaven, The Feast of Lupercal, The Mangan Inheritance, An Answer from Limbo, No Other Life, Lies of Silence *and* The Statement. *His final novel,* The Magician's Wife, *set in 19th-century French colonial Africa, where an illusionist uses his talents to demonstrate the supposed superiority of European power, shows Moore's ability to root political and religious ideas in absorbing narrative.*

READ ON >

- ● *The Doctor's Wife.*
- ▶ to *The Colour of Blood*: ▷ Saul Bellow, *The Dean's December*; ▷ Morris West, *The Clowns of God*; Arturo Perez-Reverte, *The Seville Communion.*
- ▶ to Moore's work in general: ▷ Graham Greene, *The Power and the Glory*; ▷ William Trevor, *Death in Summer;* Ronan Bennett, *The Catastrophist.*

MORRIS, William (1834–96)
British craftsman and writer

At the end of his life Morris (Pre-Raphaelite artist, designer and socialist philosopher) turned to fiction, writing historical novels and two future-fantasies, *A Dream of John Ball* (1888) and *News From Nowhere* (1891). *News from Nowhere* has the distinction of being one of the very few fantasies to predict a happy future for the human race. Its hero drifts off to sleep during a political meeting in the 1890s, and wakes up to find that he has been transported 60 years forward in time, and that every socialist dream has been fulfilled. The worker's paradise exists: war, fear, disease and poverty have been eradicated, along with money, prisons and politicians. Everyone is equal, and the harmony between human beings and their environment (the banks of the Thames) is as perfect as it was in Eden before the arrival of the Serpent. Morris's vision is poetic rather than sickly-sweet, and he writes without a twitch of irony. Whatever our hindsight-programmed cynicism a century later, *News from Nowhere* is still a fascinating and remarkable read.

Morris's other fantasies include The House of the Wolfings *(influenced by Icelandic sagas and northern European legends such as Beowulf)*, The Wood Beyond the World *and* The Sundering Flood.

READ ON >

- ● *A Dream of John Ball.*
- ▶ ▷ Robert Graves, *Seven Days in New Crete*; Edward Bellamy, *Looking Backward* (another late 19th-century utopia, anticipating a future society of peace and plenty); Michael Frayn, *Sweet Dreams* (a satire on exactly the kind of liberal-socialist paradise Morris describes – but literal: Frayn's leading character is exploring Heaven itself).

MORRISON, Toni (born 1931)
US novelist

Morrison's books explore the experience of black people in the US, from slavery to the present day. She uses history, however, not as a main subject but as the backdrop to a sensitive and witty description of ordinary people's emotions and relationships. What happened to their ancestors, and to black people in general, only partly determines who they are today. Morrison's novels include *The Bluest Eye* (1970), about an ill-treated girl's escape from reality into the fantasy that she has blue eyes; *Song of Solomon* (1977), about a man's attempts to find meaning in his life by exploring the past history of his people; *Tar Baby* (1981), whose background is the tension between today's 'successful' black people (who may, some of them think, have achieved success by compromising their racial heritage) and the poorer (possibly purer) fellow-citizens from whom they now feel alienated; and *Jazz* (1992), set in 1920s Harlem. Her most recent novel, and the only one she has published since winning the Nobel Prize in 1993, is *Paradise*, an enigmatic account of racial and cultural tension centred on an all-black township in Oklahoma.

> READ ON

- ● *Beloved* (set during the period of national reconstruction after the Civil War); *Sula* (about the friendship of two black women growing up in Ohio in the 1920s and 30s).
- ▶ ▷ Alice Walker, *Meridian*; John Edgar Wideman, *Reuben*; ▷ James Baldwin, *If Beale Street Could Talk.*

MORTIMER, John (born 1923)
British writer

Mortimer remains best known for the Rumpole series of TV comedies and books, about an eccentric, endearing lawyer who wins the cases no one else wants to touch. Mortimer's novels are affectionate comedies of manners which also concern serious subjects – British politics since 1945 in *Paradise Postponed* (1985); infidelity and possible murder in *Summer's Lease* (1988); new Labour joining hands with Thatcherism in *The Sound of Trumpets* (1998). But their light-hearted, jovial style sugars the taste of Mortimer's otherwise acid satire on the way the British upper-middle-class behaves and thinks.

Mortimer's plays include A Voyage Round My Father *and* The Judge. *His Rumpole stories are collected in several volumes, each of which has 'Rumpole' in the title, such as* Rumpole of the Bailey, Rumpole's Return *and* Rumpole and the Angel of Death. *His novels include* Charade, Dunster *and* Felix in the Underworld. Clinging to the Wreckage *is an engaging autobiography,* The Summer of a Dormouse *makes rueful reflections on growing old.*

> READ ON

- ▶ to the Rumpole stories: Carter Dickson, *The Men Who Explained Miracles.*
- ▶ to Mortimer's novels: ▷ H.G. Wells, *Tono-Bungay*; ▷ Angus Wilson, *Anglo-Saxon Attitudes*; ▷ A.N. Wilson, *Love Unknown.*

MOSLEY, Walter (born 1952)
US novelist

Mosley, reportedly Bill Clinton's favourite author, has written a series of books featuring Ezekiel 'Easy' Rawlins, a black detective/fixer and his good friend, the entertaining, if psychopathically violent, Mouse. The first to be published was *Devil in a Blue Dress* (1990), filmed in 1995 with a Mosley screenplay and Denzel Washington as Easy Rawlins. This debut was followed by *A Red Death* (1991), *White Butterfly* (1992), *Black Betty* (1994) and *Little Yellow Dog* (1996). In 1997, *Gone Fishin'*, a kind of prequel to the series originally written (and rejected by publishers) in 1988, finally appeared, bringing the Easy Rawlins books to an apparent close.

In 1995, Mosley also wrote the novel *R L's Dream*, the story of an old blues guitarist reminiscing about his meeting with Robert Johnson, king of the Delta blues singers, and a man notorious for having sold his soul to the Devil (presumably *sans* any kind of dress) in return for unrivalled musical talent and fame. In 1999, he attempted a foray into science fiction with *Blue Light*, a curious combination of mysticism and allegory that many of Mosley's fans found hard to interpret. Two more books have instigated a new series of stories featuring Socrates Fortlow, a tough, wise ex-con, trying to go straight and having a tricky time of it. *Always Outnumbered, Always Outgunned*, the first Socrates collection, appeared in 1998 and the sequel, *Walkin' the Dog,* in 2000.

DEVIL IN A BLUE DRESS (1990)
Although all of the Easy Rawlins books are memorable, *Devil in a Blue Dress* remains the best. A racial inversion of Raymond Chandler's classic noir novel *Farewell, My Lovely*, Mosley's tale sees a white man going into a Negro bar and enlisting the aid of a black man (Rawlins) to help find a missing white woman. Where Mosley's general approach differs is in the setting of Watts, the black area of Los Angeles, and its ubiquitous, if casual, threat of racially-directed violence. As he searches for a white woman with a fondness for black jazz clubs, and jazz players, Easy Rawlins enters new realms of racial tension and violence, finding himself forced to straddle two worlds in order to survive, and Mosley provides a new update on Chandler's mean streets, viewed from a black perspective.

> READ ON

▶ ▷ Raymond Chandler, *Farewell My Lovely*; Chester Himes, *A Rage in Harlem;* Gary Phillips, *Bad Night Is Falling*.

MUNRO, Alice (born 1931)
Canadian short story writer

Many of Munro's stories are set in the villages and small towns of British Columbia and Ontario, places she depicts as genteel, culturally negligible and bigoted, stagnant since the days of the Model-T Ford. Many of her characters are young people of spirit (usually women or girls), stretching the bounds of this environment. Although her themes are modern, her careful descriptions of the streets, houses, rooms and clothes of her people give the stories a strong nostalgic appeal. She is like one of the gentler Southern US writers (▷Eudora Welty, say) transported north.

Munro's story collections include Lives of Girls and Women, Friends of My Youth, Open Streets, The Love of a Good Woman, The Progress of Love, Dance of the Happy Shades *and* Who Do You Think You Are?/The Beggar Maid, *in which the stories are linked to form an episodic novel.*

READ ON >

▶ ▷ Eudora Welty, *The Golden Apples;* ▷ Katherine Mansfield, *Collected Stories;* ▷ Helen Dunmore, *Love of Fat Men;* ▷ Raymond Carver, *Will You Please Be Quiet, Please.*

READ ON A THEME: MURDER MOST MIND-BOGGLING

John Franklin Bardin, *Devil Take the Blue-Tail Fly*
Edmund Crispin, *The Moving Toyshop*
Peter Dickinson, *The Lively Dead*
Carter Dickson, *The Red Widow Murders*
▷ Umberto Eco, *The Name of the Rose*
H.R.F. Keating, *A Rush on the Ultimate*
Cameron McCabe, *The Face on the Cutting-room Floor*
Josephine Tey, *The Singing Sands*

See also: Classic Detection; Great (Classic) Detectives; Private Eyes

---

MURDOCH, Iris (1919–1999)
Irish/British novelist and philosopher

The subject of Murdoch's two dozen novels is personal politics: the ebb and flow of relationships, the way we manipulate others and are ourselves manipulated. The setting is the present day; the people are middle-class, professional, usually from the English home counties and they are all bizarre, possessed by a demon which blurs reality and dream into a single, mesmeric state. Seduction, mysticism and moral disintegration are favourite themes, and the innocent late adolescent (whose effect on other people's lives is often devastating) is a standard character.

☆ THE BELL (1958)
Should we live our lives by the conventions of society or moment by moment, defining ourselves by our changing moods and enthusiasms? This question perplexes every character in *The Bell*: all are waiting for a sudden inspiration or discovery which will define their existence, show them how they should behave. The setting is a lay community housed in a former convent, a refuge for an eccentric collection of inmates whose peace is disturbed by the arrival of two amoral 'innocents', Dora and Toby. *The Bell* was popular in the hippie 1960s, and still seems to catch the wide-eyed, distracted mood of those times. But its story and characters are fascinating and its images (for example that of the naked, startlingly white-bodied Toby diving, like a fallen angel, into the murky

convent lake to investigate a sunken bell) are as disturbing as they are unforgettable.

Murdoch's other novels include The Flight from the Enchanter, The Sandcastle, A Severed Head, The Red and the Green, The Time of the Angels, The Sea The Sea, The Book and the Brotherhood, The Message to the Planet, The Green Knight *and* Jackson's Dilemma.

READ ON ▷

- ● *The Green Knight.*
- ▶ Mary McCarthy, *A Charmed Life*. Alice Thomas Ellis, *The 27th Kingdom*. D.M. Thomas, *Birthstone*. Mary Flanagan, *Trust*. Irene Handl, *The Sioux*.

READ ON A THEME: MUSIC

- ▷ Anthony Burgess, *The Piano Players*
- ▷ Willa Cather, *The Song of the Lark*
- ▷ Hermann Hesse, *Gertrud*
  David Leavitt, *The Page Turner*
- ▷ Thomas Mann, *Doctor Faustus*
- ▷ H.H. Richardson, *The Getting of Wisdom*
- ▷ Vikram Seth, *An Equal Music*
  Joseph Skvorecky, *Dvorák in Love*
- ▷ Rose Tremain, *Music & Silence*

N

NABOKOV, Vladimir (1899–1977)
Russian/US novelist and short story writer

Nabokov wrote in Russian until 1940, when he settled in the US; thereafter, he worked in English, and also translated and revised his earlier works. He was fascinated by language, and his books are firework displays of wit, purple-prose descriptions, ironical asides and multi-lingual puns: for his admirers, style is a major pleasure of his work. Several of his novels take the form of teasing 'biographies', revealing as much about their dogged biographers as their subjects. The hero of *The Defence* (1929) is a chess-champion, crippled emotionally both by his profession and by his feeling of identity with the whole Russian cultural tradition. The heroes of *The Real Life of Sebastian Knight* (1941) and *Look at the Harlequins!* (1974) play ironical games with their would-be biographers: the more they seem to reveal themselves, the more elusive they become. ☆ *Pnin* (1957) is a sad comedy about an accident-prone Russian professor at a US university, trying to keep the customs of the Old Country in a baffling new environment. *Invitation to a Beheading* (1935) and *Bend Sinister* (1947), Nabokov's most political books, are stories of oppression and nightmare in harsh totalitarian regimes. *Despair* (1934) is a dream-like psychological thriller about a man who hunts down and murders his double, only to find that he has destroyed himself. Humbert Humbert, the tragi-comic hero of *Lolita* (1955) is led by sexual infatuation for a twelve-year-old girl into a farcical kidnapping, a flight from the police through the motels and diners of grubby middle America, and finally to murder. The book's tone of obsessive erotic reverie is repeated in *Ada* (1969), about an incestuous love-affair between two rich, spoiled people in a mysterious country midway between 19th-century Russia and the 1930s US.

★ PALE FIRE (1962)
Few novels can ever have had such an original form: a 999-line poem with introduction and commentary. The poet is an exiled Eastern European king; the commentator is a fool who fantasizes that he is the real heir to the throne, and that he is writing under the shadow of an assassination-plot. The effect is as if ▷ Anthony Hope had beefed up someone's PhD thesis: *Pale Fire* is funny, clever – and, despite its bizarre form, a delightfully easy read.

Nabokov's other novels include King, Queen, Knave; Glory; Camera Obscura/ Laughter in the Dark *and* The Gift. Nabokov's Dozen, Nabokov's Quartet, A Russian Beauty, Tyrants Destroyed *and* Details of a Sunset *are short story collections.* Speak, Memory *is a poetic account of Nabokov's privileged, pre-Revolutionary childhood.*

READ ON ▷

- ● *Pnin*.
- ▶ to Nabokov's elegant, games-playing style: ▷ Muriel Spark, *The Abbess of Crewe*; ▷ John Barth, *Giles Goat-boy*; Frederic Raphael, *California Time*; ▷ Julian Barnes, *Flaubert's Parrot*.
- ▶ to his darker novels: ▷ Franz Kafka, *The Trial*; Jerzy Kosinski, *The Painted Bird*; ▷ Martin Amis, *Success*.
- ▶ to his short stories: Donald Barthelme, *City Life*.

NAIPAUL, V.S. (Vidiadhar Surajprasad) (born 1932)
Trinidadian novelist and non-fiction writer

A Trinidadian Indian who settled in England in his early 20s, Naipaul identifies exclusively with none of these three communities, and has written about all of them. His early novels (culminating in *A House for Mr Biswas*) were gentle tragi-comedies, but from the late 1960s onwards his books grew darker. He wrote savage non-fiction about the West Indies, India, South America and the Middle East, a mixture of travel and harsh political and social analysis, and his novels dealt with totalitarian oppression and despair. *In a Free State* is about cultural alienation: its central characters are an Indian servant in Washington, a Trini-dadian in racist London and two whites in a fanatical black-power Africa. *Guerrillas* is set in a Caribbean dictatorship, *A Bend in the River* in a 'new' African country, emerging from centuries of colonial exploitation into a corrupt, Orwellian state. For most of the 1980s Naipaul wrote no fiction, but in 1987 he published *The Enigma of Arrival*, synthesizing most of his earlier themes. Its hero, a Trinidadian writer living near Salisbury, reflects on the way his ambitions and his art have changed as he has grown older, on the nature of friendship, on the passing of 'old England' and, generally, on the breakdown of the former order of the world. The book's tone is sombre, mellow and rueful; it seems more like autobiography than fiction. It is a unique and moving work.

★☆ A HOUSE FOR MR BISWAS (1961)
Mr Biswas is a free spirit shackled by circumstance. He is a poor Hindu in Trinidad, an educated man among illiterates, a good-natured soul who irritates everyone. He marries into an enormous extended family, the Tulsis, and spends the next 20 years trying to avoid being engulfed by their lifestyle, which he finds vulgar and ridiculous. The conflict – critics see it as an allegory about the absorption of political or ethnic minorities – is chiefly expressed in comedy. Mr Biswas is desperate to escape from the Tulsis's rambling mansion, thronged with disapproving relatives; his ambition is to live decently with his family in a home of his own. Although he succeeds, the book ends ironically and tragically: his victory, the vindication of all he stands for, turns to ashes even as he savours it.

Naipaul's other novels include The Suffrage of Elvira, Mr Stone and the Knights Companion, The Mystic Masseur *and* The Mimic Men. *His non-fiction books include* The Middle Passage *(on the West Indies and South America)*, An Area of Darkness *and* India: a Wounded Civilization *(two studies, a decade apart, of Indian life and politics) and* Among the Believers *and* Beyond Belief *(two investigations into the Islamic cultures of the Far East)*. Miguel Street *and* A

Flag on the Island *are collections of short stories.* Letters Between a Father and a Son *is the correspondence between Naipaul, studying at Oxford, and his father, working as a journalist in Trinidad and nursing his own literary ambitions. The correspondence is brought to a moving conclusion by the elder Naipaul's sudden death at the age of only 47.*

READ ON >

● *A Way in the World.*
▶ to the social comedies: Shiva Naipaul (V.S.'s brother), *Fireflies*; ▷ R.K. Narayan, *Mr Sampath/The Printer of Malgudi*; Amos Tutuola, *The Palm-wine Drinkard*; Timothy Mo, *Sour-Sweet.*
▶ to Naipaul's political novels: ▷ Joseph Conrad, *Nostromo*; Christopher Hope, *Black Swan.*
▶ to *The Enigma of Arrival*: P.H. Newby, *Leaning in the Wind.*

NARAYAN, R.K. (Rasipuran Krishnaswami) (1907–2001)
Indian novelist

Narayan's stories are set in the imaginary southern Indian town of Malgudi, or in the villages and farms of the nearby Mempi Hills. His characters are shop-keepers, peasant farmers, craftsmen, priests, money-lenders, teachers and housewives, and his theme is the way Hindu belief sustains them in the face of the bewildering or ridiculous events of daily life. Many of his books are comedies. In *The Maneater of Malgudi* (1961) a demented taxidermist works on a series of creatures of ever-increasing size until, to universal panic, he suggests killing and stuffing the town's sacred elephant. The narrator of *A Tiger for Malgudi* (1983) is a worldly-wise tiger who becomes a circus performer, a film star and a travelling guru. *The Painter of Signs* (1976) recounts the farcical relationship between Raman, an ambitious but under-employed sign-painter, and Daisy from the Family Planning Centre, a New Woman whose life is dedicated not to love-affairs but to preventing over-population. Other books replace knockabout with gentler, more bitter-sweet scenes from the human comedy. *The English Teacher/Grateful to Life and Death* (1945) is a beautiful story about a husband coping with grief after the death of his beloved wife. In *The Vendor of Sweets* (1967) the sweet-manufacturer Jagan is a devout Hindu who lives an austere, uncompli-cated and self-sufficient life. This life is overturned when his wastrel son Mali arrives from Delhi with a non-Indian wife, moves into Jagan's house, and undertakes a scheme for enriching himself by marketing a machine for writing novels.

Narayan's other novels include Swami and Friends *and* The Bachelor of Arts *(which with* The English Teacher *form a trilogy),* Mr Sampath/The Printer of Malgudi, The Financial Expert, The Guide *and* Waiting for the Mahatma. *Under the* Banyan Tree *and* Malgudi Days *are short-story collections;* Gods, Demons and Others *is Narayan's re-telling of stories from Hindu mythology;* My Days *is a placid autobiography.*

READ ON >

● *The Financial Expert.*
▶ Rabindranath Tagore, *The Home and the World*; Anita Desai, *The Clear Light of*

Day; S.N. Ghose, *And Gazelles Leaping*; ▷ Kazuo Ishiguro, *An Artist of the Floating World*; Tove Jansson, *The Summer Book*; Giovanni Guareschi, *The Little World of Don Camillo* (short stories).

READ ON A THEME: NEW YORK

▷ Paul Auster, *The New York Trilogy*
Kevin Baker, *Dreamland*
E.L. Doctorow, *Ragtime*
▷ Henry James, *Washington Square*
Tama Janowitz, *A Certain Age*
▷ Jay McInerney, *Brightness Falls*
▷ Toni Morrison, *Jazz*
Henry Roth, *Call It Sleep*
Damon Runyon, *Guys and Dolls*
▷ J.D. Salinger, *The Catcher in the Rye*
Hubert Selby Jr, *Last Exit to Brooklyn*

READ ON A THEME: NINETEENTH-CENTURY ENGLAND

▷ Peter Carey, *Jack Maggs*
▷ Charles Dickens, *Hard Times*
▷ John Fowles, *The French Lieutenant's Woman*
George and Weedon Grossmith, *The Diary of a Nobody*
▷ William Thackeray, *Pendennis*
▷ Anthony Trollope, *The Warden*

NOON, Jeff (born 1958)
British novelist

In the late 1980s and early 1990s a lot of inventive and adventurous fiction was being produced in the science fiction genre. Little of it was being written in Britain. The US was where the action was, 'cyberpunk' was the buzz-word and writers like William Gibson and Bruce Sterling were the leading innovators. Manchester, England seemed an unlikely setting for cutting-edge science fiction. Yet Jeff Noon's *Vurt* (1993) emerged from that unlikely setting as one of the most original science fiction books of the last twenty years. Cleverly mixing the narrative conventions of old-fashioned pulp fiction with up-to-the-minute ideas about virtual reality, Noon creates a surreal Manchester of the near future where the hallucinogenic drug of choice, vurt, carries its users into a variety of alternate realities. The narrator, Scribble, has lost his sister amidst the labyrinthine byways of one of these alternate realities and he embarks on a quest to find her. Noon has followed up his debut novel with a number of similar fictions (*Pollen*, *Nymphomation* and the stories in *Pixel Juice* all explore worlds where virtual technologies and drug cultures intermingle) but, in many ways, his most revealing novel since *Vurt* has been *Automated Alice* (1996). In interviews Noon has cited Lewis Carroll as a major influence and this updating of Alice's adventures places him in a tradition of English fantasy writers and lovers of surreal wordplay as well as within the science fiction genre.

READ ON ▷

▶ ▷ **Neal Stephenson,** *Snow Crash*; **Michael Marshall Smith,** *Only Forward*; **Tricia Sullivan,** *Someone to Watch Over Me*.

NORFOLK, Lawrence (born 1963)
British novelist

Like an English version of ▷ Umberto Eco, Lawrence Norfolk writes big, baggy novels that raid history, mythology and philosophy in search of stories to entertain and educate the reader. *Lemprière's Dictionary* (1991) took as its starting point the life of the classical scholar John Lemprière, author of an 18th-century dictionary of classical literature and the classical world. But Norfolk zigzagged back and forth through the centuries, using the dark and tangled family history of the Lemprières and the subjects of John's scholarship to introduce stories from Greek and Roman mythology, the founding of the East India Company, the siege of La Rochelle and the crime-ridden streets of Georgian London. No reader could feel short-changed by the book's ebullient concoction of corruption, conspiracy, piracy, assassinations and murders, mismatched love affairs and the misdeeds of the past returning to haunt later generations. It was an explosive debut and was followed by another sprawling monster of a book, *The Pope's Rhinoceros* (1996), which centred on 16th-century attempts to deliver a rhinoceros, an almost mythical beast at the time, to Pope Leo X. Again, this is just one of a whole gallery of interweaving stories about a Europe over which the shadow of the Reformation hangs. Norfolk's most recent book, *In the Shape of a Boar*, is shorter but, in many ways, more ambitious than his first two novels, in its linking of the mythological hunting of the Boar of Kalydon with an incident in Second World War Greece and its repercussions in the life of a Jewish poet.

READ ON ▷

▶ ▷ **Umberto Eco,** *The Island of the Day Before*; ▷ **Rose Tremain,** *Music & Silence*; ▷ **Iain Sinclair,** *Downriver*; **Adam Thorpe,** *Pieces of Light*.

O

O'BRIAN, Patrick (1914–2000).
English novelist

O'Brian's 'Jack Aubrey' novels, about an officer in the British Navy in Napoleonic times, chart his hero's progress up the ranks, and place him in great events and adventures of the time. The characters are three-dimensional (shown especially in the relationship between Aubrey and his friend, the ship's surgeon Stephen Maturin), the sailing and fighting are wonderfully described, the plots are exciting and the talk is multi-faceted, ironical and convincingly real. The novels, self-contained but adding up to one of the most impressive of all works of naval fiction, are *Master and Commander* (1970), *Post Captain* (1972), *HMS Surprise* (1973), *The Mauritius Command* (1977), *Desolation Island* (1978), *The Fortune of War* (1979), *The Surgeon's Mate* (1980) *The Ionian Mission* (1982), *Treason's Harbour* (1983), *The Far Side of the World* (1984), *The Reverse of the Medal* (1986), *The Letter of Marque* (1988), *The Thirteen Gun Salute* (1989), *The Nutmeg of Consolation* (1991), *Clarissa Oakes* (1992), *The Wine-Dark Sea* (1993), *The Commodore* (1994), *The Yellow Admiral* (1997), *The Hundred Days* (1998) and *Blue at the Mizzen* (1999).

> **READ ON**

- **The Golden Ocean** and **The Unknown Shore** are sea stories that predate the Aubrey/Maturin novels; **Collected Short Stories** were largely written in the 1950s.
- ▷ C.S. Forester, Hornblower novels. Alexander Kent, Bolitho novels, beginning with **Richard Bolitho, Midshipman**.

O'HARA, John (1905–1970)
US novelist and short story writer

In 18 novels and no less than 374 short stories, O'Hara created a one-person archive of US life and thought in the first half of the 20th century. He wrote of ordinary middle Americans coping with financial, social, religious and family crises. Many of his stories are told in the first person or in the form of letters, and are strong on irony, revealing the teller's mind or attitudes despite the words he or she uses. The prevailing mood is desperation. O'Hara's people feel that their lives and their country are like monsters out of control; all that can be done is to try to live a decent life, and even that ambition is ambushed by poverty, drink, sex, ambition or politics. This concentration on the darker side of life sometimes leads, in O'Hara's longer books, to melodrama: they deal in a soap-opera style with such issues as abortion, alcoholism or incest. His short stories, by contrast, are well-controlled, single anecdotes, remarkable for their restraint.

O'Hara's story collections include Files on Parade, Here's O'Hara, The Great Short Stories of O'Hara, 49 Stories, The O'Hara Generation *and* Pal Joey *(which he, Rodgers and Hart made into a successful musical, about an amoral, cynical 1930s night-club owner). His novels include* Butterfield 8, Ten North Frederick, A Rage to Live *and* Appointment in Samarra.

| READ ON ▷ |

▶ to O'Hara's novels: ▷ John Cheever, *The Wapshot Scandal*.
▶ to O'Hara's short stories: Sherwood Anderson, *Winesburg, Ohio*; Ring Lardner, *You Know Me, Al*; Peter Taylor, *The Old Forest*; ▷ Raymond Carver, *Cathedral*.

OKRI, Ben (born 1959)
Nigerian novelist and poet

Okri lives in England and writes in English, but his work has a lilt and cadence learned from Yoruba folk-stories and oral poetry. His best-known book is *The Famished Road* (1991), the story of a spirit born as a child to an ordinary family, who falls so in love with his human parents and with the marvellous mortal world that he chooses to remain with us, exploring and enjoying. The book's pleasures are partly the fun to be had from a mischievous little boy with supernatural powers let loose in a deeply traditional society, and partly the re-discovery, as it were through alien eyes, of the everyday wonders, mundane magic of our own existence and the world we live in.

Okri's other novels are Flowers and Shadows, The Landscapes Within *and* Astonishing the Gods, *a poetic fable about a man's search for visibility and meaning in his life.* Incidents at the Shrine *and* Stars of the New Curfew *are short-story collections;* An African Elegy *contains poems;* A Way to be Free *is a collection of essays*

| READ ON ▷ |

● *Songs of Enchantment; Infinite Riches* (sequels to *The Famished Road* following the further adventures of the spirit-child Azaro in the mortal world).
▶ Wole Soyinka, *The Interpreters*; Senbene Ousmane, *God's Bits of Wood* ▷ Salman Rushdie, *Haroun and the Sea of Stories*.

READ ON A THEME: ON THE EDGE OF SANITY

Djuna Barnes, *Nightwood*
▷ Charlotte Brontë, *Villette*
▷ Graham Greene, *Brighton Rock*
▷ Hermann Hesse, *Steppenwolf*
▷ Franz Kafka, *The Trial*
▷ Malcolm Lowry, *Under the Volcano*
▷ Vladimir Nabokov, *Despair*
▷ R.K. Narayan, *The English Teacher/Grateful to Life and Death*

See also: Depression and Psychiatry; Madness

ONDAATJE, Michael (born 1943)
Sri Lankan/Canadian novelist and poet

A poet before he was a novelist, Michael Ondaatje writes prose that is as rich, dense and allusive as poetry. Narrative is the bare bones on which Ondaatje hangs his often haunting and beautiful language and imagery. His early novels were resolutely experimental in form. Two are about real historical characters. *Coming Through Slaughter* (1979) tells the life of the legendary cornet player Buddy Bolden, allegedly the 'inventor' of New Orleans jazz, and does so in a mixture of poetry, prose, song lyrics and reminiscence. *The Collected Works of Billy the Kid* (1981) similarly presents a collage of poems, photographs and documentary evidence related to the life of, and, more significantly, the myth surrounding the teenage gunfighter. Both developed a certain cult status but were not major bestsellers. Only with *The English Patient* and the success of Anthony Minghella's film version of it has Ondaatje found the wide audience his fiction deserves

THE ENGLISH PATIENT (1992)
As the Second World War drags towards its conclusion, a nurse and her patient, an Englishman burnt beyond recognition and swathed in bandages, are holed up in a villa near Florence after the retreat of the Germans. Two other damaged individuals, a Sikh bomb-disposal expert and a former criminal who has suffered torture, are now the villa's only other occupants. As the nurse and her two companions enter into complex relations of their own and speculate about the enigma of the English patient, he returns in his own mind to North Africa before the war and an intense but doomed love affair. Written in a prose that lingers on the details of the visible, tangible world and unfolding its story in a jigsaw of interlocking scenes, *The English Patient* is a hypnotic exploration of love, memory and desire.

> READ ON

- *Anil's Ghost* (a searching tale of love and politics set in a Sri Lanka torn apart by civil war).
▶ Paul Bowles, *The Sheltering Sky*; ▷ Gabriel García Márquez, *Love in the Time of Cholera*; Alessandro Baricco, *Silk*.

ORWELL, George (1903–50)
British writer

'George Orwell' was the pseudonym of Eric Blair. In his 20s he worked for the Colonial Police in Burma (an experience he later used in the novel *Burmese Days*). He returned to England disgusted with Imperialism and determined never again to work for or support 'the system'. In fact, most of his work thereafter was literary: articles, essays and books taking a jaundiced view of British society and attitudes. Commissioned to report on the industrial north of England, he wrote *The Road to Wigan Pier* (1937), an indictment not only of unemployment and poverty but also of the failure of idealists, of all political parties, to find a cure. *Down and Out in Paris and London* (1933) is a description of the life of tramps and other derelicts; *Homage to Catalonia* (1938) is a withering account of the failure of the International Brigade in the Spanish Civil War. During the 1930s Orwell published three ▷Wellsian novels, about people dissatisfied with the constricting middle-class or lower-middle-class lives they led. It was not until 1945, when the Second World War seemed to have blown away forever the humbug and complacency which Orwell considered the worst of all British characteristics, that he published his first overtly political book, *Animal Farm*. In this Stalinist 'fairy story', pigs turn their farm into a workers' democracy in which 'all animals are equal, but some are more equal than others', and the rule of all quickly degenerates into the tyranny of the few. The success of *Animal Farm* encouraged Orwell to write an even more savage political fantasy, *1984*.

1984 (1949)

In the totalitarian future, Winston Smith's job is to rewrite history, adding to or subtracting from the record people who are in or out of Party favour. He falls in love – a forbidden thing, because it arises from free will and not by order of the Party – and is betrayed to the Thought Police. He is tortured until he not only admits, but comes to believe, that the Party is right in everything: if it says that 2 + 2 = 5, then that is so. The book ends, chillingly, with the idea that Winston has won the victory over himself: he is happy because he has chosen, of his own free will, to have no choice.

Orwell's 1930s novels are A Clergyman's Daughter, Keep the Aspidistra Flying *and* Coming Up for Air. *His essays, letters and journalism have been collected in four volumes in paperback.*

> **READ ON**

▶ to the savage politics of *1984*: Arthur Koestler, *Darkness at Noon*; ▷ Franz Kafka, *The Trial*; ▷ Vladimir Nabokov, *Bend Sinister*.

▶ Future-fantasies of a similarly bleak kind: Yevgeni Zamyatin, *We*; ▷ Aldous Huxley, *Brave New World*; ▷ Anthony Burgess, *A Clockwork Orange* (Burgess also wrote *1985*, a right-wing riposte to *1984*).

▶ ▷ Mario Vargas Llosa, *The City and the Dogs/The Time of the Hero*, set in a Peruvian military academy, is that rare thing, an Orwellian political allegory which is also funny.

READ ON A THEME: OTHER PEOPLES, OTHER TIMES

(historical novels set in remote or unusual times)
  Jean M. Auel, *Clan of the Cave Bear* (prehistoric Europe)
  Robert Edric, *The Book of the Heathen* (late 19th-century Belgian Congo)
  Shusako Endo, *Silence* (17th-century Japan)
▷ Gustave Flaubert, *Salammbô* (ancient Carthage)
  Matthew Kneale, *English Passengers* (early 19th-century Tasmania)

▷ Norman Mailer, *Ancient Evenings* (ancient Egypt)
  Naomi Mitchison, *Early in Orcadia* (prehistoric Orkneys)
▷ Jane Rogers, *Promised Lands* (18th-century Australia)
▷ Robert Silverberg, *Gilgamesh the King* (ancient Sumeria)
  Sigrid Undset, *Kristin Lavransdatter* (14th-century Norway)
▷ Mario Vargas Llosa, *The War of the End of the World* (19th-century Peru)

See also: Ancient Greece and Rome; The Bible

PATHWAYS

GEORGE ORWELL

1984
(repression and opression in grim totalitarian future)

BLEAK PROSPECTS
(nightmare scenarios for the future of human
    society)

George **Turner**, *The Sea and Summer*
Margaret **Atwood**, *The Handmaid's Tale*
Paul **Theroux**, *O-Zone*
Anthony **Burgess**, *A Clockwork Orange*
Russell **Hoban**, *Riddley Walker*
Ray **Bradbury**, *Fahrenheit 451*

THE GHASTLY PAST
(totalitarian, fundamentalist nightmares from
    'real' history)

Nathaniel **Hawthorne**, *The Scarlet Letter*
Maxim **Gorky**, *Foma Gordeev*
Willa **Cather**, *Death Comes for the Archbishop*
Graham **Greene**, *Brighton Rock*
Alexandr **Solzhenitsyn**, *One Day in the Life of
    Ivan Denisovich*

INNER HELL
(the nightmare is inside us)

William **Golding**, *Lord of the Flies*
Joseph **Conrad**, *Heart of Darkness*
Georges **Simenon**, *The Murderer*
Fay **Weldon**, *Life and Loves of a She-Devil*
Will **Self**, *My Idea of Fun*

P

PARETSKY, Sara (born 1947)
US novelist

Sara Paretsky was one of the first writers working in the hard-boiled tradition to create a convincing female central character who could support a series of novels. Her private eye, V.I. Warshawski, moves in a murky world of drug-trafficking, union corruption, medical fraud and lethal religious politics. Warshawski is a crack shot, a karate expert, and has an armoury of bruisingly unanswerable one-liners. She is also devastatingly beautiful, and combines contempt for masculine bravado with a willingness to go weak at the knees whenever a gorgeous hunk swims into view.

The Warshawski books are Indemnity Only, Deadlock, Killing Orders, Bitter Medicine, Blood Shot, Burn Marks, Guardian Angel, Tunnel Vision *and* Hard Time.

> READ ON

● *Ghost Country* (a non-Warshawski novel of life on Chicago's meanest streets).
▶ ▷ Sue Grafton, *O is for Outlaw*; Marcia Muller, *Listen to the Silence*; Janet Dawson, *Witness to Evil*; Sarah Dunant, *Fatlands* (a British version of the female private detective story).

PASTERNAK, Boris (1890–1960)
Russian poet and novelist

In the USSR Pasternak is remembered chiefly as a poet and translator (of ▷ Goethe and Shakespeare). Western readers know him for his 1957 novel ★ *Doctor Zhivago*, and for the savage reaction of the Soviet authorities of the time, who banned the book and made Pasternak renounce his Nobel Prize. *Doctor Zhivago* is about a doctor, Zhivago, and a teacher, Lara, caught up in the civil war which followed the 1917 Revolution. Although each is married to someone else and has a child, they fall in love – and the feverishness of their affair is increased by knowledge that neither it nor they will survive the war, since they come from a doomed class, the bourgeoisie. Horrified and powerless, they witness the brutality, class hatred and fury which precede the establishment of the USSR. Despite the reaction of the late-1950s authorities to all this, Pasternak was not really concerned with politics. He was more interested in the idea of people out of step with their time, star-crossed by destiny, and in the way Zhivago's and Lara's relationship was an emotional counterpart to the chaos and destruction all round them. The book ends with Zhivago's poems about Lara, like faded love-letters plucked from the rubble of the past.

> READ ON ▷

▶ ▷ Leo Tolstoy, *Anna Karenina*; ▷ Ernest Hemingway, *A Farewell to Arms*; ▷ Elizabeth Bowen, *The Heat of the Day*; ▷ Margaret Mitchell, *Gone With the Wind*; ▷ Iris Murdoch, *The Red and the Green*.

PEAKE, Mervyn (1911–68)
British novelist and artist

Peake earned his living as an artist, drawing cartoons and grotesque, sombre illustrations to such books as *Treasure Island* and *The Hunting of the Snark*. He also made portraits of the main characters in his own novels: unsmiling freaks with distorted limbs and haunted eyes, violently cross-hatched as if with giant cobwebs. He admired ▷ Poe and ▷ Kafka, and his own work lopes gleefully – and hilariously – down the same dark passages of the imagination, peering into every corner and detailing the horrors that wait behind every moss-grown, rust-hinged door.

★☆ GORMENGHAST (1946–59)
The 'Gormenghast' trilogy *Titus Groan, Gormenghast* and *Titus Alone* takes place in a mist-shrouded, monstrous kingdom surrounding the crumbling Gothic castle of Gormenghast. Evil broods, ever undefined but waiting to pounce. Everyone, from Lord Sepulchrave himself to the physician Prunesquallor, from Nanny Slagg to the demented scullion Steerpike, lives every second of each day by a precise, bizarre ritual, as compulsive and pointless as the movements of the insane. *Titus Groan* describes the fearful consequences when Steerpike, to further his own dark ambitions, starts fomenting social revolution. *Gormenghast* is about the growing-up of Titus, 77th Earl of Groan: how he learns about his inheritance, uncovers the castle's secrets and begins to chafe against the rituals which choke its people's lives. In *Titus Alone* Titus breaks free of the castle and explores the country outside, an arrogant knight-errant on a terrifying, pointless quest.

Peake's only other novel, Mr Pye, *is a gentler story about a man on Sark in the Channel Islands who shows distressing signs of turning into an angel.* Peake's Progress, *an anthology of his poems, plays and drawings, is a splendid introduction to his work and includes an extra Gormenghast story, 'A Boy in Darkness'.*

> READ ON ▷

▶ **to** *Gormenghast*: ▷ Mary Shelley, *Frankenstein*; ▷ Edgar Allan Poe, *The Fall of the House of Usher*; Stanislaw Lem, *Memoirs Found in a Bathtub*; ▷ Michael Moorcock, *Gloriana*.

READ ON A THEME: PERPLEXED BY LIFE

(people battling to understand and control their destiny)
Pearl Abraham, *The Romance Reader*
▷ **Saul Bellow, *Humboldt's Gift***
▷ **Albert Camus, *The Fall***
▷ **Erica Jong, *Fear of Flying***
▷ **Iris Murdoch, *The Sandcastle***
▷ **V.S. Naipaul, *A House for Mr Biswas***
▷ **Italo Svevo, *The Confessions of Zeno***
▷ **Anne Tyler, *The Ladder of Years***
▷ **Angus Wilson, *Anglo-Saxon Attitudes***

See also: Battling with Life; Revisiting One's Past; Teenagers

---

READ ON A THEME: PLACES

▷ **Melvyn Bragg, *The Maid of Buttermere* (English Lake District)**
▷ **Emily Brontë, *Wuthering Heights* (Yorkshire moors)**
▷ **Graham Greene, *The Comedians* (Haiti)**
▷ **Thomas Hardy, *Jude the Obscure* (rural Wessex)**
▷ **John Irving, *The Cider-house Rules* (rural Maine)**
▷ **Rudyard Kipling, *Kim* (rural India)**
▷ **R.K. Narayan, *The Painter of Signs* (small-town India)**
▷ **Graham Swift, *Waterland* (East Anglia)**

See also: Australia; Canada; Deep South, USA; Egypt; Ireland; Israel; Japan; London; New York; Scotland; Small Town Life, USA; Village and Countryside; The Wilderness

---

POE, Edgar Allan (1809–49)
US short story writer and poet

Poe's miserable life is almost as well-known as his stories. He was an orphan whose foster-father hated him; he was thrown out of university, military college and half a dozen jobs because of the instability of his character; in order to earn a living he suppressed his real ambition (to be a poet) in favour of hack

PATHWAYS

MERVYN PEAKE

GORMENGHAST
(Titus Groan uncovers his destiny
in a sinister castle-kingdom)

DARK IMAGININGS
(terror walks)

Denis **Wheatley**, *The Ka of Gifford Hillary*
James **Herbert**, *The Magic Cottage*
Bram **Stoker**, *Dracula*
Stephen **King**, *Pet Sematary*
Edgar Allan **Poe**, *Tales of Mystery and Imagination*

CASTLES AND OLD, DARK HOUSES
(– and the innocents who wander into them)

Angela **Carter**, *The Magic Toyshop*
Henry **James**, *The Turn of the Screw*
Daphne **Du Maurier**, *Rebecca*
Susan **Hill**, *The Woman in Black*
Michael **Innes**, *Lament for a Maker*

FANTASY SOCIETIES
(if you think this is the real world, beware)

Ursula **Le Guin**, *Malafrena*
Robert **Silverberg**, *Lord Valentine's Castle*
Robert **Irwin**, *The Arabian Nightmare*
Jack **Vance**, *The Blue World*

DERANGED – MOI?
(the lunatics take over the asylum)

Ken **Kesey**, *One Flew Over the Cuckoo's Nest*
Patricia **Highsmith**, *The Glass Cell*
Robert **Silverberg**, *Tom O'Bedlam*
Gore **Vidal**, *Kalki*

STARTPOINTS

POETRY

Even if we choose only from English poetry, the range is enormous. There are a thousand poets, a million poems. We may prefer book-long epics (such as Milton's *Paradise Lost*, recounting the Garden of Eden story of the Fall of Man), or short, lyric statements like the poems of Emily Dickinson or A.E. Housman. Our taste may be for ecstatic description and reflection (such as Shelley provides), gravely intellectual rumination (like that in Ezra Pound's or John Berryman's work) or jokey nonsense (such as that of Ogden Nash or Pam Ayres). And because enjoying poetry depends so much on our mood and emotions, selecting what to read is more like choosing a piece of music to listen to than picking a novel or a travel book. For many people, browsing through anthologies is a good way to discover (or rediscover) poets: five minutes' work in the poetry section of the library, or reading the reviews of new poetry in a Sunday newspaper, can open Aladdin's Cave.

Auden, W.H. (1907–73). The personal and political explored in poetry of virtuoso technical ability, wit and intellectual range. It sometimes seems as if Auden could take any subject from the Spanish Civil War to the death of a lover and address it in any poetic form he chose.

Browning, Robert (1812–89), *Men and Women* **(1855)**. Lively verse 'snapshots' of grandees, artists, soldiers, monks, all telling us their stories in dramatic monologue. Easy-flowing, character-rich verse, full of quotable (and much quoted) lines and phrases.

Chaucer, Geoffrey (*c***1343–1400),** *The Canterbury Tales* **(1387)**. 24 tales, bawdy, wise, sad, chivalric and religious, purportedly told by pilgrims to Canterbury. In 'translation', fine; in Chaucer's own English, not impossible to understand – and wonderfully 'medieval' in flavour.

Donne, John (1572–1631). Religious poems; love-lyrics. Highly personal reflections on the meaning of love (both sacred and profane), in beautiful Elizabethan English.

Duffy, Carol Ann (born 1955). Satirical, erotic, pessimistic, feminist poems on the tensions and evasions of modern life. Everyday details brought into sudden, startling focus, making you look again (and again) at what you thought you knew.

Eliot, T.S. (1888–1965). High-intellectual thought expressed in ravishing, simple images. *The Waste Land* (1922) is about psychological devastation and despair in a symbolic, ruined city. *Four Quartets* (1935–42) are meditations on how religious belief is possible for 20th-century people. *Ash Wednesday* (1930) collects shorter, lyrical poems.

Frost, Robert (1874–1963). Lyric poems, with particularly fine descriptions of nature.

▷ **Graves, Robert (1895–1985)**. Lyric poems, including some magnificent love poetry.

Heaney, Seamus (born 1939). Richly pictorial poems about the countryside and human relations, especially good on the seasons and on old age.

Hopkins, Gerard Manley (1844–89). Religious lyrics, fizzing with ecstasy at the beauty of Creation. Exuberant, ever-surprising surge of language.

Hughes, Ted (1930–98). Comedians love to parody Hughes's doomy, Nature-red-in-tooth-and-claw imagery, and his poetry is grim and dark. But few writers better describe the weather, animals, trees, rocks and water.

Keats, John (1795–1821), *Odes* (1819). 'To a Nightingale'; 'On a Grecian Urn'; 'To Melancholy' and others – Romantic, ecstatic rhapsody at its headiest. Some of the best-loved lines in the language.

Larkin, Philip (1922–85). Short, sharp poems about ordinary British life since the Second World War: sad, funny and merciless.

Masefield, John (1878–1967). Neat rhythms, simple language, obvious rhymes – and a no-nonsense way with ballad and narrative. English schoolchildren once learned him by heart more than any other poet, and though critics turn up their noses, his verse is still some of the easiest, and most haunting, of the 20 century.

McGough, Roger (born 1937). One of the 'Liverpool Poets' who became famous at the same time as the Beatles. Stand-up poetry: sly jokes about the human condition, in which the rhythms and the rhymes, comedian's patter crossed with song-lyrics, are half the fun.

Owen, Wilfred (1893–1918). Compassionate, horrifying First World War poetry, achingly memorable.

Plath, Sylvia (1932–63). Macabre imagery and ironic wit combine in Plath's poetry of despair and female alienation. Obsession with the tragic drama of her life and death have often obscured the emotional power and technical skill of her poetry

Tennyson, Alfred, Lord (1809–92). Victorian poetry, much of it inspired by Arthurian legend or by ancient Greece and Rome: sentimental, sometimes cringe-making, always eloquent.

Thomas, Dylan (1914–53). Great themes – love, Nature, aging, death – in bardic, intoxicated language, a firework-show of words.

Walcott, Derek (born 1930). Walcott examines, with immense intelligence and epic ambition, the tension between European culture and Afro-Caribbean culture and the difficulties of emerging from a colonial past with integrity and a genuine sense of self.

Whitman, Walt (1819–92). Hypnotic, free-rhythm poems on Nature, the Sublime and the Journey of Life. Grand thoughts; passionate language; a heady experience.

Wordsworth, William (1770–1850). Poems about Nature, the oddities of human life, memory ('emotion recollected in tranquillity'), in flowing, simple language: like diary jottings written up in verse.

Also recommended: John Clare, *The Shepherd's Calendar* (1827); Lawrence Durrell, *Private Country* (1943); Robert Lowell, *Poems, 1938–1949*; Andrew Marvell, *Poems* (1681); Craig Raine, *A Martian Sends a Postcard Home* (1979); Christina Rossetti, *Goblin Market and Other Poems* (1862); William Shakespeare, *Sonnets*; W.B. Yeats, *Collected Poems* (1933).

journalism and sensational fiction; he gambled, fornicated, and finally drank himself to death. He was like a man haunted by his own existence – and this is exactly the feeling in his macabre short stories, which are less about the supernatural than about people driven crazy by their own imagination. 'The Fall of the House of Usher' and 'The Premature Burial' recount the terrifying results when people are accidentally entombed alive. The murderer in 'The Tell-tale Heart' buries his victim under the floorboards, only to be haunted by what he takes to be the thud of the dead man's heartbeat. The hero of 'The Pit and the Pendulum' is psychologically tortured by the Spanish Inquisition, first by fear of a swinging, ever-approaching blade and then by the way the walls of his cell move inwards to crush him. As well as stories of this kind, Poe occasionally wrote lighter mysteries. The best-known of all ('The Murders in the Rue Morgue'; 'The Mystery of Marie Roget') centre on an eccentric investigator who solves crimes by meticulous reconstruction according to the evidence: they are the first-ever detective stories.

Poe's stories are normally collected nowadays as ★☆ Tales of Mystery and Imagination. *His other writings include poetry (*The Bells; The Raven*) and vitriolic literary criticism, savaging such contemporaries as Longfellow.*

> [!NOTE]
> **READ ON** ▷

▶ to Poe's stories of the macabre: H.P. Lovecraft, *The Call of Cthulhu and Other Weird Tales*; M.R. James, *Ghost Stories of an Antiquary*; Roald Dahl, *Switch Bitch*; ▷ Stephen King, *Nightmares and Dreamscapes*.
▶ to the detective stories: ▷ A. Conan Doyle, *The Adventures of Sherlock Holmes*; Edgar Wallace, *The Four Just Men*.

READ ON A THEME: POLICE PROCEDURAL

Wilkie Collins, *The Woman in White* (Victorian ancestor of the sub-genre)
Freeman Wills Crofts, *Death of a Train*
John Harvey, *Cold Light*
Bill James, *Eton Crop*
Quintin Jardine, *Skinner's Rules*
Ed McBain, *Killer's Choice*
▷ Ruth Rendell, *A Guilty Thing Surprised*
Maj Sjöwall and Per Wahlöö, *The Laughing Policeman*
Martin Cruz Smith, *Gorky Park*

READ ON A THEME: POLITICS

▷ Chinua Achebe, *Anthills of the Savannah*
Jorge Amado, *The Violent Land*
Benjamin Disraeli, *Coningsby*
Michael Dobbs, *House of Cards*
Joe Klein, *Primary Colours*
Arthur Koestler, *Darkness at Noon*
▷ George Orwell, *Animal Farm*

Amos Oz, *A Perfect Peace*
Howard Spring, *Fame is the Spur*
▷ C.P. Snow, *The Corridors of Power*
▷ Gore Vidal, *Burr*

POWELL, Anthony (1905–2000)
British novelist

In the 1930s Powell wrote half a dozen novels satirizing the intellectual and upper classes of the time. The optimistic, aimless young people of *Afternoon Men* drift from party to party, trying to summon up enough willpower to make something of themselves. *From a View to a Death/Mr Zouch: Superman* sets the arts and foxhunting at each other's throats. The hero of *What's Become of Waring?* has to find someone to write the biography of a best-selling travel writer who has disappeared in circumstances which grow more mysterious, and more un-savoury, by the minute. After the Second World War, during which he produced no fiction, Powell abandoned single books for a 12–novel sequence, *A Dance to the Music of Time*, a satirical portrait of 70 years of English high society and establishment life.

☆ A DANCE TO THE MUSIC OF TIME (1951–75)
The sequence follows its characters from Edwardian schooldays to nostalgic, worldly-wise old age. The narrator, Nick Jenkins, discreet as a civil servant, goes everywhere, knows everyone, and writes of his contemporaries (notably the ambition-racked Widmerpool) in elegant, ironic prose. The books move imperturbably from farce to seriousness, from knockabout to reverie. The first three novels, *A Question of Upbringing, A Buyer's Market* and *The Acceptance World*, concern the characters' schooldays, their Oxbridge careers and their entry into the glittering smart set of 1920s London. *At Lady Molly's, Casanova's Chinese Restaurant* and *The Kindly Ones* are about first jobs, marriages and the establishment of a network of sexual, social, financial and political alliances which will bind their lives. *The Valley of Bones, The Soldier's Art* and *The Military Philosophers* take the characters through two world wars, and *Books Do Furnish a Room, Temporary Kings* and *Hearing Secret Harmonies* show them coming to terms with post-war austerity, the white heat of the techno-logical revolution and flower-power, reflecting on the change not only in themselves but in every aspect of British establishment life since their school-days 50 years before.

Powell's other 1930s novels are Venusberg *and* Agents and Patients. *After finishing* A Dance to the Music of Time *he wrote an autobiography,* To Keep the Ball Rolling, *and two other (unrelated) novels,* O, How the Wheel Becomes It *and* The Fisher King.

> **READ ON**

▶ to Powell's 1930s books: ▷ Evelyn Waugh, *Vile Bodies*; Henry Green, *Party Going*; ▷ Rose Macaulay, *Crewe Train*. The mood of elegiac, upper-class malice characteristic of *A Dance to the Music of Time* is repeated in two other novel sequences – ▷ Marcel Proust, *Remembrance of Things Past (A la recherche du temps perdu*) and Simon Raven, *Alms for Oblivion*. Henry Williamson's 15–volume *Chronicles of Ancient Sunlight* similarly takes its central character through many decades of his life, from late Victorian London to Devon in the 1950s but its atmosphere of intensity, tragedy and embittered nostalgia for lost happiness is worlds away from Powell's urbane irony. So, too, are Williamson's fascist political sympathies, which mar what is otherwise a striking sequence of novels.

POWYS, John Cowper (1872–1963)
British novelist and non-fiction writer

A university professor, Powys wrote books on ▷ Dostoevsky, ▷ Homer and ▷Rabelais, dozens of articles, reviews and other non-fiction works, and a lively autobiography. His early novels (*Ducdame*; *Rodmoor*, *Wolf Solent*, all written before 1930) are sombre, ▷ Hardyish stories about the farmers and fishermen of the English West Country. After he retired from teaching Powys wrote a series of completely different novels: long, mystical books influenced by Homer and the Old Testament and drawing on English legend and dark ages history. In *A Glastonbury Romance* modern inhabitants of the Glastonbury area (including worshippers and clergy at the Abbey) find their lives mysteriously affected by local legends of King Arthur and of the Holy Grail. In a similar way, *Maiden Castle* describes how unearthing the distant past – some of the characters are archaeologists working on a prehistoric site – disturbs the present.

> READ ON ▷

- ● *Weymouth Sands*; *Owen Glendower*.
- ▶ to Powys's early novels: ▷ Victor Hugo, *Toilers of the Sea*; ▷ George Eliot, *Silas Marner*; ▷ Nathaniel Hawthorne, *The Scarlet Letter*.
- ▶ to the later fiction: ▷ Peter Ackroyd, *English Music*; ▷ Lawrence Durrell, *The Dark Labyrinth/Cefalù*; Lindsay Clarke, *The Chymical Wedding*; Charles Williams, *War in Heaven*.

PRATCHETT, Terry (born 1948)
British novelist

Pratchett writes lunatic, farcical fantasy. His books are set on Discworld, a vast disc perched on the backs of four huge elephants. Discworld is the home of a thousand thousand species of creature, from trolls and elves to mysterious beings of wood, water, air, light, mud not to mention Mafia heavies, bimbos, winos, film-directors, Death, the Three Witches from *Macbeth*, trombone-playing cows, talking trees, pyramid-builders, opera singers and wizards of every degree from Arch-chancellor Wayzygoose to Rincewind (B.mgc, failed). Each book is self-contained, but characters bob in and out like participants in some particularly demented carnival.

The Discworld novels are: The Colour of Magic *(the first)*, The Light Fantastic, Equal Rites, Mort, Sourcery, Pyramids, Wyrd Sisters, Guards! Guards!, Moving Pictures, Reaper Man, Witches Abroad, Small Gods, Lords and Ladies, Men At

Arms, Soul Music, Interesting Times, Maskerade, Feet of Clay, Hogfather, Jingo, The Last Continent, Carpe Jugulum, The Fifth Elephant *and* The Truth.

READ ON >

- *Truckers*, *Diggers* and *Wings*: a trilogy of children's/adult fantasy books about a group of 'nomes' who live under the floorboards of a department store.
- ▶ Robert Asprin, Myth series (start with *Another Fine Myth*). Tom Holt, *Odds and Gods* (not fantasy but a farce about the gods and heroes of 'real' myth).

PRICHARD, Katharine Susannah (1893–1969)
Australian novelist

Prichard was a political activist, and her best-known novels deal with matters of social concern, mainly in the 1920s and 1930s. *Working Bullocks* is the study of a community of timber workers in Western Australia, fighting the introduction of streamlined methods which will destroy their employment prospects. *Coonardoo* is about the confrontation of white people and Aborigines. The 'goldfields trilogy' *The Roaring Nineties, Golden Miles* and *Winged Seeds* (1946–50) is a densely-organized multi-generation saga, also set in Western Australia, from the gold-rush days of the 19th century, through the industrialisation and political confrontation of the 1920s to post-Second World War decline.

Prichard's other novels include Black Opal *(about a mining community threatened by big-business takeovers),* Intimate Strangers *(about a bickering couple whose marriage is saved by their shared political enthusiasms) and* Haxby's Circus *(about a husband-and-wife team struggling to run a travelling circus).* The Wild Oats of Han, *a children's book, is based on her idyllic childhood in Tasmania.*

READ ON >

- ▶ ▷ Émile Zola, *Germinal*; ▷ Mrs Gaskell, *Mary Barton*; Upton Sinclair, *The Jungle*; ▷ John Steinbeck, *The Grapes of Wrath*.

PRIESTLEY, J.B. (John Boynton) (1894–1984)
British novelist and playwright

As well as plays and non-fiction books, Priestley wrote over 60 novels. They range from amiable satire (e.g. *Low Notes on a High Level* (1956) sending up egghead BBC musicians) to sombre social realism (e.g. *Angel Pavement* (1936) about a sleepy 1930s business firm galvanized into new activity and then destroyed by a confidence trickster). His best-loved novel, *The Good Companions* (1929), tells of three people who escape from humdrum lives to join the Dinky Doos concert party in the 1920s. The novel follows the concert party's career in theatres and seaside resorts all over England, and ends with each of the main characters finding self-fulfilment in an entirely unexpected way. The book bulges with show-biz cliché – brave little troupers; lodging-house keepers with hearts of gold; leading ladies and their tantrums; cynical, hung-over leading men – and with warm-hearted nostalgia for the provincial England of the Good Old Days. It is an armchair of a novel, a book to wallow in – and if life was never really like that, so much the worse for life.

> READ ON

▶ to *The Good Companions*: *Lost Empires* is Priestley's own, darker story of life in the music-halls. ▷ Beryl Bainbridge, *An Awfully Big Adventure* is set in a 1950s repertory company in Liverpool.

▶ to Priestley's books in general: ▷ H.G. Wells, *Tono-Bungay*; James Hilton, *Goodbye, Mr Chips*; Eric Linklater, *Poet's Pub*.

PRITCHETT, V.S. (Victor Sawdon) (1900–97)
British writer

Although Pritchett has written books of many kinds (biography, criticism, novels, travel), he is best known for his short stories. He writes of ordinary people, middle class, middle income, middle aged, falling in love, quarrelling, cheating one another, enjoying small triumphs and suffering small disasters with as much concentration and effort as if they were living *War and Peace*. In 'The Fall', for example, a seedy salesman at a conference, boasting that his glamorous filmstar brother taught him how to do stage falls, has his moment of glory, time and time again, as people buy him drinks to demonstrate his skill. In 'The Camberwell Beauty' an antique dealer tries to rescue a woman hoarded like a piece of prize porcelain by a rival. In 'The Lady from Guatemala' a self-obsessed editor falls ludicrously for a girl who pursues him on a lecture tour. Drabness and seedy dignity are favourite themes of British short-story writers; Pritchett writes of them with steely detachment, as if he has understanding, but absolutely no pity, for his characters' small lives.

Pritchett's ☆ Collected Stories *were published in 1984. The best known of his individual collections are* You Make Your Own Life, When My Girl Comes Home *and* The Camberwell Beauty. *His novels – a similar blend of tartness and wistfulness – include* Nothing Like Leather, Dead Man Leading *and* Mr Beluncle. A Cab at the Door *and* Midnight Oil *are autobiography.*

> READ ON

▶ to Pritchett's short stories: ▷ William Trevor, *The Day We Got Drunk on Cake*; ▷ Katherine Mansfield, *The Garden-Party and Other Stories*; ▷ Elizabeth Bowen, *The Demon Lover*.

▶ to his novels: ▷ Angus Wilson, *The Middle Age of Mrs Eliot*; ▷ Mary Wesley, *Second Fiddle*.

READ ON A THEME: PRIVATE EYES

Lawrence Block, *A Dance at the Slaughterhouse*
James Lee Burke, *Cadillac Jukebox*
▷ Raymond Chandler, *Farewell, My Lovely*
Loren D. Estleman, *The Hours of the Virgin*
▷ Sue Grafton, *G is for Gumshoe*
▷ Dashiell Hammett, *The Maltese Falcon*
Ross Macdonald, *The Drowning Pool*

John Milne, *Dead Birds*
Robert B. Parker, *Small Vices*

See also: Classic Detection; Great (Classic) Detectives; Murder Most Mind-boggling

---

READ ON A THEME: PRIZEWINNERS

Suzanne Berne, *A Crime in the Neighbourhood* (Orange Prize 1999)
Michael Cunningham, *The Hours* (Pulitzer Prize 1999)
Keri Hulme, *The Bone People* (Booker Prize 1985)
Harper Lee, *To Kill a Mockingbird* (Pulitzer Prize 1961)
▷ David Malouf, *Remembering Babylon* (International IMPAC Prize 1996)
Arundhati Roy, *The God of Small Things* (Booker Prize, 1997)
▷ Salman Rushdie, *Midnight's Children* (Booker Prize 1981)
Zadie Smith, *White Teeth* (Guardian Fiction Prize 2000)
Jeff Torrington, *Swing, Hammer, Swing* (Whitbread Book of the Year 1992)

PROULX, Annie (born 1935)
US novelist and short story writer

Annie Proulx did not begin writing fiction until she was in her fifties but almost immediately her original (often dark) imagination, her evocative use of landscape and setting, her quirky humour and arresting use of language brought her success. A collection of short stories, *Heart Songs* (1988), was followed by her first novel, *Postcards*, the tragic saga of an American farming family and one member of it, driven into exile by an act of violence. The narrative of harsh, bleak lives lived out against the backdrop of a succession of unforgiving landscapes is held together by the novel device of a sequence of postcards, carefully reproduced in the text, sent by and to the family. Her second novel, *The Shipping News* (see below) won the Pulitzer Prize for fiction. Since this success, Annie Proulx has published a further novel, *Accordion Crimes* (1996) and a collection of stories, *Close Range,* which includes a novella, 'Brokeback Mountain', telling the poignant story of two Wyoming ranch-hands drawn into an intense sexual relationship. Their doomed struggle to accommodate their homosexual desire within a sense of self created by a macho culture is movingly portrayed.

THE SHIPPING NEWS (1993)
At the beginning of the novel Quoyle is an unsuccessful newspaperman in New York, still brooding on the humiliations of his marriage to a woman who first betrayed him and then was killed in an accident, leaving him with two small children. Accompanied by his young daughters and by a formidable maiden aunt, he returns to Newfoundland, his father's birthplace, and there he finds the fulfilment that eluded him in the city. He establishes himself at the local newspaper, finds himself drawn into the daily life of the community and emerges from the protective shell of loneliness to begin a new and rewarding relationship. More optimistic about human possibility than Proulx's other work ('And it may be that love sometimes occurs without pain or misery,' the book concludes) *The*

Shipping News is saved from the banality that a mere outline of its plot might suggest by Proulx's wit, originality and skilful unravelling of events. Quoyle's transformation becomes an offbeat celebration of the potential people have for change.

READ ON ▷

● *Accordion Crimes* (stories of immigrants to the US connected by possession of a button accordion).
▶ ▷ Carol Shields, *The Stone Diaries*; Jayne Anne Phillips, *Machine Dreams*; Joy Williams, *The Quick and the Dead*; Elizabeth McCracken, *The Giant's House*.

PROUST, Marcel (1871–1922)
French novelist

Proust's ★☆ *Remembrance of Things Past* (*À la récherche du temps perdu*) (1913–27; magnificently translated by C.K. Scott Moncrieff and Terence Kilmartin) is in seven sections (*Swann's Way, Within a Budding Grove, The Guermantes Way, Cities of the Plain, The Captive, The Fugitive, Time Regained*). Each is as long as a normal novel and each can be read both on its own and as part of the whole huge tapestry. The book is a memoir, told in the first person by a narrator called Marcel, of a group of rich French socialites from the 1860s to the end of the First World War. It shows how they react to outside events – the Dreyfus case, women's emancipation, the First World War – and how, as the world moves on, their power and social position wane. Above all, it shows them reacting to each other, to friends, acquaintances and servants: the book is full of love-affairs, parties (at which gossip is hot about who is 'in' or 'out' and why), alliances and betrayals. Through it all moves Marcel himself, good-natured, self-effacing, fascinated by beauty (both human and artistic: his accounts of music and literature are as deeply felt as those of people), and with a sharply ironical eye for social and sexual absurdity. Proust developed for the book a system of 'involuntary memory', in which each sensuous stimulus – the smell of lilac, the taste of cake dipped in tea – unlocks from the subconscious a stream of images of the past. Though this technique has structural importance in the novel – Proust believed that our present only makes sense when it is refracted through past experience – its chief effect for the reader is to provide pages of languorous, detailed descriptions, prose poems on everything from the feel of embroidery under the finger-tips to garden sounds and scents on a summer evening. Proust likes to take his time: at one point Marcel spends nearly 100 pages wondering whether to get up or stay in bed. But only the length at which he works allows him scope for the sensuous, malicious decadence which is the main feature of his work.

Proust's other writings include a collection of short stories and literary parodies, The Pleasures and the Days *(Les plaisirs et les jours), and* Jean Santeuil, *a draft of part of* Remembrance of Things Past.

READ ON ▷

▶ good parallels to the sensuous childhood evocations of the first part of *Remembrance of Things Past* : Alain Fournier, *The Lost Domain* (Le grand Meaulnes); ▷ James Joyce, *Portrait of the Artist as a Young Man*.

▶ echoing the hedonism and decadence of some of Proust's later sections: Joris-Karl
Huysmans, *Against Nature* (*À rebours*).
▶ good on 'the texture of experience': Dorothy Richardson, *Pilgrimage*; ▷ Virginia
Woolf, *The Waves*; John Dos Passos, *Manhattan Transfer*.
▶ novel sequences of comparable grandeur: ▷ Anthony Powell, *A Dance to the
Music of Time*; Henry Williamson, *The Flax of Dream*.

READ ON A THEME: PUBLISH AND BE DAMNED

(writers; publishers; agents; readers; fans)
▷ Margery Allingham, *Flowers for the Judge*
▷ Helen Dunmore, *Zennor in Darkness*
▷ P.D. James, *Original Sin*
▷ Wyndham Lewis, *The Apes of God*
▷ Anthony Powell, *What's Become of Waring?*
▷ Philip Roth, *Zuckerman Unbound*
   Bernhard Schlink, *The Reader*
▷ Tom Sharpe, *The Great Pursuit*
▷ Carol Shields, *Mary Swann*

PUZO, Mario (1920–99)
US novelist and screenwriter

Puzo began his career as a writer of children's books, but in 1969 turned to adult
fiction and had one of the biggest commercial successes in publishing history
with ★☆*The Godfather*. The story concerns the New York Mafia family the
Corleones. It centres on Don Vito Corleone's handover of authority to his son
Michael – a gift akin to being made successor to Genghis Khan – and on the
power-struggle, both with outsiders and between members of the family, to which
this leads. Present-day events are intercut with flashbacks to Don Vito's Sicilian
childhood and his early days in the US. Puzo's detail of Mafia life is as exhaustive
and compelling as a government research report. As ▷ Le Carré does with spies,
he seems to be spilling 'insider' secrets in every line, and his inventions (if they
are inventions) are so plausible that it is hard to imagine how the real Mafia could
be run in any other way. After the success of Coppola's movie version of *The
Godfather*, Puzo turned to screenwriting (among other things, he co-wrote the
first Superman film), and his later novels *Fools Die*, *The Sicilian* and the
posthumously published *Omerta*, though fast-moving and exciting, are like
novelized movies, airport-bookstall fodder lacking the documentary earnestness
which makes *The Godfather* so compulsive.

> READ ON >

▶ good Mafia follow-ups: ▷ John Grisham, *The Client*; Nick Tosches, *Trinities*;
George Dawes Green, *The Juror*; Lawrence Shames, *Sunburn* (a comedy thriller
about an ageing Mafia Don who retires to Florida and causes consternation among
his former associates when he begins to write his memoirs).

PYM, Barbara (1913–80)
British novelist

Only ▷ Jane Austen and ▷ Ivy Compton-Burnett wrote about worlds as restricted as Pym's – and she is regularly compared to both of them. Her books are high-Anglican high comedies; she is tart about the kind of pious middle-class ladies who regard giving sherry-parties for the clergy as doing good works, and she is merciless to priests. Much of the charm of her books lies in their ornate, formal dialogue: her characters all speak with the same prissy, self-conscious elegance, like civil servants taught light conversation by Oscar Wilde.

A GLASS OF BLESSINGS (1958)
Wilmet Forsyth is rich, well-bred, happy and dim. She fills her mind with fantasies about the priests and parishioners at her local church, imagining that their lives are a whirl of hidden passions, ambitions and frustrations. She imagines herself in love with a handsome evening-class teacher, and assumes that he adores her too. As the book proceeds, every one of these assumptions is proved spectacularly, ludicrously mistaken.

Pym's other novels are Some Tame Gazelle, Excellent Women, Jane and Prudence, Less than Angels, Quartet in Autumn, The Sweet Dove Died, Crampton Hodnett *and* An Academic Question.

> **READ ON**

- *Quartet in Autumn.*
- ▷ Ivy Compton-Burnett, *Pastors and Masters*; ▷ A.N. Wilson, *Kindly Light*; Alice Thomas Ellis, *The 27th Kingdom*; J.F. Powers, *Morte d'Urban*; ▷ Joanna Trollope, *The Choir.*

PYNCHON, Thomas (born 1937)
US novelist

Reading Pynchon's satires is like exploring a maze with an opinionated and eccentric guide. He leads us lovingly up every blind alley, breaks off to tell jokes, falls into reveries, ridicules everything and everyone, and refuses to say where he's going until he gets there. *The Crying of Lot 49* (1967) begins with Oedipa Maas setting out to discover why she has been left a legacy by an ex-lover, and what it is; but it quickly develops into a crazy tour of hippie 1960s California, an exploration of drugs, bizarre sex, psychic sensitivity and absurd politics, centring on a group of oddball characters united in a secret society determined to subvert the US postal system. *Gravity's Rainbow* (1973) is a much darker fable, a savage anti-war satire set in a top-secret British centre for covert operations during World War II. In a mad world, where actions have long ceased to have any moral point, where nothing on principle is ever explained or justified, the characters spend their working hours alternately doing what they are told and trying to find out the reason for their existence, and pass their leisure hours in masochistic, joyless sex. On the basis of his short stories and *The Crying of Lot 49*, Pynchon is sometimes claimed as a comic writer. But although *Gravity's Rainbow* is satirical, its jokes are knives, and its farce makes us scream with despair, not joy.

Pynchon's first and most experimental novel was V *(1963). His most recent novel is* Mason & Dixon, *a wild conflation of history and anachronism, loosely based on the two 18th-century surveyors who created the Mason-Dixon line.* Mortality and Mercy in Vienna *is a novella, and* Low-lands *is a collection of short stories.*

READ ON $\rhd$

● *Vineland.*

▶ The satirical fury of *Gravity's Rainbow* is most nearly matched in: ▷ Joseph Heller, *Catch-22*; William Gaddis, *J.R.* (about a deranged 10-year-old genius in a reform school who trades in stocks and shares and exploits other people's greed).

▶ Pynchon's more genial, loonier side is paralleled in: ▷ Mario Vargas Llosa, *Aunt Julia and the Scriptwriter*; Terry Southern, *The Magic Christian* ▷ Kurt Vonnegut, *Breakfast of Champions*; ▷ John Barth, *The Sot-Weed Factor*.

R

RABELAIS, François (c1494–1553)
French satirist

Renegade monk, doctor, scientist, philosopher and *bon viveur* – he led a crowded life – Rabelais began writing satire in his mid-30s, and quickly acquired yet another scurrilous reputation. At heart his ★☆ *Gargantua* (1534) and *Pantagruel* (1532–3) are simple fairy-tales: accounts of the birth and education of the giant Gargantua and of his son Pantagruel. But in reality, he sends up every aspect of medieval knowledge and belief. The giants study philosophy, mathematics, theology and alchemy; they build an anti-monastery whose rules are not poverty, chastity and obedience but wealth, fornication and licence. Pantagruel's mentor is no dignified greybeard but the conman Panurge, and the two of them go on a fantastic journey (through countries as fabulous as any of those visited by Sinbad or Gulliver) to find the answer to the question 'Whom shall Pantagruel marry?' Much of *Gargantua*'s first half is taken up with a fierce battle between the giants and their neighbours, and in particular with the exploits of the roistering, apoplectic Friar John of the Funnels and Goblets, who is later rewarded by being made Abbot of the Monastery of Do As You Like. Rabelais described his books as a 'feast of mirth', and their intellectual satire is balanced by celebration of physical pleasure of every kind: not for nothing has the word 'rabelaisian' entered the dictionary. The original French, already engorged with puns, jokes, parodies and over-the-top lists of every kind, was inflated to nearly twice the length by the 17th-century translator Thomas Urquhart. His English is funnier, filthier and even more fantastical than Rabelais's French: Rabelais would have loved (and stolen back) every word of it.

> READ ON

▶ ▷ Laurence Sterne, *Tristram Shandy*; ▷ Jonathan Swift, *Gulliver's Travels*; Giovanni Boccaccio, *Decameron* (short stories); Anon, *A Thousand and One Nights/ The Arabian Nights' Entertainment*.

RANKIN, Ian (born 1960)
British writer

So successful has Ian Rankin been as a crime writer in the last decade that he has established a whole new sub-genre. According to one critic, Rankin, whose novels are set in Edinburgh, is 'the king of tartan noir'. Certainly he has been successful in portraying an image of Edinburgh very different from the traditional one. He shows the darker side of the city, the skull beneath the skin of the tourist façade. He takes us away from the Royal Mile and Prince's Street and into a bleak and gritty Edinburgh of junkie squats, gangland wars and corruption in high places. Our guide through the mean streets of this other Edinburgh is the central character in most of Rankin's novels, Detective Inspector John Rebus. Rebus, although he owes something to crime fiction clichés of the lone-wolf investigator tormented by his own inner demons, is a genuinely original creation and has a complexity not often encountered in characters in 'genre' fiction. From the first novel, *Knots and Crosses* (1987), Rebus has been as interesting as the cases he investigates and, as the series has progressed, Rankin has developed the character with great skill. He has also shown increasing ambition in the subjects he covers. In *Dead Souls* (1999) the plot accommodates the human consequences of a paedophile scandal in a children's home, the return of a killer from the States to his native Scotland, Rebus's own return to his home town and the party-filled world of Edinburgh's *jeunesse dorée*. All the threads of the narrative are effortlessly woven into a satisfying whole. Rankin is not only one of the best contemporary crime novelists. He is also one of the best of modern Scottish novelists.

BLACK AND BLUE (1997)

'Bible John' was the name given by the media to a serial killer in the 1970s. He was never caught. Now a copycat killer is at work. Rebus, struggling with a drink problem and unsympathetic superiors, has been sidelined. But, as another investigation takes him from Glasgow ganglands to Aberdeen and an offshore oilrig, he is drawn into the web of intrigue and corruption that surrounds the search for the killer dubbed by the media (with characteristic inventiveness) 'Johnny Bible.'

The other Rebus novels are Hide and Seek, Tooth and Nail, Strip Jack, The Black Book, Mortal Causes, Let It Bleed, Death Is Not the End, The Hanging Garden, Set in Darkness *and* The Falls. A Good Hanging *is a collection of Rebus short stories. Rankin has also written three novels* (Witch Hunt, Bleeding Hearts and Cold Blood) *under the pseudonym Jack Harvey.*

> READ ON

● *The Hanging Garden.*
▶ ▷ Reginald Hill, *On Beulah Height*; John Harvey, *Cutting Edge*; Quintin Jardine, *Skinner's Rules* (the first in a series of Edinburgh-set police procedurals).

READ ON A THEME: RENAISSANCE EUROPE

John Banville, *Kepler*
▷ Alexandre Dumas, *The Three Musketeers*
▷ Dorothy Dunnett, *Niccolò Rising*
Carlos Fuentes, *Terra Nostra*
David Madsen, *Memoirs of a Gnostic Dwarf*
Stephen Marlowe, *The Memoirs of Christopher Columbus*
▷ Lawrence Norfolk, *The Pope's Rhinoceros*
Irving Stone, *The Agony and the Ecstasy*

See also: The Middle Ages

RENAULT, Mary (1905–83)
South African novelist

A South African by birth, Renault went to London in her 20s, and served as a nurse during the Second World War. In her 30s and 40s she wrote several novels about hospital and wartime life, culminating in *The Charioteer*, the moving story of a homosexual serviceman. In the 1950s she began writing historical novels about ancient Greece. *The King Must Die* and *The Bull from the Sea* are based on the myth of King Theseus of Athens, who killed the Cretan Minotaur; *Fire From Heaven, The Persian Boy* and *Funeral Games* are about Alexander the Great. Like ▷Robert Graves, Renault treats people of the past as though they were psychologically just like us, so that even the most bizarre political or sexual behaviour seems both rational and credible.

THE KING MUST DIE (1958)
Every year the Cretans demand tribute from Athens: seven young men and seven young women have to learn bull-dancing and be sacrificed to the Minotaur. One year, Prince Theseus takes the place of one of the young men, and sails to Crete to take revenge.

Renault's other Greek books are The Last of the Wine, The Mask of Apollo *and* The Praise Singer.

> READ ON ▷

- *The Bull from the Sea.*
▶ Colleen McCullough, *The First Man in Rome*; ▷ Robert Graves, *I, Claudius*; Tom Holt, *The Walled Orchard.*

RENDELL, Ruth (born 1930)
British novelist

Rendell's Chief Inspector Wexford novels are atmospheric murder mysteries in traditional style, set in the small towns and villages of the English Home Counties. Like ▷ P.D. James, she spends much time developing the character of her detective, a liberal and cultured man appalled by the psychological pressures which drive people to crime. Those pressures are the subject of Rendell's other books (both under her own name and as Barbara Vine): grim stories of paranoia, obsession and inadequacy.

Rendell's Wexford books include From Doon with Death, Wolf to the Slaughter, A Guilty Thing Surprised, Some Lie and Some Die, Kissing the Gunner's Daughter, An Unkindness of Ravens, Simisola, Road Rage *and* Harm Done. *Her psychological novels include* The Face of Trespass, The Killing Doll, The Tree of Hands, Live Flesh, Talking to Strange Men, Going Wrong, The Crocodile Bird *and* A Sight for Sore Eyes. Means of Evil, The Fever Tree *and* The Copper Peacock *are collections of short stories. As Barbara Vine, Rendell has written* A Dark-Adapted Eye, A Fatal Inversion, The House of Stairs, Gallowglass, King Solomon's Carpet, Asta's Book, No Night is Too Long, The Brimstone Wedding, The Chimney-Sweeper's Boy *and* Grasshopper.

READ ON ▷

▶ to the Wexford books: ▷ P.D. James, *Shroud for a Nightingale*; R.D. Wingfield, *Hard Frost*; ▷ Reginald Hill, *Exit Lines*.
▶ to the psychological thrillers: ▷ Patricia Highsmith, *The Glass Cell*; ▷ Minette Walters, *The Dark Room*; Frances Fyfield, *Undercurrents*; Nicci French, *Killing Me Softly*.

READ ON A THEME: REVISITING ONE'S PAST

▷ Margaret Atwood, *Surfacing*
▷ Anita Brookner, *A Start in Life*
David Guterson, *East of the Mountains*
Bernard MacLaverty, *Grace Notes*
▷ Hilary Mantel, *Vacant Possession*
▷ Bernice Rubens, *Our Father*
▷ Graham Swift, *Waterland*
▷ Paul Theroux, *Picture Palace*
▷ Virginia Woolf, *Mrs Dalloway*

READ ON A THEME: REWRITING HISTORY

(what might have happened if . . .)
▷ Kingsley Amis, *The Alteration*
Martin Cruz Smith, *The Indians Won*
▷ Len Deighton, *SS-GB*
Philip K. Dick, *The Man in the High Castle*
▷ Robert Harris, *Fatherland*
▷ Michael Moorcock, *Warlord of the Air*
Ward Moore, *Bring the Jubilee* (alternate reality in which the South won the Civil War)
Keith Roberts, *Pavane*
Norman Spinrad, *The Iron Dream*

RHYS, JEAN (1894–1979)
British novelist

All Rhys's novels and stories are about the same kind of person, the 'Jean Rhys woman'. She was once vivacious and attractive (an actress, perhaps, or a dancer) but she fell in love with some unsuitable man or men, was betrayed, and now lives alone, maudlin and mentally unhinged. In Rhys's first four novels (published in the 1920s and 1930s), the heroines are casualties of the Jazz Age, flappers crushed by life itself. In her last, 1960s, book *Wide Sargasso Sea* the central character is a victim of the way men think (or fail to think) of women: she is a young Caribbean heiress in the early 1800s, who marries an English gentleman, Mr Rochester, and ends up as the demented creature hidden in the attics of Thornfield Hall in *Jane Eyre*.

GOOD MORNING, MIDNIGHT (1939)

Deserted by her husband after the death of their baby, Sasha would have drunk herself to death if a generous friend had not rescued her and paid for her to spend a fortnight in Paris. She 'arranges her little life', as she puts it: a cycle of solitary meals and drinks, barren conversations with strangers, drugged sleep in seedy hotel-rooms. She is a damned soul, a husk – and then a gigolo, mistaking her for a rich woman, begins to court her, and she has to gather the rags of her sanity and try to take hold of her life once more.

Rhys's other novels are Quartet/Postures, After Leaving Mr Mackenzie *and* Voyage in the Dark. The Left Bank, Tigers are Better-looking *and* Sleep it off, Lady *are collections of short stories.*

> [READ ON]

- ● *Wide Sargasso Sea.*
- ▶ to *Good Morning Midnight:* ▷ Brian Moore, *The Doctor's Wife;* ▷ Doris Lessing, *The Golden Notebook;* Mary McCarthy, *The Company She Keeps;* ▷ Anita Brookner, *Hotel du Lac.*
- ▶ to *Wide Sargasso Sea:* Lisa St Aubin de Terán, *The Keepers of the House.*

READ ON A THEME: THE RHYTHM OF NATURE

(people in tune with or in thrall to the land)
▷ Pearl S. Buck, *The Good Earth*
  Neil M. Gunn, *The Well at the World's End*
▷ Thomas Hardy, *Far From the Madding Crowd*
  Christopher Hart, *The Harvest*
▷ Susan Hill, *In the Springtime of the Year*
  Mikhail Sholokhov, *Virgin Soil Upturned*
▷ Jane Smiley, *A Thousand Acres*
  Adam Thorpe, *Ulverton*

See also: Down to Earth; Village and Countryside

RICHARDSON, Henry Handel (1870–1946)
Australian novelist

'Henry Handel Richardson' was the pseudonym of Ethel Robertson. She was born and educated in Australia, but went to Europe in her late teens and remained there, with one three-month break, for the rest of her life. Her best-known books, however (*The Getting of Wisdom*, 1910, and the Richard Mahony trilogy) are set in Australia and reflect her own or her parents' experience. She was interested in 'psychic outsiders', people who felt that heightened awareness or sensibilities set them apart from their fellows. *The Getting of Wisdom* is about a gifted, unhappy adolescent in a late 19th-century boarding school, who uses love of the arts as an escape from the oppressive narrowness of the régime. The battle against depressive illness is a major theme of *The Fortunes of Richard Mahony* (1915–1929). In this trilogy of novels (*Australia Felix, The Way Home, Ultima Thule*) Mahony, a British doctor, goes to Australia to make his fortune in the

1850s gold rush, marries and settles. His gold-prospecting fails, and he turns first to storekeeping and then back to medicine, before making a sudden fortune from shares he thought were worthless. Unable to cope with wealth, he dissipates his money, impoverishes his family and begins a long, anguished slide into depressive mania. His devoted wife takes a job as postmistress in a remote area, nursing her husband and bringing up her uncomprehending, sorrowing family. Although the trilogy is chiefly concerned with Mahony's complex character and his relationship with his family, it is also a compelling account of 19th-century Australian pioneer and outback life.

READ ON ▷

▶ to *The Fortunes of Richard Mahony*: ▷ Gustave Flaubert, *Madame Bovary*;
  ▷ Malcolm Lowry, *Under the Volcano*.
▶ to *The Getting of Wisdom*: ▷ Antonia White, *Frost in May*.

RICHARDSON, Samuel (1689–1761)
British novelist

A successful printer, Richardson was compiling a book of sample letters for all occasions when he had the idea of writing whole novels in letter-form. He produced three, *Pamela, Clarissa* and *Sir Charles Grandison*. They are enormously long (over a million words each), and readers even at the time complained of boredom. But the books were best-sellers – not, as Richardson imagined, because of their high moral tone, but because his sensational theme (the way some people are drawn irresistibly to debauch the innocent) guaranteed success.

CLARISSA, OR THE HISTORY OF A YOUNG LADY (1748)
To escape from her parents, who have shut her in her room until she agrees to marry a man she loathes, the hapless Clarissa Harlowe elopes with Mr Lovelace, a rake. He tries every possible way to persuade her to sleep with him, and when she refuses he puts her into a brothel, drugs and rapes her. She goes into a decline and dies of shame. The story is told by means of letters from the main characters, to one another, to friends and acquaintances. One of Richardson's triumphs – which some critics claim justifies the book's inordinate length – is to reveal Lovelace's villainy only gradually, as Clarissa herself discovers it.

READ ON ▷

● *Pamela*.
▶ Pierre Choderlos de Laclos, *Dangerous Alliances* (*Les liaisons dangereuses*) is another letter-novel about moral predation, but shorter, wittier and less sentimental. A young aristocrat in pre-Revolutionary France, bored by the restrictions of polite society, devotes herself to the cynical, ice-cool shedding of all moral restraint. This book apart, Richardson's work has been more pilloried than parallelled. ▷Henry Fielding, for example, in *Tom Jones*, mocks Richardson's moral earnestness: far from shrinking from the pleasures of seduction, Tom lives for them.

RICHLER, Mordecai (1931–2001)
Canadian novelist

The heroes of Richler's vitriolic black satires are 'outsiders' (for example Jews in a gentile society), poor (they come from big-city slums) or inept (too guileless for their own good). They face a hostile world of crooks, cheats, extortionists, poseurs (often film makers or tycoons) and bullies. Like the hero of *The Apprenticeship of Duddy Kravitz* (1959), Richler's men often fight back, using the enemies' weapons and winning the battle at the expense of their own souls. The title character in *The Incomparable Atuk* (1963), an Eskimo poet who becomes a media celebrity in Toronto, adapts only too readily to the greed and scheming of city life. Richler's recent fiction has been even more scabrous, satirical and ambitious. In *Solomon Gursky Was Here* (1990) Moses Berger, Canadian writer-of-all-trades, works as speech-writer and culture-vulture to the one-time boot-legger Bernard Gursky, now a prominent Montreal billionaire. Fascinated by Gursky's enigmatic brother Solomon (supposedly killed in a plane crash) Berger is launched on a quest that takes him on a typically Richlerian roister through the history of Canada, Jewishess and, above all, through the multiple personalities of the chameleon-like Solomon Gursky. Mixing over-the-top satire, bilious rants against the modern world and a melancholy awareness of age and decline, *Barney's Version* (1997) is built around the self-serving memoirs of Barney Panofsky ('the true story of my wasted life') and his hopelessly tangled relation-ships with his three wives.

Richler's other novels include A Choice of Enemies, Cocksure, St Urbain's Horseman *and* Joshua Then and Now. The Street *is a memoir of his childhood in the backstreets of Montreal, a fascinating parallel to the opening chapters of* The Apprenticeship of Duddy Kravitz.

> **READ ON**

▶ to *The Apprenticeship of Duddy Kravitz:* ▷ Jerome Weidman, *I Can Get it For You Wholesale;* ▷ Saul Bellow, *The Adventures of Augie March.*
▶ to *Solomon Gursky Was Here* and *Barney's Version:* ▷ Joseph Heller, *Closing Time;* ▷ Philip Roth, *Sabbath's Theatre.*

ROBERTS, Michèle (born 1949)
British poet and novelist

Michèle Roberts's novels combine a sensuous and poetic appreciation of the natural world with inventive imaginings and re-imaginings of history, religion, the relationships between men and women and those between mothers and daughters. *Daughters of the House* (1992) looks at several generations of women in an obsessively Catholic household in 1940s–50s provincial France. *Flesh and Blood* (1994) is an interlocking sequence of dark, magic-realist tales, spanning centuries, of the relationships between mothers and their daughters. *Impossible Saints* (1997) juxtaposes the fictional story of Saint Josephine with Roberts's re-tellings of the lives of genuine Catholic women saints to create a portrait of female sexuality, intelligence and imagination battling through the centuries against the constraints imposed on them. *Fair Exchange* (1999) takes episodes from the emotional lives of Mary Wollstonecraft and William Wordsworth and uses them as the foundation stones for a narrative about ordinary lives caught up in the larger events of history.

THE BOOK OF MRS. NOAH (1987)

This is a dazzling fantasy, set in the present day. A woman visiting Venice with her preoccupied husband fantasizes that she is Mrs Noah. The Ark is a vast library, a repository not only of creatures but of the entire knowledge and experience of the human race. She is its curator (or Arkivist), and her fellow-voyagers are five Sibyls and a token male, the Gaffer, a bearded old party who once wrote a best-selling book (the Bible) and has now retired to a tax-heaven in the sky. Each Sibyl tells a story, and each story is about the way men have mistreated women down the centuries. Roberts channels feminist anger at male oppression into a witty and imaginative tour de force.

> READ ON ▷

- *The Wild Girl* (the gospel according to Mary Magdalene).
- ▶ ▷ Margaret Atwood, *The Handmaid's Tale*. ▷ Angela Carter, *The Infernal Desire Machines of Doctor Hoffman;* ▷ Virginia Woolf, *Orlando*; Sara Maitland, *Three Times Table*.

ROGERS, Jane (born 1952)
British novelist

Jane Rogers's two best-known novels are both historical fiction. *Mr. Wroe's Virgins* (1991), made into a memorable TV drama starring Jonathan Pryce, is the story of a charismatic fire-and-brimstone preacher in 1830s Lancashire who seizes upon a biblical text to persuade himself that he should live with seven virgins 'for comfort and succour'. Told in the very different voices of four of the virgins chosen from Mr. Wroe's congregation, this is a novel that approaches the mysteries of faith and love with intelligence and humanity. *Promised Lands* (1995) interweaves the story of the First Fleet's journey to Australia and the largely uncomprehending responses of the men in it to a new land and new peoples with a modern story of a couple with very different ideas about the nature of their handicapped son. The modern and historical strands of the narrative occasionally seem inadequately connected, two novels struggling to emerge from one, but *Promised Lands*, at its best, uses both to consider ideas of innocence, idealism and the dangers of constructing stories to explain the lives of others.

Jane Rogers's other novels are Separate Tracks, Her Living Image, The Ice Is Singing *and* Island.

> READ ON ▷

- *Island (*a woman abandoned as a baby traces her mother with the intention of killing her*)*.
- ▶ ▷ Margaret Atwood, *Alias Grace*; ▷ Thomas Keneally, *The Playmaker*; ▷ Hilary Mantel, *The Giant O'Brien*; Matthew Kneale, *English Passengers*.

READ ON A THEME: **ROMAN CATHOLICISM**

▷ **Kingsley Amis,** *The Alteration*
  Georges Bernanos, *Diary of a Country Priest*
▷ **Anthony Burgess,** *Earthly Powers*
▷ **Graham Greene,** *Monsignor Quixote*
▷ **Thomas Keneally,** *Three Cheers for the Paraclete*
  Patrick McCabe, *The Dead School*
▷ **Brian Moore,** *Catholics*
  J.F. Powers, *Morte d'Urban*
  Frederick Rolfe, *Hadrian the Seventh*
▷ **Muriel Spark,** *The Abbess of Crewe*
▷ **Morris West,** *The Devil's Advocate*
▷ **Antonia White,** *Frost in May*

ROTH, Philip (born 1933)
US novelist

One of the wriest and wittiest of all contemporary US novelists, Roth writes of Jewish intellectuals, often authors or university teachers, discomfited by life. Their marriages fail; their parents behave like joke-book stereotypes (forever making chicken soup and simultaneously boasting about and deploring their sons' brains); sexual insatiability leads them from one farcical encounter to another; their career success attracts embarrassing fans and inhibits further work; their defences of self-mockery and irony wear ever thinner as they approach unwanted middle age. In his best-known book, *Portnoy's Complaint* (1969), Roth treated this theme as farce, heavy with explicit sex and Jewish-mother jokes. The majority of his novels are quieter, the tone is more rueful, and he generalizes his theme and makes it symbolize the plight of all decent, conscience-stricken people in a world where barbarians make the running. His major 1980s work was a series of novels about a New York Jewish author, Nathan Zuckerman, who agonizes over his trade, writes an immensely success-ful (dirty) book, and is immediately harrassed by the way his fame both forces him to live the life of a celebrity, and makes him even more of an enigma to his family and friends. In the 1990s Roth produced a sequence of startling and jaundiced examinations of American dreams and nightmares, which have shown that he has lost none of his power and range as a writer. *American Pastoral* (1997), for example, is the story of Seymour 'Swede' Lvov, whose comfortable sense of himself and the America in which he lives is destroyed by events of the 1960s and by his own daughter's violent rejection of all he stands for.

☆ THE PROFESSOR OF DESIRE (1977)
Davis Kepesh, a brilliant young literature teacher, is trying to sort out his life. His views on art and literature, which once seemed the last word in wit and wisdom, now appear to him to have been engulfed by the subjects he studies: he feels like a dwarf trying to shift a mountain. His emotional life is dominated by an insistent craving for physical pleasure which he finds degrading but irresistible, and which he longs to replace by love. His mother and father are elderly, tetchy and horrified by the way their son the genius has betrayed his Jewish roots. Kepesh's

circumstances seem to him like a maze, as bewildering and terrifying as anything in ▷ Kafka and the book shows him gradually, painfully, discovering the key.

Roth's other books include Letting Go, The Great American Novel *(which uses baseball as a farcical symbol for every red-blooded US tradition or way of thought),* My Life as a Man *and* Our Gang *(a ▷ Swiftian satire about the Nixon presidency).* Goodbye Columbus *consists of an early novella and five short stories. The Zuckerman books are* The Ghost Writer, Zuckerman Unbound, The Anatomy Lesson, The Prague Orgy *and* The Counterlife. The Facts: a Novelist's Autobiography, *a fictionalized account of Roth's life, closes with a letter from 'Zuckerman' accusing Roth of living a fake life, of describing the truth of existence only when he invents fictional characters and incidents.* Deception *is a kind of pendant to this, a novel in dialogue about a novelist called Philip and his English lover.* Patrimony: a True Story *is a lacerating memoir of his father's decline and death, and of their relationship – in some ways the main inspiration for all Roth's work.* Operation Shylock *is a teasing, brilliant book, starting with a famous novelist called Philip Roth going to modern Israel (or its nightmare, Kafka-farce simulacrum), to track down an impostor called 'Philip Roth' and discover his true identity.*

> READ ON

● *When She was Good*; *Sabbath's Theatre.*
▶ Bernard Malamud, *Dubin's Lives.* ▷ Bernice Rubens, *Our Father.* ▷ Margaret Atwood, *Cat's Eye.* ▷ John Fowles, *Daniel Martin.* ▷ John Updike, *Marry Me.*

RUBENS, Bernice (born 1927)
British novelist

Rubens's heroes and heroines are people at the point of breakdown: her novels chart the escalation of tension which took them there or the progress of their cure. Some of the books are bleak: in *The Elected Member/The Chosen People* (1969), for example, a man is driven mad by feeling that he is a scapegoat for the entire suffering of the Jewish people throughout history, and the story deals with his rehabilitation in a mental hospital. In other books, Rubens turns psychological pain to comedy, as if the only way to cope with the human condition were to treat it as God's black joke against the human race. God is even a character in *Our Father* (1987): he pops up in the Sahara, in the High Street, in the parlour; in bed with the heroine and her husband, constantly nagging her to make up her mind about herself – and his persistence leads her to rummage through childhood memories (where it becomes clear that she completely misunderstood her parents' emotional relationship) and to redefine her life.

Rubens's other novels include Madame Sousatzka, I Sent a Letter to my Love, The Ponsonby Post, Sunday Best, Brothers, A Five Year Sentence, Birds of Passage, Favours, Spring Sonata, A Solitary Grief, Mother Russia, Yesterday in the Back Lane, Mr Wakefield's Crusade, Autobiopsy, The Waiting Game *and* Milwaukee.

> READ ON

● *Birds of Passage*; *I, Dreyfus* (in which a modern namesake of the Jewish officer wrongfully imprisoned in late 19th-century France suffers similarly).

▶ to *The Elected Member*: Paul Sayer, *The Comforts of Madness*.
▶ to Rubens's work in general: ▷ Paul Theroux, *Picture Palace*; ▷ Beryl Bainbridge, *A Quiet Life*; ▷ Rose Tremain, *Sacred Country*; Jane Gardam, *The Flight of the Maidens*.

RUSHDIE, Salman (born 1947)
Indian/British novelist and non-fiction writer

Rushdie's novels are magic realism: a mesmeric entwining of actuality and fantasy. ★ ☆ *Midnight's Children* (1981) is the story of a rich Indian family over the past 80 years, and especially of Saleem, one of 1,001 children born at midnight on 15 August 1947, the moment of India's independence from Britain. Saleem's birth-time gives him extraordinary powers: he is, as Rushdie puts it, 'handcuffed' to India, able to let his mind float freely through its history and to share in the experience of anyone he chooses, from Gandhi or Nehru to the most insignificant beggar in the streets. In Saleem's experience (as relayed to us) time coalesces, 'real' politics blur with fantasy, a child's memories and magnifications are just as valid as newspaper accounts. The effect is to change reality to metaphor and Rushdie uses this to make several sharp political points. In 1993 *Midnight's Children* was voted the 'Booker of Bookers', for being the finest novel awarded the prize in the 25 years of the Booker competition. In *Shame* (1983) he goes still further. This novel is set in a dream country, Peccavistan ('Sinned' rather than Sind), whose geography and history are like Pakistan's seen in a distorting mirror. We witness a power struggle between members of the Harappa dynasty and their friends/rivals/ enemies the Hyders. Interwoven with this is the story of Omar Khayyam Shakil, a bloated, brilliant physician, and his wife Sufiya Zinobia, a mental defective inhabited by a homicidal demon. *The Satanic Verses* (1988) dramatizes the conflict between good and evil in the persons of two actors, who fall out of an aeroplane and are transformed into the Angel Gibreel and Shaitan, the Devil. (The book violently offended fundamentalist Muslims, who took Gibreel's sardonic, ironic dreams about the prophet Mahound in the fantasy city Jahilia as blasphemy against their religion. Copies of *The Satanic Verses* were burned, and a *fatwa* was issued against Rushdie by Ayatollah Khomeini of Iran – events whose surreal horror beggared anything in his fiction.) *The Moor's Last Sigh* (1995), written during his sentence of living death, is another hypnotic family saga, covering the lives of the Da Gama-Zogoiby dynasty, Portuguese-Indian pepper exporters in Bombay from the 1870s to the present. Since the lifting of the *fatwa* Rushdie has published *The Ground Beneath Her Feet* (1999), a novel which boldly mixes the mythologies of East and West with the modern iconography of rock in its story of two superstar musicians and their life and love across the decades.

Rushdie's other works include Grimus *(an early, experimental novel),* East, West *(mischievous, ironic short stories),* Haroun and the Sea of Stories *(a mesmeric fable for children) and* The Jaguar Smile *(non-fiction; a politically savage look at the effect of US policies in Central America in general and Nicaragua in particular).* Imaginary Homelands *is a book of essays, chiefly on religion and literature, written during his enforced withdrawal from public life.*

READ ON $\rhd$

▶ To *Midnight's Children*: $\rhd$ Vikram Seth, *A Suitable Boy*.
▶ To *Shame*: Augusto Roa Bastos, *I, The Supreme*. $\rhd$ Günter Grass, *The Tin Drum*.
▶ To *The Satanic Verses*: $\rhd$ Angela Carter, *Nights at the Circus*. Lisa St Aubin de Terán, *Keepers of the House*.

S

SALINGER, J.D. (Jerome David) (born 1919)
US novelist and short story writer

Salinger's only novel, ☆ *The Catcher in the Rye* (1951), is a rambling monologue by 17-year-old Holden Caulfield. He has run away from boarding school just before Christmas, and is spending a few days drifting in New York City while he decides whether to go home or not. He feels that his childhood is over and his innocence lost, but he detests the phoney, loveless grown-up world (symbolized by plastic Christmas baubles and seasonal fake goodwill). He thinks that to be adult is a form of surrender, but he can see no way to avoid it. He wanders the city, talking aimlessly to taxi-drivers, lodging-house keepers, bar-tenders, prostitutes and his own kid sister Phoebe, whom he tries to warn against growing up. Finally, inevitably, he capitulates – or perhaps escapes, since we learn that what we have just read is his 'confession' to the psychiatrist in a mental home. Salinger pursued the question of how to recover moral innocence in his only other publications, a series of short stories about the gifted, mentally unstable Glass family. 'Franny and Zooey', the most moving of the stories, shows Zooey Glass, an actor, talking his sister Franny out of a nervous breakdown. It is a performance of dazzling technical brilliance and full of loving-kindness, but – and this is typical of Salinger's grim view of human moral endeavour – although it helps Franny momentarily, it contributes nothing whatever to the good of the world at large.

The Glass family stories are collected in Franny and Zooey, Nine Stories/For Esmé, with Love and Squalor *and* Raise High the Roofbeam, Carpenters.

> **READ ON**

▶ to *The Catcher in the Rye*: ▷ Carson McCullers, *The Member of the Wedding*; ▷John Updike, *The Centaur*; Truman Capote, *Breakfast at Tiffany's*; ▷ Bret Easton Ellis, *Less Than Zero* (for a 1980s view of disenchanted preppy adolescence); S.E. Hinton, *The Outsiders* (adolescent angst recorded by a writer who was herself an adolescent when she wrote the book).
▶ to 'Franny and Zooey': Sylvia Plath, *The Bell Jar*; ▷ Susan Hill, *The Bird of Night*.

SARTRE, Jean-Paul (1905–80)
French novelist, poet and philosopher

The philosophy of existentialism, which Sartre developed in essays, plays, novels and monographs, says that Nothingness is the natural state of humanity: we exist, like animals, without ethics or morality. But unlike beasts we have the

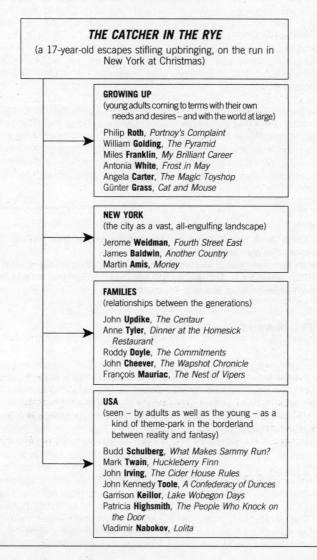

PATHWAYS

J.D. SALINGER

THE CATCHER IN THE RYE
(a 17-year-old escapes stifling upbringing, on the run in New York at Christmas)

GROWING UP
(young adults coming to terms with their own needs and desires – and with the world at large)

Philip **Roth**, *Portnoy's Complaint*
William **Golding**, *The Pyramid*
Miles **Franklin**, *My Brilliant Career*
Antonia **White**, *Frost in May*
Angela **Carter**, *The Magic Toyshop*
Günter **Grass**, *Cat and Mouse*

NEW YORK
(the city as a vast, all-engulfing landscape)

Jerome **Weidman**, *Fourth Street East*
James **Baldwin**, *Another Country*
Martin **Amis**, *Money*

FAMILIES
(relationships between the generations)

John **Updike**, *The Centaur*
Anne **Tyler**, *Dinner at the Homesick Restaurant*
Roddy **Doyle**, *The Commitments*
John **Cheever**, *The Wapshot Chronicle*
François **Mauriac**, *The Nest of Vipers*

USA
(seen – by adults as well as the young – as a kind of theme-park in the borderland between reality and fantasy)

Budd **Schulberg**, *What Makes Sammy Run?*
Mark **Twain**, *Huckleberry Finn*
John **Irving**, *The Cider House Rules*
John Kennedy **Toole**, *A Confederacy of Dunces*
Garrison **Keillor**, *Lake Wobegon Days*
Patricia **Highsmith**, *The People Who Knock on the Door*
Vladimir **Nabokov**, *Lolita*

power to make choices, and these give moral status: they are a leap from Nothingness to Being. For some people, the choice is the leap of faith, and belief in God gives them moral status; for others the choice is to make no choice at all, to drift the way the world leads them without taking moral initiatives. For Sartre's characters, the leap into being involved taking responsibility, making moral decisions from which there was no turning back. His vast novel *The Roads to Freedom* (1945–9; in three volumes, *The Age of Reason*, *The Reprieve* and *Iron in the Soul/Troubled Sleep*) tackles his theme exactly: the questions of what moral decisions to make and how to make them. It describes a group of young people trying to sort out their personal lives and at the same time to cope with the moral and intellectual challenges of fascism, communism, colonialism and the Second World War. Packed with intellectual, political and philosophical discussion and argument it is a complex read but few writings better give the intellectual 'feel' of the 1930s and 1940s.

Sartre's main philosophical monograph is Being and Nothingness. *His plays include* The Flies, The Victor/Men Without Shadows, Crime Passionel *and* Huis Clos/No Exit/In Camera. Nausea/The Diary of Antoine Roquentin *is an auto-biographical novel about a young intellectual in the 1920s and 1930s.* Words *is a memoir of his childhood spent within the stifling confines of a small French town and describes how his upbringing permanently marked his life and thought.*

> READ ON

● *Nausea*.
▶ ▷ Albert Camus, *The Plague*; Arthur Koestler, *Darkness at Noon*; Frederic Raphael, *Like Men Betrayed*.
▶ novels discussing similar personal dilemmas, but with different backgrounds and cultural conditions: ▷ Leo Tolstoy, *War and Peace*; ▷ Ford Madox Ford, *The Good Soldier*; ▷ Olivia Manning, *The Levant Trilogy*.

SAYERS, Dorothy L. (Leigh) *(1893–1957)*
British novelist

At various times, Sayers worked as an Oxford don, an advertising copywriter and a radio dramatist. She is best known, however, for a series of detective novels cruelly but accurately described (by the writer Colin Watson) as 'snobbery with violence'. The fascination of her books is not only in the solving of bizarre crimes in out-of-the-ordinary locations (an advertising agency; an Oxford women's college; an East Anglian belfry), but also in the character of her detective, the super-sleuth Lord Peter Wimsey. He is a languid, monocled aristocrat, whose foppish manner conceals the facts that he has a first-class Oxford degree, was in army intelligence during the First World War, collects rare books, plays the piano like Rubinstein, dances like Astaire and seems to have swallowed a substantial dictionary of quotations. He is aided and abetted by his manservant Bunter, a suave charmer adept at extracting confidences from the cooks, taxi-drivers, waitresses, barbers and vergers who would collapse in forelock-tugging silence if Wimsey himself ever deigned to speak to them. Several of the novels describe the unfolding relationship between

Wimsey and the crime novelist Harriet Vane. Seldom have detective stories been so preposterous or so unputdownable.

The Wimsey/Vane romance is featured in Have His Carcase, Strong Poison, Gaudy Night *and* Busman's Honeymoon. *Sayers's other Wimsey books – which some admirers prefer to those involving Harriet Vane – include* Murder Must Advertise, Clouds of Witness *and* The Nine Tailors.

READ ON ▷

- ● *Gaudy Night.*
- ▶ Amanda Cross, *No Word from Winifred*; ▷ Michael Innes, *Hamlet, Revenge!*; Robert Robinson, *Landscape with Dead Dons*; ▷ P.D. James, *A Certain Justice*; ▷ Ruth Rendell, *Some Lie and Some Die.*

READ ON A THEME: SCHOOLS

Jonathan Coe, *The Rotters Club*
▷ Charles Dickens, *Nicholas Nickleby*
James Hilton, *Goodbye, Mr Chips*
Thomas Hughes, *Tom Brown's Schooldays*
▷ James Joyce, *Portrait of the Artist as a Young Man*
▷ John Le Carré, *Call for the Dead*
▷ H.H. Richardson, *The Getting of Wisdom*
Susan Swann, *The Wives of Bath*
▷ John Updike, *The Centaur*
▷ Evelyn Waugh, *Decline and Fall*

See also: Adolescence

READ ON A THEME: SCOTLAND

George MacKay Brown, *Greenvoe*
Lewis Grassic Gibbon, *A Scots Quair*
▷ Alasdair Gray, *Lanark*
Neil M. Gunn, *Morning Tide*
James Kelman, *How Late It Was, How Late*
▷ Walter Scott, *The Heart of Midlothian*
▷ Robert Louis Stevenson, *Kidnapped*
Jeff Torrington, *Swing, Hammer, Swing*
Alan Warner, *Morvern Callar*
▷ Irvine Welsh, *Trainspotting*

SCOTT, Sir Walter (1771–1832)
British novelist and poet

Scott began his career not with novels but with poems, in a style similar to Scottish folk-ballads and the lyrics of Robert Burns. In 1814, piqued because his

STARTPOINTS

SCIENCE FICTION AND FANTASY

The origins of science fiction have been hotly debated (some experts take them back to the ancient world) but it was the industrial revolution that led to the birth of modern SF and writers such as ▷ Jules Verne and ▷ H.G. Wells gave it its first mass audience. They took advantage of public interest in the discoveries of 'real' science to write stories featuring such topics as space travel, invasions from other planets and the exploration of 'worlds that time forgot'. Ever since, SF authors have exploited every new scientific discovery and, more seriously, have used the genre to examine such ideas as 'green issues', fascism or the ethics of colonization. Some write about not physical space but the worlds of dreams and the imagination. Two kinds of SF have become separate genres: 'future-shock' books, projecting the problems of present-day society into the future, and 'space opera', about good-versus-evil battles on exotic planets. 'Space opera' is similar to the fantasy literature which mushroomed after the success of ▷ J.R.R. Tolkien's *The Lord of the Rings* (1954-5). The heroes of fantasy novels undertake magical quests – usually serious, but since the 1980s, in the hands of ▷ Terry Pratchett and others, sometimes no-holds-barred farce.

▷ **Asimov, Isaac (1920–92),** *I, Robot* **(1950)**. Collection of linked future-detective stories in which the protagonists have to tackle crimes which may have been committed by robots.

▷ **Banks, Iain M. (born 1954),** *Consider Phlebas* (1987). First of Banks's space operas, traditional SF tales of galaxy-spanning empires and high intrigue, told in a refreshingly modern style.

Bester, Alfred (1913–1987) *Tiger! Tiger!/The Stars My Destination* **(1956)**. High-energy story of revenge and transcendence told in a dazzling prose by a writer in love with the possibilities of language.

Card, Orson Scott (born 1951), *Ender's Game* **(1985)**. The world is under threat from loathsome aliens and junior geniuses train in war games to combat it.

▷ **Clarke, Arthur C. (born 1917),** *Rendezvous with Rama* **(1973)**. Classic story of the exploration of Rama, a world which drifts into the solar system from deep space and seems, until humans land on it, to have no life of its own.

▷ **Gibson, William (born 1948),** *Neuromancer* **(1984)**. The novel that created 'cyberpunk', the story of hacker Case who electronically projects his streetwise consciousness into the virtual-reality matrix that the Internet has in truth become.

▷ **Heinlein, Robert (1907–88),** *Stranger in a Strange Land* (1961). A new messiah is raised on Mars and his psychic powers lead him to the foundation of a new religion.

Holdstock, Robert (born 1948), *Mythago Wood* **(1984).** A dark and particularly English fantasy in which mysterious Jungian archetypes haunt a Herefordshire forest.

Holt, Tom (born 1961), *Flying Dutch* **(1991).** Brilliantly funny, tongue-in-cheek exploration of the story of the Flying Dutchman, doomed to an eternal life of loneliness on the seas unless he can find true love.

▷ **Moorcock, Michael (born 1939),** *Elric* **(2001).** Moorcock creates one of the great anti-heroes of fantasy literature in Elric of Melnibone, the albino sorcerer and betrayer of his own, non-human race on an earth only just coming under the domination of mankind.

▷ **Pratchett, Terry (born 1948),** *Small Gods* **(1992).** This episode in Pratchett's hilarious and ever-increasing Discworld series tells of the Grand Inquisitor's secretary: a lad who never forgets anything, ever, and who has a unique and meaningful personal relationship with God (a very tiny turtle). All the Discworld books are self-contained; this is one of the funniest.

Priest, Christopher (born 1943), *The Glamour* **(1984).** An enigmatic love triangle becomes a disturbing search for identity, as the three central characters all possess (or believe they possess) an uncanny quality that sets them apart.

Stephenson, Neal (born 1959), *Snow Crash* **(1992).** Witty, complex tale of conspiracy theories fronted by a skateboarding pizza-delivery boy. The paranoia of *The X-Files* combined with irony and a grunge sensibility.

Vonnegut, Kurt (born 1922), *The Sirens of Titan* **(1959).** Classic story of Niles Rumfoord, condemned by a scientific accident to live all moments of his life simultaneously and how, on a lunatic rollercoaster ride through the universe and time, he tries to shake off his condition.

Wolfe, Gene (born 1931), *The Book of the New Sun* **(1980–3).** This classic four-book series uses fantasy form to explore ideas of the duality between good and evil, the nature of cruelty and the possibility of redemption. Severian, exiled to the mysterious, dying planet Urth, first explores, then exploits, then seeks to save it. Individual titles: *The Shadow of the Torturer*, *The Claw of the Conciliator*, *The Sword of the Lictor*, *The Citadel of the Autarch*.

Also recommended: Poul Anderson, *The Broken Sword*; Greg Bear, *Blood Music*; Ray Bradbury, *Fahrenheit 451*; Samuel R. Delany, *Nova*; Philip José Farmer, *A Feast Unknown*; M. John Harrison, *Viriconium Nights*; Russell Hoban, *Riddley Walker*; Daniel Keyes, *Flowers for Algernon*; Stanislaw Lem, *Solaris*; Walter Miller Jr., *A Canticle for Leibowitz*; Kim Stanley Robinson, *Red Mars*; Joanna Russ, *The Female Man*; Norman Spinrad, *Bug Jack Barron*; Sherri S. Tepper, *Grass*; Jack Womack, *Elvissey*.

See also: Atwood, Ballard, Blish, Crace, Dick, Donaldson, Eddings, Fantasy Adventure, Fantasy Societies, Harrison, Herbert, Le Guin, Lessing, McCaffrey, Rewriting History, Silverberg, Wyndham.

verse was outsold by Byron's, he turned instead to historical novels, and wrote 29 in the next 18 years. They are swaggering tales of love, bravery and intrigue, many of them centred on events from Scottish history and set in the brooding landscapes of the highlands and islands.

ROB ROY (1817)

In the 1710s, Osbaldistone and Rashleigh are rivals for the hand of Diana Vernon. Rashleigh embezzles money and frames Osbaldistone. Osbaldistone escapes to the highlands of Scotland, where he seeks help from Rob Roy, an outlaw who (like Robin Hood centuries before him) robs the rich to help the poor, rights wrongs and fights a usurping power (in his case, the English) on behalf of an exiled, true royal prince (James Stuart, the Old Pretender). Osbaldistone's quest to clear his name becomes inextricably bound up with the Jacobite Rebellion, and it is not until Rashleigh (who, not unexpectedly, supports the English and betrays Rob Roy to them) is killed that justice prevails and Osbaldistone and Diana at last find happiness.

Scott's other novels include Waverley, Guy Mannering, Old Mortality, The Heart of Midlothian, The Bride of Lammermoor, Ivanhoe, Kenilworth, The Fortunes of Nigel, Quentin Durward, Redgauntlet *and* Castle Dangerous.

> **READ ON**

- ● *Ivanhoe, The Heart of Midlothian.*
- ▶ Harrison Ainsworth, *The Tower of London*; James Fenimore Cooper, *The Last of the Mohicans*; ▷ Victor Hugo, *Nôtre-Dame de Paris*; ▷ Alexandre Dumas, *The Man in the Iron Mask*; Nigel Tranter, *Montrose: the Captain General.*

SELF, Will (born 1961)
British writer

Since first coming to attention with his 1991 collection of short stories *The Quantity Theory of Insanity*, Will Self has successfully maintained an ambivalent profile in contemporary fiction. On the one hand he is the perennial bad boy and outsider, a former heroin addict who writes with brutal directness about sex, drugs and urban violence. On the other, he is the Oxford-educated, middle-class satirist once described by Martin Amis as 'thrillingly heartless, terrifyingly brainy'. Like most satirists, much of Self's anger and indignation is directed at the hypocrisies and corruptions of the city. His fiction is mostly set in London and, in Self's work, London is an almost hallucinatory city in which no one and nothing is to be trusted, not even the ongoing humanity of its inhabitants. In *Great Apes* (1997) the artist Simon Dykes wakes after a night of dissipation to find that the human city has slipped away from him while he slept. His girlfriend has become a chimpanzee and so too have the rest of the inhabitants of London. Self is very definitely not a writer for the squeamish or the easily offended but for those who like their fiction to be thrillingly heartless and terrifyingly brainy, he is an essential read.

MY IDEA OF FUN (1993)

Ian Wharton has – or fantasizes that he has – eidetic powers, the ability to see into people's lives and minds as easily as into their pockets. Seeking to understand

and control these powers, he becomes in thrall to 'Mr Broadhurst', alias 'Samuel Northcliffe', alias 'the Fat Controller', who leads him a Mephistophelean dance of alchemy, sexual fantasy and sadistic violence in return for his soul. The novel recounts Ian's twenty-year struggle to break free from the Fat Controller and his henchman Gyggle, a nightmare spiral through the underbelly of 1990s big-city Britain – or possibly through the drug-blasted synapses of his own imagination.

Self's other books include Cock and Bull, *two interlinked novellas which explore and undermine traditional ideas about male and female sexuality, the novel* How The Dead Live *and the short story collections* Grey Area *and* Tough, Tough Toys for Tough, Tough Boys. Junk Mail *is a collection of his hard-hitting and witty journalism.*

> READ ON

▶ to *Great Apes*: John Collier, *His Monkey Wife* ; ▷ Peter Høeg, *The Woman and the Ape*.
▶ to *My Idea of Fun*: William Burroughs, *The Naked Lunch*.
▶ to Self's work in general: ▷ Martin Amis, *Dead Babies*; ▷ Irvine Welsh, *Marabou Stork Nightmares*; Christopher Fowler, *Spanky*.

READ ON A THEME: SEQUELS

('what happened next' to characters from famous novels of the past)
  Elaine Feinstein, *Lady Chatterley's Confession* (after *Lady Chatterley's Lover*)
▷ George MacDonald Fraser, *Flashman* (after *Tom Brown's Schooldays*)
  Lin Haire-Sargeant, *Heathcliffe* (after *Wuthering Heights*)
▷ Susan Hill, *Mrs de Winter* (after *Rebecca*)
  Nikos Kazantzakis, *The Odyssey* (after Homer's *Odyssey*)
  Bjorn Larsson, *Long John Silver* (before and after *Treasure Island*)
  Valerie Martin, *Mary Reilly* (after *Doctor Jekyll and Mr Hyde*)
  Alexandra Ripley, *Scarlett* (after *Gone With the Wind*)
  John Spurling, *After Zenda* (after *The Prisoner of Zenda*)
  Emma Tennant, *Pemberley* and *An Unequal Marriage* (after *Pride and Prejudice*)
  Angela Thirkell, *High Rising* (after Anthony Trollope's 'Barsetshire' novels)

SETH, Vikram (born 1952)
Indian writer

Could two contemporary novels by the same author be more different in form and content than *The Golden Gate* and *A Suitable Boy*? *The Golden Gate* (1986) is a novel in verse, a sequence of nearly 700 sonnets telling of the loves and lives of a group of twentysomething professionals in California. *A Suitable Boy* (1993) is a huge 1500 page book which sets the stories of four families in newly independent India against the backdrop of the social and political changes that independence has brought. Yet both are the work of Vikram Seth. What links two such different books are Seth's easy wit, his readability and his acute eye for manners and mores both in 1980s California and in Nehru's new India. Seth's only other novel is *An Equal Music* (1998), in which a classical violinist struggles to revitalize a love he thought he'd lost and to find artistic fulfilment through his music.

Vikram Seth has also written several volumes of poetry, a book about his travels in Sinkiang and Tibet, From Heaven Lake and a collection of animal fables, Beastly Tales from Here and There.

> READ ON ▷

▶ to *A Suitable Boy*: ▷ Salman Rushdie, *Midnight's Children* and Arundhati Roy, *The God of Small Things* (for two very different ways of treating post-independence India in fiction); Rohinton Mistry, *A Fine Balance* (another epic of Indian lives caught up in wider social change, this time set in the 1970s).

▶ to *An Equal Music*: Bernard MacLaverty, *Grace Notes*.

READ ON A THEME: SEX

▷ Nicholson Baker, *Vox*
  Georges Bataille, *The Story of the Eye*
▷ J.G. Ballard, *Crash*
▷ D.H. Lawrence, *Lady Chatterley's Lover*
  Henry Miller, *The Rosy Crucifixion Trilogy (Sexus, Plexus, Nexus)*
  Anaïs Nin, *Delta of Venus*
  Pauline Reage, *The Story of O*
  D.M. Thomas, *The White Hotel*

SHARPE, Tom (born 1928)
British novelist

If, as many foreigners maintain, British humour is obsessed with the functions of the lower body, then Sharpe is our comic Laureate. In each of his books he chooses a single target – polytechnic life, publishing, Cambridge University, the landed gentry – and demolishes it magnificently, comprehensively, by piling slapstick on crudity like a demented circus clown. Sharpe's heroes live in a state of unceasing, ungovernable panic, and are usually crippled by lust, forever tripping over their own erections. His old men are gluttonous, lecherous and senile, prone to perversion and prey to strokes and heart attacks; his matrons are whooping, whip-wielding Boadiceas, scything down every beddable male in sight. If your humorous fancy is for penises trapped in briar-patches, condoms ballooning above Cambridge spires or maniacs burying sex-dolls in wet cement, Sharpe's books are for you.

☆ RIOTOUS ASSEMBLY (1973)
Kommandant van Heerden, police chief of the sleepy South African town of Piemburg, wants a quiet life and an invitation to join the exclusive British Country Club. His assistant Verkramp wants van Heerden's job. Konstabel Els wants to keep on playing with his electrodes and fucking kaffirs. But Miss Hazelstone phones to say that she has just shot her black cook – and that it was not a 'garbage-disposal operation' but the result of a lovers' tiff. Van Heerden, thinking

that she must be covering up for her brother the bishop, sets out on an investigation which spirals into an orgy of transvestism, voyeurism, bestiality and murder. The South African setting gives this book devastating point: given the situation, even Sharpe's most slapstick satirical excess seems a model of self-restraint.

Sharpe's other books include Wilt *and its sequels* The Wilt Alternative *and* Wilt on High; The Throwback; Porterhouse Blue *and its sequel* Grantchester Grind; Ancestral Vices, Vintage Stuff *and* The Midden.

READ ON ▷

● *Indecent Exposure; Blott on the Landscape.*
▶ Colin Douglas, *The Houseman's Tale*; Thorne Smith, *The Bishop's Jaegers*; Howard Jacobson, *Peeping Tom*; ▷ J.P. Donleavy, *The Ginger Man.*

SHELLEY, Mary (1797–1851)
British novelist

After the death of her husband (the poet) in 1822, Shelley developed a literary career of her own, editing her husband's work, writing essays, journals and travel-books, and publishing short stories and novels. Her best-known book is ★*Frankenstein, or the Modern Prometheus* (1818), about a man who tries to prove the superiority of scientific rationality to the supernatural by usurping God's function and creating life. Although, thanks to Hollywood, Frankenstein's monster has nudged his creator from centre-stage, even the worst Frankenstein films keep to one of Shelley's most fascinating ideas: that the monster is an innocent, as pure as Adam before the Fall, and that its ferocity is a response learned by contact with 'civilized' human beings. Shelley developed the theme of the contrast between innocence and the corruption of civilization in other books, most notably the future-fantasy *The Last Man* (1826), set in a world where all human beings but one have been destroyed by plague, and the survivor wanders among the monuments of the glorious past like a soul in Hell.

READ ON ▷

● to *Frankenstein*: ▷ H.G. Wells, *The Island of Doctor Moreau*; ▷ Bram Stoker, *Dracula*; Gerald Du Maurier, *Trilby.*
▶ to *The Last Man*: ▷ Daniel Defoe, *Robinson Crusoe*; Bernard Malamud, *God's Grace.*

SHIELDS, Carol (born 1935)
US/Canadian novelist and short story writer

In most of her novels Carol Shields writes about very ordinary people who lead lives that might be considered narrow and restricting by outside observers. In *The Stone Diaries* (see below) Daisy Goodwill's life is a long one and it certainly has its dramas but she comes to feel that she has sleepwalked through life, entering a number of roles expected of women but never reaching down to her essential self. Larry in *Larry's Party* is not a man caught up in large-scale events or swept along by strong passions. Yet Shields has a gift for locating the extraordinary that lurks within apparently ordinary people. The novelist can highlight an individuality that is not only hidden from other characters in the novel but may even be hidden from the person herself. In the short stories collected in volumes like *Dressing Up for the Carnival* and *Various Miracles* this sense of the mystery and worth of the individual is apparent. Her novels have been various in subject matter but all have had at their core people working through the maze of life in search of an elusive sense of self at its heart. *Mary Swann* is the story of four very different people whose lives are linked by an obsessive interest in the work and life of a Canadian poet unrecognized before her violent death. Different versions of Mary Swann, satisfying to the varied interpreters, are finally presented at a symposium on her work. *The Republic of Love* is the story of two people, with the wreckage of several relationships in the past, embarking on yet another hopeful journey towards emotional fulfilment.

THE STONE DIARIES (1993)

The Stone Diaries is the story of an 'ordinary' woman's life from birth in rural Canada to her death in a Florida nursing home ninety years later. Daisy Goodwill Flett, as the chapter headings of the book (Birth, Childhood, Marriage, Love etc) ironically underline lives, in one sense, a conventional life as (in her son's words at her memorial service) 'wife, mother, citizen of our century.' In another sense her life is most unconventional, including elements that might not have looked out of place in a magic-realist novel. Her mother dies in childbirth without even realizing she is pregnant. A neighbour returns to his native Orkney Islands and lives to the age of 115, proud of his ability to recite *Jane Eyre* from memory. And the novel in which Daisy's life is told is far from being conventional. It mimics the form of a non-fiction biography with family tree, photographs of family members, excerpts from letters, journals, newspaper articles etc. In a poignant, funny and knowing narrative, Carol Shields carefully unfolds the extraordinary story of the ordinary 'wife, mother and citizen of the century.'

Carol Shields's other books include Happenstance, The Box Garden, Small Ceremonies *and* A Celibate Season *(a collaboration with Blanche Howard). She has also written a biography of Jane Austen.*

> READ ON

- ● *Mary Swann.*
- ▶ to the novels: ▷ Margaret Atwood, *The Blind Assassin*; ▷ Anne Tyler, *Breathing Lessons*; ▷ Jane Smiley, *Moo*; Anita Shreve, *The Pilot's Wife.*
- ▶ to the short stories: ▷ Alice Munro, *Dance of the Happy Shades.*

READ ON A THEME: SHIPS AND THE SEA

▷ Joseph Conrad, *The Nigger of the Narcissus*
  Paul Gallico, *The Poseidon Adventure*
▷ William Golding, *Rites of Passage*
▷ Herman Melville, *Moby-Dick*
  Nicholas Monsarrat, *The Cruel Sea*
▷ Patrick O'Brian, *Master and Commander*

▷ Barry Unsworth, *Sacred Hunger*
▷ Jules Verne, *Twenty Thousand Leagues Under the Sea*
  Herman Wouk, *The Caine Mutiny*

READ ON A THEME: SHIPWRECK

▷ Daniel Defoe, *Robinson Crusoe*
▷ William Golding, *Pincher Martin*
▷ Muriel Spark, *Robinson*
▷ Kurt Vonnegut, *Galápagos*
▷ Patrick White, *A Fringe of Leaves*
  Marianne Wiggins, *John Dollar*

READ ON A THEME: SHORT STORIES

▷ John Cheever, *The Stories of John Cheever*
  Roald Dahl, *Kiss, Kiss*
  Junot Diaz, *Drown*
▷ Helen Dunmore, *Ice Cream*
  Nathan Englander, *For the Relief of Unbearable Urges*
  Aleksander Hemon, *The Question of Bruno*
▷ James Joyce, *Dubliners*
▷ Franz Kafka, *Metamorphosis and Other Stories*
  Garrison Keillor, *Lake Wobegon Days*
  Ring Lardner, *Collected Short Stories*
  Lorrie Moore, *Birds of America*
  Saki, *The Complete Stories*
  Helen Simpson, *Four Bare Legs in a Bed*

See also: Borges, Calvino, Carver, Chekhov, Doyle, Fitzgerald (F. Scott), Hemingway, Mansfield, Maugham, de Maupassant, Munro, O'Hara, Poe, Pritchett, Stevenson, Taylor, Trevor, Updike, Welty, Wilson (Angus), Wyndham.

SHUTE, Neville (1899–1960)
British/Australian novelist

'Neville Shute' was the pseudonym of Neville Shute Norway. In the 1920s he worked as an aeronautical engineer, and he later served as a Second World War naval commander – experiences which inspired two of his finest books, *Pied Piper* (1942), about a mild-mannered man who rescues a group of children from the Nazis, and *No Highway* (1948), about an aircraft engineer trying desperately to warn sceptical superiors and politicians of the existence of metal fatigue. In 1950 Shute settled in Australia, and made it the setting for most of his later books. He wrote of ordinary people in a self-effacing style; his books have the immediacy of 'in-depth' newspaper reporting. But the characters of each story are in crisis, and the plot shows them working out moral or ethical dilemmas which have implications far beyond the novel's bounds. *On the Beach* (1957) is his best-known book, set in the Melbourne suburbs at some unstated time in the near future. We see perfectly ordinary people (a young couple with a baby; a woman and her US sailor-lover) bustling about their mundane lives. But the background is anything but ordinary: the whole human race is facing imminent annihilation from the nuclear fallout of World War III. As the novel proceeds, and Shute explores the implications of this theme, his characters' attempts to preserve everyday decencies are shown to be not so much survival strategy as a pitiable, pointless evasion of reality.

Shute's early books include So Disdained, Lonely Road *and the excellent war-story* Landfall. *His later novels include* The Far Country, In the Wet, Requiem for a Wren *and* Trustee from the Toolroom. Slide Rule *is an autobiography up to 1938.*

READ ON ⟩

- *A Town Like Alice* (about two survivors from the Japanese occupation of Malaya who decide to develop one small settlement in the Australian Outback).
- ▶ to *On the Beach*: John Christopher, *The Death of Grass*; George Turner, *The Sea and Summer*.
- ▶ to Shute's other novels: Nigel Balchin, *The Small Back Room*; H.E. Bates, *The Purple Plain*; ▷ Morris West, *The Navigator*.

SILVERBERG, Robert (born 1935)
US novelist

Silverberg has written some of the most intelligent and thought-provoking science fiction of the last fifty years. Key themes of his mature work are transcendence and transformation, especially of states of consciousness, and he handles them with great skill and emotional insight. *Dying Inside*, the story of a man losing the telepathic powers which made sense of his world, is as bleak and affecting as the title suggests. *Nightwings* envisages an alien invasion that is benign rather than threatening. *Downward to the Earth*, which deliberately echoes Conrad's *Heart of Darkness,* uses science fiction techniques to explore the nature of colonialism. *Towers of Glass* movingly depicts the struggle of android slaves to turn their inventor into their god. Silverberg is also known for fantasy series set in worlds of the far future. Majipoor, for example, is a giant planet where magic and science, medieval politics and high technology, aliens and humans, co-exist. In ☆*Lord Valentine's Castle* (first volume of the 'Majipoor' Trilogy, 1979–83), a wandering juggler discovers, by chance use of his psychic powers, that he is the rightful ruler of the planet, and gathers a company of warriors to win his inheritance. In *The Majipoor Chronicles* a boy discovers the planet's computer archives, and embarks on a psychic exploration of its teeming, magical history. In *Valentine Pontifex* the ruler of Majipoor has to undertake his most demanding task yet, a battle against the Metamorphs who are destroying crops, trying to starve Majipoor's people into submission and take over Valentine's throne.

Silverberg's other books include The Book of Skulls, The Second Trip, Thorns, A Time of Changes *and two inspired by Biblical and other ancient myths*, Shadrach in the Furnace *and* Gilgamesh the King.

READ ON ▷

▶ to the science fiction: ▷ Robert Heinlein, *Job*; Frederick Pohl, *The Reefs of Space*; Ray Bradbury, *The Illustrated Man*.
▶ to the fantasies: Piers Anthony, *Vicinity Cluster*; ▷ Iain M. Banks, *Consider Phlebas*; ▷ Anne McCaffrey, *Dragonflight*.

SIMENON, Georges (1903–89)
Belgian novelist

Simenon began work as a seaman, then as a journalist, and finally began writing in his 20s. He produced over 500 books, sometimes writing them in a week or less. In his most productive year as a hack writer of potboilers he produced no less than 44 books. Simenon is best known for some 150 crime-stories featuring the pipe-smoking, Calvados-drinking Commissaire Maigret of the Paris Police. The books are short and spare; they concentrate on Maigret's investigations in bars, lodging-houses and rain-soaked Paris streets, and on his casual-seeming, fatherly conversations with suspects and witnesses. But Simenon is a far more substantial writer than this, and his relentless produc-tivity, suggest. Many of his non-Maigret novels are compelling studies of people distracted by fear, obsession, despair or hate. *Act of Passion* (1947) is the confession of a madman who kills his lover to keep her pure, to prevent her being contaminated by the evil which he feels has corroded his own soul. The hero of ★☆ *The Man Who Watched the Trains Go By* (1938), outwardly placid and controlled, is in fact so gnawed by the sense of his own inadequacy that he chooses murder as the best way to make his mark on the world. *Ticket of Leave* (1942) is about a woman who falls in love with a paroled murderer. All these books are written in a sinewy, unemotional style, as plain as a police report. Only in one novel, *Pedigree* (1948), does Simenon break out of his self-imposed limits. It is a 500-page account of a boy's growing-up in Belgium in the first 15 years of this century, an evocation not only of trams, gas-light, cobble-stones and teeming back-street life, but of an emerging personality. A fictionalized autobiography, it is one of Simenon's most unexpected and rewarding works.

READ ON ▷

▶ to *Pedigree*: ▷ Jerome Weidman, *Fourth Street East*.
▶ to the Maigret books: Nicolas Freeling, *Love in Amsterdam*; Maj Sjöwall and Per Wahlöö, *The Laughing Policeman*; Friedrich Dürrenmatt, *The Quarry*.

SINCLAIR, Iain (born 1943)
British writer

For the last twenty five years, Iain Sinclair has been conducting his own intense, idiosyncratic fictional study of the topography, history and inhabitants of his adopted city, London. His work does not often make easy reading. In Sinclair's imagination there are interconnections between the most disparate phenomena and the city is a network of links between people (past and present), buildings, sites of numinous significance, books, rituals and power-structures. This, and his highly wrought, linguistically inventive prose, make demands on the reader but the rewards are considerable. *Lud Heat* (1975), influential on ▷ Peter Ackroyd's *Hawksmoor*, is a mixture of prose and poetry which centres on the London churches of the architect Nicholas Hawksmoor. Sinclair's first novel *White Chappell, Scarlet Tracings* (1987) follows the antics of a group of seedy, unscrupulous book-dealers as they try to track down arcane editions of Victorian novels and joins to this a sequence of meditations and revelations about the Whitechapel murders of Jack the Ripper. Sinclair's finest novel to date is *Downriver* (1991), as ambitious to encompass the possibilities of London as ▷ Joyce's *Ulysses* is to memorialize Dublin. Built around twelve interlocking tales centred on the Thames and the life surrounding it, and incorporating characters from Victorian boatmen and visiting Aboriginal cricketers to sixties gangsters and nuclear-waste train-drivers, *Downriver* is an extraordinary, ebullient celebration of the splendours and squalor of the city.

Sinclair's other novels are Radon Daughters *and* Landor's Tower. Lights Out for the Territory *is a collection of essays.* Rodinsky's Room *(written in collaboration with the artist Rachel Lichtenstein) is an exploration of the Jewish East End focused on the mysterious disappearance of a reclusive scholar from his room above a synagogue in Princelet Street.*

> **READ ON** ⟩

- **Landor's Tower** (Sinclair deserts his usual setting of London in a story set entirely in the borderlands of England and Wales).
- ▶ ▷ Peter Ackroyd, *Hawksmoor*; ▷ Michael Moorcock, *Mother London*; Paul West, *The Women of Whitechapel*; Chris Petit, *Robinson*; Nicholas Royle, *The Matter of the Heart*; Maureen Duffy, *Capital*.

SINGER, I.B. (Isaac Bashevis) (1904–91)
Polish/US novelist and short story writer

Singer wrote in Yiddish, and maintained that even when he translated his work himself, English diluted its force. His characters are either Middle European Jews – merchants, yeshiva-students, gravediggers, rabbis, drunks – from the ghettos and peasant villages of the 17th-19th centuries, or (in several of his finest stories) present-day settlers in Israel or the US. They struggle to lead decent lives, uplifted or oppressed by the demands of orthodox Jewish belief and ritual. They are haunted by outside forces beyond their control: supernatural beings – several stories are narrated by dybbuks, ghosts and even the Devil himself – or mindless, vicious anti-Semitism. *Satan in Goray* (1955), *The Magician of Lublin* (1960) and *The Slave* (1962) are about dark forces, demonic evil breaking out in small, closed communities. In *The Manor* (1967), *The Estate* (1970) and *Enemies, a Love Story* (1972) the destructive forces are internal, as people's orthodox beliefs are challenged by love-affairs, business-deals, friendships and other such worldly claims. *Shosha* (1978) and its sequel *Meshugah* (published 1995) are about a Jewish writer seen first in pre-Holocaust Poland and then in 1950s literary New York.

☆ THE FAMILY MOSKAT (1950)

This is a warm, multi-generation story about a large Jewish family in Warsaw –
and Singer's finest novel. The focus is on the human relationships within the
family, magnificently and movingly described; but the novel's edge comes from
the constant intrusion of grim outside reality, the tormented history of Poland
between the Congress of Vienna in 1815 and the Second World War Nazi
storming of the Warsaw Ghetto. Counterpoint between inner and outer reality,
between public and private life, between flesh and spirit, makes this book not just
another family saga but a statement about Jewish (and non-Jewish) humanity at
large.

Singer's other novels include The Certificate, The Penitent, The King of the Fields
and Shadows on the Hudson, *posthumously published in book form although it
had only appeared as a magazine serial in Singer's lifetime. Short story collections inclue* Gimpel the Fool, The Spinoza of Market Street, A Friend of Kafka, A
Crown of Feathers, Passions, Love and Exile *and* Old Love. ★☆ Collected Stories
is a fat anthology. In My Father's Court *is a memoir of Singer's Warsaw days as the
son of a rabbi, a theological student and a budding writer.*

> [!NOTE]
> READ ON

▶ to the short stories: S.Y. Agnon, *The Bridal Canopy*; Isaac Babel, *Odessa Tales*;
  ▷ Nikolai Gogol, *Arabesques*.
▶ to *The Family Moskat*: I.J. Singer (I.B.'s brother), *The Brothers Ashkenazy*.
▶ to Singer's other novels: Bernard Malamud, *The Fixer*; Nikos Kazantzakis, *The
  Greek Passion*; ▷ Mario Vargas Llosa, *The War of the End of the World*; Jerzy
  Kosinski, *The Painted Bird*.

READ ON A THEME: SMALL TOWN LIFE, USA

  Sherwood Anderson, *Winesburg, Ohio*
  Russell Banks, *Affliction*
▷ John Cheever, *Bullet Park*
▷ John Irving, *The Cider House Rules*
  Garrison Keillor, *Lake Wobegon Days*
  William Maxwell, *Time Will Darken It*
  Larry McMurtry, *The Last Picture Show*
  Jayne Anne Phillips, *Machine Dreams*
  Dawn Powell, *My Home Is Far Away*
  Richard Russo, *The Risk Pool*

See also: Deep South, USA

SMILEY, Jane (born 1951)
US novelist

A story set in the Midwest that echoes the events described in *King Lear* (*A
Thousand Acres*); a satire on the academic pretensions of a small college (*Moo*);
a historical novel of immense ambition that takes place in the battleground
between pro- and anti-slave factions that was Kansas in the 1850s (*The All-True*

Travels and Adventures of Lydie Newton) – Jane Smiley's fiction is immensely varied. Her novels have few common denominators beyond the subtlety of her intelligence and the supple flexibility of her prose, which she can adapt to whatever requirements her story demands. She has a particularly strong feeling for rural life, both its pleasures and its pitfalls. In *A Thousand Acres* the Lear-like character is a farmer and the inheritance he bestows on his two daughters is not a kingdom but a farm in Iowa. The tragedy, which is as much that of the daughters as it is of the father, is played out against the ordinary, everyday details of farm life and is the stronger because of that. In *The All-True Travels and Adventures of Lydie Newton* the idealistic settlers of Kansas Territory find that they have to face not only the belligerence of their pro-slave neighbours but the intransigence of a land that is far from being the one of milk and honey that they imagined. The women of the book face the challenges more realistically than the men. (Smiley's fiction is full of strong women characters who get on with the daily tasks of life while the men have a tendency to make fine speeches and adopt noble postures.) Yet even the likeable and resourceful heroine Lydie is caught up in forces she cannot understand. Her husband is killed by pro-slavers and her attempt to make her own stand for his ideals (by helping in the escape of a slave) turns to tragedy. Jane Smiley is clear-sighted and unsentimental about both men and women and about the relationships between them, which is another of the qualities that make her one of America's most interesting contemporary novelists.

Jane Smiley's other novels include Horse Heaven, The Greenlanders *(an epic set in medieval Greenland),* Barn Blind, Duplicate Keys, At Paradise Gate *and* Ordinary Love. The Age of Grief *is a collection of short stories.*

> READ ON

▷ **Annie Proulx,** *Accordion Dreams*; ▷ **Barbara Kingsolver,** *The Bean Trees*; ▷ **Carol Shields,** *The Stone Diaries.*

SMITH, Wilbur (born 1933)
South African novelist

Smith's novels, set in southern Africa, are swaggering adventure yarns in the tradition of ▷ H. Rider Haggard. Their backgrounds are war, mining and jungle exploration; their heroes are free spirits, revelling in the lawlessness and vigour of frontier life. *Shout at the Devil* (1968) is typical: the story of lion-hunting, crocodile-wrestling, ivory-poaching Flynn O'Flynn whose Robin Hood humiliations of the sadistic German commissioner Fleischer take a serious turn when war is declared – this is 1914 – and he falls into a German trap.

Smith's other novels include A Falcon Flies, Men of Men, The Angels Weep, The Leopard Hunts in Darkness *(the four Ballantyne books),* A Time to Die, The Burning Shore, Birds of Prey *and* Monsoon. *The Courtneys of Africa trilogy* (The Burning Shore, Power of the Sword *and* Rage) *is about the lifelong feud of two half-brothers during the last turbulent century of South African affairs.* River God *is set in ancient Egypt and has been followed by two other books with a similar setting,* The Seventh Scroll *and* Warlock.

READ ON ▷

- *A Time to Die* (about Sean Courtney, a white safari guide who agrees to lead his rich US clients across the border into Mozambique, where the daughter is promptly kidnapped by guerrillas).
- ▶ ▷ Hammond Innes, *Campbell's Kingdom*. ▷ H. Rider Haggard, *King Solomon's Mines*.

SNOW, C.P. (Charles Percy) (1905–80)
British novelist

Snow's main work is the novel-sequence 'Strangers and Brothers' (1950–74). Though many characters recur, each book is self-contained. As the series proceeds, Lewis Eliot (the narrator of all 11 novels) rises from humble provincial beginnings to become a barrister, a civil servant and a senior government official. Snow's preoccupation was power: how people influence each other, the working of committees and hierarchies, the morality of office. He coined the phrase 'the corridors of power' – and he offers unrivalled glimpses of the people who tramp those corridors, of real individuals behind the establishment façade. ☆ *The Masters*, one of the key books in the sequence, describes the alliances and compromises required to elect a new master for a Cambridge college. *The New Men*, about scientists working on the first atomic bomb, is a study of responsibility: should we use our skills for ends we feel are wrong? Snow's themes are large, but his books are blander and less agonised than this suggests. His characters – especially the imperturbable committee-men (never women) who keep things going and the mavericks who let feelings interfere with common sense – are fascinating, and his scenes of discussion and persuasion are brilliantly done: he keeps us on the edge of our seats about such apparently trivial matters as whether someone will end up saying 'yes' or 'no'.

The books in the sequence are Strangers and Brothers, The Light and the Dark, A Time of Hope, The Masters, The New Men, Homecomings, The Conscience of the Rich, The Affair, The Corridors of Power, The Sleep of Reason *and* Last Things. *Snow's other novels include two thrillers*, Death Under Sail, A Coat of Varnish, *and* The Search, *a fascinating study of the excitement and passion of scientific research.*

READ ON ▷

- ▶ ▷ Anthony Trollope, *Can You Forgive Her?* (the first novel in the 'Palliser' sequence); ▷ Angus Wilson, *The Old Men at the Zoo*; Pamela Hansford Johnson (Lady Snow), *Error of Judgement*; ▷ Gore Vidal, *Washington, D.C.*; ▷ Neville Shute, *No Highway*.

SOLZHENITSYN, Alexandr (born 1918)
Russian novelist and non-fiction writer

Denounced for treason in 1945 (he was a Red Army soldier who criticized Stalin), Solzhenitsyn spent eight years in a labour camp where he developed stomach cancer, and after nine months in a cancer hospital was sent into internal exile. He turned this bitter experience into novels: the prison-camp books *One Day in the Life of Ivan Denisovich* (1961) and *The First Circle* (1968), and *Cancer Ward* (1968), a story of patients in a Soviet hospital. Their publication outside the USSR made him one of the most famous of the 1960s Soviet dissidents. He was finally expelled from the USSR in 1974, for writing an exhaustive description of the location, history and methods of the Russian prison-camp system, *The Gulag Archipelago* (1974–8). Few writers have ever surpassed him as a chronicler of human behaviour at its most nightmarish: his personal history authenticates every word he wrote.

Solzhenitsyn's only other fiction is the vast (and partially untranslated) 'Red Wheel' sequence of which August 1914 *and* November 1916, *about the stirrings of the Russian Revolution, are two volumes.* Invisible Allies *is a memoir and a tribute to those people who kept his work alive in Russia when to do so was to risk imprisonment.*

> READ ON ▷

▶ ▷ Fyodor Dostoevsky, *Notes from the House of the Dead*; Arthur Koestler, *Darkness at Noon*; ▷ Vladimir Nabokov, *Bend Sinister*; ▷ André Brink, *Looking on Darkness*; ▷ Thomas Pynchon, *Gravity's Rainbow*; William Styron, *Sophie's Choice*.

READ ON A THEME: SOMETHING NASTY . . .

▷ Iain Banks, *The Wasp Factory*
 Roald Dahl, *Kiss Kiss* (short stories)
 Christopher Fowler, *Soho Black*
 Thomas Harris, *The Silence of the Lambs*
 James Herbert, *Sepulchre*
▷ Stephen King, *Pet Sematary*
 H.P. Lovecraft, *The Call of Cthulhu and other Weird Tales*
▷ Ruth Rendell, *Live Flesh*
▷ Anne Rice, *Interview with the Vampire*

See also: Good and Evil

READ ON A THEME: SOUTH AFRICA

▷ André Brink, *Imaginings of Sand*
▷ J.M. Coetzee, *Disgrace*
▷ Nadine Gordimer, *Burger's Daughter*
▷ H. Rider Haggard, *King Solomon's Mines*
 Bessie Head, *When Rain Clouds Gather*
 Dan Jacobson, *A Dance in the Sun*
 Alan Paton, *Cry, The Beloved Country*
▷ Tom Sharpe, *Riotous Assembly*
 Anthony Sher, *Middlepost*
▷ Wilbur Smith, *Rage*

SPARK, Muriel (born 1918)
British novelist

Spark made her name in the 1960s: her tart black comedies seemed just the antidote to the fey optimism of the time. Her books' deadpan world is a distorted mirror-image of our own, a disconcerting blend of the bland and the bizarre. In *Memento Mori* old people are mysteriously telephoned and reminded that they are about to die. In *Robinson* a plane-load of ill-assorted people (among them the standard Spark heroine, a Catholic with Doubts) crashes on an island where laws and customs are hourly remade at the whim of the sole inhabitant. In *The Prime of Miss Jean Brodie* an Edinburgh schoolmistress tries to brainwash her pupils into being nice, non-conforming gels. *The Abbess of Crewe* reworks convent politics in terms of Watergate; the hero of *The Only Problem*, a scholar working on the Book of Job, finds its events parallelling those in his own life. Spark develops these ideas not in farce but in brisk, neat prose, as if they were the most matter-of-fact happenings in the world. The results are eccentric, unsettling and hilarious.

☆ THE GIRLS OF SLENDER MEANS (1963)
A group of young ladies lives in a run-down London club for distressed gentlefolk. It is 1945, and there is rumoured to be an unexploded bomb in the garden. The girls are excited by the possibility of imminent destruction: they find it almost as thrilling as the thought of sex. They bustle about their busy, vapid lives: pining after film stars, writing (unanswered) letters to famous writers, bargaining for black-market clothing coupons. The book is an allegory about seedy-genteel, self-absorbed Britain under the threat of nuclear extinction; for all Spark's breezy humour, the novel is haunted by the questions of where we'll be and how we'll behave when the bomb goes up.

Spark's other novels include The Mandelbaum Gate *(her most serious book, about a half-Jewish Catholic convert visiting Jerusalem at the height of Arab-Israeli tension),* The Driver's Seat, The Ballad of Peckham Rye, A Far Cry from Kensington, Symposium, Loitering with Intent, Reality and Dreams *and* Aiding and Abetting. The Complete Short Stories *gathers together all her previously published stories and some that have not appeared before.* Curriculum Vitae *is autobiography.*

> READ ON

- *The Ballad of Peckham Rye, The Bachelors.*
▶ Ronald Firbank, *The Eccentricities of Cardinal Pirelli*; ▷ Rose Macaulay, *The Towers of Trebizond*; Alice Thomas Ellis, *The 27th Kingdom*; Christopher Hope, *Serenity House*; ▷ Hilary Mantel, *An Experiment in Love*; Elizabeth Jolley, *Miss Peabody's Inheritance.*

READ ON A THEME: SPIES AND DOUBLE AGENTS

  James Buchan, *Heart's Journey in Winter*
▷ Joseph Conrad, *The Secret Agent*
▷ Frederick Forsyth, *The Fourth Protocol*
  Alan Furst, *The World at Night*
▷ W. Somerset Maugham, *Ashenden*

▷ John Le Carré, *A Perfect Spy*
  Gavin Lyall, *Spy's Honour*
▷ Ruth Rendell, *Talking to Strange Men*

See also: Action Thrillers; High Adventure

STEAD, Christina (1902–83)
Australian novelist

Although Stead was born in Australia, she lived most of her life, and set many of her books, in Europe (especially Paris) and the US. She writes of these places, however, not as a native but as a visitor, in a detached, ironic tone. In *The Beauties and Furies*, a savage moral tale about adultery, a young wife runs off to 1930s Paris and has an affair with a handsome but ruthless sexual adventurer; in the end he drops her and goes in search of younger prey. *The Man Who Loved Children*, set in the US but based on Stead's own experience, is a story of stifling family life at the turn of the century, presided over by a monstrous, bullying father; the whole thing is seen through the eyes of his daughter, Louise, as she grows from terrified, adoring childhood to rebellious adolescence and adulthood.

Stead's other novels include For Love Alone, Dark Places of the Heart/Cotter's England, The People With the Dogs, Miss Herbert (The Suburban Wife) *and the long, ironic 'romance'* Letty Fox, Her Luck. The Salzburg Tales *is a collection of macabre, satirical and bawdy short stories modelled on Chaucer's* Canterbury Tales.

> READ ON

▶ to *The Beauties and Furies*: ▷ Jean Rhys, *After Leaving Mr Mackenzie*; Patrick Hamilton, *Hangover Square*; Djuna Barnes, *Nightwood*.
▶ to *The Man Who Loved Children*: ▷ Ivy Compton-Burnett, *A Family and a Fortune*; ▷ Angela Carter, *The Magic Toyshop*.

STEINBECK, John (1902–68)
US novelist

Until Steinbeck settled to writing in 1935, he moved restlessly from one job to another: he was a journalist, a builder's labourer, a house-painter, a fruit-picker and the caretaker of a lakeside estate. This experience gave him first-hand knowledge of the dispossessed, the unemployed millions who suffered the brunt of the US Depression of the 1930s. Their lives are his subject, and he writes of them with ferocious, documentary intensity and in a style which seems exactly to catch their habits of both mind and speech. The ruggedness of his novels is often enhanced by themes borrowed from myth or the Old Testament. *To A God Unknown* (1933) is about an impoverished farmer who begins worshipping ancient gods and ends up sacrificing himself for rain. *Tortilla Flat* (1935) about 'wetbacks' (illegal Mexican immigrants to California) uses the story of Arthur, Guinevere and Lancelot from British myth. *East of Eden* (1952) is based on the story of Cain and Abel. Though Steinbeck never thrusts such references down his readers' throats, they add to the grandeur and mystery which, together with documentary grittiness, are the overwhelming qualities of his work.

★☆ THE GRAPES OF WRATH (1938)

The once-fertile Oklahoma grain-fields have been reduced to a dust-bowl by over-farming, and the Joad family are near starvation. Attracted by leaflets promising work in the fruit-plantations of California, they load their belongings into a battered old car and travel west. In California they find every plantation surrounded by destitute, desperate people: there are a thousand applicants for every job. The plantation-owners pay starvation-wages and sack anyone who objects; the workers try to force justice by strike action – and are beaten up by armed vigilantes. When Tom Joad, already on the run for murder, is caught up in the fight for justice and accidentally kills a man, it is time for Ma to gather the family together again and move on. There must be a place for them somewhere; there must be a Promised Land.

Steinbeck's shorter novels include Cannery Row, The Pearl *and* The Short Reign of Pippin IV. *His short stories, usually abut 'wetbacks', share-croppers and other victims of the US system, are in* The Red Pony *and* The Long Valley. The Acts of King Arthur and his Noble Knights *is a straightforward retelling of British myth;* The Portable Steinbeck *is a packed anthology.*

> READ ON ⟩

- *Of Mice and Men* (a tragedy about the friendship between two ill-matched farmworkers, Lennie – a simple-minded giant of a man – and the weedier, cleverer George).
▶ Erskine Caldwell, *God's Little Acre*. ▷ Edith Wharton, *Ethan Frome*. ▷ William Faulkner, *The Hamlet*. Upton Sinclair, *The Jungle*; Frank Norris, *McTeague*; James T. Farrell, *Studs Lonigan*.

STENDHAL (1783–1842)
French novelist and non-fiction writer

'Stendhal' was a pseudonym used by the French diplomat Henri-Marie Beyle. As well as fiction (four novels; a dozen short stories) he published essays on art, literature and philosophy and several autobiographical books. Unlike most early 19th-century writers – even ▷Balzac and ▷Dickens – who concentrated on surface likenesses, painting word-pictures of events, people and places without introspection, Stendhal was chiefly interested in his characters' psychology. The main theme of his novels was the way outsiders, without breeding or position, must make their way in snobbish, tradition-stifled society by talent or personality alone. His books give the feeling that we are watching the evolution of that personality, that we are as intimate with his people's psychological development as if they were relatives or friends.

★ SCARLET AND BLACK (LE ROUGE ET LE NOIR) (1830)

The book is a character-study of Julien Sorel, a carpenter's son who rises in the world by brains, sexual charm and ruthlessness. He becomes, first, tutor to the children of the local Mayor, then the Mayor's wife's lover, and finally secretary to an aristocratic diplomat whose daughter falls in love with him. In ten years he has travelled from humble origins to the verge of a dazzling marriage and a brilliant career. But then the Mayor's wife writes a letter denouncing him as a cold-hearted adventurer, his society acquaintances reject him, and he returns to his native town to take revenge.

Stendhal's other completed novels are Armance, The Abbess of Castro *and* The Charterhouse of Parma. The Life of Henri Brûlard *and* Memoirs of an Egoist *are fictionalized autobiography.* Love *is a collection of reflections on the subject, prompted by the failure of one of Stendhal's many unrequited passions.*

> **READ ON**

- ● *The Charterhouse of Parma.*
- ▶ to *Scarlet and Black*: ▷ André Gide, *Strait is the Gate*; ▷ Nikolai Gogol, *Dead Souls*; ▷ George Eliot, *Middlemarch*; ▷ Honoré de Balzac, *Lost Illusions.*
- ▶ to *The Charterhouse of Parma*: ▷ Umberto Eco, *The Name of the Rose.*

STERNE, Laurence (1713–68)
British novelist

Sterne was a Yorkshire clergyman and a lover of wine, good talk, travel and song. His only novel, ★☆ *The Life and Opinions of Tristram Shandy, Gentleman* (1760–7) is less a story than a gloriously rambling conversation. Tristram sets out to tell his life-story (beginning with the moment of his conception, when his mother's mind is less on what she is doing than on whether his father has remembered to wind the clock). But everything he says reminds him of some anecdote or wise remark, so that he constantly interrupts himself. It takes 300 pages, for example, for him to get from his conception to the age of seven, and in the meantime we have had such digressions as a treatise on what the size and shape of people's noses tell us about their characters, an explanation of how the boy came to be called Tristram by mistake for Trismegistus (and what each name signifies), accounts of the Tristapaedia (the system devised for Tristram's education), the curse of Ernulphus of Rochester and the misfortunes of Lieutenant le Fever; we have also had the novel's preface (placed not at the beginning but as the peroration to Book III), and many musings on life, love and the pursuit of happiness by Tristram's father, Uncle Toby and Corporal Trim. The reader is constantly exhorted, nudged and questioned; there is even a blank page in case you have urgent thoughts of your own to add. We never know how Tristram's life turns out; instead, we are copiously informed about Uncle Toby's love-affairs, Tristram's travels in France and the adventures of the King of Bohemia. Sterne himself called *Tristram Shandy* 'a civil, nonsensical, good-humoured book'; it is the most spectacular shaggy-dog story ever told.

Sterne's other writings include sermons – he was a Yorkshire parson – and A Sentimental Journey, *a discursive, half-fictionalized account of the towns and people he saw and the tales he heard during six months' travelling in France.*

READ ON >

▶ ▷ François Rabelais, *Gargantua*. Miguel de Cervantes, *Don Quixote*; Tobias Smollett, *The Expedition of Humphry Clinker*; ▷ John Kennedy Toole, *A Confederacy of Dunces*; Flann O'Brien, *At Swim-Two-Birds*; ▷ Saul Bellow, *Henderson the Rain King*.

STEVENSON, R.L. (Robert Louis) (1850–94)
British writer of novels, short stories and non-fiction

Apart from the brief psychological thriller *Dr Jekyll and Mr Hyde* (1886), about a man who uses drugs to change himself from kindly family doctor to deformed killer and back again, Stevenson's chief works are historical adventure-stories. It is often assumed that these are books for children, but (except perhaps in *Treasure Island*, 1883) there is also plenty to interest adults: Stevenson's evocation of scenery (especially Scotland), the psychological complexity of his characters, and the feeling (which he shared with ▷Tolstoy) that each human life is part of a vast historical, moral and cultural continuum.

READ ON >

● *Kidnapped*.
▶ to *Dr Jekyll and Mr Hyde*: ▷ H.G. Wells, *The Invisible Man*; Gaston Leroux, *The Phantom of the Opera*; James Hogg, *Confessions of a Justified Sinner*; James Robertson, *The Fanatic*.
▶ to the adventure stories: ▷ George MacDonald Fraser, *The Candlemass Road*; ▷ Walter Scott, *The Heart of Midlothian*; ▷ John Buchan, *Castle Gay*; ▷ A. Conan Doyle, *The Valley of Fear*; Bjorn Larsson, *Long John Silver*.

STOKER, Bram (1847–1912)
Irish writer

Forget all sendups and tawdry horror-film exploitation. ★ *Dracula* (1897) is still one of the most blood-curdling novels ever written. The reader may begin by counting off the clichés – foggy cemeteries, vaults under the madhouse, the blazing crucifix, the bat-count climbing down the castle walls – but the sheer power of the story, its conviction and its exotic (and erotic) eeriness soon grip like tiny pointed teeth. Stoker was not a genius, but *Dracula* is a work of genius, the Gothic novel (written in the form of diaries and letters to give added authenticity) to end them all.

READ ON >

▷ Edgar Allan Poe, *Tales of Mystery and Imagination*; ▷ Stephen King, *Salem's Lot*; Anne Rice, *Interview with the Vampire*.

STOUT, Rex (1886–1975)
US novelist

Stout was one of the great US names of the Golden Age of detective fiction, writing some 50 novels of an unvarying high standard. His stories centre on a double act. Nero Wolfe is a woman-hating eccentric who lives in a large, old house with his cook, gardener, books, 10,000 orchids and a brain the size of a planet. His secretary, Archie Goodwin, does all the legwork and narrates the stories. Stout's plots are bizarre and complicated; the dialogue is sharp; the relationship of Wolfe and Goodwin is endlessly intriguing. Good sample novels are *Fer-de-Lance, Where There's a Will, The League of Frightened Men* (Stout's own favourite) and *Death of a Dude*.

> READ ON

▶ Robert Goldsborough, *The Last Coincidence* (one of many Nero Wolfe books by Goldsborough, who catches Stout's manner so well that he could be the master reincarnated); Lawrence Block, *The Topless Tulip Caper* (a spoof); H.R.F. Keating, *A Rush on the Ultimate*.

SVEVO, Italo (1861–1928)
Austrian/Italian novelist

Svevo was a businessman in Trieste; his firm made underwater paint. Despite encouragement from his friend ▷ James Joyce, he never took his writing seriously until the last year of his life, when a French translation of ★☆*The Confessions of Zeno* (1922) brought him European fame. His books are ironical comedies. Their ineffective, bewildered heroes blunder about in society, looking for some point to their existence – and the chief irony is that they are genuinely the 'zeros' they think they are, their existence has no point at all. *The Confessions of Zeno* is the autobiography of a man who wants to give up smoking. He explains that his addiction is actually psychological, since every cigarette he smokes reminds him, in ▷Proustian fashion, of some past experience, so that to give up smoking would be to surrender his own history; he writes of his Oedipal relationship with his father (whom he accidentally killed), of his prolonged, ludicrous courtship of the wrong woman, and of his treatment by a psychiatrist sicker than himself. The book is as dreamlike and terrifying as ▷Kafka's novels – indeed, Svevo exactly shared Kafka's vision of the world as an absurd, endless and sinister labyrinth.

Svevo's other novels are A Life, As A Man Grows Older *and the shorter* Tale of the Good Old Man and the Pretty Girl.

> READ ON

▶ ▷ Franz Kafka, *The Castle*; ▷ Saul Bellow, *Herzog*; Alberto Moravia, *The Conformist*; Machado de Assis, *The Heritage of Quincas Borba*; William Cooper, *Scenes from Married Life*; ▷ William Boyd, *The New Confessions*; ▷ Gabriel García Márquez, *Love in the Time of Cholera*.

SWIFT, Graham (born 1949)
British novelist

Swift's novels centre on apparently ordinary people – shopkeepers, housewives, clerks – under psychological stress. They have reached turning-points in what have seemed boring, routine lives, and the novels show them mentally rerunning the past to find explanations for their feelings, either to themselves or to others. In *Waterland* (1983) the main character is an elderly history teacher, and the event he is remembering is the discovery, forty years before, of a boy's body in a drainage-ditch in the English Fens. In front of a bored, cheeky class, he begins thinking aloud about the reasons for the boy's death – and his monologue ranges through the history of the Fens (one of the remotest and most mysterious English regions), the story of several generations of his own family, and, not least, an account of the rivalry between his mentally subnormal brother Dick and Freddie Parr, the boy found drowned.

Swift's other novels are The Sweet Shop Owner, Shuttlecock, Out of This World, Last Orders *and* Ever After, *about a despairing man working himself away from suicide by researching the death of his father – and the events, further back in the past, which may have had a bearing on that. The Booker Prize-winning* Last Orders *tells a deceptively simple story of four ageing men on a journey to the coast where they plan to scatter the ashes of an old friend in the sea. The journey forces them all into reassessments of their own lives and relationships.* Learning To Swim *is a collection of short stories.*

> READ ON

- *Out of This World* **(in which, in alternate monologues, the son and granddaughter of a First World War hero, an arms manufacturer, reflect on the way the old man's obsessive love for them has poisoned both their lives).**
- ▶ ▷ Ian McEwan, *The Child in Time* ; ▷ Julian Barnes, *Staring at the Sun*; Peter Benson, *The Levels*; ▷ Jane Rogers, *Promised Lands*.

SWIFT, Jonathan (1667–1745)
British/Irish satirist and journalist

Swift was a savage satirist, pouring out poems, articles and essays attacking the follies of his time. ★☆ *Gulliver's Travels* (1726) differs from his other work only in that the edge of its satire is masked by fairy tale – indeed, the satire and scatology are often edited out so that the book can be sold for children. Gulliver is a compulsive explorer, despite the moral humiliation he suffers after every landfall. In Lilliput the people (who are six inches high) regard him as an uncouth, unpredictable monster – particularly when he tells them some of the ideas and customs of his native England. In Brobdignag he becomes the pet of giants, and tries without success to convince them of the value of such civilized essentials as lawcourts, money and guns. He visits Laputa and Lagado, cloud-cuckoo-lands where science has ousted common sense; on the Island of Sorcerers he speaks to great thinkers of the past, and finds them in despair at what has become of the human race. Finally he is shipwrecked among the Houynhyms, horses equipped with reason who regard human beings as degenerate barbarians, and who fill him with such distaste for his own species that when he returns to England he can hardly bear the sight, sound or smell of his own family. Throughout the book, Gulliver doggedly preaches the glories of European 'civilization' (that is, the customs and belief of the Age of Enlightenment), and arouses only derision or disgust.

READ ON ▷

▶ Voltaire, *Candide*; Samuel Butler, *Erewhon*; ▷ Nathanael West, *A Cool Million*.
▶ Equally lacerating satires on aspects of late 20th-century life: Michael Frayn, *A Very Private Life*; ▷ Thomas Pynchon, *The Crying of Lot 49*; ▷ Angela Carter, *The Passion of New Eve*.

T

TAYLOR, Elizabeth (1912–75)
British novelist and short story writer

A large part of Taylor's art consists of appearing to have no art at all: few authors have ever seemed so self-effacing in their work. As each novel or story begins, it is as if a net curtain has been drawn aside to reveal ordinary people in a normal street. The setting is the outskirts of some large English town; the people are housewives, bus-conductors, labourers, schoolchildren; there seems to be no drama. But as the story proceeds, an apparently unfussy chronicle of ordinary events and conversations builds up enormous psychological pressure, which Taylor then releases in a shocking or hilarious happening which opens speculation wide about whatever will happen when the book is closed. Her artistry – subtle, gentle and unsettling – is at its peak in short stories; her novels, thanks to larger casts, more varied settings and longer time schemes, tend more to wry social comedy than to the sinister.

☆ THE DEVASTATING BOYS (1972)
The people in this story collection are typical Taylor characters: an elderly couple in the countryside who decide to offer a holiday to two black children from the city slums; a young West Indian, utterly alone in London on the eve of his birthday; an 11-year-old child taking a bus home from a hateful piano lesson; a blue-rinsed widow with an orderly routine of life. Something unexpected happens to each of them, a psychological bombshell. They were as unremarkable as our neighbours – but after these stories, our neighbours will never seem the same again.

Dangerous Calm *is an aptly titled selection from Taylor's short stories. Her novels include* Angel, At Mrs Lippincote's, A View of the Harbour, The Wedding Group, Blaming, A Wreath of Roses, Mrs Palfrey at the Claremont *and* The Soul of Kindness.

> **READ ON**

- *Dangerous Calm; The Wedding Group* (novel).
- ▶ to the stories: ▷ V.S. Pritchett, *The Camberwell Beauty and Other Stories;* ▷ William Trevor, *Angels at the Ritz*; Mary Gordon, *Temporary Shelter*.
- ▶ to the novels: ▷ Susan Hill, *A Change for the Better*; ▷ Barbara Pym, *Excellent Women*; ▷ Angus Wilson, *Late Call*; Theodor Fontane, *Effi Briest*.

READ ON A THEME: TEENAGERS

▷ Julian Barnes, *Metroland*
S.E. Hinton, *The Outsiders*

READ ON A THEME: TERRORISTS/FREEDOM FIGHTERS

THACKERAY, William Makepeace (1811–63)
British novelist and journalist

Until the success of *Vanity Fair*, when he was 36, Thackeray earned his living as a journalist and cartoonist (especially for *Punch* magazine) and as a humorous lecturer. His first intention in his novels was to write 'satirical biographies', letting the reader discover the follies of the world at the same time as his naive young heroes and heroines. But the characters took over, and his books now seem more genial and affectionate than barbed. He invented characters as grotesque as ▷ Dickens's, caricatures of human viciousness or folly, but he wrote of them with a kind of disapproving sympathy, a fellow-feeling for their humanity, which Dickens lacks. Humbug, ambition and the seven deadly sins are Thackeray's subjects – and so are friendship, kindness and warm-heartedness. At a time when many English novels were more like sermons, clamorous for reform, he wrote moral comedies, showing us what fools we are.

★ VANITY FAIR (1847–8)
The book interweaves the lives of two friends, gentle Amelia and calculating, brilliant Becky Sharp. Becky is an impoverished orphan determined to make her fortune; Amelia believes in love, marriage and family life. Each of them marries; Amelia's husband has an affair with Becky, and dies at Waterloo with her name on his lips; Becky's husband finds her entertaining a rich, elderly admirer and abandons her. In the end, each girl gets what she longed for, but not in the way she hoped. Amelia, after ten years pining for her dead husband, is cruelly told by Becky of his infidelity, and turns for comfort to a kind man who has worshipped her from afar, and who now offers her marriage, a home and all the comforts of obscurity. Becky's son inherits his father's money and gives her

an annuity on condition that she never speaks to him again; we see her at the end of the book, queening it in Bath, an idle, rich member of the society she has always aspired to join and whose values Thackeray sums up in the title of the book.

Thackeray's other books include Pendennis *(the story of a selfish young man, spoilt by his mother, who goes to London to make his fortune as a writer) and its sequel* The Newcomers, Henry Esmond *and its sequel* The Virginians, *and* Barry Lyndon.

> [READ ON]

● *Pendennis.*
▷ Jane Austen, *Emma*; ▷ Arnold Bennett, *The Card*; ▷ H.G. Wells, *Tono-Bungay*; ▷ Eudora Welty, *The Ponder Heart*; ▷ Barbara Pym, *No Fond Return of Love.*

THEROUX, Paul (born 1941)
US novelist and non-fiction writer

Some of Theroux's most enjoyable books are about travelling: *The Great Railway Bazaar, The Old Patagonian Express, The Kingdom by the Sea, The Iron Rooster, The Happy Isles of Oceania, The Pillars of Hercules.* In all of them the narrator, the writer himself, feels detached, an observer of events rather than a participant – and the same is true of the people in Theroux's novels. They live abroad, often in the tropics; like the heroes of ▷Graham Greene (the author Theroux most resembles) they feel uneasy both about the society they are in and about themselves; they fail to cope. The hero of *Saint Jack* (1973), a US pimp in Singapore, hopes to make a fortune providing rest and relaxation for his servicemen compatriots, but the pliability of his character makes him the prey for every conman and shark in town. In *The Mosquito Coast* (1981) an ordinary US citizen, depressed by life, uproots his family and tries to make a new start in the Honduran jungle, with tragic, farcical results. *Honolulu Hotel* (2000) is an episodic novel set in run-down hotel in Hawaii. The manager is an unsuccessful writer, battling with the personal demons that beset so many of Theroux's characters, who acts as witness to the tragi-comedies and mini-dramas that unfold in the seedy rooms of the hotel.

MY SECRET HISTORY (1989)
André Parent is an American writer, born at the time of the Second World War, randy for women and hot for every experience the world can offer. He teaches in Africa, writes novels and stories, makes a fortune from a travel book. He fulfils his adolescent ambition, 'to fuck the world', only to find that he has lost moral identity. The book is wry, funny, and no comfort to Americans, intellectuals, writers, the middle-aged, or indeed anyone else at all.

Theroux's other novels include Waldo, The Family Arsenal, Doctor Slaughter, Picture Palace, Chicago Loop, Millroy the Magician, *an acid science fiction fantasy* O-Zone, My Other Life *(a kind of companion to* My Secret History*) and* Kowloon Tong. Sinning With Annie, The Consul's File *and* The London Embassy *are collections of short stories.* Fresh Air Fiends *is a collection of travel essays;* Sir Vidia's Shadow *is a memoir of Theroux's thirty-year friendship (now ended) with*

▷ *V.S. Naipaul, horribly compelling in its revelations of the insecurities and jealousies of the literary life.*

READ ON ▷

► to *My Secret History*: John Fowles, *Daniel Martin*; ▷ Graham Greene, *The Honorary Consul.*

► to Theroux's novels in general: ▷ P.H. Newby, *Leaning in the Wind*; Timothy Mo, *Sour-Sweet*; ▷ William Boyd, *Stars and Bars.*

► to the travel books: Jonathan Raban, *Coasting.*

TÓIBÍN, Colm (born 1955)
Irish writer

In three very different novels Colm Tóibín has used an unobtrusive, un-demonstrative but highly effective prose style to tell stories about Irish people, both past and present, caught in emotional dilemmas and crises in their lives. *The Blackwater Lightship* (see below) is his most recent novel and, arguably, the one in which his economic, unflamboyant use of language is most movingly deployed but his first two novels are also well worth reading. *The South* (1990) is set in 1950s and 1960s Spain. A young Irishwoman, an aspiring painter, arrives in Barcelona in flight from her family in Ireland. Her relationship with a Spanish painter, at odds with Franco's regime, moves towards a tragic conclusion. *The Heather Blazing* (1992) is the story of an Irish judge, reflecting on his own life, his family memories and the resonance of Irish history. In a fourth novel, *The Story of the Night* (1996) Tóibín produced a haunting and sensuous exploration of a young gay man in Falklands War-era Argentina, discovering his sexuality against the backdrop of a country in transition.

THE BLACKWATER LIGHTSHIP (1999)
Declan O'Doherty is a young man, dying of AIDS. He asks to be taken to the isolated house by the sea where his grandmother lives and which he remembers from his childhood. Three generations of the women in his family – grandmother, mother and sister – join him there, as do two gay friends, who have known of his illness far longer than his family. Mutual antagonism and estrangement have characterized all the relationships between the women in the family and unresolved conflicts simmer beneath the surface, occasionally breaking out in harsh exchanges, as they all try to come to terms with Declan's illness and with one another. Tóibín is too intelligent and subtle a writer to offer easy resolutions to the essentially unresolvable realities his characters face and his prose is so spare and draws so little attention to itself that it is easy to miss just how controlled and well-crafted it really is. In the end, the restraint and understatement of Tóibín's narration, leaving space for the reader's own imagination to work, are what make this novel so moving.

Tóibín's non-fiction books include Bad Blood *(travels along the border between the Republic and Northern Ireland),* The Sign of the Cross *(travels in Catholic Europe) and* Homage to Barcelona. *He has also edited* The Penguin Book of Irish Fiction.

READ ON >

▶ Seamus Deane, *Reading in the Dark*; John McGahern, *Amongst Women*; David Leavitt, *The Page Turner*; John Banville, *Eclipse*; Niall Williams, *Four Letters of Love*; Dermot Bolger, *Father's Music*.

TOLKIEN, J.R.R. (John Ronald Reuel) (1892–1973)
British novelist

In 1937 Tolkien, a teacher of Anglo-Saxon literature at Oxford University, published a children's book (*The Hobbit*), about a small furry-footed person who steals a dragon's hoard. Bilbo Baggins was a hobbit, and his quest was the prologue to an enormous adult saga in which elves, dwarves, wizards, ents, human beings and hobbits unite to destroy the power of evil (embodied by the Dark Lord Sauron and his minions the Ring-wraiths and the orcs). The three volumes of ☆*The Lord of the Rings*, published in the mid-1950s, started a vogue for supernatural fantasy-adventure which has spread world-wide and taken in films, quiz-books and role-play games as well as fiction. Tolkien outstrips his imitators not so much because of his plot (which is a simple battle between good and bad, with the moral issues explicit on every page) as thanks to his teeming professorial imagination. He gave his made-up worlds complete systems of language, history, anthropology, geography and literature. Reading him is like exploring a library; his invention seems inexhaustible.

Although The Hobbit *and* The Lord of the Rings *are self-contained, Tolkien published several other volumes filling in chinks of their underlying history, explaining matters only sketched in the main narrative, and adding even more layers of linguistic, historical and anthropological fantasy. The chief books are* The Silmarillion *and* Unfinished Tales. Lost Tales *(three volumes) and* The History of Middle Earth *(five volumes) contain notes and drafts, chiefly of interest to addicts.* Farmer Giles of Ham *and* The Adventures of Tom Bombadil *are short stories for children.*

READ ON >

▶ ▷ Stephen Donaldson, *The Chronicles of Thomas Covenant*; Piers Anthony, *A Spell for Chameleon*; ▷ David Eddings, *The Belgariad Quintet*. ▷ Terry Pratchett, *The Colour of Magic* is a spectacular spoof.

TOLSTOY, Leo Nikolaevich (1828–1910)
Russian novelist

In his 60s and beyond Tolstoy became famous as a kind of moral guru or secular saint: he preached the equal 'value' of all human beings, and suited actions to words by giving away his wealth, freeing his serfs and living an austere life in a cottage on the edge of his former estate. A similar view underlies his fiction. His ambition was to enter into the condition of each of his characters, to show the psychological complexity and diversity of the human race. His books are not tidily organized, with every event and emotion shaped to fit a central theme, but reflect the sprawl of life itself. The result was a psychological equivalent of ▷Balzac's

STARTPOINTS

THRILLERS

Thrillers grew out of the adventure novels of the 19th century, such as ▷ Jules Verne's *Twenty Thousand Leagues Under the Sea* or ▷ H. Rider Haggard's *King Solomon's Mines*. ▷ Rudyard Kipling's *Kim* (1901) and Erskine Childers' *The Riddle of the Sands* (1903) were among the first novels to add politics to adventure – a blend which has dominated thrillers ever since. The many wars of the 20th century, in particular the (non-fighting) Cold War, gave thriller writers exciting backgrounds and ready-made 'good guys' and 'bad guys'. 'Their' chaps are out to use any trick, wile or murderous plot to control the world, and are thwarted only by the grit and pluck of 'our' chaps. In subtler thrillers (pioneered by ▷ Graham Greene in his 1940s 'entertainments', and since the 1960s by ▷ John Le Carré) writers dealt not in moral blacks and whites but in myriad shades of grey. During the Cold War anti-communist feeling in the West led to a mass of thrillers casting the former USSR as the villain and Soviet thrillers returned the compliment by blackening the West. But since the early 1990s thrillers of this kind have become as dead as dodos, and writers either set their stories in the past (for example in World War II), or find new enemies (such as terrorists, serial killers, organized crime or religious fundamentalists), and leave East-West politics alone.

▷ **Ambler, Eric (born 1909), *The Mask of Dimitrios* (1939)**. Classic. A writer on holiday in Turkey sees the body of a criminal in the morgue, and sets out, despite all attempts to stop him, to discover his story.

▷ **Clancy, Tom (born 1947), *The Sum of All Fears* (1991)**. In the near future, Palestinian terrorists get control of nuclear weapons.

▷ **Deighton, Len (born 1929), *City of Gold* (1992)**. In Cairo, during the 1942 Desert War, someone in Allied High Command is feeding Rommel military secrets, and must be stopped.

Easterman, Daniel (born 1949), *Name of the Beast* (1992). In 1999 portents of the end of the world begin to appear in Egypt then an archaeologist, examining a mummy in the Cairo Museum, finds links with the devilish, black-magic past.

Alan Furst, *The World at Night* (1997). Film producer becomes involved in the dark and dangerous world of resistance to the Nazis in wartime France.

▷ **Grisham, John, *The Pelican Brief* (1992)**. A young law student is the only person in the US to see a connection between two simultaneous political assassinations, on the right and the left. From that moment on her life is in deadly danger.

Harris, Thomas, *The Silence of the Lambs* (1990). Hannibal Lecter, the favourite film bogeyman of the 1990s, leads FBI agent Clarice Starling a merry dance as she tries to track down a serial killer.

▷ **Higgins, Jack (born 1929), *Thunder Point* (1993)**. Secret World War II documents, found in a sunken U-boat in the Caribbean 50 years later, reveal a conspiracy to keep Nazism alive after the war and implicate many of those still in power in the 1990s.

Household, Geoffrey (1900–88), *Rogue Male* (1939). Classic thriller about an agent who escapes from the Nazis and is forced, literally, to 'hole up' like a fox in a burrow while they hunt him.

Kerr, Philip, *A Philosophical Investigation* (1992). Detective in the not-so-distant future pits his wits against a serial killer with a fondness for Wittgenstein.

▷ **Le Carré, John (born 1931), *The Quest for Karla* (1974–90)**. Classic quartet of Cold War, house-of-mirror novels, involving George Smiley's search not just for Soviet agents but also for traitors in his own service, the ironically named 'Circus'. Individual titles: *Tinker Tailor Soldier Spy*, *The Honourable Schoolboy*, *Smiley's People* and *The Secret Pilgrim*.

▷ **Ludlum, Robert (born 1927), *The Road to Omaha* (1992)**. Amerindian fighter for justice defends the interest of the Wopotami people against Strategic Air Command, who have taken over their land and are prepared to fight dirty to keep it.

Pattison, Eliot, *The Skull Mantra* (2000). Original and moving thriller in which a disgraced Chinese investigator is drawn into the mystery surrounding a headless corpse found on a Tibetan mountainside.

▷ **Smith, Wilbur (born 1933), *Elephant Song* (1991)**. Action adventure in Zimbabwe, as film-maker and anthropologist try to thwart a conspiracy involving ivory-poaching, international business interests and the projected elimination of an entire country and its people.

Also recommended: Richard Condon, *The Manchurian Candidate*; Michael Connelly, *The Poet*; Bernard Cornwell, *Storm Child*; Clive Cussler, *Dragon*; Jeffrey Deaver, *The Coffin Dancer*; Ken Follett, *Night Over Water*; Colin Forbes, *Cross of Fire*; Jonathan Kellerman, *Time Bomb*; David Mason, *Shadow over Babylon*; Richard North Patterson, *The Outside Man*; Piers Paul Read, *On the Third Day*.

See also: Action Thrillers, Buchan, Forsyth, High Adventure, MacLean, Spies and Double Agents, Terrorists/Freedom Fighters.

'snapshots' in *The Human Comedy*. Whether Tolstoy is showing us a coachman who comes and goes in half a page, or a major character who appears throughout a book, he invites us to feel full sympathy for that person, makes us flesh out his or her 'reality' in terms of our own.

★☆ WAR AND PEACE (1869)

The book begins with people at a St Petersburg party in 1805 discussing the political situation in France, where Napoleon has just been proclaimed emperor. Tolstoy then fills 100 pages with seemingly random accounts of the lives and characters of a large group of relatives, friends, servants and dependants of three aristocrats, Andrey Bolkonsky, Pierre Bezuhov and Natasha Rostov. Gradually all these people become involved both with one another and with the gathering storm as Napoleon's armies sweep through Europe. The story culminates with the 1812 French invasion of Russia, Napoleon's defeat and his retreat from Moscow. The war touches the lives of all Tolstoy's people, and in particular resolves the triangle of affection between his central characters. The effects of war are the real subject of *War and Peace*. It contains 539 characters – the range is from Napoleon to the girl who dresses Rostov's hair, from Bolkonsky to an eager young soldier sharpening his sword on the eve of battle – and Tolstoy shows how their individual nature and feelings are both essential to and validated by the vast tapestry of human affairs of which they are part.

Tolstoy's other novels include Anna Karenina *(in which an adulterous and tragic love affair is used to focus a picture of the stifling, morally incompetent aristocratic Russian society of the 1860s),* The Death of Ivan Illich, The Kreutzer Sonata, Master and Man *and* Resurrection. *His autobiographical books include* Childhood, Boyhood, Youth *and* A Confession.

READ ON

● *Anna Karenina.*
▶ to *War and Peace*: ▷ Émile Zola, *The Downfall (Le débâcle)*; ▷ I.B. Singer, *The Family Moskat*; ▷ Bernice Rubens, *Mother Russia.*
▶ to *Anna Karenina*: ▷ Ivan Turgenev, *On the Eve*; ▷ George Eliot, *Romola*; ▷ Gustave Flaubert, *Madame Bovary*; ▷ Boris Pasternak, *Doctor Zhivago.*

TOOLE, John Kennedy (1937–69)
US novelist

A Confederacy of Dunces (1980), Toole's only novel, was published posthumously: it had collected so many rejection slips that he killed himself. It is a no-holds-barred comic grumble against the 20th-century world in general and the city of New Orleans in particular. Its anti-hero, Ignatius J. Reilly, is a narcissistic, hypochondriacal, towering genius who regards himself as too good for the world. He has successfully avoided working for 30 years, living in a fetid room in his mother's house and alternately masturbating, playing the lute and scribbling brilliant thoughts on a succession of supermarket notepads. At last his mother sends him out to find a job – with catastrophic results. Bored after one hour in a trouser factory, he sets about destabilizing staff-management relations; hired to sell hot-dogs, he eats his stock; in all innocence, he takes up with drug addicts, whores and corrupt police. If Ignatius were likeable (say, like Voltaire's Candide),

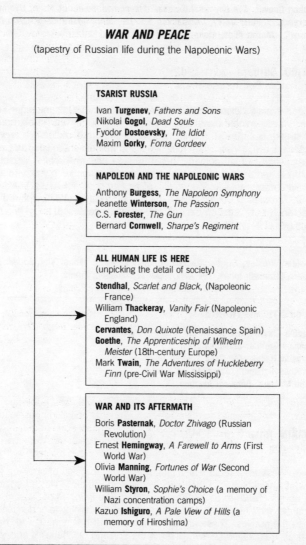

PATHWAYS

LEO TOLSTOY

WAR AND PEACE
(tapestry of Russian life during the Napoleonic Wars)

TSARIST RUSSIA

Ivan **Turgenev**, *Fathers and Sons*
Nikolai **Gogol**, *Dead Souls*
Fyodor **Dostoevsky**, *The Idiot*
Maxim **Gorky**, *Foma Gordeev*

NAPOLEON AND THE NAPOLEONIC WARS

Anthony **Burgess**, *The Napoleon Symphony*
Jeanette **Winterson**, *The Passion*
C.S. **Forester**, *The Gun*
Bernard **Cornwell**, *Sharpe's Regiment*

ALL HUMAN LIFE IS HERE
(unpicking the detail of society)

Stendhal, *Scarlet and Black*, (Napoleonic France)
William **Thackeray**, *Vanity Fair* (Napoleonic England)
Cervantes, *Don Quixote* (Renaissance Spain)
Goethe, *The Apprenticeship of Wilhelm Meister* (18th-century Europe)
Mark **Twain**, *The Adventures of Huckleberry Finn* (pre-Civil War Mississippi)

WAR AND ITS AFTERMATH

Boris **Pasternak**, *Doctor Zhivago* (Russian Revolution)
Ernest **Hemingway**, *A Farewell to Arms* (First World War)
Olivia **Manning**, *Fortunes of War* (Second World War)
William **Styron**, *Sophie's Choice* (a memory of Nazi concentration camps)
Kazuo **Ishiguro**, *A Pale View of Hills* (a memory of Hiroshima)

the satire might seem more genial and sympathetic; but he is a revolting example of how, in Toole's view, there is no excuse for the clinical brilliance of the brain being shackled to such a bag of guts as the human body. *A Confederacy of Dunces* is witty, slapstick, ▷Rabelaisian, Falstaffian – and offers the human species no reason at all for self-congratulation or for hope.

READ ON ▷

- ● *The Neon Bible* (written at 16; not as good, but good enough).
- ▶ Robert Coover, *The Universal Baseball Association*. Frederick Rolfe, *Hadrian the Seventh*; ▷ Peter Carey, *Illywhacker*; B.S. Johnson, *Christie Malry's Own Double-Entry*; ▷ Martin Amis, *Money*.

TRAPIDO, Barbara (born 1942)
South African/British novelist

Trapido's novels begin quietly, establishing a handful of characters (usually young, usually middle-class) and a setting (school, university, big house in a quiet street). But then she springs surprises on her characters – a new arrival, unexpected love, a visitor from long ago – and watches them squirm. Her books turn Aga-saga to high comedy: her witty style, the characters' likeability and foolishness and the bubbly good humour and invention keep you reading to the end. Her novels are *Brother of the More Famous Jack* (1982), *Noah's Ark* (1986), *Temples of Delight* (1990), its sequel *Juggling* (1994; about the same characters twenty years on but just as delightfully confused) and *The Travelling Hornplayer* (1997).

READ ON ▷

- ▶ ▷ Mary Wesley, *The Vacillations of Poppy Carew;* ▷ Anne Tyler, *Ladder of Years*; Elizabeth Jolley, *The Newspaper of Claremont Street.*

READ ON A THEME: TRAINS

- ▷ Agatha Christie, *Murder on the Orient Express*
- ▷ Graham Greene, *Stamboul Train*
- ▷ Jaroslav Hašek, *The Good Soldier Svejk*
- ▷ Patricia Highsmith, *Strangers on a Train*
- ▷ John Masters, *Bhowani Junction*

TREMAIN, Rose (born 1943)
British writer

Early success as a radio writer taught Tremain the skill of showing people's emotions and attitudes in their own words, and without a wasted syllable. Her early novels (*Letter to Sister Benedicta*, *The Swimming Pool Season*) are outstanding at showing people developing emotionally, coming to understand and to change themselves. These are contemporary, but her richest work has been historical. *Restoration* (1989), is set in the England of Charles II and is told by

Robert Merivel, an ambitious nonentity who is favoured by Charles, falls from grace by his own foolishness, and then gradually discovers, through suffering, the inner strength of his own character. The book's settings are Charles's court, Bidnold House in Norfolk (for Merivel, a kind of earthly paradise), New Bedlam lunatic asylum in Whittlesea, and a run-down house in Cheapside, London, in the months leading up to the Great Fire. *Restoration* engulfs the reader; its gusto never flags; but its underlying theme, how Merivel first damns and then redeems himself, and its beautiful ending, give it the depth and sadness characteristic of all Tremain's work. In *Music & Silence* (1999) Peter Claire, an English lutenist, travels to the court of the 17th-century king of Denmark, Christian IV. Christian, a charismatic man fallen into melancholy, depends on music to raise his fallen spirits. His wife hates music and longs only for the energetic attentions of her German lover. Claire, in flight from a love affair with an Italian-born Irish Countess, is drawn to one of the Queen's ladies-in-waiting, herself an escapee from a dark family background. Told in a variety of voices, *Music & Silence* harmonizes them all into a powerful and sensuous narrative.

Tremain's other novels include, The Cupboard, Sacred Country *and* The Way I Found Her. *Her short stories are collected in* The Colonel's Daughter, The Garden of the Villa Mollini *and (the particularly fine)* Evangelista's Fan.

| READ ON ▷ |

- ● *The Way I Found Her.*
- ▶ to *Restoration* and *Music & Silence*: ▷ Robert Graves, *Wife to Mr Milton*; ▷ Jeanette Winterson, *Sexing the Cherry*; Tracy Chevalier, *Girl with a Pearl Earring*; ▷ Jane Rogers, *Mr. Wroe's Virgins.*
- ▶ to Tremain's other books: ▷ Anita Brookner, *Lewis Percy*; Jane Gardam, *The Queen of the Tambourine.*

TREVOR, William (born 1928)
Irish writer

Trevor worked briefly as schoolteacher (history and art), sculptor and advertising copywriter before becoming a full-time writer in 1964. He is a leading author of short stories, many of which have been adapted for TV with outstanding success. He writes of sad, unfulfilled and remorselessly ordinary people, trapped by age, unattractiveness, miserable marriages or deadend jobs and struggling to make sense of lives in seedy, run-down cities and out-of-season holiday resorts. The world is in a state of creeping, half-genteel decay – and only the glimmer of ambition in his people's minds, flaring sometimes into obsession, keeps them from surrender.

☆ MRS ECKDORFF IN O'NEILL'S HOTEL (1969)
Mrs Eckdorff, a photo-journalist, comes to Dublin to investigate a run-down hotel which the barman on a cruise-liner told her is being run as a brothel. No one wants to publish the story: she is photographing it for a book, and for her own satisfaction. As she intrudes ever more into the barren-seeming lives of the men and women connected with the hotel, trying to rouse them from lethargy and dispiritedness, she comes gradually to feel that the gulf she perceives is not in

TRAVEL

Travel writing has a long history. Some 2,500 years ago Herodotus travelled widely in the Middle East and Egypt, researching his *History of the Persian War*, and wrote up the unexpected peoples and customs he encountered. Six centuries later Pausanias walked every kilometre of Greece, recording local legends and customs in a guidebook which, incredibly, can still be used today. Some 1,100 years later still, the Venetian Marco Polo produced, in *Travels* (1298), one of the first travel bestsellers, a wide-eyed account of the wonders of medieval Asia and travel writing has flourished ever since. For the reader it has a double attraction: we hear about exotic places and people, and the writer takes all the strain. Nowadays, when so much of the world is documented, it is often this last feature, the personal spin each author puts on familiar experience, which gives a book life: personal grouchiness, comedy, fine descriptive prose, interesting reflections, or (in the best books of all) all four.

Bryson, Bill (born 1951), *Made in America* (1993). Hilarious musings on everything American, from popcorn to gridlock, pegged loosely to a narrative of perfectly ordinary tourist travel except that nothing, in Bryson's eyes, is ever ordinary.

Burton, Richard (1821–90), *A Personal Narrative of a Pilgrimage to Al-Madinah and Mecca* (1855). Burton, disguised as an Arab, was the first European to visit the holy places of Islam, and tells the tale as if he were writing an adventure novel.

Cherry-Garrard, Apsley, *The Worst Journey in the World* (1922). Classic account, using letters, diaries and the author's own polar experience, of Captain Scott's doomed explorations in the 1910s.

Dalrymple, William (born 1967), *In Xanadu* (1989). Erudition and entertainment combined in Dalrymple's account of his undergraduate journey in the footsteps of Marco Polo.

Durrell, Gerald (1925–95), *The Bafut Beagles* (1953). Funny account of animal-collecting in Africa, by the author of *My Family and Other Animals*. Also: *Three Singles to Adventure*, *A Zoo in My Luggage*, *The Whispering Land*.

Fermor, Patrick Leigh (born 1915), *A Time of Gifts* (1977). An 18-year-old rebel sets out in 1933 to travel from the Hook of Holland to Istanbul on foot. Classic of the genre. *Between the Woods and the Water* (1987) is a sequel.

Heyerdahl, Thor (born 1914), *The Kon-Tiki Expedition* (1948). Across the Pacific on a huge balsa-wood raft, to show that Polynesians may have been settlers from ancient South America.

Kingsley, Mary (18621900), *Travels in West Africa* (1897). Unflappable Victorian lady walks and rides through jungles, crosses rivers, climbs mountains, camps near hostile villages and savours every moment.

Moorhouse, Geoffrey (born 1931), *Om* (1993). Well-known travel writer tours South India, looking for enlightenment. Fascinating places and people and a thoughtful account of the author's spiritual journey.

▷ **Naipaul, V.S. (born 1932), *An Area of Darkness* (1964)**. West Indian Hindu writer spends a year in India and writes dazzling, caustic account.

Newby, Eric (born 1919), *A Short Walk in the Hindu Kush* (1958). Author and laconic friend go for walk in the Himalayas, in true Boy's-Own-Paper style. Very funny.

Raban, Jonathan, *Passage to Juneau* (1999). Raban sails from Seattle to Alaska, accompanied only by ghosts of his own past and of the men who made the journey before him.

▷ **Sterne, Laurence (1713–68), *A Sentimental Journey Through France and Italy* (1768)**. By the author of *Tristram Shandy*.

▷ **Theroux, Paul (born 1941), *The Old Patagonian Express* (1979)**. Splendidly grumbly novelist specializes in horrendous train journeys. This one takes him from Boston, Massachusetts, all the way to Patagonia and back. A modern classic.

Thesiger, Wilfred (born 1910), *Arabian Sands* (1969). Across the Sahara with the Bedouin. One of the great travel books of the past 50 years.

Thubron, Colin (born 1939), *Behind the Wall* (1987). Modern China, its landscape, its people and its uneasy links with a glorious past.

Also recommended: Robert Byron, *The Road to Oxiana*; Peter Fleming, *Brazilian Adventure*; Heinrich Harrer, *Seven Years in Tibet* (mountain-climber trapped in pre-Chinese Tibet during World War II); Norman Lewis, *Dragon Apparent*; Rory Maclean, *Stalin's Nose*; Claudio Magris, *Danube*; Philip Marsden, *The Spirit-Wrestlers*; Peter Matthiessen, *The Snow Leopard*; Dervla Murphy, *Full Tilt: Ireland to India on a Bicycle*; P.J. O'Rourke, *Holidays in Hell*; Mary Russell, *The Blessings of a Good Thick Skirt* (famous women travellers of the past); Jeremy Seal, *A Fez of the Heart*; Freya Stark, *Riding to the Tigris*; John Steinbeck, *Travels With Charley*.

them, but in her own soul. Emptiness of spirit is the novel's theme, and its outcome is almost entirely the opposite of what Trevor cunningly leads us to suspect.

Trevor's short story collections include The Day We Got Drunk on Cake, Angels at the Ritz, After Rain *and* The Hill Bachelors. *His novels include* The Old Boys, Elizabeth Alone, The Children of Dynmouth, The Love Department, Other People's Worlds, The Silence in the Garden, Felicia's Journey *and* Death in Summer. *A number of books (*Fools of Fortune, The News from Ireland, Family Sins*) deal more specifically than his other work with the effects of recent Northern Irish politics.*

> **READ ON**

- **Two Lives** (two short novels). In **Reading Turgenev** a woman is stirred into awareness of the world (and to passion) when a friend introduces her to the stories of Turgenev. In **My House in Umbria** Emily Dalehunty, an ex-prostitute now running a **pensione** in Chiantishire, takes up writing romantic fiction, exploring the nature of passion, sex and love in her own life as well as those of her characters); **The Children of Dynmouth** (about a disturbed teenager terrorizing a run-down seaside town).
- ▶ to *Trevor's short stories:* ▷ Susan Hill, *A Bit of Singing and Dancing;* ▷ V.S. Pritchett, *The Camberwell Beauty;* ▷ John Cheever, *The Collected Stories.*
- ▶ to his novels: John Banville, *Eclipse* ▷ Angus Wilson, *The Middle Age of Mrs. Eliot;* ▷ Mary Wesley, *A Dubious Legacy;* ▷ Anita Brookner, *Look at Me.*

TROLLOPE, Anthony (1815–82)
British novelist

Until Trollope was 52 he worked for the Post Office, travelling in Europe, the US, north Africa and all over the British Isles. He turned his foreign experience into travel books, and used his British observations in 47 novels, many of them written, in the fashion of the time, for serial publication in magazines. His style is genial and expansive, and his books deal with such characteristic Victorian themes as class, power, money and family authority. His favourite characters are the upper-middle class of small towns and the surrounding estates. His plots involve the exercise of authority by the older generation and, by the young, all kinds of pranks, kicking over the traces, unsuitable love-affairs and mockery of their elders' stuffiness. Trollope's best-loved novels are in two six-book series, the 'Barsetshire' books (1855–67), about intrigue and preferment in a cathedral city, and the 'Palliser' books (1864–80), about politics on the wider stages of county and country. Each novel is self-contained, but recurring characters and cross-references between the books, added to Trollope's easy-going style, give the reader a marvellously comfortable sensation, as of settling down to hear about the latest scrapes of a group of well-loved friends.

☆ BARCHESTER TOWERS (1857)
The second novel in the Barsetshire sequence is high comedy. Imperious Mrs Proudie, wife of the timid new Bishop of Barchester, brings the Reverend Obadiah Slope into the Palace to help dominate her husband and run the diocese. But Slope is a snake in the grass, determined to make a rich marriage

for himself, to win preferment in the church, even to defy Mrs Proudie if that will advance his cause. Their power struggle is the heart of the book, a stately but furious minuet which soon sweeps up all Trollope's minor characters: rich, pretty Widow Bold, apoplectic Archdeacon Grantly, flirtatious Signora Vesey-Negroni, saintly Mr Harding, bewildered Parson Quiverful and his 14 squalling brats.

The Barsetshire novels are The Warden, Barchester Towers, Doctor Thorne, Framley Parsonage, The Small House at Allington *and* The Last Chronicle of Barset. *The Palliser novels are* Can You Forgive Her?, Phineas Finn, The Eustace Diamonds, Phineas Redux, The Prime Minister *and* The Duke's Children. *Trollope's other novels include* The Bertrams, Orley Farm, The Belton Estate, The Way We Live Now *and* Mr Scarborough's Family.

> READ ON

▶ **to the Barsetshire books:** ▷ Joanna Trollope, *Parson Harding's Daughter*; Angela Thirkell, *High Rising* (first of a series set in Barsetshire and borrowing Trollope's characters); Elizabeth Goudge, *Cathedral Close*; ▷ Susan Howatch, *Absolute Truth* ▷ Barbara Pym, *Crampton Hodnett.*
▶ **to the Palliser books:** ▷ John Galsworthy, *The Forsyte Saga*; Benjamin Disraeli, *Coningsby*; ▷ Christina Stead, *House of All Nations.*

TROLLOPE, Joanna (born 1943)
British novelist

In 1980 Trollope's *Parson Harding's Daughter*, a sequel to her forebear ▷ Anthony Trollope's *The Warden*, was garlanded as the Historical Novel of the Year. She has also written a modern 'Barsetshire chronicle': *The Choir* (1988), set among the musicians in a squabble-filled Anglican Cathedral close. But she is best known for a series of novels about the lives and problems of ordinary contemporary people. She is particularly good at describing the ebb and flow of relationships, between siblings, parents and children, husband and wives. Her evocations of 'village Britain' – especially the gossip and machinations under the serene soap-opera surface – are much admired.

A SPANISH LOVER (1993)
Lizzie, an Earth Mother with four lively children, an 'artistic' husband and a career to juggle, relies on the detached strength of her twin Frances – particularly at Christmas. But one year Frances announces that she is spending the holiday in Spain, and both women's lives start to unravel, till they learn to stand on their own feet without their sibling to support them.

Trollope's other novels include A Village Affair, A Passionate Man, The Rector's Wife, The Best of Friends, Next of Kin, Other People's Children *and* Marrying the Mistress. *She has also written period romances (as Caroline Harvey), and a non-fiction account of women in the British Empire,* Britannia's Daughters.

> READ ON

● *The Men and the Girls.*
▶ ▷ Margaret Forster, *The Battle for Christabel*; ▷ Penelope Lively, *According to Mark.* Penelope Mortimer, *The Pumpkin Eater.*

TURGENEV, Ivan Sergeevich (1818–83)
Russian novelist and playwright

A rich man, Turgenev spent much of his life travelling in Europe, and was welcomed abroad as the leading Russian writer of his time. He was less popular in Russia itself. Although his limpid style (influenced by his friend ▷ Flaubert) and his descriptions of nature were admired, his wistful satire, treating all human endeavour as equally absurd, won favour with neither conservatives nor radicals. His favourite characters are members of the leisured class, and his stories of disappointed ambition, failed love affairs and unfocused dissatisfaction anticipate not so much later revolutionary writings as the plays of ▷Chekhov.

★ FATHERS AND SONS (1861)
Arkady, a student, takes his friend Bazarov home to meet his father. The old man is impressed by Bazarov's vigorous character and outspoken views – which are that none of the old moral and social conventions have intrinsic validity, and that people must decide for themselves how to live their lives. (This attitude to life, 'nihilism', was widespread among Russian intellectuals in the 1860s and 1870s.) The novel soon leaves politics to explore the effects of Bazarov's character on his own life. He falls in love, and disastrously misinterprets his beloved's wish for friendship as the proposal of a 'free' liaison; he visits his parents, who cannot reconcile their admiration for their son with bewilderment at his ideas; he quarrels with the traditionalist Pavel, Arkady's uncle, and fights an absurd duel with him; he nurses serfs during a typhus epidemic and becomes fatally infected. Although Bazarov always regarded his own existence as futile, after his death it becomes apparent that he has changed the lives and attitudes of every other person in the story.

Turgenev's novels include Rudin, A Nest of Gentlefolk, On the Eve, Smoke *and* Virgin Soil. A Hunter's Notes/A Sportsman's Sketches *contains short stories and poetic descriptions of country scenes.* A Month in the Country, *a Chekhovian comedy, is his best-known play.*

> READ ON

- *Torrents of Spring* **(the story of a man torn by love for two women, a beautiful girl and the wife of an old school friend).**
- ▶ ▷ **Gustave Flaubert,** *A Sentimental Education*; **George Moore,** *The Lake*; ▷ **L.P. Hartley,** *The Go-Between*; ▷ **Willa Cather,** *The Professor's House*; ▷ **Anton Chekhov,** *The Lady With the Lapdog and Other Short Stories.*

TWAIN, Mark (1835–1910)
US novelist and journalist

'Mark Twain' was the pseudonym of Samuel Clemens. A former steam-boat captain on the Mississippi, soldier, gold-miner and traveller, he wrote breezy, good-humoured accounts of his experiences, with an eye for quirky customs, manners and characters. His favourite form was the short story or comic, factual 'sketch' of half a dozen pages, and several of his books are collections of such pieces. He wrote three historical novels: *Personal Recollections of Joan of Arc* (serious; the biography of Joan by a former page and secretary), *The Prince and the Pauper* (about a beggar-boy changing places with King Edward VI of England, his exact double) and *A Connecticut Yankee in King Arthur's Court* (in which a man, transported back in time, startles Camelot with such 'magic' items as matches, a pocket watch and gunpowder). In Twain's best-loved books, *The Adventures of Tom Sawyer* (1876) and ★☆ *The Adventures of Huckleberry Finn* (1886), he wove reminiscences of boyhood and of life on the Mississippi into an easy-going, fictional form. *Tom Sawyer* is about the scrapes, fancies and fears of boyhood. The heroes of *Huckleberry Finn*, a boy and a runaway slave, pole a raft down the Mississippi, beset by conmen, bounty-hunters and outraged citizens, and fall into slapstick adventures each time they land.

Twain's satires include Pudd'nhead Wilson *and* Extract from Captain Stormfield's Visit to Heaven *(funny) and* The Mysterious Stranger *(serious).* Tom Sawyer Abroad *and* Tom Sawyer Detective *are novels, following Tom's adventures in adult life. Twain's short stories are collected in* The Celebrated Jumping Frog of Calaveras County and Other Sketches *and* The Man That Corrupted Hadleyburg. *His books of travel and reminiscence include* The Innocents Abroad, Roughing It, A Tramp Abroad *and* Life on the Mississippi.

> **READ ON**

▶ to *Huckleberry Finn*: Alphonse Daudet, *Tartarin of Tarascon*; ▷ Henry Fielding, *Tom Jones*; H.E. Bates, *The Darling Buds of May*.
▶ to Twain's travel books: ▷ Robert Louis Stevenson, *Travels With a Donkey* (and its sibling, ▷ John Steinbeck, *Travels With Charley*); ▷ Laurence Sterne, *A Sentimental Journey*; Laurie Lee, *As I Walked Out One Midsummer Morning*.

TYLER, Anne (born 1941)
US novelist

Tyler writes, in cool, stylish prose, of the anguish of people caught up in the pains of everyday emotional life. She is especially good on relationships: between husbands and wives, brothers and sisters, parents and children. Her plots are as simple as those of any romantic novelist: people finding one another, drifting apart, coming together again. But the elegance of her writing, and the extra-ordinary lifelikeness of her characters, take her into the literary company of ▷ Lurie or ▷ Updike, worlds away from most romance.

☆ THE ACCIDENTAL TOURIST (1985)
Ethan, the 12-year-old son of Macon and Sarah Leary, is brutally murdered, and his death destroys his parents' marriage. The story centres on Macon, a writer of rueful travel books, as he struggles against the need to rebuild his life, and in particular against the possibility of finding happiness with Helen (a dog-trainer many years his junior). Just as emotional scar tissue begins to form, Sarah comes back into his life, reopening the wound and confronting him once more with the need for choice.

Tyler's other novels include The Clock Winder, Celestial Navigation, Searching for Caleb, Breathing Lessons, Saint Maybe, Earthly Possessions, Ladder of Years, A Patchwork Planet *and* Back When We Were Grownups.

READ ON >

● *Dinner at the Homesick Restaurant.*

▶ ▷ Alison Lurie, *The War Between the Tates*; Anita Shreve, *Strange Fits of Passion*; ▷ Carol Shields, *Larry's Party*; Alice Hoffman, *Turtle Moon*; Gail Godwin, *The Good Husband.*

U

UNSWORTH, Barry (born 1930)
British novelist

Unlike, say, ▷ Robert Graves, whose historical novels project onto people of ancient times the sensibilities and preoccupations of our own century, Unsworth gets under the skin of the past, showing us not merely long-ago manners and ways of behaviour but a whole philosophical and ethical outlook, sometimes as remote from today as if his characters came from other planets. His dozen novels include *Pascali's Island*, *Stone Virgin*, *Sugar and Rum*, *Sacred Hunger* (a blockbuster set on an eighteenth-century slave ship) and the spare, moving *Morality Play* (1995), whose leading character is a fourteenth-century priest who leaves his vocation because of boredom and takes up with a company of strolling actors – only to find that they are creating a play about a recent child-murder whose perpetrator may next turn on them themselves. *Losing Nelson* (1999) cleverly fuses past, present and the present's interpretation of the past in the story of a man obsessively researching a biography of Nelson. As he struggles to reconcile what he learns with what he wants to believe about the great naval hero, he slowly begins to lose his grip not only on his idea of Nelson but on his own sense of self.

READ ON ▷

▶ ▷ William Golding, *The Spire, Rites of Passage;* ▷ Thomas Keneally, *The Playmaker;* ▷ Brian Moore, *Black Robe;* ▷ Rose Tremain, *Restoration*.

UPDIKE, John (born 1932)
US novelist and short story writer

Updike's short stories (most of them written for the *New Yorker*) are witty anecdotes about the snobberies and love affairs of ambitious Long Island couples, or single, brilliant jokes (for example treating bacteria under a microscope as if they were guests at a trendy cocktail party). Some of his novels are in a similarly glittering, heartless style. In *Couples* (1968) a small group of bored Connecticut commuters changes sex-partners as carelessly as if playing a party game. In *The Witches of Eastwick* (1984) three bored young widows set themselves up as a coven of amateur witches, only to become sexually ensnared by a devilishly charming man. The hero of *A Month of Sundays* (1975) is a 'progressive' clergyman tortured by lust. Updike's other novels are deeper, concentrating more on the underlying pain than on the ludicrous surface of his characters' lives. The Rabbit books (*Rabbit, Run*; *Rabbit Redux*; *Rabbit is Rich*; *Rabbit at Rest*, 1960–90) follow the life of an ex-school sports champion who finds emotional maturity and happiness almost impossible to grasp. The hero of *Roger's Version* (1986), a middle-aged professor, is thrown into moral turmoil by the possibility of devising a computer program to prove the existence of God. Updike's more recent novels have included *Gertrude and Claudius*, an ambitious and witty retelling of events familiar from *Hamlet* and *Toward the End of Time,* set in 2020, in which a typical Updikean man muses on his life.

☆ THE CENTAUR (1963)
George Caldwell, an eccentric, ineffective science teacher at Olinger High School in the 1950s, deflects his feelings of inadequacy by fantasizing that he is Chiron, the centaur who taught the heroes of Greek myth (which makes his headmaster Zeus and his colleagues Athene, Hephaestus and Hercules), and that he has terminal stomach cancer. The book describes three days in his life, during which he is forced to come to terms with himself and with his adolescent son Peter, who idolizes him. Myth-reminiscences start and end the book; its heart is more straightforward, a moving account of small-town life and of the inarticulate love between Peter and his perplexed, exasperating father.

Updike's other novels include The Poorhouse Fair, Of the Farm, The Coup, S, *the savage black farce* Memories of the Ford Administration *and two made from stories about a neurotic writer:* Bech, a Book *and* Bech is Back. Brazil *is an unusual, and unusually rich, departure: a love story, retelling the myth of Tristan and Isolde and set in South America. His story collections include* The Same Door, Pigeon Feathers, Museums and Women, The Music School, Trust Me *and* The Afterlife. Self-consciousness *contains six autobiographical essays, fascinating background to his fiction.* Hugging the Shore *is a large collection of Updike's reviews and criticism.*

> READ ON

▶ ▷ Philip Roth, *The Ghost Writer*. Arthur Laurents, *The Way We Were*. ▷ Anne Tyler, *Dinner at the Homesick Restaurant*. Frederic Raphael, *Heaven and Earth*. ▷ Angus Wilson, *Hemlock and After*. ▷ Brian Moore, *The Great Victorian Collection*.

V

VARGAS LLOSA, Mario (born 1936)
Peruvian novelist

An admirer of ▷ Márquez, Vargas Llosa uses magic realism to give an even more biting view of South American life and politics. *The City and the Dogs/The Time of the Hero* (1962) is a satire on fascism set in a gung-ho, brutal military academy. *The War of the End of the World* (1981) is about the oppression, by the authorities, of a 19th-century Utopian community for derelicts and dropouts, deep in the magic wilderness. *The Storyteller* (1991) is set among a fast-disappearing tribe of Amazonian Indians, whose stories *are* their history – and, as the book progresses, their only real existence. *The Notebooks of Don Rigoberto* (1998) is an erotic fantasia in which the protagonist, recording his sexual longings and memories, draws himself and the reader into a world of uncertainty and transgression.

★☆ AUNT JULIA AND THE SCRIPTWRITER (1977)
Mario, a student, works part-time for a decrepit radio station, and idolizes the extraordinary man who writes and stars in half a dozen daily soap operas. Mario's own life is complicated by his love affair with his aunt, Julia. The book alternately gives us extracts from the soap operas, as weird as dreams, and Mario's own farcical story, as romantic and over-the-top as any soap.

Vargas Llosa's other novels include The Green House, Who Killed Palomino Molero, The Time of the Hero *and* Death in the Andes. The Cubs *is a collection of short stories.* The Perpetual Orgy *is a book-length musing about* ▷ Flaubert's Madame Bovary, *part literary criticism, part reconstruction, part anthology – it is magic realism and non-fiction, hand in hand.* A Fish in the Water *is the story of Llosa's own involvement in Peruvian politics, often as surreal as the events of his fiction.*

> READ ON

● *In Praise of the Stepmother.*
▶ ▷ Louis de Bernières, *Señor Vivo and the Coca Lord*; ▷ Isabel Allende, *Eva Luna*; Augusto Roa Bastos, *I, the Supreme.*
▶ to *The Perpetual Orgy*: ▷ Julian Barnes, *Flaubert's Parrot.*

VERNE, Jules (1828–1905)
French novelist

Verne began writing in the 1860s, the heyday of both exploration and popular science – and his inspiration was to mix the two. His stories mimic the memoirs of real-life explorers of the time, fabulous adventures narrated in sober, business-like prose – and, by stirring in scientific wonders impossible or unlikely at the time, he tips them into fantasy. His heroes are not tethered to the surface of the Earth: they tunnel towards its core (*Journey to the Centre of the Earth*), live underwater (*Twenty Thousand Leagues Under the Sea*) and ride rockets into space (*From the Earth to the Moon*; *Round the Moon*). Alternately with these 'scientific' adventure-stories, Verne produced tales of more orthodox derring-do: *Michel Strogoff*, for example, is a gentleman-adventurer whose bravery saves Civilisation as We Know It; in *Round the World in Eighty Days* Phileas Fogg embarks on a crazy journey to win a bet. Modern science has outstripped most of Verne's inventions, but few later science fiction writers have bettered him for straight-down-the-line, thrill-in-every-paragraph adventure.

READ ON

▶ ▷ A. Conan Doyle, *The Lost World*; ▷ H.G. Wells, *The First Men in the Moon*; ▷ H. Rider Haggard, *She*; C.S. Lewis, *That Hideous Strength*; Edgar Rice Burroughs, *Pirates of Venus*; ▷ Kurt Vonnegut, *The Sirens of Titan*.

VIDAL, Gore (born 1925)
US novelist and non-fiction writer

Vidal made his name as a tart-tongued, witty commentator on 1960s and 1970s life, a favourite chat-show guest. Whatever the topic, from the rotation of crops to the horror of Nazi concentration camps, from zen to flower-arranging, he had some-thing interesting to say. The same protean brilliance fills his novels. Whether their subject is homosexuality (*The City and the Pillar*, 1948/65), the excesses of the film industry (*Myra Breckinridge*, 1968) or US politics (the series *Burr, Lincoln, 1876, Washington DC, Empire, Hollywood: a Novel of The Twenties* and *The Golden Age* 1967–2000), they are original, stimulating and engrossing. This is particularly so in his historical novels, where he makes his alternative view of past events seem more attractive than reality itself. *Julian* is a study of the last pagan Roman emperor, who tried to stop the rush of Christianity in the name of (as Vidal sees it) the more humane, more generous Olympian religion. *Creation* is the memoirs of an imaginary Persian nobleman of the 5th century BC, who went as ambassador to India, China and Greece and knew Confucius, Buddha and Socrates.

Vidal's other novels include Williwaw, Myron, Kalki, Live from Golgotha, Messiah *and* Duluth. *He has also written detective stories (including* Death in the Fifth Position) *under the name* Edgar Box. A Thirsty Evil *is a collection of short stories.* Palimpsest *is a malicious, gossipy memoir which occasionally surprises the reader by the poignancy of Vidal's recollections, particularly of his grandfather and of a lover killed in the Second World War.* United States *is a massive selection of Vidal's often brilliant essays.*

READ ON

● *Duluth.*
▶ to Vidal's historical novels: Peter Green, *The Sword of Pleasure* (set in republican Rome); John Hersey, *The Wall* (about US missionaries in China); ▷ John Barth, *The Sot-weed Factor* (set in Maryland in the time of the Pilgrim Fathers); ▷ Rose Tremain, *Restoration* (set in 1660s Britain).

▶ to Vidal's novels in general: ▷ Kingsley Amis, *The Alteration*; ▷ Patrick White, *The Twyborn Affair*; ▷ Muriel Spark, *The Ballad of Peckham Rye*.

READ ON A THEME: VILLAGE AND COUNTRYSIDE

▷ Bruce Chatwin, *On the Black Hill*
  Isabel Colegate, *The Shooting Party*
  Christopher Hart, *The Harvest*
▷ V.S. Naipaul, *The Enigma of Arrival*
  Tim Pears, *In the Place of Fallen Leaves*
▷ Graham Swift, *Waterland*
  Adam Thorpe, *Ulverton*
▷ Joanna Trollope, *A Passionate Man*

See also: The Rhythm of Nature; Small Town Life, USA

VINE, Barbara: see RENDELL, Ruth

VONNEGUT, Kurt (born 1922)
US novelist

Science fiction ideas shape Vonnegut's novels and so do autobiography, political and social satire, loonish humour and a furious, nagging rage at the way the human race is pillaging the world. ☆ *Galápagos* (1985) begins at the moment of nuclear apocalypse (which is triggered by a bomber-pilot fantasizing that firing his missile is like having sex). A group of people, gathered in Ecuador for the 'Nature Cruise of the Century', find that their ship has become a Noah's Ark: they are the sole survivors of humankind. They land in the Galápagos Islands, equipped with no technology save a computer whose memory is stuffed with 1,000 dead languages and a million quotations from the world's great literatures, and set about survival. At first they are hampered, as (Vonnegut claims) the human race has been handicapped throughout its existence, by the enormous size of their brains, attics of unnecessary thought. But Galápagos is the cradle of the evolutionary theory and that may be humanity's last hope.

Vonnegut's other novels are Player Piano; The Sirens of Titan; Mother Night; Cat's Cradle; God Bless You, Mr Rosewater; Slaughterhouse Five; Breakfast of Champions; Slapstick; Jailbird; Palm Sunday, Deadeye Dick *and* Hocus Pocus. Canary in a Cathouse *and* Welcome to the Monkeyhouse *contain short stories.*

READ ON ▷

● *Cat's Cradle*; *The Sirens of Titan*.
▶ Brian Aldiss, *The Primal Urge*. Frederick Pohl, *The Coming of the Quantum Cats*.
  ▷ Michael Moorcock, *The Final Programme*. ▷ Russell Hoban, *Riddley Walker*.
  Walter M. Miller, *A Canticle for Leibowitz*. Bamber Gascoigne, *Cod Strewth*.

W

WALKER, Alice (born 1944)
US novelist, poet and non-fiction writer

The background to Walker's books is the struggle for equal rights in the US over the past 40 years, first by blacks and then by women. Radical politics are not, however, her main concern. She writes wittily, ironically, about the follies of human life, and she is as merciless towards her idealistic, college-educated activists as she is to their slobbish, mindless opponents. *Meridian* (1976), Walker's second novel, is the splendidly ironical study of a southern black activist, educated to be a 'lady' (in the 1920s white meaning of the term), who becomes a leader in the equal rights movements of the 1960s. When we see Meridian years later, all battles won, holed up in the small southern town of Chickokema, where apart from the coming of equality, nothing momentous has ever happened, she is totally confused about where all her energy, her driving force, has gone. Was this really what her life was for? *The Color Purple* (1986) uses a number of imaginative narrative devices to tell the story of Celie, a black woman in the segregated Deep South who has known nothing but abuse and exploitation until she meets Shug Avery, a female singer who offers her the chance of love and emotional support.

Walker's other novels are The Third Life of Grange Copeland, The Temple of My Familiar, Possessing the Secret of Joy *(about African tribal women, and especially Tashi, facing a horrific initiation into adult life) and* By the Light of My Father's Smile. In Love and Trouble, You Can't Keep a Good Woman Down *and* The Way Forward Is With a Broken Heart *are short story collections. She has also published poetry (*Once; Revolutionary Petunias; Horses Make a Landscape Look More Beautiful: Willie Lee, I'll See You in the Morning*) and three books of essays:* In Search of Our Mother's Garden, Living by the Word *and* Anything We Love Can Be Saved. The Same River Twice *is autobiography.*

> **READ ON**

- ● *The Temple of My Familiar.*
- ▶ To Walker's elegant, tart style: Mary McCarthy, *The Group*; ▷ Muriel Spark, *The Girls of Slender Means.*
- ▶ To her view of the bizarreness lurking inside perfectly ordinary-seeming human beings: ▷ John Irving, *The World According to Garp*; Tove Jansson, *Sun City.*
- ▶ To her politics: Gayl Jones, *Corregidora*; Lisa Alther, *Kinflicks*; Ralph Ellison, *Invisible Man.*

WALTERS, Minette (born 1949)
British novelist

Like so many of the best contemporary writers of crime fiction (▷Ruth Rendell, Frances Fyfield, Andrew Taylor) Minette Walters produces books that are not so much 'whodunnits' as 'whydunnits'. Our interest is held not so much by the twists and turns of a convoluted, puzzle-like plot but by the way the narrative progressively reveals more and more about the psychology and hidden depths of her characters. This has been the case since her first novel *The Ice House*, about three women who may or may not have got away with murder ten years before the book opens, was published in 1992. Her second novel, *The Sculptress* (1993), introduced the kind of pairing of disparate characters that has recurred in later books. The obese, unloved Olive Martin, imprisoned for the apparent murders of her mother and sister, represents a terrible enigma, an affront almost, to the middle-class complacency of the woman intent on writing a book about her crimes. In her more recent novels Minette Walters has increasingly concentrated on stories which gradually unveil the hidden motivations of her characters. In *The Shape of Snakes* (2000) a teacher refuses to accept that the death of an alcoholic neighbour is an accident. For twenty years she obsessively amasses evidence to prove that murder took place. Narrated by the teacher and reproducing many of the documents which constitute her evidence, the book moves relentlessly towards the revelation of dark, unsettling and moving truths about its characters. Retaining its tension and mystery until its last page, it is the best example yet of Minette Walters's ambition to press forward into territory not usually occupied by writers of crime fiction.

Minette Walters's other novels are The Scold's Bridle, The Echo, The Breaker *and* The Dark Room.

> **READ ON**

- **•** *The Dark Room.*
- **▶** ▷ Barbara Vine, *A Fatal Inversion*; Nicci French, *The Safe House*; Val McDermid, *Killing the Shadows*; Andrew Taylor, *The Barred Window*.

READ ON A THEME: **WAR: BEHIND THE LINES**

Noel Barber, *A Woman of Cairo*
▷ Elizabeth Bowen, *The Heat of the Day*
▷ Louis de Bernières, *Captain Corelli's Mandolin*
▷ Sebastian Faulks, *Charlotte Gray*
▷ Jaroslav Hašek, *The Good Soldier Svejk*
▷ Ernest Hemingway, *A Farewell to Arms*
▷ Thomas Keneally, *Schindler's Ark*
▷ Leo Tolstoy, *War and Peace*

See also: Terrorists/Freedom Fighters

READ ON A THEME: **WAR: FRONT LINE**

▷ Pat Barker, *The Ghost Road*

Stephen Crane, *The Red Badge of Courage*
▷ Len Deighton, *Bomber*
▷ Sebastian Faulks, *Birdsong*
▷ Joseph Heller, *Catch-22*
▷ Ernest Hemingway, *For Whom the Bell Tolls*
▷ Alistair MacLean, *The Guns of Navarone*
▷ Norman Mailer, *The Naked and the Dead*
Frederic Manning, *Her Privates We* (also known as *The Middle Parts of Fortune*)
R.H. Mottram, *The Spanish Farm Trilogy*
Bao Ninh, *The Sorrow of War*
Erich Maria Remarque, *All Quiet on the Western Front*

See also: War: Behind the Lines

WAUGH, Evelyn (1903–66)
British novelist

Waugh's main work was a series of tart satires on 1930s attitudes and manners. His vacuous, amiable heroes stumble through life, unsurprised by anything that happens. By chance, they land in the centre of affairs (political, business and sexual) and their presence triggers a sequence of ever more ludicrous events. Innocence is their only saving grace: Waugh's views were that the world is silly but dangerous, and that those who think they understand it are the most vulnerable of all. He was particularly venomous about British high society, depicting the ruling class as a collection of alcohol-swilling Hooray Henries or Henriettas, whose chief pastimes are partying (if young) and interfering in public life (if old). That class apart, the range of his scorn was vast. *Decline and Fall* sends up (among other things) the English prep school system, *Black Mischief* mocks tyranny in an African state emerging from colonialism, *Scoop* satirises gutter journalism and *The Ordeal of Gilbert Pinfold* (1957) mercilessly details the hallucinations of an alcoholic author on a detestable ocean cruise. The Second World War trilogy *Sword of Honour* (1965) sets Waugh's foolish heroes in the context of truly dangerous, genuinely lunatic real events, and *Brideshead Revisited* (1945) is a more serious book still, the study of an aristocratic Catholic family collapsing under the weight of centuries of unconsidered privilege.

☆ A HANDFUL OF DUST (1934)
The book begins with standard Waugh farce: a pin-headed society wife, Brenda Last, takes a lover to occupy her afternoons. But the effect on her husband Tony and son John is devastating, and the book moves quickly from farce to tragedy. Waugh never abandons the ridiculous – no one else would have placed his hero in impenetrable tropical jungle, the slave of a megalomaniac who makes him read *Edwin Drood* aloud – but he also writes with compassion for his characters, involving us in their loneliness as his more farcical novels never try to do.

Waugh's other novels are Vile Bodies, Put Out More Flags *and* The Loved One. *His travel books include* Remote People *and* Waugh in Abyssinia. *His*

Diaries, Letters *and his autobiography* A Little Learning *are a revealing blend of pity for himself and mercilessness to others. Like all his work, they are also very funny.*

> READ ON >

● *Scoop.*

▶ ▷ William Boyd, *A Good Man in Africa*; ▷ Malcolm Bradbury, *Eating People is Wrong*; ▷ David Lodge, *How Far Can You Go?*; P.H. Newby, *The Picnic at Sakkara*; ▷ John Updike, *The Coup*; Paul Micou, *The Music Programme*.

READ ON A THEME: WEEPIES

▷ Charlotte Brontë, *Jane Eyre*
▷ Louis de Bernières, *Captain Corelli's Mandolin*
▷ Daphne Du Maurier, *Rebecca*
  Nicholas Evans, *The Horse Whisperer*
▷ Margaret Mitchell, *Gone With the Wind*
▷ Boris Pasternak, *Doctor Zhivago*
  Erich Segal, *Love Story*
  Robert Waller, *The Bridges of Madison County*

WELDON, Fay (born 1933)
British novelist and screen-writer

A former advertising executive ('Go To Work On an Egg') and TV dramatist, Weldon writes novels in short, screenplay-like scenes full of dialogue: her books are like sinister sitcoms turned into prose. In the 1970s she was regarded as a leading feminist writer, and 'women's experience' is a major theme in all her books. Her heroines are ordinary people resisting the need to define themselves as someone else's wife, lover or mother, and missing the traditional cosiness such roles afford. Individuality can only be bought at the cost of psychic discomfort – and this is often intensified by the malice of others and by the hostility of the environment: witchcraft and the venomousness of nature regularly add spice to Weldon's plots. Her books are fast, funny and furious; but their underlying ideas are no joke at all.

PUFFBALL (1980)

Liffey, married to boring, ambitious Richard, longs to live in a country cottage; Richard wants a child. They strike a bargain, move to the wolds near Glastonbury and do their best to get Liffey pregnant. Almost at once the idyll turns to nightmare. The cottage has few facilities; there are no commuter-trains to London; their neighbour is a child-beater and an amateur witch. As the baby grows in Liffey's womb and Richard, alone in London for five days a week, consoles himself, Mabs (the neighbour) tries every trick of witchcraft, from potions to pin-stuck wax models, to make Liffey abort her child. *Puffball* is a romantic novel for grown-up people – and the games Weldon plays with our longing for a happy ending give the plot some of its most devastating, satisfying twists.

Weldon's other novels include Down Among the Women, Female Friends, The President's Child, Little Sisters, Praxis, Watching Me Watching You, The Life and Loves of a She-Devil, The Shrapnel Academy, The Heart of the Country, The Fat Woman's Joke, Life Force, Splitting, Worst Fears, Big Women *and* Rhode Island Blues. A Hard Time to Be a Father *is a collection of short stories.*Godless in Eden *is a selection of essays.*

READ ON >

● *Darcy's Utopia.*
▶ ▷ Margaret Atwood, *Life Before Man*; Marge Piercy, *The High Cost of Living*; Mary Gordon, *The Company of Women*; Penelope Mortimer, *Long Distance*; Alice Thomas Ellis, *Unexplained Laughter*; Maggie Gee, *Light Years*.

WELLS, H.G. (Herbert George) (1866–1946)
British writer of novels, short stories and non-fiction

Wells's early novels were science fantasies, imagining what it would be like if people could travel in time (*The Time Machine*, 1895) or space (*The First Men in the Moon*, 1901), or how the Earth might defend itself against extra-terrestrial attacks (*The War of the Worlds*, 1898). Like ▷Verne, Wells predicted many inventions and discoveries now taken for granted: in *The War in the Air* (1908) for example, he forecast fleets of warplanes and bombers in the days when the Wright brothers were still headline news. For all their scientific wonders, these novels are full of pessimism about society: wherever people go, they find barbarism, oppression and misery. *The Island of Doctor Moreau* (1896), about a mad scientist hybridizing humans and animals on a lonely island, brings the pessimism nearer home. Side by side with such morbid fantasies, Wells wrote a series of utterly different books. These are genial social comedies, about ordinary people (shop-assistants, clerks) who decide that the way to find happiness is to break out and 'make a go of things'. Sometimes (as in *Ann Veronica*, 1909, about a girl determined on emancipation despite the wishes of her family) Wells's message is polemical; but most of the books – *Love and Mr Lewisham* (1900), *Kipps* (1900), *The History of Mr Polly* (1910) – replace propaganda with an indulgent, enthusiastic view of human enterprise.

☆ TONO-BUNGAY (1909)
George Ponderevo goes to live with his uncle Teddy. He helps Teddy market a marvellous new elixir, Tono-Bungay: it is the answer to the world's problems, the health, wealth and happiness of humankind in a bottle. The Tono-Bungay fortune swells by the minute – and then George discovers that the product is 99% distilled water. The discovery presents George with unresolvable moral dilemmas of all kinds. Does it matter what Tono-Bungay is made of, if it does what it claims to do? Is Teddy a crook or does he genuinely believe he is benefiting humankind? How can George bankrupt those he loves – and in the process destroy his own chances of a happy marriage and a prosperous home? He puts off the decision, and in the meantime continues his hobby: pioneer aviation. In the end, technology – the lighter-than-air-machine itself – comes to the rescue: a charming example of Wells's view that all moral and social dilemmas can be solved by science.

Wells's other science-fantasies include When the Sleeper Wakes, The Food of the Gods *and the story collections* Tales of Space and Time *and* The Country of the Blind and Other Stories. *His other novels include* A Modern Utopia, The New Machiavelli *and* Mr. Britling Sees It Through.

READ ON ▷

▶ **to Wells's science fiction:** ▷ **Jules Verne,** *Twenty Thousand Leagues Under the Sea*; **C.S. Lewis,** *Out of the Silent Planet*; **H.P. Lovecraft,** *The Shadow over Innsmouth*; **Brian Aldiss,** *Moreau's Other Island* (*Wells's nightmare vision transplanted to space).*
▶ **to his social comedies:** ▷ **Arnold Bennett,** *The Card*; **Hugh Walpole,** *Mr Perrin and Mr Traill*; ▷ **J.B. Priestley,** *The Good Companions.*

WELSH, Irvine (born 1958)
British novelist

Revealing an Edinburgh at odds with the tourist image of tartan tweeness, *Trainspotting* (1993), Irvine Welsh's portrait of heroin users on bleak council estates, was a landmark in Scottish (and British) fiction and, through a successful film adaptation, became a cult book for a generation. Welsh adopts no easy tone of moral condemnation. Heroin is presented simply as an everyday part of the lives of his characters – source of pleasure as well as desolation – and even the most shocking descriptions of cheap sex, violence and the desperate urge to score are shot through with dark humour. Told in energetic, phonetically reproduced Scots language, awash both with obscenity and accidental poetry, *Trainspotting* is a black but utterly compelling narrative. Welsh followed the book with *Marabou Stork Nightmares* (1995), an ambitious attempt to fuse another story of blighted, violent lives with excursions into the fantasy world of its central character. Roy Strang lies in a coma in hospital. As his real past, as both victim and perpetrator of sexual violence, unfolds in his mind, so too does a surreal safari through a half-imagined, half-remembered Africa where Strang, re-cast as some kind of gentleman explorer, hunts the marabou stork. The book is not a complete success. The reality of Strang's past life carries more conviction than the stork hunt his imagination, in search of redemption from his demons, has conjured up. But *Marabou Stork Nightmares* shows Welsh to be a writer of much greater ambition than *Trainspotting* alone might have suggested. His most recent novel, *Glue* (2001), is once again set in the now-familiar Welsh terrain of Edinburgh slum estates and is again told in the now-familiar vernacular but, in carrying the story of four friends through three decades of their lives, he is once more attempting to stretch his range as a writer.

Welsh's other fictional works are Filth *(a novel),* Ecstasy *(a collection of three novellas) and* The Acid House *(short stories).*

READ ON ▷

▶ **James Kelman,** *A Chancer*; **Alan Warner,** *Morvern Callar*; **John King,** *The Football Factory*; **Laura Hird,** *Born Free.*

WELTY, Eudora (1909–2001)
US novelist and short story writer

Unlike such writers as ▷ Faulkner or ▷ McCullers, who saw the southern United States as a kind of hell tenanted by freaks and degenerates, Welty treats them as paradise. The countryside is lush; birds and animals teem; all nature is in harmony. Human beings are at the heart of the idyll – and Welty shows them as uncomprehending innocents. The 'Negroes' – she is writing about times long gone – are children of nature, at peace with their environment. The 'White Folks', by contrast, feel edgy. They sense that they are corrupt, that their presence threatens Eden; but they have no idea why this should be so, and all they can do is live as they always have and hope that things will be all right, that nothing will change. The surface events in Welty's books are a mosaic of ordinariness – parties, children's games, chance meetings in town or at the bathing-station – but underlying them all is a sense of fragility, of impending loss. Her characters are living in a dream, comfortable and comforting, but it is only a dream, and already we, and they, sense the first chill of wakefulness.

DELTA WEDDING (1946)
In the 1920s, nine-year-old Laura travels to her uncle's plantation in the Mississippi Delta, to help in preparations for her cousin's wedding. She revels in the eccentric, affectionate rough-and-tumble of cousins, great-aunts, visitors (and dozens of blacks, as friendly and unconsidered as household pets); she climbs trees, bakes cakes, guesses riddles, listens to gossip as the wedding-dress is sewn. Welty also shows the preparations through the eyes of the bride's parents, the bride and groom themselves, and an assortment of servants, friends and neighbours. The wedding brings a whole community into focus – and we are shown, with persistent, gentle irony, that it is not just the bride and groom who must undergo a rite of passage, but the South itself.

Welty's other novels are The Robber Bridegroom, The Ponder Heart, The Optimist's Daughter *and* Losing Battles. *Her short stories are collected in* A Curtain of Green, The Wide Net, The Golden Apples *and* The Bride of Innisfallen. One Writer's Beginnings *is a series of essays, originally lectures, that describe the people and places that shaped her development as a writer.*

READ ON ▷

- *The Optimist's Daughter.*
▶ Randall Jarrell, *Pictures from an Institution*; ▷ L.P. Hartley, *The Go-Between*; ▷ Colette, *The Ripening Seed*; ▷ Evelyn Waugh, *Brideshead Revisited*; Robert Penn Warren, *All the King's Men.*

WESLEY, MARY (born 1912)
British novelist

Wesley's first adult novel, *Jumping the Queue*, was published when she was 70, and since then she has had runaway success. In several of her novels she writes of elegant elderly people, usually women, whose efficient outward lives depend on unsuspected and eccentric thoughts, rituals or long-held secrets. Her stories tell what happens when some chance event – often falling in love with a younger person – brings eccentricity to the surface, rippling the apparently tranquil pool in ways which are bizarre, hilarious, often joyously sexy, and very, very sad. In others (*The Camomile Lawn*, for instance) she looks back at the Second World War, not for nostalgic purposes, but to examine, often astringently, the lives and loves of ordinary young people caught up in larger events.

☆ NOT THAT SORT OF GIRL (1987)
Rose is 69, recently widowed, and hard as nails. For 50 years her 'ideal' marriage had been a polite fiction, sustained (for her) by an intermittent, passionate and secret love affair. Sex has been the calm centre of her existence, her reason for living – a matter usually of music-hall farce, but here treated seriously and sensitively, and no joke at all.

Wesley's other books include Harnessing Peacocks, The Vacillations of Poppy Carew, The Camomile Lawn, A Sensible Life, Second Fiddle *and* Part of the Furniture.

READ ON >

- *Jumping the Queue* (about a middle-aged woman, a would-be suicide, who gives refuge to a charming murderer, and finds that his presence makes her life flower anew).
- ▶ Elizabeth Jolley, *Palomino*; ▷ Joanna Trollope, *A Village Affair*; Jenny Diski, *Happily Ever After*; Joanne Harris, *Five Quarters of the Orange*.

WEST, Morris (1916–99)
Australian novelist

West's books (old-fashioned yet still immensely readable) are fast-moving moral thrillers, stories not of espionage or crime but of the solution of ethical dilemmas. The hero of *The Shoes of the Fisherman* (1963) is a saintly Iron Curtain prelate who is elected Pope. *The Clowns of God* (1981) is about another Pope forced to abdicate because he has seen a vision predicting the imminent end of the world, and proposes to publicize the fact. In *The Navigator* (1976) a group of people sails to find the Polynesian paradise to which all human souls, the myth says, go after death; they are led by a man who is either a visionary, a charlatan or mad. *The World Is Made of Glass* (1983) is set in Vienna in 1913. The psychiatrist Jung treats a woman who regards him more as a confessor than a healer – and the experience brings him hard up against his sense of his own moral failure, both as a doctor and as a man.

West's other novels include Children of the Sun, The Devil's Advocate, Daughter of Silence, The Tower of Babel, Summer of the Red Wolf, The Salamander *and* Harlequin.

READ ON >

- *The Devil's Advocate*.
- ▶ Jerome Weidman, *The Temple*; Frank Slaughter, *Epidemic*; ▷ Neville Shute, *Requiem for a Wren*; ▷ C. P. Snow, *The Sleep of Reason*; ▷ Thomas Keneally, *Three Cheers for the Paraclete*; ▷ Brian Moore, *The Colour of Blood*.

WEST, Nathanael (1906–40)
US novelist and screenwriter

West wrote rubbishy films for a living: their titles include *Rhythm in the Clouds, Born to be Wild* and *Hallelujah I'm a Bum*. To please himself, he wrote four satirical novels, dark black comedies a million miles from Hollywood. The hero of *Miss Lonelyhearts* (1933) is a cynical newspaperman assigned to the agony column. He begins by despising the wretches who write for advice, but soon begins to pity them and finally leaves his desk to intervene in one case personally, with fatal but farcical results. In *The Day of the Locust* (1939) West used his experience of screenwriting to produce a mordant satirical portrait of the under-side of the Hollywood dream factory. The bit players of the film business, the would-bes and never-weres, strut and shuffle through West's narrative which culminates in a terrifying riot at a movie premiere.

West's other novels are The Dream Life of Balso Snell *and* A Cool Million.

> READ ON

▶ Joe Orton, *Head to Toe*; Budd Schulberg, *What Makes Sammy Run?*; ▷ Aldous Huxley, *After Many a Summer*; ▷ Mordecai Richler, *Cocksure*.

READ ON A THEME: THE WEST (THE GREAT AMERICAN FRONTIER)

Desmond Barry, *The Chivalry of Crime*
Thomas Berger, *Little Big Man*
Pete Dexter, *Deadwood*
Zane Grey, *Riders of the Purple Sage*
Ron Hansen, *Desperadoes*
Larry McMurtry, *Lonesome Dove*
▷ Jane Smiley, *The All-True Travels and Adventures of Lydie Newton*

WHARTON, Edith (1862–1937)
US writer of novels, short stories and non-fiction

A society hostess, Wharton caused outrage by writing with ironical rage about the complacency and shallowness of her own class. (She later described high society as 'frivolous . . ., able to acquire dramatic significance only through what its frivolity destroys'.) In 1907 she moved to Europe and broadened her scope, writing two Hardyesque rural tragedies (*Ethan Frome, Summer*), several books set in Europe (including *The Reef*, which her friend ▷Henry James admired) and some atmospheric ghost stories. But she regularly returned to her favourite theme, the stifling conventions of 1870s–1920s New York high life – and it is on this that her reputation rests. Her enemies put her down as a clumsy imitator of James. But whereas he showed his characters' psychological innerness, she was interested in manners, in events. She also wrote shorter, wittier sentences, and crisper dialogue. Except that her subject matter is so sombre, she is more like Oscar Wilde than James.

THE HOUSE OF MIRTH (1905)

Lily Bart, a beautiful, sharp-witted girl, has been conditioned to luxury from birth. Unfortunately she is an orphan, living on a small allowance. She gambles at cards, loses, and because of her moral scruples (she refuses to pay off her debts by becoming the mistress of a wealthy creditor), she ends up poorer and more desperate than ever. Faced with the choice of marrying either a rich man she despises (not least because he is a Jew, something her WASPish upbringing has taught her to abhor) or the penniless man she loves, she chooses neither – and soon afterwards, as the result of scandalous accusations, loses her position in society. She moves into cheap lodgings and sinks into despair. She has achieved moral integrity, broken free of her upbringing, but in the process, because of that upbringing, she has destroyed herself.

Wharton's other novels include The Custom of the Country, The Age of Inno-cence, Old New York *and* The Reef. *Her short stories, published originally in several volumes, have been collected in one volume.* A Backward Glance *is autobiography, interesting on her friendship with Henry James.*

> READ ON

- ● *The Custom of the Country.*
- ▶ Ellen Glasgow, *Barren Ground*; Louis Auchincloss, *A World of Profit*; ▷ George Eliot, *Middlemarch*; ▷ William Thackeray, *Vanity Fair*; ▷ Elizabeth Taylor, *The Wedding Group*; ▷ Mary Wesley, *Not That Sort of Girl.*

WHITE, Antonia (1899–1979)

British novelist

A journalist and translator (notably of ▷Colette), White is remembered for four deeply felt autobiographical novels. *Frost in May* (1933) is the story of a child at a grim convent boarding school. The nuns' mission is to 'break' each pupil like a horse – to tame her for Christ – and the book remorselessly charts the series of small emotional humiliations they inflict on the heroine, which have entirely the opposite effect from the one intended. In the later novels White's heroine works as an actress (*The Lost Traveller*, 1950), tries to combine serious writing with work as a copy-writer (*The Sugar House*, 1952), and finally (*Beyond the Glass*, 1954), in the course of a terrifying mental illness, exorcises the ghosts of Catholicism and her relationship with her father, the influences which have both defined and deformed her life.

White's other books include the short story collection Strangers, *and* The Hound and the Falcon, *an account in letter form of her return to Catholicism.*

> READ ON

- ▶ to *Frost in May*: ▷ James Joyce, *Portrait of the Artist as a Young Man*; Jane Gardam, *Bilgewater*; ▷ Thomas Keneally, *Three Cheers for the Paraclete.*
- ▶ to *Beyond the Glass*: Sylvia Plath, *The Bell Jar*; Janet Frame, *Faces in the Water.*
- ▶ to White's work in general: ▷ Rosamond Lehmann, *Dusty Answer*; ▷ Rose Macaulay, *The World My Wilderness.*

WHITE, Patrick (1912–90)
Australian novelist and playwright

White was interested in Nietzsche's idea of 'superbeings', people endowed with qualities or abilities which set them apart from the rest of the human race. But White's characters are cursed, not blessed, by difference: their chief attribute is a cantankerous individuality which makes it impossible for them to adjust to society or it to them. In some books (e.g. *Riders in the Chariot*, 1961, about anti-semitism, or *The Vivisector*, 1970, about a convention-defying painter) the 'enemy' is the stifling gentility of lower-middle-class Sydney suburbanites. In others (e.g. *The Tree of Man*, 1956, about a young farmer in the 1900s, or *A Fringe of Leaves*, 1976, see below), the battle is symbolic, against the wilderness itself. But wherever conflict takes place, it is of epic proportions: White's craggy prose puts him in the company of such past writers as ▷ Melville or ▷ Conrad, and in the 20th century only ▷ Golding equals his blend of fast-paced story-telling and brooding philosophical allegory.

★ VOSS (1957)
In 1857, financed by a group of Sydney businessmen, a group of explorers sets out to cross Australia. The expedition is led by the German visionary Voss: physically awkward, ill-at-ease in towns and houses, speaking a tortured, poetic English which sounds as if he learned it by rote, phrase by painful phrase. The other members include an ex-convict and a dreamy aboriginal boy, Jackie, torn between the white people's culture and his own. White balances reports of the expedition's struggle against the desert and to understand one another with accounts of the life of Laura Trevelyan, a young woman fascinated by Voss (at first as a larger-than-life character, an epic personality, and then as a vulnerable human being) as she waits in Sydney, like a medium hoping for spirit-messages, for news of him.

White's other novels are Happy Valley, The Living and the Dead, The Aunt's Story *(a comedy about an indomitable spinster travelling alone)*, The Solid Mandala, The Eye of the Storm *and* The Twyborn Affair. The Burnt Ones *and* The Cockatoos *are collections of short stories.* Flaws in the Glass *is an autobiography, good on White's own battles against the wilderness (he was an outback farmer) and against convention (he was homosexual).*

> **READ ON**

- ● *A Fringe of Leaves* (about a woman shipwrecked in Queensland in the 1840s, who is captured by Aborigines and brought to terms not only with an alien culture but with her feelings about the 'civilization' she knew before).
- ▶ to *Voss*: ▷ William Golding, *Darkness Visible*; ▷ H.H. Richardson, *The Fortunes of Richard Mahony*; ▷ Peter Carey, *Oscar and Lucinda*; Paul Bowles, *The Sheltering Sky*; ▷ Joseph Conrad, *The Nigger of the 'Narcissus'*.
- ▶ to *A Fringe of Leaves*: ▷ D.H. Lawrence, *The Plumed Serpent*; ▷ Katharine Susannah Prichard, *Coonardoo*; ▷ Jim Crace, *Signals of Distress*.
- ▶ to White's work in general: ▷ Christina Stead, *The Man Who Loved Children*; Joyce Cary, *The Horse's Mouth*; ▷ Elizabeth Taylor, *Blaming*.

WILDER, Thornton (1897–1975)
US novelist and playwright

Wilder is known for plays as well as novels: *The Matchmaker* (source of the musical *Hello, Dolly*), *Our Town, The Skin of Our Teeth* and many others. His works explore an idea he called 'simultaneity'. Time is not progressive but circular, our destinies move in cycles, and when people's cycles coincide (like the overlapping Olympic rings), that is the moment of simultaneity, of crisis, in all their lives. In his best-known novel, *The Bridge of San Luis Rey* (1927), the moment of simultaneity is the collapse of a bridge in 18th-century Peru; the book tells the lives of each of the five people killed in the disaster, reaching a climax at the exact instant when the bridge falls in. *The Ides of March* (1948) is a historical novel which charts, in a series of imaginary letters, the converging destinies of a group of people in ancient Rome; it ends on the morning of the Ides of March, 44 BC, as Julius Caesar leaves for the senate-house where (history tells us) he was due to be assassinated.

Wilder's other novels are The Cabala, The Woman of Andros, Heaven's My Destination, The Eighth Day *and* Theophilus North.

> READ ON >

- ▶ **to *The Ides of March*:** ▷ Marguerite Yourcenar, *Memoirs of Hadrian*; John Arden, *Silence Among the Weapons*; ▷ Mary Renault, *The Last of the Wine*; Hilda Doolittle ('H.D.'), *Hedylus*.
- ▶ **other books, of different periods and on different themes, but all concerned with our perception of time:** ▷ James Joyce, *Ulysses*; ▷ Lawrence Durrell, *Tunc* and *Numquam*; ▷ Salman Rushdie, *The Satanic Verses*.

READ ON A THEME: THE WILDERNESS

   Andrea Barrett, *The Voyage of the Narwhal*
▷ Willa Cather, *Death Comes for the Archbishop*
▷ Joseph Conrad, *Heart of Darkness*
   Fenimore Cooper, *The Last of the Mohicans*
   Charles Frazier, *Cold Mountain*
▷ Brian Moore, *Black Robe*
▷ Jane Rogers, *Promised Lands*
▷ Paul Theroux, *The Mosquito Coast*
▷ Patrick White, *Voss*

WILSON, A.N. (Andrew Norman) (born 1950)
British novelist

Wilson's early books (*The Sweets of Pimlico*; *Unguarded Hours*) were comic novels in the style of ▷ Evelyn Waugh, and just as funny. Then, in the mid-1980s, he began to write more serious books, tragi-comedies about the fears and despair of educated, upper-class people, usually women. Their sad hilarity, and a slightly donnish touch in the writing, are reminiscent of the books of ▷ Barbara Pym.

LOVE UNKNOWN (1986)

Three women who shared a London flat in the 1960s have gone their separate ways in the 20 years since. One has flitted from man to man like a wind-up butterfly. Another inherited money and has lived a celibate life in Paris. The third has made an 'idyllic' marriage to the man they all once idolized. Now, as the novel begins, adultery is discovered and the three women's lives intersect once more, unstoppably and painfully.

Wilson's tragi-comedies include The Healing Art, Who Was Oswald Fish, Wise Virgin, Gentlemen in England, *the trilogy (*Incline Our Hearts, A Bottle in the Smoke *and* Daughters of Albion) *and* Dream Children. *He has also written non-fiction: re-examinations of the life of Christ and St. Paul,* God's Funeral (*about the secularization of Western society in the 19th century) and biographies of Milton,* ▷ *Scott,* ▷ *Tolstoy and Belloc.*

> **READ ON**

- ● *Dream Children.*
- ▶ ▷ **Barbara Pym,** *A Glass of Blessings*; ▷ **Bernice Rubens,** *Our Father*; ▷ **Muriel Spark,** *The Girls of Slender Means*; ▷ **Alison Lurie,** *Foreign Affairs.*

WILSON, Angus (1913–91)

British novelist and short story writer

Wilson is a post-Second World War successor to the great Victorian novelists. His plots are expansive, his pages teem with characters and his style is pungently satirical. His middle-class heroes and heroines, often members of the professions, have large, quarrelsome families; adultery, homosexuality, shady dealing and the conflict between public and private duty shape their lives. The 'public' plot of *Hemlock and After* (1952) is about a novelist trying to establish a writers' centre in a large, old house; the 'private' plot concerns his anguish about his own homosexuality. *The Old Men at the Zoo* (1961) is a satire set in a future Britain threatened by a united Europe and defeated by its own penchant for replacing action with committee rhetoric. The heroine of *The Middle Age of Mrs Eliot* (1958), unexpectedly widowed, throws off the Home Counties mask and embarks on a raffish odyssey across the world, a quest to find herself. In *Late Call* (1964) another lower-middle-class matron, forced to live with her widowed, unloved son, has to come to terms with the soulless New Town he lives in, a reflection both of his own inner desolation and of the emotional wasteland between them where once was love. *Setting the World on Fire* (1980) is a study of the lives and relationships of two brothers, one a finicky lawyer, the other an artist (an experimental theatre director). As well as his novels, Wilson's short stories are much admired. They are sharp anecdotes of emotional ineptness, often involving the clash between middle-aged parents and their children or between ill-matched lovers.

☆ ANGLO-SAXON ATTITUDES (1956)

Gerald Middleton is a rich, successful academic (a historian of Anglo-Saxon England). His personal life is a shambles: he lives apart from his wife, dislikes his children and grandchildren, squabbles with his colleagues and has lost touch with his friends. Faced with the need to accept or reject an important academic task, he begins to think again about the greatest, and oddest, archaeological discovery of his youth 50 years before: an obscene pagan statue in the tomb of a 7th-century Christian missionary. Was it a hoax – and if so, if this is yet another lie on which he has built his life, what can he do now to set things right?

Wilson's other novels are No Laughing Matter *and* As If By Magic. The Wrong Set, Such Darling Dodos *and* A Bit Off the Map *are collections of short stories.*

READ ON >

● *As If By Magic.*
▶ to Wilson's novels: ▷ Iris Murdoch, *The Sandcastle*; ▷ Willa Cather, *The Professor's House*; Peter Taylor, *A Summons to Memphis.*
▶ to the short stories: ▷ V.S. Pritchett, *The Camberwell Beauty*; Mary Gordon, *Temporary Shelter.*

WINTERSON, Jeanette (born 1959)
British novelist

Several of Winterson's early novels are tart, magic-realist fables which set characters with modern sensibilities in riotously chaotic historical settings: Noah's Ark (filled with grumbling women) in *Boating for Beginners*, the rank back-canals of Venice and the battlefields of Napoleonic France in *The Passion*, the mud-flats and brothels of 17th-century London in *Sexing the Cherry*. Her more recent books have continued to use all the resources of myth, fairy-tale and language itself to construct ever more daring and demanding fictions. *The Powerbook* (2000) flits between Capri and Paris, London and cyberspace in a series of interlocking narratives that invite the active participation of the reader in creating its stories.

☆ SEXING THE CHERRY (1989)
A giantess known as the Dog Woman rescues an infant from the Thames, names him Jordan and brings him up until he is apprenticed to the naturalist John Tradescant and starts to travel the world in search of exotic plants. The place is London, in the grip of Puritans whose Christian fervour has no truck with compassion or even with simple truth. Jordan's dreams of far countries, and of a princess who exists beyond the grasp of gravity, are intertwined, page by page, with his mother's account of her brutal daily life, as fundamentalist to its violent principles as the Puritans she preys on are to theirs.

Winterson's other novels include Oranges Are Not the Only Fruit *(about a young girl who escapes a harsh Plymouth Brethren upbringing by asserting her lesbian identity),* Written on the Body *(a bizarre love story in which the book we are reading is the body, and the body is the book),* Art and Lies *and* Gut Symmetries. Art Objects *is a collection of characteristically impassioned essays on writing and writers*

READ ON >

● *The Passion.*
▶ ▷ Michèle Roberts, *The Book of Mrs Noah*; ▷ Angela Carter, *The Magic*

Toyshop; ▷ Italo Calvino, *The Cloven Viscount* (in *Our Ancestors*); ▷ Iain Sinclair, *Radon Daughters.*

WODEHOUSE, P.G. (Pelham Grenville) (1881–1975)
British novelist

In the 1920s and 1930s Wodehouse wrote Broadway shows, and he once described his novels as 'musical comedy without the music'. There are over 100 of them, gloriously frivolous romps set in high society 1920s England or among dyspeptic US newspaper magnates and film tycoons. Wodehouse's gormless heroes are in love with 'pips' and 'peacherinos'. Before they can marry they must persuade dragon-like relatives (usually aunts) to give reluctant consent or to part with cash – and the persuasion often involves stealing valuable jewels (to earn undying gratitude when they are 'found' again), smuggling the girl into the house disguised (so that the radiance of her personality will charm all opposition) or blackmail (threatening to reveal embarrassing secrets of the relative's misspent youth). There are two main novel-series, the Jeeves books (in which Bertie Wooster consistently makes an ass of himself, usually by being the fall-guy in Jeeves's machiavellian schemes), and the Blandings books (in which Lord Emsworth's prize pig bulks large). Other books tell of the multifarious members of the Mulliner family and the Drones Club, of golfers, cricketers and incompetent crooks; in all of them the season is high summer, every cloud is lined with silver, and happy endings are distributed 'in heaping handfuls' (to quote Wodehouse's own immortal phrase).

☆ LEAVE IT TO PSMITH (1923)
Before Eve Halliday will marry him, Freddie Threepwood needs £1000 to start a bookmaker's business. He goes to Blandings Castle to ask his father Lord Emsworth. But Lord Emsworth has no access to his own fortune: that route is guarded by Lady Constance Keeble and her sidekick the Efficient Baxter. The plot spirals to include poets who are not everything they seem, stolen jewels, a purloined pig – and above all the machinations of the endlessly, irritatingly good-humoured Psmith.

Wodehouse's Blandings books include Galahad at Blandings, Heavy Weather, Pigs Have Wings *and* Uncle Fred in the Springtime. *His Jeeves books include* Joy in the Morning, Carry On, Jeeves, The Inimitable Jeeves, Jeeves in the Offing, Much Obliged, Jeeves, Right Ho,Jeeves, Stiff Upper Lip, Jeeves *and* The Code of the Woosters. *His other novels include* Money in the Bank, Uncle Dynamite, The Luck of the Bodkins *and* Quick Service. The Man Upstairs, The Clicking of Cuthbert, Eggs and Crumpets *and* Meet Mr Mulliner *are short-story collections, and* Performing Flea *is autobiography.*

>[READ ON]▷

● *Summer Lightning.*
▶ Ben Travers, *Rookery Nook* (novel version); Richard Gordon, *Doctor in the House*; Patrick Denis, *Auntie Mame*. The same kind of gormless farce, transplanted to California, updated to the 1980s and set among incompetent crooks and gangsters is in Donald E. Westlake's Dortmunder books, e.g. *Bank Shot* or *Who Stole Sassi Manoon?*

WOLFE, Thomas (1900–38)
US novelist

Wolfe's life's work was an incoherent, multi-million-word torrent of autobiographical prose, an attempt to make epic fiction of ordinary US life. His models were ▷Homer, Shakespeare and ▷Dickens – and his work is every bit as grand as that suggests. He and his publishers organized some of the material into two long novels, telling the story of Eugene Gant, a young Carolina writer, from boyhood to first success. The first and most accessible book, *Look Homeward, Angel* (1929), tells of Eugene's childhood as the youngest member of a sprawling, bickering slum family, of his awakening to culture and of his heart-breaking realization that to 'follow art' he must abandon his family and everything it stands for and chop off his own roots. *Of Time and the River* (1935) continues the story, following Eugene through college and to Paris, charting his artistic friendships, his learning about sex and love, and his first attempts at writing. After Wolfe's death two other novels, *The Web and the Rock* and *You Can't Go Home Again*, were assembled from his manuscripts. They follow another writer, George Weber – an adult version of Eugene Gant – through marriage, divorce, disillusion with the US and hostility to European fascism in the 1930s.

> READ ON

▶ ▷ John O'Hara, *From the Terrace*; ▷ Lawrence Durrell, *The Black Book*; ▷ H.H. Richardson, *The Fortunes of Richard Mahony*; James Jones, *From Here to Eternity*.

WOLFE, Tom (born 1931)
US journalist and novelist

The 1960s creator and practitioner of New Journalism (non-fiction writing that ignored traditional attempts at objectivity and impersonality in favour of an exuberant adoption of many of the techniques of fiction) Tom Wolfe had long hinted that he would one day turn his attention to the novel. When ☆ *The Bonfire of the Vanities* finally arrived in 1987 it fulfilled most of the expectations advance publicity had aroused. It is a big and bold novel, attempting to do for 1980s New York what Dickens had done for 1840s London – provide an all-encompassing vision of urban society from its richest citizens to the dwellers in its ghettos. Sherman McCoy is a wealthy Wall Street investment banker, one of the 'Masters of the Universe', as Wolfe ironically calls him. His life seems an embodiment of the American Dream until, driving his Mercedes through the Bronx, he hits a black pedestrian. From that point dream turns rapidly to nightmare and Sherman is pitched into a world of politicians on the make, sleazy media hacks and the assorted lowlife caught up in a legal system that offers its own strange versions of 'justice'. Alive with satirical observation, peopled by a rich cast of over-the-top characters and narrated in the pyrotechnic language that Wolfe had perfected in his non-fiction, *The Bonfire of the Vanities* is a highly entertaining study of a status-mad society. It was another eleven years before Wolfe's second novel, *A Man in Full*, was published in 1998. After such a long wait this story of racial tensions and financial scams in Atlanta seemed something of a disappointment. Painted on the same large canvas as the first novel it none the less lacks the drive and frenetic energy that make *The Bonfire of the Vanities* one of the best and funniest American novels of the last three decades.

Wolfe's non-fiction books include The Right Stuff *(the story of the early years of the American space programme),* The Electric Kool-Aid Acid Test *(classic 1960s account of Ken Kesey, his Merry Pranksters and their bus ride across America),* The Kandy-Kolored Tangerine Flake Streamline Baby *and* From Bauhaus to Our House. Hooked Up *is a collection of essays that also includes a novella,* 'Ambush at Fort Bragg'.

> **READ ON**

▶ **to the fiction:** ▷ **Don Delillo,** *Underworld*; ▷ **John Irving,** *A Prayer for Owen Meany.*

▶ **to the non-fiction: Hunter S. Thompson,** *Fear and Loathing in Las Vegas*; ▷ **Norman Mailer,** *The Executioner's Song.*

WOOLF, Virginia (1882–1941)
British novelist and non-fiction writer

As well as novels, Woolf published two dozen non-fiction books: biographies (one of Flush, Elizabeth Barrett Browning's pet dog), diaries, essays on feminism and on literature. She was fascinated by psychology, and her nine novels set out to show, in prose, the workings of the subconscious mind. Instead of narrating strings of events she lets her characters run on in a 'stream-of-consciousness' style which gradually builds a clear picture of their personalities. She tells us the jumble of thoughts and memories in ordinary men and women, and she is particularly good at showing moments of radiant inner happiness. *Mrs Dalloway* (1925), the interior monologue of a middle-class woman preparing to give a dinner-party, reveals her feelings about herself and her past as well as the urgent claims of the coming evening. In *To the Lighthouse* (1927) a group of adults and children is shown on a summer holiday – the trip to the lighthouse is a promised birthday treat for one of the children – and then in the same place ten years later, when the trip is finally made. Despite war and death in the intervening years, the influence of the dead mother is as strong as in her lifetime. *The Waves* (1931), Woolf's most complex book, traces six people's reactions to experiences from childhood to maturity, showing how apparently small 'real' past events continue to affect the personality as waves shape and reshape the shore.

Woolf's other novels are The Voyage Out, Night and Day, Jacob's Room, Orlando, The Years *and* Between the Acts. Haunted House *and* Mrs Dalloway's Party *are collections of short stories.*

> **READ ON**

▶ ▷ **Marcel Proust,** *Swann's Way* **(Part One of** *Remembrance of Things Past)*; ▷ **Jean Rhys,** *Good Morning, Midnight*; **D.M. Thomas,** *The White Hotel*; **Dorothy Richardson,** *Pilgrimage*; **Anaïs Nin,** *Seduction of the Minotaur*; ▷ **Margaret Atwood,** *Surfacing*; **Gertrude Stein,** *Three Lives*; ▷ **Iris Murdoch,** *The Sea, The Sea.*

WYNDHAM, John (1903–69)
British novelist and short story writer

'John Wyndham' was one of the pseudonyms of John Wyndham Lucas Beynon Harris, who wrote straightforward science fiction and thrillers under the names

'John Wyndham Parkes' and 'Lucas Beynon'. The 'John Wyndham' novels are less science fiction than thrillers, set on Earth, with science fiction overtones: he called them 'logical fantasies'. In *The Midwich Cuckoos* (1957) an alien race seeks to colonize Earth not by force of arms but by fertilizing women – and the story begins, in the quiet English countryside (a favourite Wyndham location) as the half-alien children approach puberty. In *Chocky* (1968) a small boy has an invisible confidante – not a figment of his imagination, but a being from outer space. ☆*The Day of the Triffids* (1951) begins with two simultaneous disasters, the sudden blinding of all human beings and the growth of enormous, mobile, predatory plants; the novel concerns the hero's attempts to organize resistance and save the human race.

Wyndham's other novels include The Chrysalids, The Kraken Wakes *and* Trouble With Lichen. *His short stories are collected in* The Seeds of Time, Consider Her Ways *and* Web.

READ ON ⟩

▶ Bob Shaw, *Night Walk*; James Herbert, *The Magic Cottage*; ▷ H.G. Wells, *The Time Machine*.

Y

READ ON A THEME: YOUNG ADULTS

   Lisa Alther, *Kinflicks*
▷ Ford Madox Ford, *Parade's End*
▷ Johann Wolfgang von Goethe, *The Apprenticeship of Wilhelm Meister*
▷ Nadine Gordimer, *A Sport of Nature*
▷ Marcel Proust, *Within a Budding Grove* (Part Two of *Remembrance of Things Past*)
▷ Philip Roth, *Goodbye, Columbus*
   Charles Webb, *The Graduate*

See also: Emotionally Ill-At-Ease; Perplexed by Life; Teenagers

YOURCENAR, Marguerite (1903–88)
French writer

Yourcenar is best known for her novel ★☆ *Memoirs of Hadrian* (1951), a study of the urbane, civilized man who ruled the Roman Empire in the second century AD. Unlike ▷ Robert Graves's *I, Claudius*, which is chiefly the tale of an outrageous family power struggle, *Memoirs of Hadrian* is a philosophical auto-biography, concerned not only with politics and conquest but with Hadrian's intellectual and emotional growth. It is a quiet, understated book, balancing Hadrian's descriptions of his search for tranquillity of soul with the torments and ecstasies of his passion for the beautiful boy Antinous.

Yourcenar's other novels include A Coin in Nine Hands, Alexis *and* The Abyss *(in which a Flemish scholar wanders Renaissance Europe in search of 'knowledge untrammelled by doctrine').*

READ ON ▷

▶ ▷ Mary Renault, *The Mask of Apollo*; ▷ Gore Vidal, *Julian*; ▷ Thornton Wilder, *The Ides of March*.

Z

ZOLA, Émile (1840–1902)
French novelist and non-fiction writer

Zola won scandalous fame at 27 with his novel *Thérèse Raquin*, about a pair of lovers who murder the woman's husband. The book's financial success let him take up fiction full-time, and he began a 20-novel series designed to show – in a scientific way, he claimed, as species are described – every aspect of late 19th-century French life. Although each novel is self-contained, their main characters are all members of the two families which give the series its name, The Rougons and the Macquarts. Zola's scheme echoed ▷Balzac's in *The Human Comedy*, and like Balzac he was interested in exact description, what he called 'naturalism'. But his morbid and pessimistic nature led him to concentrate on the harsher aspects of human existence, so that his characters often seem less like real human beings than the people dragged into sermons to illustrate the effects of drink, lust or poverty. Outside France, Zola's best-known books are *Germinal* (1885, about conditions in the coalmines, and including a strike and a major accident), *Earth* (*La Terre*) (1887, about subsistence farming), *The Belly of Paris* (*Le ventre de Paris*) (1873, about the food markets of the city), *The Boozer* (*L'assommoir*) (1871) and *For Women's Delight* (*Pour le bonheur des dames*) (1883, about the staff and customers of a department store).

NANA (1880)
The subject is sex. Nana's mother was a country girl who went to Paris to seek her fortune, became a laundress but was destroyed by drink – this is the story of *The Boozer*. Nana grows up as a street-urchin, and later becomes an actress and singer. She is beautiful but corrupt, morally brutalized by her childhood. She sets out systematically to destroy men: Zola thinks of her first as one of the Sirens in myth, drawing men irresistibly to her by the beauty of her voice, and then as a spider, preying on them even as she mates with them. He pities neither Nana nor her victims: like his other novels, this panorama of big-city life is painted entirely in shades of black.

Other books in the series include The Human Beast *(La bête humaine) (about the gangs of navvies who built railroads),* Money *(set among financiers) and* The Downfall *(Le débâcle) (a devastating picture of the 1870 Commune and siege of Paris, which Zola saw as a cleansing operation, ridding the city of the corruption which had led to the misery described in his other books). In his last years he finished the first three books of another series,* The Four Gospels: *their titles are* Fertility, Work *and* Truth.

READ ON $\triangleright$

- *Thérèse Raquin.*
- ▶ ▷ W. Somerset Maugham, *Liza of Lambeth*; Theodor Fontane, *Effi Briest;* Frank Norris, *The Pit*; Theodore Dreiser, *An American Tragedy*; ▷ John Steinbeck, *The Grapes of Wrath*; George Gissing, *New Grub Street*.

INDEX

Bold page numbers indicate main references

Brodkey, Harold **39**
Broken Sword, The 245
Bronson, Po 194
Brontë, Anne 40
Brontë, Charlotte **40–1**, 66, 82, 106, 107, 207, 293
Brontë, Emily **40–1**, 214
Brook Kerith, The 29
Brookner, Anita 5, **41**, 88, 125, 173, 177, 231, 232, 277, 280
Brooks, Terry 90
Brother of the More Famous Jack 144, 276
Brothers 237
Brothers and Sisters 58
Brothers Ashkenazy, The 255
Brothers Karamazov, The 77
Brown, Alan 151
Brown, George Douglas 41
Brown, George MacKay 243
Browning, Robert 169, 216
Brunner, John 125
Bryson, Bill 278
Buchan, James 259
Buchan, John **42**, 60, 119, 122, 263
Buck, Pearl S. 53, 232
Buddenbrooks 92, 105, 185, 186, 188, 189
Buddha of Suburbia, The 3, 32, 174, 268
Budrys, Algis 56
Bug Jack Barron 245
Bukowski, Charles 34, 94
Bulgakov, Mikhail 111
Bull from the Sea, The 230
Bullet in the Ballet, An 6
Bullet Park 52, 255
Bullfighters, The 184
Bunyan, John 26
Burger's Daughter 112, 258
Burgess, Anthony 29, **42–3**, 67, 118, 137, 139, 155, 200, 209, 211, 236, 275
Burglar Who Thought He Was Bogart, The 58, 64
Burke, James Lee 65, 68, 222
Burmese Days 208
Burn Marks 212
Burney, Fanny 169
Burning Bright 82, 285
Burning Shore, The 256
Burnt Ones, The 300
Burnt-out Case, A 119
Burr 219, 288
Burroughs, Edgar Rice 288
Burroughs, William 6, 21, 73, 161, 247
Burton, Richard 278
Business, The 22
Busman's Honeymoon 243
Butler, Samuel 58, 212, 266
Butterfield 8 207
Buyer's Market, A 219
By the Light of My Father's Smile 290
Byatt, A.S. 41, **43–4**, 79, 120, 178
Byron, Robert 279
Byron: Selected Letters and Journals 169
Bystander 114
Byzantium Endures 195

C

C is for Corpse 114
Cab at the Door, The 222
Cabal 64, **72**

Cabala, The 301
Cack-Handed War, A 14
Cadillac Jukebox 65, 68, 222
Cain, James M. 122
Caine Mutiny, The 129, 251
Cain's Book 6
Cairo Trilogy 183
Cakes and Ale 191, 192
Cal 91
Calder, Richard 63
Caldwell, Erskine 261
California Time 94, 202
Caligula **46**
Call for the Dead 167, 243
Call if You Need Me 49
Call It Sleep 27, 39, 166, 204
Call of Cthulhu and Other Weird Tales, The 218, 258
Call of the Toad, The 34, 115
Call of the Wild, The 175
Calvino, Italo 17, 35, **45–6**, 63, 139, 194, 304
Camberwell Beauty and Other Stories, The 222, 267, 280, 303
Cambridge 48
Camera Obscura 201
Cameron, Jeremy 33
Camomile Lawn, The 297
Campbell, John W. 10
Campbell's Kingdom 146, 257
Camus, Albert 27, **46–7**, 77, 214, 242
Can You Forgive Her? 105, 257, 281
Canal Dreams 22
Canary in a Cathouse 289
Cancer Ward 258
Candide 266
Candlemass Road, The 104, 263
Candy 129
Candy, Edward 41
Cannery Row 261
Canopus in Argus 172
Canterbury Tales, The 216, 260
Canticle for Leibowitz, A 104, 139, 245, 289
Capital 195, 254
Capote, Truman 240
Captain and the Enemy, The 119
Captain Blood 81, 134, 142
Captain Corelli's Mandolin 67–8, 93, 291, 293
Captain Horatio Hornblower 99
Captain Pantoja and the Special Service 4
Captain Singleton 69
Captains and the Kings, The 187
Captains Courageous 164
Captive, The 224
Card, Orson Scott 127, 244
Card, The 28, 269, 295
Cardinal of the Kremlin, The 55
Carey, Peter 16, 17, 25, **47–8**, 158, 159, 165, 174, 185, 189, 204, 276, 300
Carol 134
Carpe Jugulum 221
Carpenters 240
Carpentier, Alejo 4, 157, 189
Carr, Caleb 136
Carr, John Dickson 64, 78, 117
Carrie 111, 113, 161
Carroll, Lewis 204–5
Carry On, Jeeves 304
Carter, Angela 5, 6, 11, 12, 46, **48–9**, 104, 137, 165, 189, 215, 235, 239, 241, 260, 266, 303

Carter, P. Youngman 5
Carter, Peter 138
Cartwright, Justin 4, 174
Carver, Raymond **49**, 53, 199, 207
Cary, Joyce 9, 34, 155, 173, 192, 300
Casanova's Chinese Restaurant 219
Case Book of Sherlock Holmes, The 78
Case of Conscience, A **33**
Case of Spirits, A 65
Case of the Gilded Fly, The 5
Cassandra, Princess of Troy 9
Cast Iron Shore, The 82
Castle, The **156**, 264
Castle Dangerous 246
Castle Gay 263
Castle of Otranto, The 66
Castle of the Crossed Destinies, The 45
Castle of Wizardry 86
Casualty, The 34
Casuarina Tree, The 191
Cat and Mouse 115, 241
Cat Jumps, The 35
Cat Who Walks Through Walls 127
Catalina 191
Catastrophist, The 3, 163, 196
Catch-22 91, 126, **128**, **129**, 158, 227, 292
Catcher in the Rye, The 3, 155, 204, 240, **241**, 268
Cathedral 49, 207
Cathedral Close 281
Cather, Willa **50**, 178, 200, 211, 282, 301, 303
Catholics 195, 236
Cat's Cradle 289
Cat's Eye 11, 12, 53, 237
Cause for Alarm 7
Cause of Death 61
Caves of Steel, The 10
Cefalù 83, 102, 220
Celebrated Jumping Frog of Calaveras County and Other Sketches, The 283
Celestial Navigation 283
Celestial Omnibus 100
Celibate Season, A 250
Cement Garden, The 18, 180, 181
Cemetery Nights 76
Centaur, The 52, 212, 240, 241, 243, **286**
Certain Age, A 104, 204
Certain Justice, A 151, 243
Certificate, The 255
Cervantes Saavedra, Miguel de 26, 94, 109, 110, 141, 263, 275
César Birotteau 21
Chamber, The 120
Chamber Music 154
Chancer, A 295
Chandler, Raymond **50–1**, 122, 198, 222
Chang, Jung 14, 53
Change for the Better, A 267
Change of Gravity, A 133
Changing Places 37, 120, 174
Chant of Jimmie Blacksmith, The 158, 185
Chaos and Order 76
Chaplin, Charlie 14
Chapterhouse of Dune 131
Charade 197
Charioteer, The 230
Charity 70
Charlotte Gray 68, 93, 291
Charlotte Mew and her Friends 96